WITHDRAWN

W9-CKE-325

MONTGOMERY COLLEGE
GERMANTOWN CAMPUS LIBRARY
GERMANTOWN MARYLAND

UNFINISHED WORK

Building Equality and Democracy in an Era of Working Families

EDITED BY JODY HEYMANN AND CHRISTOPHER BEEM

THE NEW PRESS

NEW YORK
LONDON

308094

JUN 1 5 2005

Compilation © 2005 by Jody Heymann and Christopher Beem
Individual essays © 2005 by each author

All rights reserved.
No part of this book may be reproduced, in any form, without written permission
from the publisher.

Requests for permission to reproduce selections from this book should be mailed to:
Permissions Department, The New Press, 38 Greene Street, New York, NY 10013

Published in the United States by The New Press, New York, 2005
Distributed by W. W. Norton & Company, Inc., New York

LIBRARY OF CONGRESS CATALOGING-IN-PUBLICATION DATA
Unfinished work : building equality and democracy in an era of working families /
edited by Jody Heymann and Christopher Beem.
     p.   cm.
   Includes bibliographical references and index.
   ISBN 1-56584-991-4—ISBN 1-56584-922-1 (pbk.)
   1. Work and family—United States.   2. Family—United States.
I. Heymann, Jody, 1959–   II. Beem, Christopher.
HD4904.25.U54   2005
306.3'6'0973—dc22   2004059240

The New Press was established in 1990 as a not-for-profit alternative to the large,
commercial publishing houses currently dominating the book publishing industry.
The New Press operates in the public interest rather than for private gain, and is committed to publishing, in innovative ways, works of educational, cultural, and community value that are often deemed insufficiently profitable.

www.thenewpress.com

Composition by dix!

Printed in Canada

10   9   8   7   6   5   4   3   2   1

To Ann and Phil Heymann,
Ray and Marilyn Beem, and
all those caring for their families

How ashamed are we that one-quarter of our children, in one of the richest countries in the world, live in poverty? How much do we care that those who raise children, *because* of this choice, have restricted opportunities to develop the rest of their potential, and very little influence on society's values and direction? . . . How much do we *want* the just families that will produce the kind of citizens we need if we are ever to achieve a just society?

—Susan Moller Okin

CONTENTS

PREFACE

This book is a product of the Johnson Foundation's Work, Family and Democracy Project and of the Work, Family and Democracy Initiative at Harvard University led by Jody Heymann. We are grateful to the David and Lucile Packard Foundation for additional support, and to Jody Heymann for chairing the project.

For decades, the Johnson Foundation has sponsored Wingspread conferences that focus on the well-being of children and families. We initiated the Work, Family and Democracy project because we were frustrated by the truncated nature of the work and family debate, and its deleterious effects on both. As many acknowledge, our society has undergone a revolution. Fifty years ago, most families had an adult present at home. Now most families have both parents working. The issues surrounding work and family arise from our failure to develop institutions to replace the former arrangement.

This failure is not merely economic; it is social, civic, and moral. Work and family issues cannot be adequately addressed within the confines of the employer-employee relationship. This is a chief reason for our frustration. The principle objective of the Work, Family and Democracy Project is to restore the debate to this broader frame.

By bringing together a wide range of disciplines and perspectives, this book promises to help develop a richer and more productive exchange. Beyond the divisive categories of left and right in American politics, there lies great potential for finding common ground, and thereby bettering the condition of America's children, families, and neighborhoods.

Boyd H. Gibbons III
President
The Johnson Foundation

[xi]

UNFINISHED
WORK

INTRODUCTION

Societal Crossroads

Jody Heymann

In order to endure, democracies need to be able to adapt to new and unexpected challenges. Civil liberties and rights need to be protected even while democracies combat new external and internal threats. But the challenges nations face are not only the sudden and cataclysmic ones. The long-term survival of societies may be equally challenged by major economic and demographic shifts. The United States, like many countries throughout the world, is currently facing changes that present just such a dramatic challenge: in the last 150 years, there has been a revolution in where, how, and by whom paid work is done in industrialized countries. The response to these changes will be critical to the success of American society. Importantly, these circumstances also present an opportunity to greatly deepen equality of opportunity for all women and men, across social class, to participate fully in the work of society, in shaping the next generation, and in governance.

DRAMATIC DEMOGRAPHIC AND ECONOMIC SHIFTS

During the nineteenth and twentieth centuries, revolutionary changes in the nature of work occurred throughout North America and Europe. In the United States, with the end of the Civil War and the rise of the industrial era, men and a significant number of single women left their farms and homes for wage and salaried work. After World War II, as bans on and barriers to their employment declined, married women and mothers increasingly joined the paid labor force. The cumulative effect of these changes was profound.

Instead of working in the same place where they care for their children or their elderly and sick family members, most adults now work far from their caretaking responsibilities. Most adults used to have one geographic community: they lived, worked, and cared for their family members in the same locality. Now, many adults live in one community, work in a second, and have parents and sometimes children they are caring for in a third.

Just as the location of work has changed, so too has the ability of individuals to determine when they labor. Nineteenth-century parents who worked at home or on farms could more readily interrupt their jobs to meet children's needs. The number of hours they worked was subject to the necessities of finishing essential tasks, but nonetheless their schedules were under their control. With the rise of wage and salaried work in a formal industrial sector, employers came to dictate work schedules—including when work began, when it ended, what days adults had to show up, when breaks could be taken, and whether and when leave was permitted for family or community emergencies.

While the world of work has changed dramatically over the past 150 years, much of American society has effectively stood still. Public schools continue to follow an agrarian calendar, with a long summer vacation and a short school day. Work schedules and demands continue to reflect a time when at least one adult caregiver labored at home. Similarly, community leaders frequently assume that adults will be home and available in neighborhoods that are, in fact, sometimes nearly void of adults during working hours.

Civil institutions and public policies in the United States have barely adapted to address the challenges that these changes have brought to the lives of working individuals and their families. In contrast to the host of governmental policies and civic programs that have emerged to adapt to advances in transportation, communications, and technology, the response to the changing circumstances facing working families has been meager. Yet making the most of these changes is important to the future of any society, and particularly crucial to a democracy.

ESSENTIAL FOUNDATIONS OF DEMOCRACY

In order to survive over the long run, every society needs to accomplish certain essential tasks: completing productive work, raising subsequent generations well, preventing and addressing threats, and responding effectively to change. Like all other societies, democracies must accomplish these same four essential tasks, but they face one additional challenge: to become fully democratic, they must ensure all citizens have an equal opportunity for civic and political participation. The success and long-term survival of democracies are maximized by having the highest-quality participation.

Democracies are the only form of government that places sovereignty in the hands of the whole population—either directly or through representatives. American democracy, like many subsequent ones, evolved in response to a period of abuse of power by the aristocracy. By being the sole form of government to attempt to place power and responsibility in the hands of the whole population, democracies inherently have the greatest interest in supporting the education, development, and welfare of the whole population.

The notion of a truly democratic society is grounded in the belief that when they grow up, children from every neighborhood may serve in and determine the leadership of each branch of governance. They can be lawyers and judges. They can serve on juries, zoning commissions, school boards, and the like. And by voting they can decide who among them will govern. Because the sum of how a nation's children grow up determines the future quality of life in a democracy, children in a democracy are uniquely seen as a public good. Democracies, therefore, have a particular incentive to invest in the quality of care, education, and rearing children receive. James Madison argued that without educated citizens, American democracy would be "but a prologue to a farce or a tragedy, or perhaps both."[1]

At the same time, democracies have an inherent reason to invest in equality in governance. While the origins of democracy may have occurred in Athens in the fifth century B.C.E., large-scale representative democracy was born with the United States in the eighteenth century. The early precursors in ancient Greece were small city-states with direct political participation by all citizens—but with only an elite allowed to claim citizenship. Early elected representatives in Europe served under monarchs and did not have the full power to govern. It was with the beginning of true democratic governance at a national level that the indelible link between successful democracies and equality became evident. In writing about early American democracy, Tocqueville noted the essential role of equality in protecting freedom: "As no one is different from his fellows, none can exercise a tyrannical power; men will be perfectly free because they are all entirely equal; and they will all be perfectly equal because they are entirely free. To this ideal state, democratic nations tend."[2]

Democracy's particular reliance on the quality of education of all and on equality in civic and political participation increases the importance of understanding how demographic and economic shifts may affect these features in American society.

ADDRESSING HISTORICAL INEQUALITIES

In nineteenth- and early-twentieth-century America, the jobs of both paid work and rearing the next generation—essential to every society—were accomplished, but with great inequality. Social constraints, along with legal bans and barriers to work by married women and mothers, left women with far fewer choices than men, fewer leadership opportunities, fewer resources, and less income. While gender-specific bans in employment have been prohibited since the passage of the 1964 Civil Rights Act, the disproportionately high barriers women and the working poor must surpass in order to succeed at work, while caring for family members, continue to contribute to the fault lines of gender and economic inequality in our country. Working women continue to carry significantly more of the caregiving burden than men do, and yet, as this book will document, they still grapple with worse working conditions. Likewise, workers living in poverty face the doubled and relentless obstacles of far worse working conditions while having far greater caregiving responsibilities—particularly when it comes to caring for sick family members and helping children get educated in spite of poor schools. Just as addressing the needs of working families is essential to democracy because of its impact on the next generation who will run the nation, addressing these needs is crucial because of their impact on equality of opportunity among adults. In short, prior to the dramatic demographic transitions, the United States was getting its economic work accomplished and was raising the next generation of citizens—but these tasks were being carried out at the expense of creating enormous inequalities in the public and private lives of women and men, and the poor and nonpoor.

Creating a successful and lasting democracy is as much an evolutionary process as a revolutionary one. Few nations have been created as fully formed democracies; rarely have full and equal rights to participate in every aspect of a society been effectively shared by all members from the start. The limitations of early American democracy are well known and provide an example of this. At its inception, the United States allotted all the rights of citizenship only to white men with property. It took the United States nearly two centuries before all citizens—irrespective of their race, gender, and wealth—even had equal rights to vote and work. Today, while *in jure* these and other fundamental rights are assigned to all, they are not, in practice, equally available to all. If the United States is to continue to evolve and succeed as a democracy, it needs to address the essential societal tasks of completing work and rearing the next generation while increasing equality of opportunity—not increasing disparities. As a country, we will need to find a way to manufacture goods, provide services, operate buses and trains, teach teenagers, and raise children without relying on gender inequality. Moreover, we will need to accomplish these tasks in a way that gives low-income families the same opportunity as high-income families at succeeding in the workplace and successfully raising healthy children.

ADDRESSING FUNDAMENTAL SOCIETAL NEEDS

Thus, a central question for American democracy—and indeed any democracy—is how to simultaneously enhance equality and ensure that adults can be productive at work, rear the next generation well, and participate in civic life. In theory, there are three possible approaches: (1) place the responsibility solely on individuals and families, (2) rely on the private sector alone, or (3) have the public sector also support families that work. In practice, for any society that is not going to survive by exploiting inequalities, the evidence to date provides a clear answer: all three groups need to be involved in finding a solution. Families play an essential role, and workplaces have critical responsibilities, but a balance between work and family needs will not be achieved without a public role.

Families' Roles

While there is no substitute for parents' commitment to their children and no replacement for family members willingly caring for their elderly relatives, most adults simply cannot work in the paid labor force and by themselves meet all the needs of the children and adults in their families. To expect this would be as unrealistic as to expect that most laborers could grow their own food, spin their own thread, and weave and sew their own clothes.

Beyond the need for affordable, high-quality routine child and elder care services, adults need decent working conditions and basic benefits. Without these, adults cannot succeed at work and, at the same time, meet their families' unpredictable needs. Without the availability of leave or flexibility in their work schedule, adults often cannot provide urgently needed care for sick family members. When children face serious troubles at school, too many parents have no possibility of meeting with teachers and specialists without risking losing their jobs or essential income.

Public and Private Sector Roles

Throughout the past half century in the United States, it has become clear that while a select few businesses excel at providing decent working conditions and basic benefits, in the absence of public policies that guarantee these conditions for all members of a society, most companies do not. Popular magazines have posted lists of companies with good benefits in order to boost voluntary private sector efforts. Similarly, the U.S. Department of Labor has highlighted companies that have begun work-family programs and initiatives. But while individual companies may lead in developing improved policies, their voluntary initiatives have not to date and are unlikely in the future to result in universal coverage for American employees. That this is the state of affairs should not be entirely surprising. CEOs' performances are evaluated by share price, not by social policy or family care. Consequently, even when the societal benefits would be large, corporate leaders have little incentive to improve working conditions and benefits; in fact, there may be a *disincentive* if it means the company will have to bear a cost while its competitors choose not to provide any coverage. As a result, most Americans continue to lack reliable paid leave and work flexibility. Few receive any support from their employers for child or elder care. Moreover, there are profound inequalities in who receives any workplace benefits, with the affluent receiving significantly more than the middle class, and the middle class receiving substantially more than the poor.[3]

The importance of a public sector role in these labor areas and services should not be surprising. Most marked strides in guaranteeing decent working conditions that the United States has taken as a nation in the past—from child labor laws to the minimum wage to occupational safety laws—have required public sector action to become universal.

Moreover, history clearly demonstrates that a public role was necessary to guarantee primary and secondary education. No industrialized country now relies on companies to provide education for their employees' children. Nations have recognized that providing education for employees' children is not closely related to the work of many companies and would thus be poorly attended to and poorly funded if left in the companies' hands. Furthermore, there would be frequent educational disruptions for children when parents changed jobs, and the education of children whose parents cobbled together several part-time jobs would, at best, be uncertain. Just as it does not make sense for the private sector to be solely responsible for the education of their employees' older children, it does not make sense for companies to be solely responsible for supporting early childhood education or extended school days or calendars.

In sum, the need for a public sector role in ensuring basic services for children is as relevant as the need for ensuring decent working conditions for parents and other caregivers. The quality of care and education this generation of children receives will determine the nature of society in the future, as well as its economic success.[4]

THE WORK, FAMILY AND DEMOCRACY INITIATIVE

Because meeting the needs of working families is fundamental to our success as a society, to increasing equality, and to strengthening our democracy, Christopher Beem and I developed an initiative on work, family, and democracy. Addressing a problem of this breadth and depth requires, within academia, a wide range of expertise and, within society, leaders from every sector. We were fortunate to be able to assemble an exceptional group of leaders and scholars for the task at hand. Over the course of three years, with the support of the Johnson Foundation and the David and Lucile Packard Foundation, we brought together academics and policy makers whose work is grounded in governmental, nongovernmental, and private sector organizations. Participants shared their perspectives from political science, sociology, economics, religion, history, and public policy. This edited volume is one of the products of this initiative. Through this book, we hope to engage many more in the dialogue. It is our hope that by broadening the discussion, we can help to transcend our current impasse, thereby reinvigorating public debate, improving the lives of families, and in the long run strengthening the democracy of this nation.

OVERVIEW OF THE BOOK

Section I: Historic Changes

In Section I, the book analyzes the tectonic shifts in American work, family, and civil society. Chapter 1 presents a century's worth of census data on the evolving demographics of American families. Chapter 2 provides a detailed history of the fundamental changes in work and labor experiences during the past century. Chapter 3 places the transformation of work and family lives in the context of the simultaneous complex transformation of civil society.

Section II: Inequalities Across Gender and Class

Section II examines the extent to which the poor and the affluent, men and women, differ in their experiences of work, family, and democracy. Chapter 4 examines the commonalities as well as the disparities in the caretaking and work lives of women and men. Both Chapters 4 and 5 detail the untenable choices low-income families currently face as adults try to work while providing adequate care for their children, elderly parents, and disabled family members. Chapter 6 provides a striking view of the contrasting challenges faced by high-income families. Chapter 7 places the earlier detailed analyses of the experiences of men and women, low-income families and high earners, in a national context of how Americans across social class spend their time working, caring for family members, and contributing to their communities.

Section III: Challenges to Moving Forward

Section III provides insights into why we have not yet seen an effective national response to the problems working families face in America. Chapters 8 and 11 raise provocative questions about the extent to which the current economic paradigm in the United States is standing in the way of effective responses to the crises working families face. Chapter 9 examines why the corporate response has been inadequate. Chapter 10 highlights what the impediments are to changes originating solely from unions.

Section IV: Seeking Solutions

Section IV makes the case for why a public sector response is needed and what that might look like. Chapter 12 illustrates how other nations have successfully addressed work-family and equity issues in their democracies. Chapter 13 makes a passionate argument for eliminating the heavy penalties paid by Americans who are both workers and caregivers. Finally, Chapter 14 details a sample set of policy solutions that would decrease inequalities abundant in work and caregiving across gender and class in America.

Section I

Historic Changes

I

Changes in the Demographics of Families over the Course of American History

Donald J. Hernandez

America's families have undergone three major transformations: the first between the beginning of the Industrial Revolution and the Great Depression, the second after World War II, and the third beginning now. In this chapter, I examine the profound transformations in each of these time periods, and I use children as the lens through which to view, analyze, and evaluate them.

The first reason for using children as my focal point is that much of the growing interest and concern about changes in the work-family nexus arise from apparent incompatibilities between work and parenting in America. These tensions often have potentially detrimental consequences not only for the work roles of parents but also for the current well-being and future prospects of children. Second, children, as compared to adults, have relatively little control over the forces and decisions that impair or improve their circumstances.

Third, the family is the institution most directly responsible for children's well-being because parents make the day-to-day decisions that determine the quality of care—plus the quality of the nutrition, clothing, housing, health care, schools, and neighborhoods—available to children. But the choices parents make are shaped by opportunities and constraints flowing from social and economic forces as well as from federal, state, and local public policies. Most notably for present purposes, the resources that parents can make available to their children are determined largely by parents' access to paid employment, as well as by the timing and financial rewards associated with their paid work.

Finally, I focus on children because they are at the leading edge of the current demographic transformation of the American family and society, which is creating a new American majority. Historically, racial and ethnic minorities, including Hispanics, blacks, Asians, American Indians, and other nonwhite groups, have constituted only a small portion of the American population. But taken as a whole, these racial and ethnic minorities are growing much more rapidly than the non-Hispanic white population, and these groups are destined to become the numerical majority within the lifetime of today's children. The emergence of racial and ethnic minorities as the majority population is occurring most rapidly, and will become a reality first, among children.

REVOLUTIONARY TRANSFORMATIONS
FROM THE CIVIL WAR TO WORLD WAR II

The lives of children were completely altered between the mid-1800s and the mid-1900s by three revolutionary changes in the family: a radical change in fathers' work, the approaching extinction of the large nuclear family, and the flowering of mass education. In the mid-1800s, 70 percent of children lived in two-parent farm families, a majority lived in families with seven or more siblings, and only about one-half attended school (Figures 1-1 and 1-2). By 1930, only 30 percent of children lived on farms, 55 percent lived in two-parent families with a breadwinner father and a homemaker mother, and most children had only one or two brothers or sisters in the home. By 1940, the length of the school year had doubled, and about 90 percent of children ages seven to seventeen were enrolled in school.

During the mid-1800s, then, most children spent little time in school, and they lived in two-parent farm families, working side by side with their fathers and mothers and a large number of siblings to sustain themselves in small farming communities. By the 1930s and 1940s, most children lived in nonfarm families where the fathers left home for most of the day to earn the income required to support their families, while mothers remained in the home to care for their children and to perform unpaid household labor. After age six, children

FIGURE 1-1. Children Ages 0–17 in Farm Families, Father-as-Breadwinner Families, and Dual-Earner Families, 1790–2000

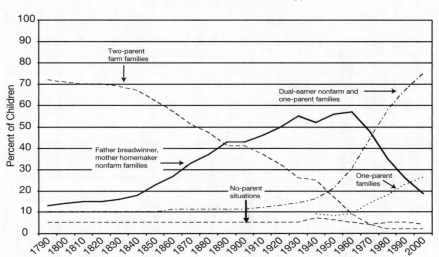

Two-parent farm families were estimated at 2 percent for year 2000. Estimates are for ten-year intervals from 1970 to 2000.

D.J. Hernandez, *America's Children: Resources from Family, Government, and the Economy* (New York: Russell Sage Foundation, 1993).

spent most of the day and the year in school. Although a hundred years may seem like a long time, it is important to note that the life expectancy of middle-aged adults today is more than seventy-five years. Consequently, the hundred-year transformation in the family economy, family size, and schooling occurred in little more than a single human lifetime, by today's standards.

Explaining the Transformation of Fathers' Work, Family Size, and Schooling

What explains these three revolutionary changes in the family lives of children? During the first century of the Industrial Revolution, these changes reflected the three major pathways available to parents who wanted either to improve their family's relative social and economic status or to keep from losing too much ground compared to others

FIGURE 1-2. Median Number of Siblings, 1865–2004

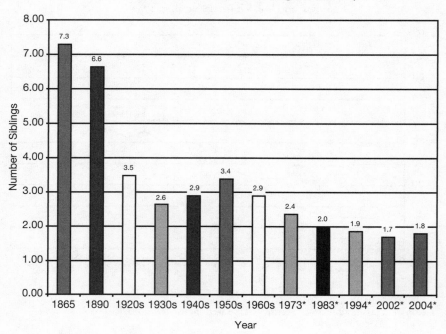

* Expected

Source: D.J. Hernandez, *America's Children, Resources from Family, Government, and the Economy* (New York: Russell Sage Foundation, 1993) and unpublished census tabulations kindly provided by Martin O'Connell.

who were taking advantage of emerging economic opportunities.[1] First, as the mechanization of agriculture created an increasingly precarious economic situation for many rural families, the attraction of comparatively well-paid jobs for fathers in the expanding urban-industrial economy motivated mass migration from farms to urban areas. Thus the rise of capitalism in the late nineteenth and twentieth centuries increasingly drew workers, especially fathers, into expanding urban areas, serving as an engine not only for the transformation of fathers' work but also for the transformations in fertility and schooling that followed.

But the move to urban areas meant that food, clothing, and other necessities had to be purchased, making the costs of supporting each child more demanding. Meanwhile, laws restricting child labor and mandating universal education, along with comparatively low wages for children in urban areas, greatly reduced the potential economic contributions of children to their urban families. Also, as the quality and quantity of consumer products and services increased with economic growth, expected consumption standards rose; people had to spend more money simply to maintain the new "normal" standard of living, and the newly available goods and services competed with children for parental time and money. For all these reasons, more and more parents limited their family size to a comparatively small number of children, allowing available income to be spread less thinly.

Schooling increased dramatically for three broad reasons. First, as the economic value of children's work declined relative to adults', parents became less motivated to keep their children in the labor force. Second, the child protection movement and labor unions successfully sought legislation restricting child labor and mandating universal schooling.[2] Third, as time passed and higher educational attainments became increasingly necessary to obtain jobs that offered higher incomes and greater prestige, parents encouraged and fostered higher educational attainments for their children as a path to success in adulthood.

REVOLUTIONARY TRANSFORMATIONS SINCE WORLD WAR II

The post–World War II era was marked by three additional revolutionary changes: the expansion of mothers' participation in the paid labor force, the rise of one-parent-family living arrangements, and the drop and subsequent rise in child poverty.

The Rise of Mothers' Labor Force Participation

During the last half of the twentieth century, children witnessed an enormous increase in the proportion of mothers working for pay (Figure 1-3), just as the children in an earlier era had experienced a massive movement by fathers out of the home to work in the urban-industrial economy. The revolution in mothers' work occurred twice as fast, however. The decline for children in the two-parent farm family from 60 percent to 10 percent occurred from 1860 to 1960. But the corresponding rise in working mothers from 10 percent to 60 percent

FIGURE 1-3. Proportion of Children with Mothers in the Labor Force, 1940–2000

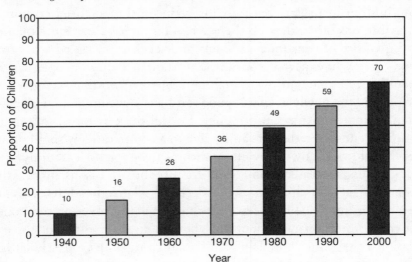

D.J. Hernandez, *America's Children: Resources from Family, Government, and the Economy* (New York: Russell Sage Foundation, 1993).

Data for 2000 are from U.S. Bureau of the Census, Current Population Survey, 2000.

required only half that time—from 1940 to 1990. By 2000, seven in ten children lived with mothers who worked for pay.

What caused this revolutionary increase in mothers' labor force participation? Much of the answer lies in the earlier historic changes in the family and the economy. Before 1940, many parents had three major avenues for maintaining, improving, or regaining their economic status. They could move off the farm for fathers to obtain comparatively well-paid jobs, they could have fewer children to allow available income to be spread less thinly, or they could increase their education. But by 1940, only 23 percent of Americans lived on farms, and 70 percent of parents had only one or two dependent children in the home. In addition, many adults found it difficult or impractical to pursue additional schooling after age twenty-five. Thus, the historical avenues to improving the relative economic status of their families had already effectively closed for a large majority of parents age twenty-five or older.

However, a fourth major possibility for improving the relative economic status of their families emerged between 1940 and 1960. In the post–World War II economy, white-collar jobs for women were increasingly open, and comparatively few unmarried women were available to take these jobs.[3] Meanwhile, mothers were becoming increasingly available and increasingly well qualified for paid employment, for at least three reasons. First, the historic increases in school enrollment and in the school year's length had effectively released mothers from personal child care responsibilities for the equivalent of about two-thirds of an eight-hour workday, for about two-thirds of a full-time adult workyear. Second, many mothers were highly educated, because their educational attainments, along with men's, had increased historically (Figure 1-4).

FIGURE 1-4. Proportion of Children Born Between 1920s and 1990s
Whose Parents Have Specified Educational Attainment

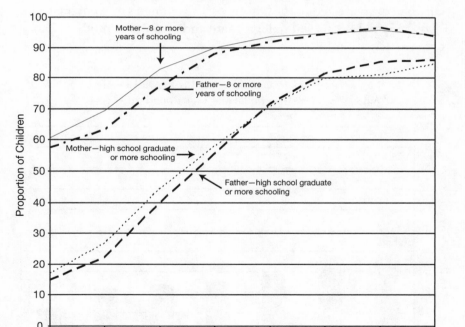

D.J. Hernandez, *America's Children: Resources from Family, Government, and the Economy* (New York: Russell Sage Foundation, 1993).

* Note: Nine or more years of schooling

Third, immediate economic insecurity and need, associated with fathers' lack of access to full-time employment, made mothers' work attractive. Full-time year-round work increased for fathers after the Great Depression. But through the subsequent decades up to 1990, and despite the enormous increase in mother-only families, at least one-fifth of children lived with fathers who, during any given year, experienced part-time work or joblessness (Figure 1-5). This has been a powerful incentive for mothers to enter the paid labor market. It also is plausible that paid work offered an attractive hedge for some women against the increasingly likely economic disaster of losing most or all of their husbands' incomes through divorce. In addition, the Equal Pay Act in 1963 and the prohibition of sex discrimination under Title VII of the 1964 Civil Rights Act facilitated the rise in mothers' paid employment by easing legal barriers to women's employment that initially had been erected in the late 1800s; the women's movement of the 1970s, meanwhile, served to legitimate and encourage mothers' labor force participation.[4]

FIGURE 1-5. Proportion of Children Living with a Father Who Works Less than Full Time Year-Round, 1940–2000

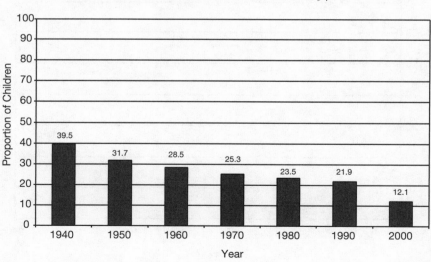

D.J. Hernandez, *America's Children: Resources from Family, Government, and the Economy* (New York: Russell Sage Foundation, 1993).

Data for 2000 are from U.S. Bureau of the Census, Current Population Survey, 2000.

The Rise of Mother-Only Families

Twenty years after mothers' labor force participation began to expand, another revolution in family life began—an unprecedented increase in mother-only families. A remarkably steady increase in divorce occurred between the 1860s and 1960s, with only three short-lived jumps around the world wars and the Great Depression (Figure 1-6). Expanding urban employment for fathers fueled the increase in divorce.[5] Preindustrial farming had literally required fathers and mothers to work together to support the family. But as fathers obtained nonfarm jobs, they could, if they wanted, leave the family home and take their incomes with them. At the same time, in moving to urban areas, husbands and wives left behind the small-town social controls that had once censured divorce. The economic interdependence of husbands and wives was weakened further by the revolutionary rise in mothers' labor force participation after 1940. With a nonfarm job, a mother could, if she and her husband separated or divorced, support herself with her own income. This fact contributed to the rapidly rising divorce rates during the late 1960s and 1970s.[6]

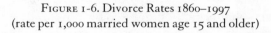

Figure 1-6. Divorce Rates 1860–1997
(rate per 1,000 married women age 15 and older)

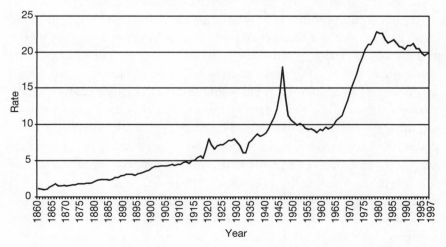

Reprinted from National Center for Health Statistics, "Advance Report of Final Divorce Statistics, 1988," *Monthly Vital Statistics Report* 39, no. 12, supp. 2, May 21, 1991.

Economic insecurity and need also have contributed greatly to the rise in separation and divorce. Glen Elder, Rand Conger, and their colleagues have shown that instability in fathers' work and resulting drops in family incomes lead to increased hostility between husbands and wives, reduced quality of the marital relationship, and increased risk of divorce.[7] In fact, each of the three economic recessions between 1970 and 1982, as compared to each preceding nonrecessionary period, led to sharp increases in mother-only families.[8]

Between 1940 and 1960, however, black children experienced much larger increases than white children in mother-only families with separated or divorced mothers, and especially after 1970, they experienced extremely large increases in mother-only families with never-married mothers.[9] The much higher proportion of black children who lived in mother-only families between 1940 and 1960 may be accounted for by disruptions associated with the startling drop in the proportion of blacks living on farms following the Great Depression, from 44 percent in 1940 to only 11 percent by 1960, and by the extraordinary economic pressures black families confronted as they moved to urban areas.

Turning to the rise in out-of-wedlock childbearing, the second component of the rise in mother-only families—and a major contributing factor—has been, as suggested by William Julius Wilson, the lack of employment among young men, especially black men.[10] In 1955, black men and white men ages sixteen to twenty-four were nearly equal in their chances of having a job (Figure 1–7). But by the late 1970s and 1980s, young black men were 15 percent to 25 percent more likely than young white men to be without a job, representing a large and rapid reduction in the availability of young-adult black men (that is, those of the main family-building ages) who might provide significant support to families.[11] The size of this racial gap in employment is at least two-thirds as large as the 23 percentage point increase between 1960 and 1988 in the comparative proportion of black and white children living in mother-only families with never-married mothers.

The proportion of children with a mother but no father in the home jumped from the narrow range of 6 percent or 8 percent during the 1940s and 1950s to 23 percent in 2000. Little change occurred before 1960, because, during the prior century, the effect of increasing divorce

FIGURE 1-7. Percentage Points by Which White Male Employment
Exceeds Black Male Employment, 1955–2000

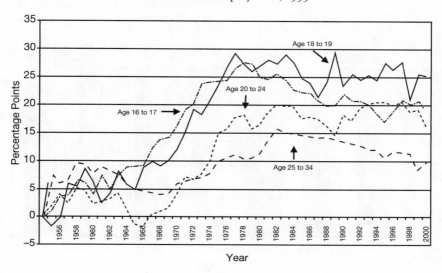

D.J. Hernandez, *America's Children: Resources from Family, Government, and the Economy*
(New York: Russell Sage Foundation, 1993).

U.S. Bureau of Labor Statistics (2001).

had been counterbalanced by declines in parental death rates. From a
child life-course perspective, however, very high proportions of children, historically, spent at least part of their childhood living with
fewer than two parents, at about 30 percent for whites and between 55
percent and 60 percent for blacks, mainly because of parental death or
divorce (Figure 1-8).

The Myth of the Traditional Ozzie and Harriet Family

Drawing together the changes in fathers' and mothers' employment
and family structure, we can then calculate estimates—for any given
time period—of the proportion of children living in families where
the father worked full time year-round, the mother was a full-time
homemaker without paid employment, and all the children were born
after the parents' only marriage. These are the so-called traditional
Ozzie and Harriet families.[12] Taking into account the effects not only
of divorce, out-of-wedlock childbearing, and mothers' employment

FIGURE 1-8. White and Black Children Ever Living with Fewer
than Two Parents by Age 17, 1920s to 1980s Cohorts

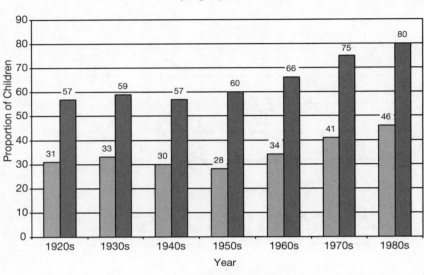

Note: More recent estimates cannot be calculated from the decennial census because of
changes in data collection. Since 1980, however, the proportions of white and black children
ever living with fewer than two parents may have increased and almost surely have not
declined. Parental divorce and births to unmarried women are the primary determinants of
these trends. Although the divorce rate has changed little since 1980, the proportion of all
births accounted for by unmarried women increased substantially between 1980 and 2000
from 10 to 29 percent for whites and from 49 to 68 percent for blacks.

D.J. Hernandez, *America's Children: Resources from Family, Government, and the Economy*
(New York: Russell Sage Foundation, 1993).

but also of instability in fathers' employment, we see that never since
the Great Depression have a majority of children lived in the idealized
Ozzie and Harriet families that have remained a myth throughout the
postwar era. While 31 percent of seventeen-year-olds lived in these
mythologized families in 1920, the prevalence of such families fell over
time to only 15 percent in 1960, and less than one-half of U.S. children
have been born into such families since at least 1940. In fact, the fraction of children born into these families fell from 44.5 percent in the
1950s to only 27.4 percent in 1980.

Furthermore, the limited evidence available for earlier times regarding marital dissolution and women's work suggests that it was

never the case that a majority of children lived in such idealized families. About one-fifth of newborns in 1940 and 1950 were not living in intact, two-parent families, and from 1920 to 1950 about one-third of seventeen-year-olds were not living in such families.[13] In addition, the overall rate of marital dissolution was steady between 1860 and 1960 because declining mortality rates were counterbalanced by rising divorce rates.[14] Therefore, it is likely that as far back as 1860 roughly

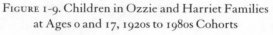

FIGURE 1-9. Children in Ozzie and Harriet Families
at Ages 0 and 17, 1920s to 1980s Cohorts

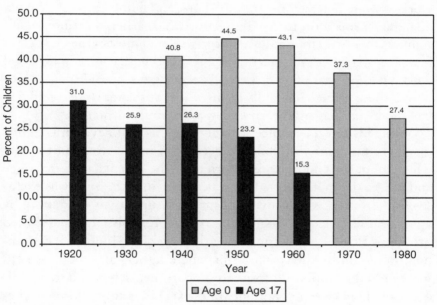

Note: More recent estimates cannot be calculated from the decennial census because of changes in data collection. The proportion of children ages 0 and 17 living in Ozzie and Harriet families has, however, no doubt declined further since 1980, when the most recent estimates in this figure were calculated. A primary determinant of decline in Ozzie and Harriet families has been the fall in the proportion with two parents in the home where the father works full time year-round and the mother did not work last year, which by 2000 had dropped for children ages 0 and 17, respectively, to 18 percent and 11 percent. These proportions are less than the corresponding estimates of the proportions in Ozzie and Harriet families of 27 percent and 15 percent, respectively, calculated as of 1980. If it were possible to take into account parental divorce and births to unmarried women, the proportions as of 2000 would be smaller still.

D.J. Hernandez, *America's Children: Resources from Family, Government, and the Economy* (New York: Russell Sage Foundation, 1993).

one-fifth of children were not born into intact, two-parent families, and that by age seventeen this proportion increased to about one-third. Insofar as mortality rates were still higher before 1860, the proportion of children not living in intact, two-parent families may also have been greater prior to the middle of the nineteenth century.

Mothers' employment was also substantial prior to 1940, if work that was not counted as employment in historical census data collection is included. For example, the 1900 census counted only 22.5 percent of women as employed in the formal economy, but the rate of women's employment rises to 46.4 percent if work is defined as including the taking in of boarders and lodgers, along with the uncounted work of women in factories, family shops, and family farms.[15] Women on family farms at the turn of the century, and earlier, contributed substantial labor to their families' enterprises,[16] and most of the increase in female employment in 1900 that is associated with counting informal work (16.9 percent of 23.9 percent) results from considering as employed those women on family farms whose husbands were counted as labor force participants because they were family farmers.[17]

While historical evidence strongly suggests that never in U.S. history have a majority of children been born into or lived in families where all of the children were born after the parents' only marriage and where the mother acted only as a homemaker and it was exclusively the father who provided economic support to the family by working full time year-round, the reasons for this fact have shifted over time. Prior to and during the early years of the Industrial Revolution, most children lived on farms where fathers and mothers both worked in the family enterprise to support themselves and their children, and high parental mortality rates exposed many children to one-parent families. As farming diminished and mortality declined, levels of often-insecure urban employment for fathers increased and were followed by mothers' increased employment in the formal labor market, as well as rising levels of divorce and, then, out-of-wedlock childbearing. Though the series of revolutionary changes in children's family lives during the past two centuries was not without its moments of continuity, what is important nevertheless is that from the perspective of children's actual living situations, the idealized vision of traditional family life has been a myth.

The Fall and Rise of Child Poverty

The third postwar revolution in children's lives has involved income and poverty trends. Median family income more than doubled between 1947 and 1973, but it increased by only 7 percent in the next twenty years, despite the enormous jump in mothers' paid work in the formal economy. Not until the seven years spanning 1993 to 2000 did a sustained increase of 18 percent occur in median family income.

With regard to poverty, social perceptions about what income levels were "normal" and "adequate" changed substantially because of the enormous increase in real income and the real standard of living between 1940 and 1973. The relative nature of judgments about what income level is sufficient has been noted for more than two hundred years. In *Wealth of Nations,* for example, Adam Smith emphasized that poverty must be defined in comparison to contemporary standards of living. He defined economic hardship as the experience of being unable to consume commodities that "the custom of the country renders it indecent for creditable people, even of the lowest order, to be without."[18] In 1958, the economist John Kenneth Galbraith also argued, "A people are poverty-stricken when their income, even if adequate for survival, falls markedly behind that of the community. Then they cannot have what the larger community regards as the minimum necessary for decency; and they cannot wholly escape, therefore, the judgment of the larger community that they are indecent. They are degraded for, in a literal sense, they live outside the grades or categories which the community regards as respectable."[19]

Historical changes in public perceptions about the amount of income needed by families have generally mirrored actual changes in family income.[20] In a review of evidence spanning 1937 through the 1960s, Rainwater found that throughout the era, Americans had viewed a "low" or "poverty-level" income in any given year as an amount equal to less than 50 percent of median family (disposable) income in that year; "enough to get along" as an amount equal to at least 50 percent of the median but less than 75 percent of it; "comfortable or prosperous" as an amount equal to at least 75 percent of the median but less than 150 percent of it; and "rich or super-rich" as an amount at least 150 percent of the median.[21] Therefore, the relative poverty measure adopted here sets the value of the poverty threshold at one-half of median family income in specific years, with adjustment for family size.[22]

According to this measure, child poverty declined sharply during the 1940s and then more slowly during the 1950s and 1960s. But after 1979, child poverty increased sharply, and it has since remained at high levels (Figure 1-10). The 1999 relative poverty rate for children of 27 percent was identical to the rate experienced by children in 1949. Meanwhile, the proportion of children living in official poverty also increased from a low of about 14 percent in 1969 to a high of 21 to 23

FIGURE 1-10. Children Ages 0 to 17 Years by Relative Income Level, 1939–1999

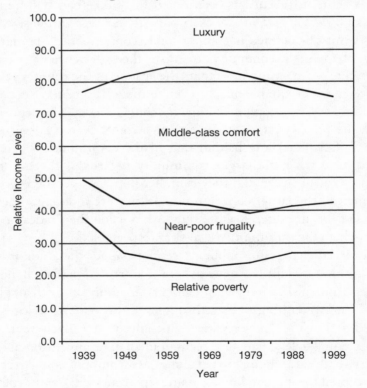

D.J. Hernandez, *America's Children: Resources from Family, Government, and the Economy* (New York: Russell Sage Foundation, 1993).

Data for 1999 are from U.S. Bureau of the Census, Current Population Survey, 2000.

percent between 1990 and 1996, although official child poverty subsequently declined to 16 percent as of 2000.[23]

Why did childhood poverty increase between the early 1970s and early 1980s and then remain at high levels through the early 1990s? One important and sometimes overlooked relevant change has been the large declines in the incomes of working men, especially those in the prime ages for fathering and rearing children. Large increases have occurred since the early 1970s—but especially since 1979—in the extent to which men working full time year-round have earnings that are less than the official poverty level for a four-person family. From 1992 to 1994, the proportions of men working full time year-round with such low incomes were 40 percent for ages eighteen to twenty-four, 13 percent for ages twenty-five to thirty-four, and 8 percent for ages thirty-five to fifty-four. Despite small declines subsequently, the proportions remained high in 1997, at 35 percent, 12 percent, and 8 percent, respectively.[24]

Of course, the amount of income available to children from their fathers is substantially less for children living in mother-only families than for children living with two parents. The best available evidence indicates, however, that only about one-third of the increase in child poverty during the 1980s could be accounted for by the rise in mother-only families, while about two-thirds of the increase was directly accounted for by declining income.[25] Thus, trends in childhood poverty have not mainly followed patterns in mother-only families that are independent of economic factors. Instead, trends in poverty have changed mainly because of the economic and employment experiences of fathers and mothers.

THE NEW AMERICAN MAJORITY OF THE TWENTY-FIRST CENTURY

Looking to the future, the U.S. fertility rate is near or below the level required to replace the population, and the baby boom generation is moving beyond childbearing age. Consequently, driven by population growth in other countries and U.S. economic opportunities, future growth in the U.S. population will occur primarily through immigration and births to current and future immigrants and their

FIGURE 1-11. Children in Immigrant Families from Various Regions of Origin: 1910, 1960, 1990, and 2000

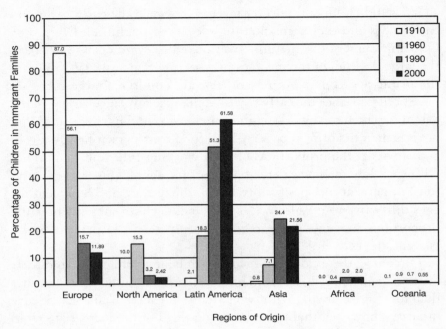

D.J. Hernandez and K. Darke, "The Well-Being of Immigrant Children, Native-Born Children with Immigrant Parents, and Native-Born Children with Native-Born Parents," in *Trends in the Well-Being of America's Children and Youth* (Washington, DC: Office of the Assistant Secretary for Planning and Evaluation, U.S. Department of Health and Human Services, 1998.)

Data for 2000 are from U.S. Bureau of the Census, Current Population Survey, 2000.

descendants. As of 2000, 20 percent of children in the United States were children of immigrants, with one or both parents foreign-born; more than three-fifths of these children were Hispanic, and more than one-fifth were Asian (Figure 1-11).

Because most children in immigrant families are Hispanic or non-white, Census Bureau projections indicate that children younger than eighteen who are Hispanic, black, Asian, or of some other racial minority will grow to account for more than one-half of the child population before 2040. But the timing of growth among racial and ethnic minorities varies greatly by age. The most recent projections by the U.S. Census Bureau indicate that in the year 2030, when the baby boom

FIGURE 1-12. Past and Projected Percentages of Children
in Specified Race/Ethnic Groups

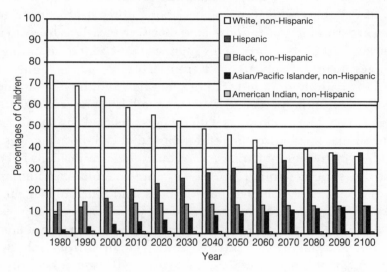

Source: Population Projections Program, Population Division, U.S. Census Bureau, January 13, 2000.

generation born between 1946 and 1964 will be in the retirement-age range of sixty-six to eighty-four years, 74 percent of the elderly will be non-Hispanic whites, compared to only 59 percent of working-age adults and 52 percent of children (Figure 1-12).[26] Consequently, as the growing elderly population of the predominantly white baby boom generation reaches retirement age, its members will increasingly depend on the productive activities and civic participation (that is, voting) of working-age adults who are members of racial and ethnic minorities (many of whom lived in immigrant families as children) for their economic support during retirement.

The Outlook for Immigrant Children's Families

A critical question for the future, then, is: What are the circumstances of children in immigrant families today? A recent study by the National Academy of Sciences' Institute of Medicine and the National Research Council found the following.[27] Children in immigrant families were, as of the 1990 census, less likely than children in U.S.-born families to have only one parent in the home. The overwhelming majority of children in immigrant families, like those in U.S.-born families, had fathers who were in the labor force—at 88 percent to 95 percent across the generations—and they were nearly as likely to have mothers in the labor force. This suggests that children in immigrant families are more likely to benefit from stable two-parent family situations than are children in U.S.-born families, and that the families of children of immigrants and those native-born have equally strong work ethics. The proportions with college-educated parents also were quite similar for children in immigrant and in U.S.-born families. But children in immigrant families were, on average, more likely to be exposed to socioeconomic risks. For example, children in immigrant families experienced higher poverty rates, and much higher proportions of their parents had completed eight years of schooling or less.

The higher levels of poverty among children in immigrant families are, however, highly concentrated among children from only twelve countries of origin. Five of these countries are the source of many officially recognized refugees: the former Soviet Union, Cambodia, Laos, Thailand, and Vietnam. Immigrants from four of the twelve nations have fled countries experiencing war or political instability: El Salvador, Guatemala, Nicaragua, and Haiti. Two others are small countries sending many migrants who seek unskilled work: Honduras and the Dominican Republic. The twelfth country is Mexico, which currently sends the largest number of both legal and illegal immigrants, and which has been an important source of unskilled labor for the U.S. economy throughout the twentieth century. The overall official poverty rate for children in immigrant families from these twelve countries was 35 percent in the 1990 census.

With regard to work issues in these families, 90 percent of children in immigrant families from these twelve countries had fathers who were in the labor force. But, in sharp contrast, 40 percent had fathers who did not work full time year-round, 46 percent had fathers with eight years of schooling or less, and 40 percent lived in linguistically isolated households where no one in the home age fourteen or older spoke English exclusively or very well. Thus, the much higher poverty rate for children from these twelve countries is not strongly related to a lack of labor force participation by fathers but instead is strongly associated with a lack of full-time year-round work among fathers, with extremely low educational attainments among parents, and with linguistic isolation from English-speaking society.

Available evidence suggests, then, that compared to third- and later-generation children, those in immigrant families were, on average, exposed to greater socioeconomic risks, particularly if their origins were in Southeast Asia, the former Soviet Union, Central America, or Mexico. In addition, children in immigrant families had less access to health insurance and health care, and those living at greatest socioeconomic risk were less likely to live in families receiving a range of welfare benefits and services.

Surprisingly, then, children in immigrant families were doing at least as well as or better than third- and later-generation children for a wide variety of indicators measuring physical health, mental health, and school adjustment.[28] This conclusion must be tempered, however, for three reasons.[29] First, although available evidence regarding the health and well-being of children in immigrant families is consistent across a wide variety of domains, it is limited both in its quality and in the number of domains for which research exists. Second, available evidence suggests there is enormous variability across children with different countries of origin for many indicators.[30] Third, health and well-being of children in immigrant families appear to deteriorate through time and across generations.[31] Since children in immigrant families are the fastest-growing component of the new American majority, the prospects for them are enormously important to the nation's future.

PUBLIC POLICIES FOR CHILDREN AND FAMILIES IN THE TWENTY-FIRST CENTURY

The policy implications of these transformations in the nature of childhood, work, and family in America will be discussed in detail throughout this book. In particular, the number of children living in families in which all adults work has important implications for the creation of a private and public system that universally provides the resources children and families require for their current well-being, their future success, and their basic human dignity. What kind of system might this be? Four components appear essential: paid parental leave, pre-kindergarten early education and care, guaranteed income supports, and access to health insurance and health care.

Universal paid leave for parents with infants is essential if parents are to have the time necessary for the care and nurturing of their newborns while working.[32] Currently, the United States has a two-class system in which a small group of parents can afford to take time off to be with their babies, whereas a very large second tier is effectively shut off from the opportunity of spending significant time with their newborns. All newborns would benefit from universal paid parental leave.

Universal pre-kindergarten early education and care programs would also benefit all children and families.[33] The United States has experienced two child care revolutions: the first for children age five or six and older as fathers entered the urban-industrial labor market, and the second for preschool-age children as mothers entered the paid labor force. The first child care revolution was legally mandated and funded by the government through universal public education systems that provided the intellectual foundation for the enormously successful American economy. Are the development, education, and success of America's youngest children any less important today as the nation competes for well-paid jobs in the global economy?

Public support for child care is currently a two-class system. For middle-income and high-income families, federal tax credits are available. But the working poor and working near-poor have access only to stigmatized and inadequate child care services and vouchers, or to no public child care resources at all. Reliance on the corporate world is not likely to reduce inequality of access to child care, because only the most successful companies with highly paid employees have the resources to provide such child care benefits. A caring society will provide early care and education, universally, for its children.

Guaranteed income supports are also essential. While nearly all families in America are working families, many live in poverty because their wages are low or their jobs are part-time or part-year. The single most successful policy to reduce poverty among working Americans during the past decade has been the earned income tax credit. Refundable earned income tax credits have proven to be a politically viable vehicle for creating an income floor for working Americans.

Closely related is the need for a refundable child care credit for parents of many working-poor families who must work nonstandard hours to support themselves. Among all employed women ages eighteen to thirty-four in 1991 with children younger than fourteen, for example, only 60 percent worked a fixed daytime weekdays-only schedule. These workers are especially likely to provide many services in the American economy, working as cashiers, waitresses, or cooks; nursing aides, orderlies, or attendants; supervisors or proprietors in sales occupations; hairdressers or cosmetologists; or maids, janitors, or cleaners.[34] In order to survive, these workers must work nights, weekends, or irregular hours, which pose special difficulties for making child care arrangements. For these families, universal, refundable child care credits are an essential adjunct to universal pre-kindergarten early education.

Lastly, access to health insurance and health care is needed. For the past half century, Americans have relied primarily on employers to provide health care coverage for their families, with a limited public system only for the most destitute. Yet 29 percent of children in 2000 were not covered by employee-based private insurance, and including government-supported coverage, 12 percent remain uninsured. Among poor children, 76 percent were not covered by employee-based private insurance, and 33 percent had no coverage from either private or government sources.[35] Low-income working families often do not have access to health insurance. Children and adults require health care to survive and thrive. As one of the wealthiest nations in the world, the United States can surely afford health care for all.

CONCLUSION

In sum, if Americans care about all their children and families, then universal approaches to meeting their needs may be not only appropriate but also essential because the piecemeal approaches of the past have left many children and families without adequate child care, without adequate income, and without adequate health care. As the new American majority emerges, the work and family experiences of non-Hispanic whites and of racial, ethnic, and cultural minorities are becoming bound together ever more tightly, and the future of each is increasingly becoming the future of all.

2

Changing Work and Family Lives:
A Historical Perspective

Eileen Boris

From its founding in World War I, the Women's Bureau of the U.S. Department of Labor had focused on what a later generation named the "double day," the dilemma faced by women of having to combine wage labor with household responsibilities, particularly the bearing and rearing of children.[1] At its 1948 conference "The American Woman, Her Changing Role—Worker, Homemaker, Citizen," it defined "democracy to include what we mean by [a] decent living and a chance to make a decent living . . . education for all, decent conditions of work, rights of everyone to a job, social insurance, maternity benefits, child welfare, health, rights to culture and recreation."[2] During the prosperity of the decades following the conference, only some Americans would obtain these accoutrements of a decent life.

The problems of reconciling workplace demands with families' needs and of determining the proper relation between women's and men's wage earning and their domestic responsibilities dominated public discussion throughout the twentieth century. These continue to vex policy makers and families alike, despite shifts in a host of social and cultural factors, such as gender norms, labor force participation, household composition, the role of government, and the meaning of democratic participation itself.

In this chapter, I concentrate on work and family policies, such as social assistance to poor mothers and their children, labor standards legislation, child care, and health care, during the origins of the American welfare state in the Progressive Era of the early 1900s and the

New Deal of the 1930s and 1940s. I then more briefly consider changes after 1960. Three assumptions guide the analysis that follows. First, social policies shape cultural constructions of the worker and normative conceptions of proper homes and families.[3] Second, the state sector in the United States has remained underdeveloped compared to that sector in European welfare states. Specifically, instead of benefits or programs available for all, a residualist paradigm under the U.S. "liberal" welfare regime limited programs to individuals and families marked "at-risk" or unable to survive without a government safety net.[4] Finally, U.S. public and private social policies have long reflected socially constructed hierarchies that, in general, have disadvantaged women more often than men and people of color more often than whites.[5]

For over a century, the relationship between work and family lay at the center of debates over the state's responsibility to its citizens and citizens' obligations to society. Social policy sought to reinforce gendered expectations of work and family based on a white, middle-class, Protestant, and married heterosexual norm of female domesticity and male breadwinning. In the Progressive Era, local and state governments began to supplant private, often religiously based charities in the relief of needy families judged deserving of aid. These were families where industrial accidents, the death of a male breadwinner, maternal incapacity, and the overall capriciousness of capitalist workplaces had created economic dependency. Policies would reduce maternal wage earning through monetary supplements, while courts would punish men who failed to support families through garnishment of wages and the threat of incarceration. Protective legislation sought to safeguard the childbearing and child rearing capabilities of female industrial workers at a time when mostly white women held such jobs, but when initially there was little public or private provision of child care for employed mothers.

The New Deal promised "security" against the hazards of industrial life and economic dislocation to a nation scared by the Great Depression. Its programs focused on providing adequate support to male breadwinners through unemployment insurance and pensions and also encouraging their unionization. By basing social security on employment, and then omitting agriculture and domestic service, a result of political struggle between business, labor, northern liberals, and southern segregationists, social security excluded most minority men and women as well as most white women. Housewives gained old age and other benefits only if their husbands "earned" coverage through their jobs. Over the next decades, civil rights and women's rights advocates, along with organized labor, fought for expanded social security provisions, so by 1980 these were nearly universal.

During World War II, labor shortages and higher wages offered new opportunities for women, suggesting alternative ways of organizing work and family. While some of these new services and programs, such as public provision of child care, faded with war's end, they reemerged as demands of the postwar rights movements for gender and racial justice. Others became commercialized, such as cleaning services and prepared food that offered relief from the double day—at least for those women with enough income to purchase them. Feminists gained parental leave and protections against pregnancy discrimination for those women who labored in jobs covered by these laws. Reproductive rights, however, remained tenuous: abortion was heavily restricted, and poor women, disproportionately African American and Latina, found their right to bear children undermined by the new welfare regime.

The 1980s and 1990s reinforced a widening gap in time, goods, and quality of life between families at the top of the income pyramid and those without resources at the bottom.[6] The Reagan revolution and devolution of federal power undermined the New Deal order after it finally had become more inclusive. Fueled by a gender gap, in which women more consistently supported spending for social services and the improvement of work and family life, public policy stood at a crossroads at the beginning of the twenty-first century.[7] Whether or not the New Deal legacy could provide the foundations for a revitalized welfare state, one that met the work and family needs of all, remained unresolved as a new era, fueled by fears of terrorism and war, began.

DEFINING THE STATE'S ROLE IN THE SUPPORT OF HOMES AND FAMILIES AT THE BEGINNING OF THE TWENTIETH CENTURY

During the opening decades of the twentieth century, reformers and philanthropists wrestled with the problem of the "home slacker,"[8] meaning the failed male breadwinner, and "the mother who must earn,"[9] that is, the woman who had to take up employment to compensate for her partner's economic failure. Social provision during this period grew as a mixture of public and private services, while states regulated women's working conditions and courts attempted to enforce men's family responsibilities. Without suffrage, women influenced social policy through lobbying campaigns and through support of candidates for whom men could vote.[10]

In the wake of new immigration from eastern and southern Europe, increased industrialization, and urban expansion, early-twentieth-century reformers attempted to address the impact of poverty—with its resulting deterioration of living conditions—on working-class families.[11] In the process, they began to forge an activist state, especially on the local level, responsible for the general welfare of its inhabitants. Prior to the late nineteenth century, the most prominent form of state intervention into families' lives came through judicial decisions that addressed marriage, divorce, inheritance, and child custody.[12] According to various scholars, there existed a dual system of family law: the law for the middle and upper classes, which sought to allocate resources, and the law for the indigent, which sought to curb public expenditures, forcing support back onto an extended kin network whenever possible.[13] Some industrial states, such as New York, formed boards of charity, and many municipalities maintained earlier forms of poor aid through either workhouses or outdoor relief (provision of food, clothing, fuel, and so on to the noninstitutionalized poor). Religious and other private charities tended, however, to predominate over state aid. The Progressive movement would reconfigure this pattern by enacting legislation mandating new social services and by regulating industrial practices.[14] As with much of U.S. history, however, the South exhibited the regional pattern of longer dependency on private initiatives. Significantly, a growing Jim Crow regime stymied work and family social provisions not only for African Americans but also for poor whites; both groups, then, except for those eligible for "Confederate pensions," faced stingy public services and a lack of state aid.[15]

Mothers' Wage Earning and Mothers' Pensions

In the late 1800s and early 1900s, about 90 percent of all men ages fifteen to sixty-four were engaged in gainful employment. According to most estimates, fewer than 25 percent of women were employed, but new calculations, including both home-based and formal-economy labor, have indicated that nearly half the women in the same age bracket were generating income. Slightly more than 40 percent of wives could be classified as workers, though most either engaged in unpaid labor for family farms and shops or took in boarders. The home location of their work masked the difficulties of caring for their children while simultaneously earning money.[16]

Nonetheless, in public discourse and social policy, the term *worker* was predominantly used to mean a man who left the home to earn wages. However, men from racial or ethnic minority groups were often considered inadequate as men, or workers, primarily because they failed to earn a wage large enough to support a stay-at-home wife and school-attending children, but also because they often labored in service industries and performed care work, which was generally viewed as the province of women.[17] The "woman worker" existed, but as a special kind of worker—that is, a woman who was temporarily in the labor force before marriage and motherhood or who had to re-turn to employment, as a wife or widow, because of family necessity.[18] The concerns of African American women were widely ignored or disparaged because these women often had to enter the labor force and had to work by caring for the houses and children of privileged social groups.[19] Such complex cultural conceptions about work and workers—and related notions about children's needs and worth— would shape evaluations of male unemployment, the "woman worker," and child labor throughout the century.[20]

Family preservation represented a major reform goal. Mothers became the objects of social reform when husbands and fathers were unable to fulfill their breadwinning duties—whether because of in-dustrial accidents, unemployment, low wages, death, or desertion. While the divorce rate dropped from one in every 13.9 marriages in 1887 to one in every 15.6 marriages by 1906,[21] poor people deserted, rather than divorced, their partners and thus remained uncounted by such statistics.[22] Male nonsupport led mothers "to carry the double burden of earning the support and of performing the domestic duties which, under our present habits of thinking, are inextricably inter-twined with her maternal duties," social work educator Sophonisba Breckinridge noted in 1910. "When any one of these phases of her work must be neglected," Breckinridge further observed, "it is the side of nurture and personal care which is slighted, since the dollars and cents with which to pay for the daily meal and the weekly rent must be found, while the discipline and coddling can, of course, be deferred."[23] Child neglect and juvenile delinquency, reformers such as Breckinridge predicted, would result.

In the 1910s, mothers' pensions, or state monies given to families without breadwinners, were one solution. Reformers fashioned widows' or mothers' pensions from the same gender ideology that embraced the search for a higher "American Standard of Living" through collective bargaining on the part of restrictive (and overwhelmingly white and male) craft unions, while simultaneously criminalizing men's desertion of families.[24] Pensions represented a form of state provision for social reproduction and enabled widows judged "fit and worthy" to remain at home.[25] The labor market participation of mothers often had necessitated the breakup of their families, with children sent to orphanages or left to roam the streets.[26] As President Theodore Roosevelt told the 1909 White House Conference on the Care of Dependent Children, "The goal toward which we should strive is to help the mother, so that she can keep her own home and keep the child in it; that is the best thing possible to be done for the child."[27]

Children's Health and Welfare: Questions of Public Versus Private Support

Such an understanding—also held by middle-class white women in voluntary organizations such as the National Congress of Mothers and the General Federation of Women's Clubs, whose mobilization had pushed twenty states to enact mothers' pensions between 1911 and 1913 and forty states by 1920[28]—seriously curtailed day care as an alternative.[29] Child care, maternity leave, and medical benefits for childbirth would entice women to remain in the labor force, charged Florence Kelley, the leader of the National Consumers' League, which campaigned against sweatshops. Philanthropic agencies exacerbated the "double burden," she claimed, by establishing "day nurseries, charity kindergartens, charity sewing rooms, and doles of home sewing." To her, the idea of a nursery so women could "work at night after they have cared for their children by day" appeared "monstrous."[30] Worried about such overwork, Kelley fought to eliminate the necessity of mothers' wage earning. If men could not support wives, then the state either had to force men's support through laws against desertion, provide pensions for "orphans and widowed mothers of young children," or help men obtain living wages. "Prevention of accidents and disease" further would lengthen men's work lives. For "detached" women without children, Kelley advocated factory work with wages high enough to sustain them. Regarding "deliberately idle men," Kelley said they should be "sen[t] to the workhouse for the week-end . . . just to remind them of their obligation."[31]

In contrast, African American women activists accepted the wage earning of married women and mothers. They established nurseries, but they generally had less access to the state to translate their private programs into public policy.[32] In Chicago during this period, however, black clubwomen engaged in partisan politics, gaining appointments to school boards, the Domestic Relations Court, and other agencies to serve their community. As the historian Patricia A. Schechter concluded from the career of Ida B. Wells-Barnett (an activist and founder of the Women's Era Club, the first civic organization for African American women), they could not afford the disinterestedness that white women reformers cultivated—even when involved with the political parties—to give them moral clout with government and politicians.[33]

The actual impact of day nurseries, or crèches, was limited. At the turn of the century, the philanthropist-run National Federation of Day Nurseries operated centers in cities with large immigrant populations, such as Chicago, Philadelphia, Cleveland, and New York, with the goal of "Americanizing" the next generation of workers. By 1916, there were seven hundred affiliated nurseries. Social settlements, such as Chicago's pioneer Hull House, also offered child care for wage-earning mothers. Religious institutions organized their own centers, and black women's clubs in both the South and the North sponsored day care in their own settlements and churches. The public schools functioned as caretakers for older children, abetted by compulsory education laws, which thirty-two states had passed by 1900 to battle child labor.[34] The National Child Labor Committee, in fact, offered "scholarships" to substitute for wages and, thus, keep would-be child laborers in school, but literacy and age requirements for work permits varied, and enforcement of child labor legislation was often lax.[35]

Day care remained a private, rather than state-funded, service. In contrast, the development of mothers' pensions "led to a major expansion of administrative capacity at the level of state and local government," the historian Sonya Michel has concluded, making pensions "the government's principal policy toward low-income mothers and their children."[36] Yet implementation of mothers' pensions undermined the care rationale expressed by reformers, who, like Julia Lathrop, the first head of the U.S. Children's Bureau, also viewed the "rearing of children" as a "duty of citizenship."[37] Underfunded by reluctant state and municipal governments, pensions were rarely generous enough. They never included a caretakers' grant, only monies for the children, and they usually excluded women with one child from coverage. In Chicago, officials eliminated from eligibility those mothers with earnings sufficient to support their families. But because rules also precluded full-time wage labor, mothers were forced into the low-paying and casual sectors of the economy, such as piece-rate sewing in their homes, split-shift waitressing, and domestic service. Local conceptions of worthiness determined who received pensions in the first place, and that fact led to the disproportionate exclusion of African Americans and immigrants (without citizenship standing), the barring of unwed mothers, and the elimination of those lacking "good habits."[38]

Fiscal strains on charities and the pension system encouraged states and localities to separate widowed women, who received aid, from the deserted, who rarely received any. So did the belief among family reformers that pensions would encourage either collusion by husbands and wives to "cheat the charities" or desertion by fathers who believed that someone else would care for their charges. Social workers agreed that nonsupport, rather than actual family breakup, was the crime. By 1916, every state had criminalized the act of nonsupport.[39] Thus, charities sent women seeking assistance to the New York City Domestic Relations Court, established in 1910 to enforce rulings and laws mandating that husbands support their wives. The Department of Public Charities dispersed alimony until 1919, when local bureaus took up this function.[40] Similarly enforcing such "breadwinner regulation," the Chicago Court of Domestic Relations maintained the fiction of the family wage—a wage earned by one adult that was sufficient to support a family. The court resented public policing of what was labeled as a "private" obligation, but its very actions challenged any simple separation of public and private.[41]

The Impact of Labor Laws on Women and Families

The question of public involvement was not limited to pensions and support. Potential motherhood also elicited state intervention in labor contracts. Labor laws for women and children provided reformers an entering wedge related to wage, hour, and other workplace standards in an era when the Supreme Court upheld "freedom of contract" for men. Court protection arose from a "public interest in women as reproducers."[42] In 1905, the Supreme Court struck down New York's attempt to legislate shorter hours for bakers in the precedent-setting *Lochner* case, but three years later it upheld an hours law for women in *Muller v. Oregon.* As Justice David Brewer wrote for the majority, "That woman's physical structure and the performance of maternal functions place her at a disadvantage in the struggle for subsistence is obvious . . . and, as healthy mothers are essential to vigorous offspring, the physical well-being of a woman becomes an object of public interest and care in order to preserve the strength and vigor of the race."[43] Gender-based understandings of the worker thus provided a terrain upon which reformers, unionists, employers, and the courts fought over the extent of state responsibility for work and its subsequent impact on the family.

Between 1908 and World War I, seventeen states passed various laws stipulating the conditions under which women could labor. These restricted employment in some occupations; for example, foundries were deemed dangerous for pregnancy or childbearing. In addition, they established minimum wages to alleviate exploitation, but some hoped also to save young women from lives of prostitution (though state minimums never offered the potential for economic independence because they set wages too low for self-support). Bans on night work promised to protect morals as well as health, though they kept women from lucrative jobs in trades such as printing and bartending. (Entertainment forms dependent on sexuality and the allure of female beauty remained uncovered by such regulations.) These so-called protective labor laws usually failed to cover part-time and home labor, encouraging employers to reorganize their work so as to bypass the laws altogether. In addition, laws banning home-based industrial work proved nearly impossible to enforce. Protective laws improved the conditions of women in female-dominated manufacturing but encouraged their concentration in jobs unwanted by men. Beset by lower wages, many young women saw marriage as an escape from wage labor. But men could not always support their families, leading mothers to return to a labor market where women's work earned fewer rewards and where women of color, concentrated in agricultural and personal service occupations, stood outside of labor laws.[44]

The Supreme Court's 1923 decision in *Adkins v. Children's Hospital,* which overturned the minimum wage law for Washington, D.C., pulled the plug on minimum wage boards that calculated wages on the basis of women's needs rather than on the rate for the job, an approach that equal pay advocates had advanced during World War I. The Court's majority determined that "revolutionary . . . changes . . . in the contractual, political and civil status of women, culminating in the nineteenth amendment," superseded the reasoning of *Muller.*[45] By 1925, the Women's Bureau was pressing for "a living wage without discrimination because of sex" as "the recommended wage standard."[46] It recognized that women also were breadwinners and thus appropriated the term *living wage* to apply to them as well. A woman's wage, then, was both an individual expression of worth and a reflection of a woman's familial responsibilities.[47]

Public and Private Responses to Health Care Needs

Progressive Era reform thus generated protections from private or market-driven actions that would have undermined wage earners' family lives, but it provided state services or benefits only for those in the most desperate circumstances. Reformers, however, were committed to the idea that society as a whole could benefit from programs that targeted the needy. Advances in public health affected all urban dwellers, even if tenement house reform, pure food and drug laws, and better sanitation most directly impacted those who resided in deteriorating urban environments.[48] Private solutions particularly predominated in the area of health care, an activity that was still located in the home and performed by female kin but was gradually moving into hospitals and becoming dominated by health professionals.[49] Nongovernmental groups, such as the New York Charity Organization Society, "collaborated closely" with public authorities to quarantine people with contagious diseases.[50] Free clinics and settlement houses offered outpatient services, while visiting nurses made calls to tenement dwellers in their homes. Men's fraternal and worker benevolent societies were more likely than charities to provide sick pay, death benefits, and medical care, however inadequate. Women wage earners lacked equivalent organizations, though some gained benefits directly from their employers. Furthermore, within the "welfare capitalism" of the 1910s and 1920s employers granted women workers, if anything, recreational and educational programs, rather than the health insurance and financial pensions that they offered to men. With the exception of miners in the West and garment workers in New York City, who responded to occupational diseases by establishing their own facilities, only a quarter of the unionized had sickness benefits and health care by 1916, when slightly more than 5 percent of laborers were unionized. Only industries with exceptionally high rates of accidents and illness tended to offer health care, usually through company doctors.[51]

The Sheppard-Towner Act of 1921 proved an exception to the paucity of state provision of health care. It represented Congress's political response to the perceived power of women as a newly enfranchised bloc of voters. The act addressed infant and maternity health, as had previous advice-focused programs of the agency that implemented it: the U.S. Children's Bureau, which was established in 1912 after a campaign by child welfare reformers and middle-class women's clubs to save children from premature employment in industries and improve children's health and welfare.[52] Rather than establish maternity leave for wage-earning women, which reformers continued to believe would encourage mothers' employment, the bureau, under Sheppard-Towner, gave matching grants to states for infant protection, educational programs and rural clinics.[53] Nearly all states participated in the program; they set up training classes for midwives, conducted immunization campaigns, and sponsored visiting nurses and health conferences. Opposed by physicians, who wanted both to control baby care and to relieve illness, and the U.S. Public Health

Service, which wanted to take over all federal health programs, the Children's Bureau found itself on the defensive by mid-decade; ultimately, physicians' opposition kept it from implementing sustained medical care. When no unified women's vote materialized, Congress easily sided with the American Medical Association, which labeled the Sheppard-Towner Act " 'an imported socialistic scheme' of 'state medicine' " and ended the program in 1929.[54] By then, according to the historian Molly Ladd-Taylor, "Sheppard-Towner workers had held 183,252 prenatal and child health conferences and helped establish 2,978 permanent health clinics."[55] Universal in its intent, if not its coverage (though it did reach Native American reservations and African Americans in rural areas), the act extended the arena of federal responsibility in health care while maintaining the states as the locus of government programs.

In the early twentieth century, then, local governments joined private philanthropies in beginning to address the work and family issues that rapid industrialization, increased immigration, and expansive urbanization had generated. But they worked under traditional understandings of maternal domesticity and male breadwinning. Under the regulatory function and police power, law and social policy restrained unbridled capitalism and wayward husbands more often than they guaranteed social benefits. Nonetheless, social reformers pushed for labor legislation and mothers' pensions in the states that would eventually become incorporated into federal social policies during the Great Depression. The limited life of the Sheppard-Towner Act foreshadowed the difficulties ahead for the establishment of any universal national health policy, but Progressive reformers set in motion a mixed private-public welfare state.

ESTABLISHING A SOCIAL SAFETY NET: THE NEW DEAL ORDER

During the Great Depression, work and family policies broadened beyond their focus on immigrants, dependents, and paupers to include a greater proportion of the nation, whose sense of security the economic crisis had undermined. With net farm income rapidly falling, foreclosures on family farms numbered in the hundreds of thousands. Nine million had lost their savings during the bank collapse; nearly a quarter of wage earners were unemployed by 1933, and millions worked reduced hours. Initially, occupational segregation protected women from unemployment, although not from low wages; in some families, wives and children entered the labor market to make up for lost male wages. Yet married women in public sector jobs faced dismissal under the 1932 Economy Act out of the general belief that they were taking jobs away from "real providers." In blue-collar occupations, where women were scarce, black and white men, especially in the Northeast and Midwest, felt the downturn most. However, the black rate of unemployment was double that of whites in hard-pressed cities such as Detroit. Until World War II, a fifth of the possible labor force remained out of work.[56]

The New Deal response was security: "economic security, social security, moral security," President Franklin Roosevelt reiterated during World War II in calling for a "Second Bill of Rights" that would assure people of the right to a job, housing, education, medical services, and other components of a decent standard of living.[57] Initially, the Roosevelt administration attempted to shore up the nation's financial system and its productive and distributional capabilities for both industry and agriculture. It also concentrated on the immediate needs of the unemployed through various work relief programs, such as the Civilian Conservation Corps, the National Youth Administration, and the Works Progress Administration (WPA). Only then did it turn to more structural approaches in the arena of social welfare.[58]

The New Deal order that emerged from the Great Depression and World War II forged a limited welfare state based on two tracks. The first track, which was federally funded and administered, embraced the economy's core-sector workers—most often white men—and their dependents. The National Labor Relations Act (also known as the Wagner Act) facilitated the collective bargaining crucial for industrial workers to wrestle better wages, working conditions, and, with World War II, fringe benefits such as pensions and health care from their employers, inscribing a private welfare state within this federal one. The second track, which was left to the states and their greater arbitrariness, covered the most socially and economically disadvantaged people, who were more often men of color and women.[59] Beset by divisions within the Democratic Party on race and states' rights, business mobilization through the Republican Party, and Cold War priorities, the New Deal's comprehensive social democratic vision remained unrealized.[60] What emerged was a mixed private-public welfare state that favored employment over nonwage care work, in which tax incentives and other state policies facilitated the growth of pensions and health insurance in private firms; the result was the linking of people's welfare to the vagaries of the market.[61]

A Limited Security Net: Relief Programs and Labor Standards

New Dealers believed "that 'the worker and his family' deserved 'a living wage,'" and the assumption remained that family life would improve when male wages increased.[62] Relief programs, such as the WPA, usually provided employment for only one family member, the household head.[63] The 1935 Social Security Act—with provisions for old age insurance, unemployment insurance, and Aid to Dependent Children (ADC), and later the 1962 Aid to Families with Dependent Children (AFDC)—solidified the model of the citizen-worker, basing eligibility on an individual's employment record or family relation to a covered breadwinner. Labor standards—the minimum wage, maximum hour, and child labor restrictions embodied in the 1938 Fair Labor Standards Act (FLSA)—applied only to industries engaged in interstate commerce. The act covered only 34 percent of workers, slightly more of whom were men than women.[64] The New Deal thus created an unequal system, linking its most generous provisions—administered by the federal government—to employment, but excluding agricultural and service occupations dominated by white women and people of color.[65] Millions still found themselves outside the net of security.[66]

"Security," as the historian Jennifer Klein has shown, was limited in its components as well as its clients. For example, the labor movement and advocates of health insurance alike demanded that society assume responsibility for individual health care, which a member of the Women's Auxiliary of the Steel Workers Organizing Committee referred to as one of "the 'inalienable rights' of every citizen."[67] But New Dealers were unable to ensure such coverage. A medical model eclipsed the Progressive Era focus on public health even as doctors, consumers, employers, and unions experimented with "programs that would enable patients to pool the risks and costs of sickness and injury, thus bringing medical care within the reach of more people."[68] Strong opposition from the American Medical Association, insurance companies, and hospitals stymied national health insurance throughout the 1930s and 1940s. Instead, cooperatives, "the Blues" (Blue Cross and Blue Shield), and group clinics formed the backbone of a nongovernmental system of health insurance, enhanced by collective bargaining over the next decades.[69] Patchwork coverage resulted. Thus, New Deal programs such as the Tennessee Valley Authority provided some poor families with medical services, and the Social Security Act revived maternal and child health as a federal concern. Meanwhile, the families of rank-and-file servicemen became eligible for the Emergency Maternity and Infant Care program initiated by the Children's Bureau during World War II.[70] Whether or not a workplace was unionized and whether or not a union could wrestle benefits through collective bargaining further contributed to the irregular shape of health coverage.[71]

The Fair Labor Standards Act

Labor standards legislation federalized earlier state regulations, bringing security to covered workers. As the economic historians Figart, Mutari, and Power have observed, "The Fair Labor Standards Act legitimated and institutionalized the idea that living standards and workers' needs mattered in setting wages."[72] It also helped both restore the family wage and curtail child labor. The FLSA did not specifically address issues associated with gender or race, but Figart, Mutari, and Power have concluded that the act "was constructed so that white, male, unskilled workers could come closer to a male breadwinner wage." After all, many skilled male workers were already earning more than its initial minimum (25¢ an hour), and men of color generally were not covered by the law because of where they worked. Labor organizations, whose support of the legislation ranged from the lukewarm response of the American Federation of Labor (AFL) to the more adamant advocacy of the Congress of Industrial Organizations (CIO), also emphasized the FLSA's focus on unskilled male workers. The mineworker chief and CIO head John L. Lewis concurred with AFL spokesmen at hearings on the FLSA: "Normally, a husband and father should be able to earn enough to support his family," he testified. "This does not mean, of course, that I am opposed to the employment of women, or even of wives, when this is the result of their own free choice. But I am violently opposed to a system which by degrading the earnings of adult males makes it economically necessary for wives and children to become supplementary wage earners."[73] Furthermore, labor leaders only reluctantly accepted legislated floors on wages, since no one thought that the minimum wage would, in fact, enable a man to support his family; the point of such legislation was to hamper low-wage competition from undermining other workers. "It is only those low-wage and long-working-hour industrial workers, who are the helpless victims of their own bargaining weakness, that this bill seeks to assist to obtain a minimum wage," the Senate Committee on Education and Labor remarked about the FLSA. Although labor leaders viewed collective bargaining as central to ensuring workers' freedom, according to John P. Davis of the National Negro Congress, labor standards legislation ended up bringing no help "to those workers whose lack of collective bargaining power render[ed] them capable of exploitation by employers."[74]

Barriers to Work-Related Benefits for Women

Women, in general, went in and out of the labor market, worked part time, and concentrated in workplaces uncovered by either law or union contract;[75] women's labor in the home—paid as well as unpaid—remained underrecognized.[76] According to the political scientist Suzanne Mettler, while women in the garment and textile industries benefited from the FLSA, exemption from the law hurt women more than men. Sales clerks, laundry operatives, beauticians, clerical workers, and a host of other women laborers belonged to intrastate commerce and thus remained uncovered. Except for those working in agriculture (22.8 percent of the workforce in 1940), most uncovered men earned more than the minimum wage. Women were twice as likely to be exempt from the FLSA and to earn less than the FLSA-mandated wage.[77]

Among workers who lost their jobs, the federally controlled unemployment insurance (UI) program would cushion those who had earned benefits as a "right" because they had contributed to the program through a tax on their earnings and on employer payrolls. However, benefit levels corresponded to prior income, which disproportionately aided people with higher salaries or wages, thereby disadvantaging men of color and women.[78] UI extended only to those with employment histories that met a threshold of earnings and hours. There was a "work test" in that unemployment had to result from employer actions, not from laziness or quitting with "good cause," and the involved person had to search for a new job.[79] The vagueness of criteria allowed assessments of the worker to creep into eligibility evaluations, and administrators of the system would turn down those who refused offers of jobs with standard business hours. Among those part-time, seasonal, and causal laborers targeted for exclusion were "those who ha[d] more than one leg in the home."[80] The Committee on Economic Security (CES), the crafter of social security, rejected unemployment compensation for housewives. UI thus would not contain allowances for dependents of unemployed wage earners—as did the British or Belgian systems—nor did it extend to women temporarily out of work due to maternity. Pregnant workers, as well as women who had no child care or who quit jobs to move for their husbands' employment or to fulfill other "marital obligations," were not "available for work" and thus could not be considered unemployed.[81]

The housewife, however, would gain old age benefits with 1939 amendments to the Social Security Act that added "a supplementary allowance equivalent to fifty percent of the husband's own benefits."[82] A woman could draw from her own "contribution," rather than her husband's, if, by doing so, she would receive more. But this was still a period when the majority of wives lacked sustained labor force participation; the 1939 amendments both subsidized female domesticity and provided real material gains for women. In 1956, amendments lowered the pension eligibility age for women to sixty-two but reduced the amount of benefits, on the assumption that women would follow usually older husbands into retirement. These shifts increased couples' overall income, but it did little for single women, who often could not afford early retirement.[83]

Title I of the 1935 act had provided Old Age Assistance (OAA) through the states to indigent elderly people who did not qualify for Old Age Insurance (OAI, commonly called social security). OAA's relatively generous administration in subsequent years became a political problem for OAI, which was not scheduled to pay benefits—ones that would have been, on the average, less than those under OAA—until

1942, but the OAA program was accumulating a surplus from its tax on employers and employees.[84] The 1939 amendments shored up popular support for social security while extending "security" to "normal" families. Under the concept of "equity for covered men," survivor's insurance distributed funds to children of deceased fathers. Meanwhile, widows with children younger than eighteen received three-fourths of the pension coming to their husbands, unless they remarried or entered the workforce. In contrast, divorced or never-married women had to rely on the more arbitrary, state-run ADC program for any publicly funded benefits.[85]

The 1939 amendments transformed social security, as the historian Alice Kessler-Harris has noted, from "a labor regulation device meant to preserve the dignity of workers who made way for the next generation into something more clearly approximating a promise of economic security freed of its rigid requirement for an equitable return on individual contributions."[86] Rather than an insurance program in the technical sense, it relied on a "pay-as-you-go formula."[87] Over the next decades, this necessitated expansion to new groups of workers—including "regularly employed farm and domestic workers" in 1950 and 1954—and thus turned OAI into the most universal of work and family programs.[88]

Shifts in Women's Work Patterns and Societal Responses to Child Care Needs

During the Depression, when the government sought to remove those judged less efficient from the labor force, many formulators of ADC celebrated motherhood but also assumed that "worthy" widows would earn something toward their upkeep. Arguing for passage, one Arkansas congressman envisioned "the careworn and dejected widow shout[ing] with joy upon returning from the neighbor's washtub after having received assurance of financial aid for her children."[89] ADC originally provided monies only for the children and lacked any grant for caregivers. When the referent for *mother* came to include nonwhites, states—beginning with Louisiana in 1943—adopted "employable mother" rules that forced would-be recipients into the labor market if any form of employment was available.[90] Not only did the numbers under ADC expand during the 1940s, but the type of family shifted as well, away from widows to the never-married (from 2 percent in 1938 to 14.1 percent in 1948). Simultaneously, the proportion of African Americans doubled to 31 percent of all aided, even with the often limited assistance of the southern states.[91]

Welfare rarely came without arbitrariness or discrimination, as "employable mother," "suitable home," and "man in the house" rules restricted the eligibility of poor, single mothers.[92] Moreover, federal funds to the states for ADC fell below those for OAA, the other means-tested program. State fiscal burdens, added to the local control of eligibility, further reinforced ADC's patchwork character, expressed through geographical arbitrariness. Children and their caregivers would not receive the same assistance throughout the nation. As with earlier mothers' pensions, states discriminated against poor, single mothers on the basis of moral and racial criteria, excluding "illegitimate" children from coverage and instituting racial quotas and citizenship requirements.[93]

The children of families on relief, however, gained access to nursery schools as part of New Deal aid to their families. With half-day programs, these schools aimed to employ teachers more than to provide child care for wage-earning parents. As early as 1933, the relief czar Harry Hopkins explained, "The education and health programs of nursery schools can aid as nothing else in combating the physical and mental handicaps being imposed upon these young children." By 1935, the WPA ran about nineteen hundred of these schools for around seventy-five thousand pupils.[94]

Women's Work and Children's Care During and After World War II
Conditions during World War II reflected tension between the need for womanpower and defense of "the democratic family" with its stay-at-home mother. As the head of the War Manpower Commission directed in 1942, "No women responsible for the care of young children should be encouraged or compelled to seek employment which deprives children of essential care until all other sources of supply are exhausted."[95] But millions of women responded to the high wages offered by war industries, with more than six million entering the labor force between 1940 and 1945, thus doubling the number of employed women. Few mothers with children younger than six left their homes; their numbers rose from 9 percent to 12 percent during the war years,

at a time when women headed nearly one in five families.[96] In manufacturing, business, and government, white women gained access to higher-paying positions; African American women, however, remained last hired, first fired and found it difficult to break into war work. The same was true for African American men.[97]

Though never adequate to meet the need of women war workers, child care centers existed in more than forty-four hundred communities by mid-1943. Still, a year later, at least 16 percent of mothers in defense-related industries lacked child care; by war's end, federal monies under the Lanham Act had led to the establishment of only 3,102 centers.[98] Parents from all racial and ethnic groups avoided such institutional care and, instead, relied on babysitters and family day care.[99] Government funding stopped in most places within a year of demobilization, despite organized protests by mothers in Philadelphia, New York City, Washington, D.C., Cleveland, and elsewhere. In California, state-supported child care, previously available to war workers, became means-tested and was offered only to families of limited income.[100]

But the war also offered ways to organize wage work and family labor that did not rely on mothers. Kaiser Shipyards in Portland, Oregon—a public-private venture involving buildings funded by the Maritime Commission, with red tape waived by federal authorities—housed model child care centers with low fees, with the government picking up the cost by reimbursing the Kaiser Corporation.[101] Other factories experimented with shopping, laundry, and meal services, prefiguring the transfer of domestic labor from the home to the market—a process that intensified with the growing employment of mothers with small children during the twentieth century's last decades.[102]

At war's end, many women lost their higher-paying jobs and returned to pink-collar (and no-collar) labor, rather than fully leaving the labor market. This shift in the location of women's labor existed alongside an ideological assault on mothers' wage earning itself.[103] The failure to institute maternity leave particularly marked the persistence of norms that classified women as temporary workers. Among the states, only Rhode Island established paid leave under the disability provisions of its unemployment program in 1942, while 1946 amendments to the Railroad Retirement Act included pregnant women in expanded employee entitlements that actually covered few women, given the sex ratios in that industry.[104] Proposals to formalize maternity leave for government employees through the civil service in the late 1940s met defeat in a Congress under the sway of Republican conservatives and southern Dixiecrats.[105]

Changes Forged Through Collective Bargaining

With public policies stymied, workers turned to collective bargaining. During the 1940s, private insurance plans increasingly included maternity benefits. Most plans for female-dominated workforces possessed some sort of provision, though the needle trades and retail stores less often provided weekly cash benefits than did industries with fewer women, such as the metal trades and automobile manufacturers. By 1951, the New York Department of Labor found that of 304 plans with maternity benefits, 171 covered dependent wives, and only 161 covered women unionists themselves. Industries with few women workers, such as construction and transportation, included only wives. In contrast, the United Steelworkers of America and the United Automobile Workers, CIO unions that had seen an increase in women members during the war, offered national plans with maternity benefits. The Amalgamated Clothing Workers offered obstetrical benefits from $25 to $100, while the International Ladies' Garment Workers' Union—despite extensive health and welfare funds and viable local health centers—hardly covered maternity. Its health centers usually lacked prenatal clinics or any special services for pregnant women. Plans generally included hospitalization and surgical benefits.[106]

Many unions had "negotiated for maternity leave, job security, and retention of seniority." In a 1952 study, the Women's Bureau found that three-fourths of manufacturing firms and half of other firms provided some job security for absences due to maternity. Four-fifths of union contracts contained leave-of-absence clauses, though only a sixth of unions, mostly in manufacturing, specified maternity leaves. Teachers who worked in large cities (of over 100,000 residents) had leave, but those in small cities did not; they often were on year-to-year contracts to begin with. Some school districts required teachers to leave as soon as they became aware of being pregnant—meaning, for a large majority, before the sixth month. Because reinstatement could take place only at the beginning of the year or semester, the length of time away from work could extend to over a year. If no suitable position existed when a teacher was ready to return, she waited for an appropriate vacancy. None of this leave was paid.[107]

Whether or not a workplace benefit such as maternity leave was a women's right depended on the terms in which it was argued and the manner in which it was administered. In the late 1940s, advocates for children endorsed paid leave for pregnant workers out of concern for the babies—a pronatalist argument. But trade unionists reformulated leave as a worker's right and argued that the denial of maternity leave interfered with women's "freedom to choose the kind of lives they wish, including the right to marriage and to have children." One representative of government workers contended, "When they marry, as is their right, they should have the right to retain their jobs. . . . If this is a real right, they must have maternity leave with pay." Otherwise, women were "denied effective opportunity for marriage."[108]

Major Shifts in the Labor Market

As historians now recognize, the 1950s presented less a retreat to domesticity than a reconfiguration of the labor market.[109] By 1953, half of employed women were married and a third had children at home.[110] In the early 1950s, the U.S. Women's Bureau advocated for a child care tax deduction to benefit married wage-earning women. The resulting measure in 1954 permitted such a deduction, but only women of modest income could qualify.[111] In the context of the Cold War need for womanpower, part-time and temporary work appeared to be the key to reconciling domestic responsibility, national security, and labor force demands.[112]

But social supports for women's wage earning became a public responsibility only during wartime, and even then individual solutions predominated. Like the New Deal before them, unions and employers framed benefits around employment, similarly excluding those whose work lay outside those perimeters. For African Americans, Latinos, and other racial or ethnic minorities, the family and the community, rather than the state or the market, supported women's attempts to combine wage earning and child rearing.[113]

By midcentury, then, an American welfare state promised economic security to workers and their families in the core sectors of the economy through labor standards, collective bargaining, and social security. The promissory note that came with employee contributions to social security and private pensions and health insurance, however, maintained a racialized and gendered order: the service and agricultural jobs of men and women of color and many white women made them ineligible for benefits. Such families, then, stood outside the protection of the state. Their jobs were more precarious, and their family life was strained by inadequate income amid growing affluence. The division between worthy widows and lone mothers intensified as the state placed into the stigmatized category of public assistance women who never married or had married men uncovered by unemployment insurance or other job supports. World War II showed that social policies could help families balance employment and family labor even if funding of child care and provision of health care and maternity leave proved inadequate. But the American solution to combining work and family emphasized market solutions over public resources except during wartime.

FROM THE RIGHTS REVOLUTION TO THE ERA OF PERSONAL RESPONSIBILITY

The so-called rights revolution of the 1960s and early 1970s, anchored by the 1964 Civil Rights Act and the 1965 Voting Rights Act, expanded the New Deal order through including those left out, especially African Americans and Latinos, and extending benefits to new areas, such as health coverage for elderly and indigent people.[114] It advanced equal opportunity and attempted to combat on-the-job discrimination for white women and racial minorities.[115] The Johnson administration launched the War on Poverty as a social welfare extension to formal civil rights.[116]

Expansion of Women's Paid Work and of the Women's Rights Movement

Meanwhile, rising labor force participation of mothers with young children from all social groups transformed the double day from a working-class problem into a crisis in social reproduction. The "time bind," expressed through the expansion of the working day beyond nine to five, and the care deficit, marked by the floating location of caregiving between the home and other places, dramatized the middle class's concern with balancing work and family.[117]

The President's Commission on the Status of Women, appointed by John F. Kennedy in 1961, recommended a wide range of services to enable women to enter the labor market, such as "childcare . . . at all economic levels."[118] It further sought equal rights in the courts without abandoning Progressive Era protective labor laws. The goal was to "enable women to continue their role as wives and mothers while making a maximum contribution to the world around them."[119] Congress responded to the commission by passing the Equal Pay Act of 1963 but limited equality of pay to the same, rather than comparable, work, which failed to challenge inequalities of wages resulting from occupational segregation by sex. Women who moved into "nontraditional" fields such as construction during the 1970s benefited, but since the undervaluation of "women's work" persisted, the wage gap remained. The narrow construction of equal pay generated a movement for comparable worth, which by the early 1980s had some success in reformulating the job-specific pay rates in public sector employment.[120]

With Title VII of the 1964 Civil Rights Act, issues relating to sex found a place in antidiscrimination law, even if Title VII's supporters had hoped to kill the entire Civil Rights Act through its inclusion.[121] The National Organization for Women's (NOW) 1967 "Bill of Rights" called for enforcement of Title VII, as well as the establishment of new social policies in the realms of both home and work. NOW asked for maternity leave and nondiscriminatory social security benefits for women. Its proposals included tax deductions for working parents, day care centers, equal job-training opportunities, and higher payments for women on public assistance. While much of this agenda duplicated what trade union women had been advocating since the late 1940s, support for reproductive rights was new.[122] In embracing abortion, the new feminists reinterpreted the politics of work and family to include bodily integrity and motherhood. A later, more radical reproductive rights movement agitated for the rights of poor women and their children. By the 1990s, protests against "family caps" and birth control as conditions of receiving public assistance sought to guarantee women's right to have children.[123]

The NOW agenda was partially realized during the next decades. For example, in contrast with only minor changes in social security, private pension reform extended women's benefits to include "super-annuated divorcees and disabled widows in 1983." [124] Child care became more readily available, but—despite some attempts at universal provision—it varied tremendously in terms of cost and location.[125] Through struggle, feminists were perhaps most successful in obtaining maternity leave, one of the more traditional work and family agenda items they were pursuing. In response to Supreme Court decisions that refused to consider unequal treatment of the pregnant as sex discrimination, feminists launched the Campaign to End Discrimination Against Pregnant Workers, which led to passage of the Pregnancy Discrimination Act. This amended Title VII and became effective in 1979. Rejecting the association of maternity with disability and seeking to break the link between women and parenting, trade union women—for example, in the Coalition of Labor Union Women—and others pushed for the Family and Medical Leave Act, which Republican presidents vetoed twice before it became law in 1993. Though this act protected seniority and maintained health benefits, the stipulated leave was unpaid and covered only workplaces with more than fifty employees.[126]

Increased Attention to Poor Women's Work and Family Needs

While many middle-class (and, often, white) feminists were focusing on ensuring women's right to earn, many poor, single mothers were demanding the choice to care for their children at home. Through the National Welfare Rights Organization, they called for a right to welfare, and during the 1960s and 1970s this newly rights-conscious group demanded and gained greater access to resources. The number of families on welfare assistance grew by half between 1960 and 1966 and then jumped threefold in the next decade, to more than 2.7 million by 1976. In addition, legal services and civil rights lawyers established the right to a fair hearing for people to obtain or maintain benefits.[127]

Those opposed to "big government" and its supposed encouragement of irresponsibility criticized the increase in the number of welfare recipients, referring especially to women dubbed "welfare queens." [128] The so-called Reagan revolution, a period of backlash against women's rights and civil rights, sought to reverse public responsibility for meeting working families' needs by privatizing many governmental functions and promoting market-based services. Through tax cuts and military buildup, it appeared that President Ronald Reagan would dismantle the New Deal order.[129] Although the Clinton administration advanced a more family-friendly agenda, its political weakness and "New Democratic" politics led to the "era of personal responsibility," which ended welfare, or AFDC, in 1996.[130] The new program, Temporary Assistance for Needy Families (TANF), made work a requirement for public assistance, placed time limits and other restrictions on eligibility, and encouraged marriage as a solution to the poverty of mothers and their children.[131] The "compassionate conservatism" of George W. Bush envisioned a return to the private system of charity that the Progressives had found so wanting but still had depended upon. Social security itself came under attack through privatization plans that were to secure its finances before baby boomers' retirement, and the enacted revisions in Medicare saw government shoring up the private system of insurance and for-profit drug companies.[132]

Conclusion

Until the early twentieth century, state policies sought to buttress the family wage, an earning large enough for a man to provide for a wife who stayed home to care for their children. Nonetheless, reformers and policy makers alike recognized that some families needed additional income, better obtained by maternal than by child labor. During the Progressive Era, the rise of maternal employment in response to a perceived decrease in paternal responsibility generated interference in families of the poor. The Great Depression turned the problem of sustaining family life in the face of under- and unemployment into a national issue, while the New Deal established social benefits and labor rights for industrial workers and their families. World War II offered wage-earning women opportunity to gain higher wages by leaving service, retail, and light manufacturing for war production, but its experiments in public services, such as child care, proved temporary. The rights revolutions of the 1960s and early 1970s opened up welfare state and private benefits to many previously left out by curbing discriminatory practices.

But the new social movements failed to restructure the organization of work in relation to family life. Women's demands for equality at work were stymied by their continued responsibilities for care work and other forms of domestic labor. White professional women thus hired other women, usually recent immigrants or members of racial minority groups, to clean their homes and watch their children or elderly. Feminists sought to go out to work and to control reproduction without state restrictions; poor, single mothers fought against welfare policies that forced them from the home into the low-wage labor market and interfered with their reproductive decisions. By century's end, some women had too little time outside their jobs, while others were searching for jobs that would bring in adequate income. Meanwhile, conservative politicians defended the limited welfare state, making citizens and noncitizens alike dependent more on the vagaries of the labor market.

Closely related to race and immigrant status, class continued to impact how women combined family and wage labor, as it had a century before. Whether or not the New Deal legacy could provide the foundations for a revitalized welfare state—one that met the work and family needs of all—remained unresolved at the dawn of a new era, fueled by fears of terrorism, outsourcing of jobs, corporate undermining of private pensions, and assaults by concentrated wealth and monopolized media on the democratic process itself.

3

Civil Society: Changing from Tight to Loose Connections

Robert Wuthnow

Several summers ago I set out to find the country church where my grandparents had been married and my father baptized. After driving seemingly endless miles along a dirt road rutted by a recent Kansas thunderstorm, I came upon the building—a once-magnificent wooden structure with a commanding view of the surrounding valley. Here had lived a thriving community of German farmers, drawn by cheap land and new markets. For them, community meant living among people who spoke the same language, practiced the same religion, sent their children to a nearby one-room schoolhouse, and seldom ventured the twenty miles it took to reach the nearest town. In their community, work was nearly always done within a few hundred yards of home, and child rearing involved older sisters and brothers, extended family members, and neighbors, as well as parents. Today, most of these people's descendants have moved away, seeking community in new places and in new ways.

In every era the ways in which people seek community are profoundly shaped by the social circumstances in which they live. Country churches and one-room schools have been replaced by shopping malls and universities. Except among recent immigrants, community is now less often a function of ethnicity and national origin and more often a reflection of personal interests and avocational affinities. It bears the imprint of smaller families, complex work schedules, global markets, and greatly expanded communication technologies.[1]

The reason for being interested in these changes is that there is now widespread concern about our communities—and about the very basis of our democratic system. Seventy-eight percent of Americans in one national survey say they regarded "the breakdown of community" as a "serious" or "extremely serious" problem in our society.[2] Of course, people may have been worried about their communities in the past, too. But the present concern seems to correspond with what other studies reveal about an erosion of neighborhood ties. For instance, surveys show that fewer people spend social evenings with their neighbors than in the past, and memberships in such prominent community organizations as Rotary, Elks, and the League of Women Voters appear to be diminishing.[3] Little wonder, then, that social commentators worry that the ties binding us together may be unraveling.

But voicing concern about the collapse of community gets us nowhere if it leads only to moralistic pleas for people to take a more active role in meeting and helping their neighbors. We must understand the ways in which social conditions have been changing in recent decades and, armed with that understanding, consider the new ways in which people are taking part in their communities—especially those that seem particularly well suited to the new conditions under which we live. Understanding how changes in work and family are transforming our communities is the key to recognizing that community involvement is not simply weakening but rather taking on new forms.

WHY AMERICANS DISCONNECT

Although today's world is vastly different from the one in which my grandparents lived, the term *community* still has local connotations for most people, just as it did for the earlier generations. According to the Civic Involvement Survey, a national survey I conducted in 1997, 41 percent of Americans say the phrase that comes closest to their definition of *community* is "your neighborhood" and another 35 percent opt for "the town in which you live" (8 percent choose "the larger region in which you live" and 13 percent "the people you associate with").[4]

Mobility and the Sense of Community

As the survey findings suggest, the most obvious place to look for why loyalties to communities may be declining is the geographic mobility that prevents people from sinking roots in their neighborhoods and towns. The extent of this mobility is evident in the fact that 50 percent of Americans ages eighteen to thirty-five have lived at their present address less than two years. And by the time they are in their fifties, the average American has lived at more than twelve different addresses.[5] Moving this much makes it difficult for people to join community organizations—especially the kind that expect lifelong commitment.

Still, Americans have always been a mobile people. They came from other countries, leaving the older generation behind, and often followed the frontier westward in search of new opportunities. Eventually they moved from farms to towns and from cities to suburbs. In studies of towns and suburbs in the 1950s, researchers often saw this uprootedness as one of the sources of Americans' seemingly incurable penchant for joining, and some scholars doubt that mobility has actually increased very much.[6]

But if geographic mobility alone does not provide a satisfactory explanation for Americans' tendency to disconnect from their communities, mobility does point toward ways in which changes in work affect how people relate to their communities. In the past, new economic opportunities often permitted (or even encouraged) people to move in groups (like the German farmers who settled in Wisconsin and then came together to the community in Kansas where my grandparents lived). Mining communities, steel towns, and the automobile industry—all drawing on unskilled pools of labor mobilized through ethnic or racial ties—followed this pattern.[7] In contrast, the contemporary economy encourages people to move as individuals (literally, as single individuals, or as members of a nuclear family). Colleges and universities are the chief arbiters in this process: recruiting students from as many diverse groups and locations as possible, channeling them into dozens of different disciplinary specialities, and then sending them into a labor pool that rewards individual achievement.[8] When these people settle into new communities, therefore, they usually do not have networks of family, fellow churchgoers, or childhood friends already there.

The process of settling and resettling does not stop with entry-level jobs. Where loyalty to the company is rewarded, moving up is likely to require shifting from location to location in order to master the company's national or international markets. Other labor markets are characterized more by shifting from company to company. As a result, few Americans can realistically look forward to staying in a single line of work from the time they enter the labor force until they retire. Indeed, among workers ages thirty-five to forty-nine, 62 percent say they have already worked in at least three different lines of work (not counting jobs while they were growing up).[9] The unsettledness that many individual workers experience is compounded, moreover, by the growing number of companies that are involved in mergers and acquisitions and that depend on temporary workers and outsourcing.

The fluidity of contemporary work is hardly conducive to forging stable ties with one's community. Nationally, only 32 percent of American workers say the people they have contact with through their work are mostly from their own community, while 68 percent say these contacts are mostly with people from other places.[10] Moreover, people who move from job to job are also more likely to move from community to community, and those who move are less likely to know their neighbors and less likely to feel they could count on their neighbors for help.

These changes in work have been paralleled by equally profound changes in family life. A growing proportion of younger people are remaining single or childless for longer periods of time—often in order to make a successful start in their careers. Those who do marry have fewer children than was true, say, in the 1950s, and they are more likely to divorce. Moreover, the typical married couple is a two-career family, meaning that schedules are often more complicated than in the past. And retirees are more likely to live longer, remain healthier, and have savings plans or social security on which to depend for their income.

These changes in family life have had significant implications for the ways in which Americans during the 1960s and since then have come to relate to one another. Studies conducted between the late 1960s and early 1980s showed already that younger people devoted a considerable share of their energy to interacting with their own generation (both for companionship and in search of marriage partners). Parents with children are more likely to live away from grandparents and other relatives than in the past, spending more of their own nonworking time on parental activities, as well as relying on day care providers. In addition, older people have become less likely to live near or be financially dependent on their adult children.[11]

As family patterns change, Americans' ties to their communities also change. Single people are less likely to know their neighbors than are married people, and those who have no children or only one child are less likely to know their neighbors than those who have more children. The neighborhood bonds that used to be maintained by women who stayed at home also appear to be weakening as a result of more women joining the labor force. According to research, women who currently work full time know fewer of their neighbors than those who work part time, while those who say they keep house know more of their neighbors than those who are in the labor force.[12]

The Increasing Porousness of Institutions

Other changes could be considered as well (in leisure time, consumption patterns, and so on). But one change that has influenced all social institutions must be emphasized: the growing porousness of institutions. In *Loose Connections,* my 1998 book, I presented detailed evidence about the ways in which American institutions have become more porous over the past half century. Also, I examined implications of this porousness for social interaction, understandings of community, and civic involvement. By *porous,* I mean social conditions that permit goods, people, and information to flow easily across institutional boundaries. For instance, national boundaries that let immigrants and temporary workers enter and exit with relative ease are porous. Or, for another example, the institution of marriage is porous if it permits spouses to enter into and break marital vows easily or frequently. Porousness is by no means an inevitable feature of modern societies: until recently, Japan was characterized by relatively impermeable family, neighborhood, and economic structures, despite being highly advanced economically. In the United States, porousness was inhibited during the middle of the twentieth century by, among other things, the Cold War, which generated concerns about national security and about people's loyalty to God and country. But, other things being equal, market economies flourish when goods and services can be exchanged easily and often.

As the world's foremost market economy, the United States has evolved a pattern of social institutions that increasingly permit and encourage such exchange. Contemporary institutions facilitate the flow of goods, people, and information. The frequency of mergers and acquisitions and the extent of outsourcing in the corporate world are examples. So are the increased volume of transactions on the nation's leading stock exchanges, the rising number of people who have experienced divorce or who live in blended families, the ease with which people contact acquaintances by e-mail or receive information through cable television and satellite networks, and the growing number of Americans who have traveled or been reared in other countries. In all of these cases, movement is facilitated by relatively weak institutional boundaries: informal norms, as well as laws, that make it possible for people to shift loyalties fairly easily. Porous institutions are well suited to a rapidly changing economy because they permit people to break ties and forge new relationships as new conditions emerge. They reward people for having extended networks of relatively weak ties, and they depend on large numbers of people who serve as arbiters in the making and breaking of these ties (brokers, headhunters, travel agents, and divorce lawyers, to name a few).[13]

The increasing porousness of American institutions needs to be understood as a response to shifts in the economy and in the technologies on which communication and control depend, rather than being regarded only as a kind of moral failure on the part of individuals. Corporations' capacity to deal with a large number of suppliers and subcontractors depends on computing and information technology, whereas in the past these same corporations would have needed to hire a permanent workforce and bring them together in a single location. From the individual worker's point of view, it makes sense to hedge one's bets, as it were, by learning a variety of skills and by cultivating a wide network of social contacts, rather than becoming too dependent on a single employer. Although the same dynamics do not necessarily pertain to the family, individuals who know the necessity of keeping their options open in the labor market may also find themselves uprooted in ways that are not conducive to stable relationships as spouses or parents. Thus, among men who have been in only one line of work, the proportion who have been divorced is 25 percent, compared to 34 percent among men who have been in five different lines of work; among women, the comparable figures are 24 percent and 56 percent.[14]

Porous institutions do not diminish the human penchant for social relationships, but they alter people's ways of structuring relationships and thus influence the character of community. The old forms of community that depended on living for an extended period in a single neighborhood, working for a lifetime in one setting, and being rewarded for seniority in a fraternal or community organization are either less attractive to a growing number of Americans or more difficult to maintain. The relationships on which community involvement currently depends are more likely to be looser, fluid, short-term, and focused on specific tasks, as explored through the examples in the next section.

THE NEW FORMS OF COMMUNITY INVOLVEMENT

How we relate to our communities has been particularly influenced by the porous society in which we live. Community involvement is inevitably different when community means something different than it did in the past. These changes are especially evident when we consider the extent of American's current involvement in volunteer activities, examine the scope of support groups that have arisen in recent years, or think about the changes American religion is experiencing.

Today's Thriving Voluntarism

One of the most striking developments over the past thirty years has been the huge increase in volunteering. If community were simply dying, as some commentators believe, Americans would be staying at home or looking after their own interests, rather than volunteering to help others. But trends in volunteering are up, not down. In fact, Gallup polls that asked, "Do you, yourself, happen to be involved in any charity or social service activities, such as helping the poor, the sick, or the elderly?" showed an increase from only 26 percent in 1977 to 46 percent in 1991. Other surveys conducted during the 1990s showed that approximately half the public had done some kind of volunteer work during the preceding year.[15]

The fact that volunteering has increased does not mean that Americans are necessarily more interested in helping other people than they were a few decades ago. But volunteering has come to have new meaning. It is increasingly understood as a formal activity, done for several hours a week and in conjunction with some voluntary organization, such as a church, school, hospital, or service agency. Most volunteering still occurs in the neighborhoods in which volunteers live or in adjacent neighborhoods. But, unlike helping a friend or a neighbor, volunteering usually refers to assisting a stranger, such as a homeless person, a client at a soup kitchen, or a hospital patient.

Perhaps paradoxically, volunteering has become more attractive in recent decades, not so much as an antidote to self-interest but as an expression of American individualism. Volunteers say they enjoy helping others because they learn new skills, become stronger people, gain a better sense of their personal identity, or have experiences that enrich and add variety to their lives. Volunteers are also motivated by altruistic and humanitarian concerns, such as wanting to alleviate pain and suffering. But volunteering has been shaped by the market culture in which Americans live: they shop around to find a volunteer activity that interests them (and often one that will contribute to their career goals), and this shopping is made possible by the fact that volunteer organizations compete with one another and advertise to solicit volunteers; volunteers develop relatively short-term relationships with other volunteers and with the people they assist, which observers have argued is different from traditional neighborhood and kin relationships and resembles the instrumental relationships present in the workplace; and volunteers have reported that they enjoy helping organizations with proven effectiveness and evaluate these organizations using the same cost-benefit and efficiency notions that they do in their jobs.[16]

Today's Volunteers

Just who is doing this volunteer work? According to studies conducted by Independent Sector, the Washington-based umbrella group for U.S. nonprofit organizations, at least a third of people in virtually every major demographic category do some volunteer work each year. But the proportions are higher for women than for men, for middle-aged people than for older and younger people, and for those with higher incomes and higher levels of education.[17] The political scientist Robert Putnam has presented some evidence suggesting that the increase in volunteering (with the exception of some increase among young people, which he attributes to community service requirements) is all accounted for by a rise among older people (whom he terms the "civic generation").[18] But neither the Independent Sector studies nor results from studies analyzed by the sociologist Andrew

Greeley have borne out this suggestion; in those studies, increases in volunteering were evident among middle-aged people as well.[19]

The ways in which people volunteer are, of course, influenced by the nature of their obligations. Contrary to popular imagery of how it may have happened in the past, volunteering is no longer performed primarily by women who stay at home while their husbands earn a living. Among women and men who work full time, rates of volunteering are the same: in both cases, 57 percent have done some volunteer work in the previous year. It is just as common for women who work full time to do some volunteering each year as it is for women who work part time to do so. Among both women and men, those who work sixty hours a week or more are just as likely to volunteer as those who work fewer hours a week. And women and men who are employed are more likely to volunteer than those who say they stay at home to keep house or who are retired.[20]

It *is* the case that women who work part time spend more hours a week volunteering (0.9 hours on average) than women who work full time (0.5 hours). The former are also more likely than the latter to engage in several specific kinds of volunteering: helping distribute food to the needy, working at homeless shelters, volunteering at schools, and volunteering for arts and cultural activities. But for most other kinds of volunteering, the proportions of women and men who participate point to an important feature of the volunteer sector: it has become so diverse that people with almost any kind of interest or amount of time can find a niche. For instance, schools, youth programs, and churches still command the bulk of volunteer time, but newer organizations, such as crime-watch associations, AIDS-related volunteering, environmental projects, community development corporations, violence prevention programs, and community organizing now draw substantial numbers of volunteers as well.[21]

The family factors that influence volunteering favorably are being married and having children at home. Rates of volunteering are higher among men and women who are married than among those who are not married (and this is true among people of all ages). Having children at home is associated with higher rates of volunteering among women (largely because they do more volunteer work at child-related programs, such as at schools and for youth organizations), and those who have two, three, or four children are more likely to volunteer than those who have only one child. Among men, the likelihood of volunteering is unrelated to having children at home.[22]

Judging from these relationships, larger societal trends are at work that both encourage and discourage volunteering. The fact that larger numbers of women are employed full time now than a generation ago has not dampened volunteering; in fact, it may have even encouraged volunteering, especially if the larger proportion of women who now work in the professions (who volunteer at higher-than-average rates) is taken into account. At the same time, fewer people getting married and having children (or having fewer children) probably has had a dampening effect on volunteering.

The Role of Nonprofit Organizations

But we cannot fully understand volunteering without also paying attention to the role of nonprofit organizations. Between 1967 and 1992 the number of nonprofit organizations in the United States grew by almost 500 percent—from 309,000 to 1.4 million—and they currently employ approximately 8 percent of the labor force (or 18 million people). These organizations, along with churches and schools, play a large role in encouraging people to volunteer and providing them with the opportunities to volunteer. In one national survey, 41 percent of people who had done volunteer work within the past year said their involvement had included contact with nonprofit organizations; in another study, employees of nonprofit firms were themselves significantly more likely to do volunteer work than employees of for-profit firms.[23]

Nonprofit organizations have grown for a variety of reasons: support from (and competition among) religious groups, increasing social diversity, favorable tax-exemption laws, and, in many cases, financial assistance from government programs.[24] Some critics have argued that these organizations can never take the place of the service clubs that used to be more popular. Yet this criticism may be too hasty. Nonprofit organizations, like service clubs, are relatively small, and most are oriented toward local communities; they offer people—often professionals trained to assist with community needs that could not be handled by service clubs—ways of opting out of the for-profit economy; and the volunteers who work with these professionals experience many of the same benefits that club members do (including learning about their community, becoming more interested in social issues, gaining self-confidence, and learning new skills).[25]

The Focus of Volunteers' Efforts

Volunteering is, of course, directed to many social needs, not just those of families. But evidence suggests that volunteering is one of the ways in which families are being helped by the wider community. For instance, national survey data collected in 1992 showed that approximately 15 percent of all volunteers reported having been engaged during the previous year in "youth development" activities; other activities that may have helped children or needy families included "education" (15 percent), "health" (13 percent), and "human services" (12 percent).[26]

The Civic Role of Small, Supportive Groups

A second way in which Americans are creating community is through a huge variety of small, supportive groups, or support groups—ranging from therapy and counseling groups to groups for people with addictions or disabilities to religious groups, sports and hobby groups, book discussion clubs, and musical groups. Although many of these groups do not aim directly to solve community problems, people who become involved in them attest that these groups serve as ways of meeting people in the wider community, developing social networks, and gaining social and emotional support.

The Extent of Participation

Accurately gauging whether or not more people have become involved in support groups during recent decades is harder than assessing the rates of involvement with volunteer work, because standard questions have not been included in surveys and because people can define support groups in different ways. The one kind of support group that clearly has grown is the twelve-step, or anonymous, group, such as Alcoholics Anonymous (AA). Membership in AA (which was founded in 1935 and became a national phenomenon only in the 1950s) grew from approximately 445,000 in 1979 to approximately 980,000 in 1989 and then reached 1,127,471 in 1992.[27] Most twelve-step groups average approximately twenty to twenty-five members who attend weekly, and the variety of such groups has become more specialized in recent years. Al-Anon (founded in 1951) grew from 1,500 groups in 1981 to 1,900 (with approximately 500,000 members) in 1990; in the same year, there were 1,300 Adult Children of Alcoholics groups, none of which had existed prior to 1982.[28]

An estimate of the larger mutual support self-help movement—which includes groups for the bereaved, for people with disabilities and health needs, for parents, and for victims of crime and domestic violence—comes from figures compiled by the fifty state-level self-help clearinghouses, whose task is to provide annually updated lists of local self-help groups and to obtain information from these groups about memberships, goals, and activities. In 1976, membership in all such groups nationally was estimated at five million to eight million people; in 1988, the comparable figure was twelve million to fifteen million members.[29] Another way of estimating the growth of self-help groups is by comparing the results of a 1984 Harris poll with more recent results. In the 1984 study, only 3 percent of the adult public said yes when asked, "Are you now participating in a mutual support self-help group for the purpose of aiding you in coping with a specific problem or problems of everyday life?" In comparison, a 1992 Gallup survey found that 10 percent of the public were participating in a "small group that meets regularly and that provides caring and support for its members" and described their groups as "self-help group[s]."[30] Although these questions are not strictly comparable, they are consistent with the estimates drawn from other sources.

The Structure and Focus of Support Groups

The typical support group includes approximately twenty people who meet every week or every other week to talk about common problems or interests. In view of the transience of the population, most of these groups are quite stable, existing on average for more than five years and including members who typically have belonged for three to five years. Support groups are nevertheless amenable to drawing in people who may be new to their community or whose interests and needs have changed. Most members take pride in their ability to welcome newcomers; few groups have formal initiation rites or membership tests; some are anonymous, deliberately shielding people from having to divulge information about where they live or work; and many have icebreakers, parties, and dinners that encourage people to interact informally.[31] Support groups often include discussions of work-related problems (a small proportion occur in the workplace), and working women in particular have reported turning to support groups as ways of handling work-related stress. Support groups also serve as surrogate families, providing the child-rearing tips and marital advice that previously came from nearby relatives.

Because support groups generally focus on their own members' needs and interests, they have been criticized for not serving a larger role in their communities. This criticism should not be overstated, however. While it is true that many support groups are too small, too homogeneous, and too isolated to make much of an impact on social policy and other national problems, their members do benefit in many ways that have larger social implications. Overcoming addictions, helping people find friends, encouraging people to think more deeply about their religious values, and supporting people with illnesses or disabilities are all positive contributions. So are learning to interact with others, discovering the necessity of compromise, gaining self-dignity, and experiencing forgiveness.[32] Small, supportive groups sometimes play a behind-the-scenes role in social policy formation, too. For instance, AA has a national-level organization that presses for legislation on substance abuse prevention and drunk-driving laws. Similarly, the respective support groups for people with HIV, with physical disabilities, and with other health-related issues often maintain newsletters and e-mail lists that help to mobilize petitions on legislative matters of interest to the group members.

Support groups encourage their members to become involved in the wider community as well. Among those nationally who say they participate in a self-help group, for example, 74 percent have done volunteer work within the past year, compared to 48 percent of those who do not participate in a self-help group.[33] The reasons are not hard to find. Self-help groups put people in contact with others and with organizations (often religious ones) that invite them to volunteer, and many self-help groups draw people with special needs who realize the value of helping others. Small, supportive groups are thus one of the ways in which people are adapting to porous social arrangements.

These groups sometimes hold meetings at the workplace because this is where people know one another and can more easily arrange to meet than in their neighborhoods; they sometimes provide day care, at least on an emergency basis; they often discuss the emotional effects of divorce, job loss, and layoffs; and they occasionally provide financial assistance, such as loans or temporary housing.

The Reassembling of Religion

The large number of support groups that occur under religious auspices suggests that there may be something about religion that is helping it to adapt to new circumstances as well. Attendance at religious services has been strikingly constant in recent decades, rather than declining in the way that involvement in many other community organizations has.[34] At least a quarter of Americans participate regularly in religious services, and nearly 60 percent hold membership in one of the three hundred thousand local congregations of which the nation's religious traditions are composed.

Greater Fluidity and Larger Congregations
Behind its apparent stability, American religion has undergone major changes in recent years—changes that reflect the influences of new relationships at work and in the family and that, in turn, are helping congregations play a continuing role in their communities. One of these changes is a decline in the cultural barriers that used to keep different religious traditions apart and that often resulted in communities forming around distinct ethno-religious identities (such as Irish Catholic, Swedish Lutheran, or German Baptist). Today, more Catholics are marrying Protestants than a generation ago, more Jews are marrying Christians, and more Lutherans and Baptists are becoming Presbyterians or Episcopalians. These changes reflect the wider culture's greater tolerance for religious diversity, but they also stem from people interacting with those of other faiths at their jobs and in their neighborhoods. Other changes include people saying that they have "shopped" for a place of worship (that is, have switched congregations or denominations as a result of geographic mobility or shifts in personal preferences) and people piecing together a pastiche of personal spirituality that they describe as different from being loyal to organized religion.

The greater fluidity of religious identities has led to a "market-place" spirituality that some observers find troublesome because of its emphasis on self-gratification and lack of long-term connections with religious organizations.[35] Instead of taking their cues from religious authorities and instead of settling into religious communities for generations, spiritual seekers are often guided by personal experiences, momentary impulses, and a consumerist mentality that emphasizes quick results. Observers believe these forms of fluidity are more prominent now than in the past, at least partly because people have opportunities to shop for spirituality at bookstores and through mass media.[36] Still, spiritual seekers seldom pursue their religious quests entirely alone: they come together at retreat centers and workshops, often continue to participate in local congregations, and frequently engage in service projects and volunteer programs.

For those who do join religious communities, another significant change has been a gradual shift from small to larger congregations. A majority of congregations are still quite small, numbering fewer than a hundred active participants, but most of the people who attend congregations are concentrated in larger ones, often numbering a thousand members or more.[37] These larger congregations are more likely to be located in suburbs than in small towns or rural areas. Their members are more likely to be young or middle-aged college-educated professionals who have moved recently. And these members are more likely than those of smaller congregations to do volunteer work in their communities, probably because the congregations themselves help to sponsor more community service programs and are more closely linked with nonprofit service agencies and other community organizations.[38] Larger congregations are thus playing an important role in bringing people who have been uprooted from their communities of origin back together.

Coalition Building and New Work-Family Initiatives

Large and small congregations alike are also adapting to changing circumstances by forming coalitions that better enable them to serve community needs. Some of these coalitions are quite small, such as several congregations banding together to operate a soup kitchen in their neighborhood, while others consist of hundreds of congregations engaged in an alliance to provide a wide range of community services or coalitions involving both religious and nonreligious agencies, such as community development corporations. Coalitions of this kind have emerged because single congregations often cannot meet their communities' needs. By joining together, congregations can share the task of providing volunteers, work more effectively with specialists employed by nonprofit organizations, and even receive government funding for their programs. These coalitions illustrate the broader interorganizational networks that appear to be increasingly common in a porous society.[39]

Nevertheless, religious organizations face a serious challenge because of the ways in which work and family patterns have been changing. People whose jobs require them to move usually take as long as five years to become integrated into the life of a new congregation, and those who work long hours are less likely to take an active part in congregational tasks than those who work fewer hours. Congregations have generally made married couples with children feel more at home than single and divorced people, meaning that the decline of the nuclear family may also signal diminished participation rates at churches and synagogues. Some congregations are responding to these challenges by organizing group discussions about work and family, but it is unclear whether such programs are making much of an impact on how people actually behave. Other congregations, though, are experimenting with a wide variety of options, including day care programs for members and the wider community, more intensive premarital counseling, weekend retreats for couples to discuss marital problems, faith-based counseling programs, and foster parent programs.

THE "E" REVOLUTION

Volunteering, support groups, and religion all have the advantage (as far as community building is concerned) of actually bringing people together, at least for short periods and for limited purposes. The revolution in electronic technology—especially the Internet—poses a different sort of challenge: while it provides opportunities for people to exchange information at greater speeds and with relative ease, it may work against the very kinds of social interaction on which strong communities and strong democratic traditions are based. Thus, experts' opinions on the social ramifications of electronic communication have been mixed. On one hand, some observers have pointed to research in which a minority of Internet users reported *perceiving* that they were getting out and actually interacting with people less often as a result of time spent sitting at their personal computers. On the other hand, some writers have compared the Internet to such previous technological revolutions as radio, the dime novel, and the penny newspaper, suggesting that democracy has always been served when more people can keep abreast of social issues at lower cost.[40]

Internet and e-mail communications occur largely without respect to geographical distance. Thus, these forms of communication may facilitate involvement in local communities, as illustrated by the growing number of municipalities that have Web sites, churches that conduct business by e-mail, and community organizations that sponsor Internet chat rooms and news groups. It is just as possible, however, that the Internet and e-mail may keep people in touch at greater distances, at the expense of the local, face-to-face interaction that builds strong personal bonds in neighborhoods and towns.

In one national survey, a comparison of the social behavior reported by Internet or e-mail users with that of nonusers provided one way of determining whether electronic communication diminished or enhanced those people's ties to their local communities. Taking into account other factors that might be related to the use of electronic communication and to community involvement (such as age, gender, race, education, and income, as well as the suburban or central city base of each person's neighborhood), those who used the Internet or e-mail were *more likely* than those who did not use either one to say they had attended a community meeting or done volunteer work in the previous year, belonged to a community organization, and talked about social issues with their neighbors; they were also more likely to be registered to vote and were neither more nor less likely to know at least half of their neighbors or to define community in terms of their neighborhood or town, rather than in terms of some larger region.[41] These comparisons do not suggest that electronic communications somehow cause people to become more involved in their communities; nevertheless, they suggest that electronic communication (at least if it does not become an obsession that takes up all of a person's time) functions more like the telephone than the television: it is a vehicle for staying in contact with other people, rather than a way of withdrawing from social interaction.

But do people in fact use the Internet to keep informed about issues, or does it serve mainly as a way to conduct business or as a substitute for personal telephone calls? A national survey asked respondents if they have "read about social or political issues on the Internet" during the twelve months preceding the survey. Twenty-nine percent of the adult public said they have—a higher percentage than the proportion who have attended a class or lecture about social or political issues during the same time period (19 percent). The study gave no evidence that people might be substituting the one source of information for the other (those who attended classes were more likely to use the Internet, and vice versa). The study also suggested what the consequences might be of using the Internet to learn about social issues. Leaving aside those who have attended classes (who were already more politically active), those who have read about issues on the Internet were about twice as likely to have contacted an elected official during the preceding year than those who had not read about issues on the Internet. In other words, turning to the Internet for information went hand in hand with making one's sentiments known, rather than with encouraging people to remove themselves from the political process.[42]

What is not yet known is how e-mail, the Internet, and other new communication technologies are affecting the relationships between family and work. Anecdotal evidence has suggested that work may increasingly intrude on family life as a result of workers being able to connect to co-workers via e-mail at home or being more easily reached via cellular telephones. At the same time, these technologies make it easier for parents to check up on children from work, coordinate family schedules, and keep in contact with relatives who are scattered geographically.

THE PROBLEM OF MARGINALIZATION

Volunteering, support groups, religion, and the Internet are ways in which most ordinary middle-class Americans can reach out to other people, perhaps in place of the more stable community organizations they might have belonged to in the past. If so, critics of these new forms of community might still be concerned that more is being lost than gained, and for this reason they might call on Americans to do more. But such calls will be misplaced if another development in American society is overlooked. This is the widening gap between those who live comfortable (or affluent) lifestyles and those who are being marginalized by current social and economic trends.

The widening gap in economic well-being has been well documented in studies of household incomes. Between 1975 and 1997, for example, the share of aggregate income received by the top 5 percent of American families grew from 15 percent to 21 percent, while the share received by the bottom 40 percent decreased from 18 percent to 14 percent. Comparisons over a longer time span show how distinctive the last quarter of the twentieth century was in this respect. Whereas real income grew at an annual rate of 2 percent to 3 percent for all income groups between 1947 and 1973, between 1974 and 1997 real income was stagnant (or declined) for those in the lowest income groups but rose significantly for families in the highest income groups. Moreover, among lower-income families, staying even generally came as a result of women joining the workforce. Thus, when the incomes of *individual* wage earners are compared, real wages actually declined for those in the lowest categories but increased for those in the highest categories.[43] During the 1980s and 1990s, poverty also became increasingly concentrated in largely segregated inner-city neighborhoods.[44]

Like older forms of community involvement, the newer forms are highly skewed toward people with greater social and economic privileges. Volunteering seems to be less a function of whether or not a person has free time and more a function of having certain skills and opportunities. Thus, level of education is one of the main factors influencing people's likelihood of volunteering. For instance, in one large national study, those with college degrees (compared to those with high school degrees) were twice as likely to have volunteered for a youth or religious organization or to have helped the needy within the preceding year; the college-educated were nearly three times as likely to have volunteered for a neighborhood civic organization, health organization, or arts organization.[45] From qualitative interviews, it appears that being better-educated, working in professional or managerial occupations, and living in neighborhoods where volunteer opportunities are plentiful seem to give people the confidence to believe that they can make a difference by volunteering. Having the "right" clothing, having learned to speak up and to lead meetings, and having day care and transportation are all helpful if a person is interested in getting involved in community organizations. Similarly, small, supportive groups are largely peopled by the middle class, so much so that disadvantaged persons have often complained of feeling uncomfortable or out of place.[46] Access to e-mail and the Internet is highly skewed toward the middle class, and even religious organizations (which span all social strata) typically reward their better-educated and more affluent members more highly than those who may be perceived as having fewer skills and resources to offer.

Evidence also suggests that community involvement has declined more severely among the marginalized than among the privileged. For instance, the decline in association memberships that occurred during the late 1970s and 1980s was more serious among those who had been reared in lower-income households than among those who had been reared in households with above-average incomes. Similarly, the rates of association membership for people with just high school diplomas declined more than they did for people with college degrees, and the decline was much more substantial among racial minorities than among whites. Moreover, the reason for these differences appeared to be that things had gotten worse for those at the bottom: their incomes had fallen, they were more likely to be widowed or divorced, and their outlook had become more pessimistic.[47] Other evidence has shown that the decline in voter turnout during the 1970s and 1980s was much more severe in lower-income, inner-city neighborhoods than in more affluent, suburban neighborhoods.[48]

Given these results, leaders seeking to boost citizens' community involvement must pay special attention to the widening gap between rich and poor, as well as to the fact that living in lower-income, inner-city neighborhoods puts people at a significant disadvantage in being able to form stable connections with voluntary organizations. Porous institutions create opportunities for some people to reap profits by selling electronic communications technology, brokering mergers and acquisitions, investing in the stock market, or changing jobs and learning new skills. But porous institutions also permit people to fall through the cracks more easily, especially if new markets leave people without marketable skills and if slim profit margins are maintained by keeping wages at subsistence levels.

RESPONSIBLE LEADERSHIP

The problem of marginalization underscores the fact that changing social circumstances do not automatically generate the forms of community involvement on which a strong and healthy democratic society depend. People may be motivated to volunteer because of deep-seated humanitarian impulses, or they may join support groups and religious congregations in search of ways to overcome their own vulnerability. Yet these personal decisions on the part of millions of individuals do not ultimately add up to a good society as long as the ill effects of unrestrained markets are ignored or as long as democracy is assumed to be simply self-perpetuating. Porous communities appear capable of motivating and sustaining volunteerism of the kind that has increased in recent decades, but such volunteering usually depends on professional leadership in nonprofit and other community organizations. Small, supportive groups can help overcome some of the stress to which families are exposed, but these groups require committed leaders. The new information and communication technologies also need guidance if they are to help families at all levels of society.

Responsible leadership means that local, state, and national officials play an active role not only in shaping the social circumstances in which markets operate but also in redressing whatever ill effects and social dislocations emerge from changing economic relationships. For example, family leave policies that require employers to give parents time to attend to infants or tax policies that eliminate penalties for being married and provide earned income credits for low-income families make sense, not just as ways of helping workers and families but also as ways of promoting the social relationships that, in turn, lead people to volunteer, attend community meetings, and develop bonds with their neighbors.

As important as the role of elected officials is, the leadership displayed by average citizens, clergy, business managers, and the professionals who run nonprofit service organizations is equally significant. Volunteer efforts can easily focus on the schools, churches, and arts organizations in which middle-class people and their children are involved unless guidance is present to redirect these efforts toward the disadvantaged communities in which they are most needed: despite the fact that half of Americans volunteer each year, only 7 percent have done so in a poor inner-city area.[49] Support groups can become insular settings in which middle-class people gather to share tips about gardening and sports, or they can provide opportunities for searching questions to be raised about the number of hours people are working, the ways they spend their money, and whether they are realizing or abandoning their ideals. Responsible leadership means striving for both inclusion and clearer understandings of mutual social bonds. Inclusion involves "doing with" rather than "doing for," as in the case of faith-based community organizing that draws in and nurtures leadership from low-income neighborhoods. Mutual social bonds involve emphasizing the fact that privilege and disprivilege are systemically related, and that common humanity transcends class boundaries.

For strong local communities to play a role in strengthening and preserving democracy, individuals and organizations whose interests reach beyond local neighborhoods must be encouraged. Volunteering flourishes because of legal decisions that protect the right of people to associate; so do support groups and religious organizations. Volunteers frequently come to the realization that advocacy for social justice is needed in addition to deeds of kindness. Religious organizations devote much of their attention to local ministries, but they also staff denominational offices and support programs that link congregations to needs in other communities and nations.

The key to strong communities throughout American history has been recognizing that people have different skills and talents, which, when brought together, make dreams possible that cannot be realized any other way. For all the changes that have taken place over the past half century in patterns of work and family, the social fabric is still woven by hands that have been trained in highly specialized ways. Civic engagement occurs in the workplace and through the family, as well as in volunteer settings or support groups. Some people are called to start new organizations, to innovate, and to bring people together, while others find their calling in hunkering down, performing their jobs, and raising their children quietly and responsibly.

Standing there in the cemetery behind the country church overlooking the valley in which my grandparents had settled, I realized that what is left of their community still bears silent testimony to the importance of leadership and innovation. One of the graves is that of the founding settler, who, as a clergyman in Wisconsin, had organized a wagon train to carry his flock to their new community. He would have known, I suppose, that in any era, communities do not just happen but are made.

Section II

Inequalities Across Gender and Class

4

Inequalities at Work and at Home: Social Class and Gender Divides

Jody Heymann

As a nation, the United States holds dear the belief that all people should have an equal opportunity to grasp the American dream. If adults work hard, they are supposed to have a fair chance at success. Likewise, all children are supposed to have an equal chance at succeeding in school and leading a healthy and full life. But too often neither goal is realized. The barriers many working poor parents currently face in the United States make it next to impossible for them to succeed at work while caring well for their children. Moreover, women carry greater caregiving responsibilities than men and face worse working conditions.

LABOR FORCE TRANSFORMATION

In the past century and a half, two major transformations changed the makeup of the paid labor force in the United States. The first, the movement of men out of agricultural and other home-based work into the paid industrial labor force, began in the 1840s. The second began in earnest a century later when women entered wage and salary jobs in significant numbers.

From the founding of the United States until the mid-1800s, most children were raised in farm families in which both parents worked at home.[1] In 1830, 70 percent of children lived in farm families, and only 15 percent had a father who was a wage earner.[2] When most adults were working at their homes or on their land, their children and adult family members in need of care were with them or nearby. As the

Industrial Revolution progressed, the number of families in which the father was a wage earner began to rise. By the 1920s, the majority of children were growing up in families in which the father worked outside the home,[3] and by 1930, only 30 percent lived in farm families.[4]

Although women were among the first Americans to work in factories when the Industrial Revolution got under way in the early 1800s, unmarried women made up the majority of the women's labor force at that time.[5] For women of color, as for white women, single women predominated in early paid labor force participation.[6] Married women's limited labor force participation in the 1800s and early 1900s was neither an accident nor a result of women's choices: openings for men and women were advertised separately, many jobs excluded women, and many others explicitly barred married women. At the time, employers could legally discriminate against women in hiring. It was not until World War II—when large numbers of women were needed to fill the jobs left vacant by the men who had gone to war— that a dramatic decline in discrimination against married women occurred in hiring.[7]

Marked changes in the employment of mothers of school-age children began in the 1940s; equally marked changes in the employment of mothers of preschool children began in the 1960s. By 1990, more than 70 percent of children lived in households in which every parent was in the labor force.[8] Changes in labor force participation permeated the lives of women ages twenty-five to sixty-five and led to profound changes in whether and how many women were at home to care for elderly parents and young children.

In short, labor force changes during the past 150 years were the result not of women alone entering the formal labor force but rather of both men and women entering the industrial and postindustrial labor force. The fact that both men and women labor was not new, but what *had* changed were the location and conditions of work for both men and women—from home and farm, where they managed their own work, to factory and office, where others did. As the transformation in the location and nature of labor began, families became dependent on wages and salaries for food, clothing, and other essentials. By the end of the revolution, most families no longer had any adult working at home full time.

When men began to work for wages and salaries instead of directly producing goods for their own families, American communities, states, and the federal government recognized that if lone wage earners were injured, lost their jobs, or grew too old or sick to work, their families would lack money for food and clothing. As a result, a series of state and federal programs—workmen's compensation, unemployment insurance, and old age and survivors' insurance—were created in the first third of the twentieth century to ensure that families were cared for even if the single earner could no longer work.[9] Women's entry into the labor force completed the transformation in how families meet caretaking needs. However, communities, states, and the federal government in the United States—in marked contrast to their response to the first dramatic shift in labor—have responded little to this second one, with its profound implications for adults' availability to care for children and other dependents.

Little or nothing has been done to help make it feasible for families to answer the critical questions they have been facing now for decades: Who regularly cares for preschool-age and out-of-school children when parents work away from home? Who provides routine care for elderly parents who can no longer care for themselves? What happens when children and the elderly get sick and need care at unanticipated times? What happens when children have developmental or educational problems and need an adult's help during work hours?

The marked movement of men and women into the industrial and postindustrial labor force has transformed the United States. But we, as a nation, have failed to respond, leaving a rapidly widening gap between working families' needs and the combination of high workplace demands, outdated social institutions, and inadequate public policies. The cost of the United States' failure to meet the changing needs of working families is being borne by children and adults alike. Moreover, until we address the needs of working families, we will be unable to successfully provide equal opportunities for women and men, poor and middle-class children.

The research group I lead has conducted global, national, and urban studies on these issues. Among the principal sources of data for this chapter are the National Longitudinal Survey of Youth, the Survey of Midlife in the United States, a collaborative national Daily Diaries study, and the Urban Working Families Study. In research supported by the National Institutes of Health and the W.T. Grant

Foundation, my team analyzed extensive, nationally representative, longitudinal data from the Department of Labor's National Longitudinal Survey of Youth (NLSY) on more than four thousand working parents to examine parental working conditions across social class and whether parents had the paid leave and flexibility they needed to care for their children's health and development. As an associate of the MacArthur Foundation Network on Successful Midlife Development, I examined the work and family conditions faced by over thirty-five hundred Americans, ages twenty-five to seventy-four. In the Daily Diaries study, research also supported by the MacArthur Foundation, I developed questions for and analyzed the first systematic, nationally representative study to daily ask over a thousand Americans across the country whether they had to cut back on their commitments to meet family members' needs. In research supported by a Picker Commonwealth scholarship, I developed an ethnographic urban study that involved in-depth interviews of representative samples of urban families in their homes, employers at their work sites, and teachers at day care centers over the course of many months. Finally, my research team analyzed data on over twenty-eight hundred Americans in the National Study of the Changing Workforce.

Together, the studies on which this chapter is based involved interviews with more than ten thousand caregivers and included in-depth interviews with home visits, daily diaries, testing of children, and multiyear follow-ups. My research team's work examines how Americans of all ages are working while addressing the health, educational, and routine and urgent care needs of children, elderly parents, and other adults. The studies provide an unprecedented view of what experiences working Americans share and how these experiences diverge by social class. They also provide some of the first evidence about how the health and development of our nation's children are being affected—often for the worse—by the current trends.

This chapter will first present key findings from these studies and summarize findings from related research by others. My book, *The Widening Gap: Why America's Working Families Are in Jeopardy and What Can Be Done About It,* presents the complete results.[10] In particular, this chapter will examine the availability in the United States of before- and after-school care for children under five, working conditions that allow parents to be involved in their children's education, and working conditions that enable parents to care for sick children. The availability and affordability of adequate supports, services, and working conditions across social class and gender will be analyzed.

Second, this chapter will discuss how to narrow the gap between what social supports and working conditions need to be available in the United States in contrast to what currently is available. A variety of policies that can make a difference will be discussed, ranging from basic job benefits to early educational opportunities, expanding what is available to school-age children, caring for elderly and disabled adults, and bringing American social institutions into the twenty-first century. Finally, the chapter will end by discussing the implications of these policies for equality in America.

THE BARRIERS CHILDREN AND PARENTS FACE

Lack of Quality, Affordable Early Education

Preschool- and school-age children fare well when working families find affordable, available, and high-quality education and care for them. In fact, research has shown that children who have the opportunity to attend preschool have larger vocabularies and are better readers at age six than their brothers and sisters who have not had an opportunity to attend.[11] Evaluations of model early childhood programs have shown a wide range of benefits for children, including improved achievement test scores, a decreased need for special education services, decreased rates of being held back in school, and greater rates of high school graduation.[12] The problem is that the majority of families cannot find that kind of quality education or care. Many families in the United States simply cannot afford it. In all but one state, the average cost of having a four-year-old in preschool is more than the average annual cost of public college tuition. From Tucson to Anchorage, from Honolulu to Omaha, from Kansas City to Oklahoma City, preschool costs twice as much as college tuition. For example, sending a four-year-old to preschool in Seattle, Washington, costs an average of $6,604 per year, whereas college tuition at a public institution costs an average of $3,151 per year.[13]

One option available for low-income families is Head Start, the principal federal program aimed at providing disadvantaged children with early educational opportunities. But Head Start in its current form serves only a small fraction of the needs of children living in poverty. Only half of three- and four-year-olds who qualify for Head Start are able to attend at all. Due to limited funding and slots, the overwhelming majority of those who attend do so less than full time and for only one year, even though most would benefit from attending more. The availability is even more limited for early Head Start, which reaches less than 2 percent of those eligible.[14]

Insufficient Opportunities for School-Age Children

Like early education, making extended school programs available has been shown to improve children's academic achievement across social class.[15] Studies have demonstrated that children who participate in after-school programs not only spend more time on their homework but also are more likely to complete their homework and to prepare it better. The ability to read is at the core of much of elementary, middle, and high school achievement, and after-school programs have been shown to have important effects on reading. A National Academy of Sciences study on preventing reading difficulties confirmed that children who receive extra time and reading instruction beyond the current school day have significant improvements in their academic achievement.[16] Reading improves for children already succeeding in school, as well as for at-risk children receiving support in after-school programs.[17] Among at-risk youths, aspirations for completing high school also improve when they participate in after-school programs; youths in after-school programs are less likely both to drop out of school and to be held back. At the societal level, those communities that have more structured activities for school-age children have fewer students suffering from major problems including substance abuse and other behavioral and mental health problems.[18] Moreover, after-school programs have also been shown to lead to a decrease in crime and victimization.[19] This makes sense, given that the hours with the highest rates of children and youth committing and being victims of crimes are on weekdays between 2:00 and 8:00 P.M.[20]

Yet, in spite of their demonstrated importance, affordable, quality programs for school-age children are scarce. This is in part because as grossly inadequate as the public and corporate policies regarding preschool-age children currently are in the United States, they are far more developed than the policies addressing the needs of schoolchildren. Employers who pride themselves on providing benefit packages for working parents typically boast of maternity leave policies and preschool child care programs, while they often neglect parents of school-age children. Since the federal government has done little more, school-age children's needs have been largely ignored. In 1998, twice as many parents wanted to have an after-school program available to their children as had them available, according to the U.S. Department of Education.[21] And the situation is getting worse, not better. The Government Accounting Office has estimated that the demand in some urban areas for out-of-school programs will be four times as great as the supply.[22] As a result, many schoolchildren—from both low- and middle-income families—lack access to supervision and care during out-of-school hours.

Barriers to Parents' Involvement in Education

One of the key factors affecting how children fare in school is parental involvement in different aspects of children's education.[23] When parents are involved in their children's education, children achieve more in elementary school, junior high school, and high school.[24] Parental involvement is associated with children's higher achievement in language and mathematics, improved behavior, greater academic persistence, and lower dropout rates.[25] Intermittently, working parents are called to take time off from work to meet with teachers, principals, and learning specialists; to visit schools; and to help guide their children through difficult periods. Our analyses of nationally representative data showed that across the country, too many parents lacked the paid leave and flexibility they needed to take time from work to help their children with school problems. Disastrously, those who most needed such benefits had the fewest.[26]

In our studies, we found that families in which a child was in the bottom quartile in reading or math were significantly more likely to face working conditions that made it difficult or impossible for the parents to adequately assist their children. Of parents who had a child scoring in the bottom quartile in math, more than half at times lacked any kind of paid leave, and nearly three-fourths could not consistently

FIGURE 4-1. Do Parents of Children at Risk Educationally
Have the Chance to Take Leave from Work to Assist?

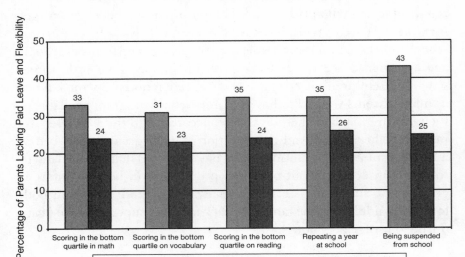

Note: The figure is based on analyses we conducted with data from the National
Longitudinal Survey of Youth. We examined whether parents lacked paid leave and
scheduling flexibility in their primary job some or all of the time over a six-year period.

rely on flexibility at work to meet with teachers or learning specialists.
One out of three found themselves in double jeopardy, that is, simultaneously lacking paid leave *and* work flexibility (see Figure 4-1). One in
six were not able to be available routinely in the evenings to help with
homework (see Figures 4-2 and 4-3).

Families in which a child scored in the bottom quartile in reading
were equally constrained by working conditions. More than half of
these parents lacked paid leave, and nearly three out of four lacked
flexibility they could rely on to meet with schoolteachers and specialists (see Figure 4-1). Furthermore, as in the case of the parents of children scoring in the bottom quartile in math, one in six parents of
children scoring in the bottom quartile in reading worked evenings,
when their children most needed academic help (see Figures 4-2 and
4-3). These patterns also held for the parents of children who were at
greatest risk: those who had had to repeat a grade in school or who had
been suspended from school. Four out of ten of these parents found
themselves, some or all of the time, lacking both paid leave and flexi-

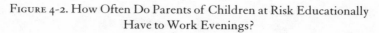

FIGURE 4-2. How Often Do Parents of Children at Risk Educationally
Have to Work Evenings?

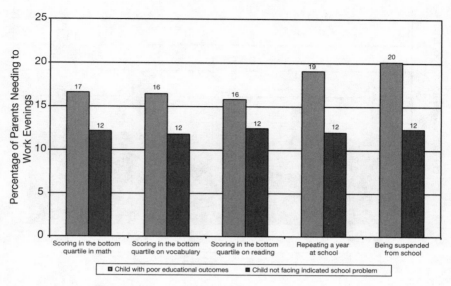

Note: The figure is based on analyses we conducted with data from the National
Longitudinal Survey of Youth. Parents needing to work evenings reported working an
evening shift at their primary job for some or all of their working years over a six-year
period.

bility (see Figure 4-1). Nearly one out of five of these parents worked
evenings (most without any choice), when their children needed them
most (see Figures 4-2 and 4-3).

In all these cases, poor parental working conditions disastrously
limited the extent to which parents could be available to help children
whose education was in trouble. Could the relationship between
parental working conditions and children's poor school performance
be explained by other factors? Even when statistical methods were
used to control for differences in family income and in parental education, marital status, and total hours parents worked, we found that the
more hours parents had to be away from home in the evening, the more
likely their children were to test in the bottom quartile on achievement
tests. Similarly, after controlling for other differences, we still found
that parents who had to work at night were 2.7 times as likely to have a
child who had been suspended from school (see Appendix A).

FIGURE 4-3. How Often Do Parents of Children at Risk Educationally
Have to Work Nights?

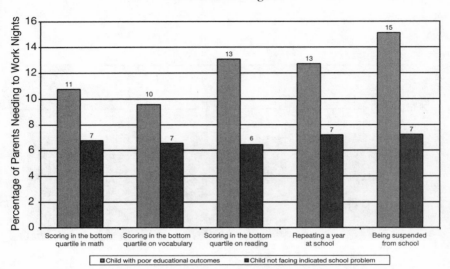

Note: The figure is based on analyses we conducted with data from the National
Longitudinal Survey of Youth. Parents needing to work nights reported working a night
shift at their primary job for some or all of their working years over a six-year period.

Barriers to Parents' Involvement in Children's Health Care

Parents have long played an essential role in the health care, as well as
the education, of their children, and many studies over the course of
decades have demonstrated the importance of parents' involvement
when their children are sick. When their parents are present, sick children have better vital signs and fewer symptoms; they recover more
rapidly from illnesses and injuries.[27] Furthermore, the presence of parents shortens children's hospital stays by 31 percent.[28] Despite the compelling evidence about the value of having parents involved in their
children's health care, little attention has been paid to the factors that
influence whether working parents can participate.

In the Baltimore Parenthood Study, we asked young parents a series of questions about the factors that affected their ability to care for
their children who became sick. Only 42 percent of parents were able
to stay at home when their children were sick on a regular workday.
Of those who were able to stay at home with their sick children, more

than half said they could do so because they received some type of paid leave. Twenty-nine percent reported that they used paid vacation or personal days; 14 percent, paid leave designated for care of sick family members; 11 percent, their own paid sick leave; 11 percent, unpaid leave; and 7 percent, flexible working hours. Twenty-one percent used different work benefits on different occasions.

Our research confirmed that the parents who received some type of paid leave were significantly more likely to stay home with their sick children (see Figure 4-4). In fact, the availability of paid leave proved to be the key determinant of parents' actions. After controlling statistically for other relevant factors, those parents who had either sick leave or vacation leave were 5.2 times as likely to care for their sick children as those who did not have such benefits.[29] Parents who were single, who were living near or below the poverty line, or who had a high school education or less had worse working conditions; therefore, they

FIGURE 4-4. Percentage of Parents Who Stay Home with
Sick Children, by Job Benefit

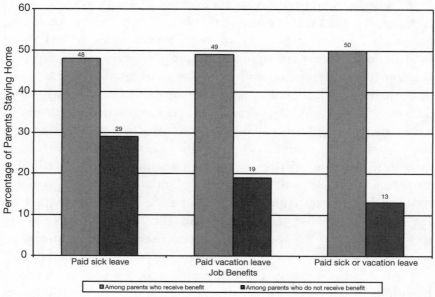

Note: The figure is based on analyses we conducted with data from the Baltimore Parenthood Study.

were significantly less likely to have stayed at home when their children became sick.

In spite of the critical need, the majority of U.S. parents do not consistently have paid leave they can use to care for children; as a result, children are left home alone or are sent to school sick.[30]

Unequal Burdens Across Social Class

The toll on children and adults of our nation's inadequate policies is exacerbating damaging and persistent income inequalities in the United States. While there is no doubt that families across the country—from every ethnic and racial group, as well as from both middle-income and poor families—are dramatically affected by the gap between American institutions and families' needs, the poor are affected first and worst. When social institutions fail families, middle-income families have more resources of their own with which they can try, at least for a time, to plug some of the holes in the dike; low-income families, however, are left to resolve the problems themselves, often without any other resources to rely upon.[31]

As noted earlier, paid leave and flexibility at work can critically affect a worker's chances of meeting family members' needs. Analyzing nationally representative data, we found that families in the bottom quartile of income were significantly more likely to lack paid sick leave, paid vacation leave, and flexibility than families in the upper three quartiles of income. Even people who earned just above the median income were less likely than those in the top quartile of income to have either paid sick leave, paid vacation leave, or flexibility (see Figure 4-5). At the same time, they were more likely than those in the top quartile to have to work evenings or nights. Among employed parents, 20 percent of those in the lowest income quartile worked evenings, compared to 14 percent and 13 percent of those in the middle quartiles and 7 percent of those in the highest quartile; for night work, the respective figures were 10 percent, 9 percent (for both middle quartiles), and 6 percent.

On nearly every measure of job flexibility that would enable working adults to care for family members, the middle-income employees we studied were worse off than higher-income ones (see Figure 4-6).

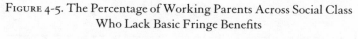

FIGURE 4-5. The Percentage of Working Parents Across Social Class
Who Lack Basic Fringe Benefits

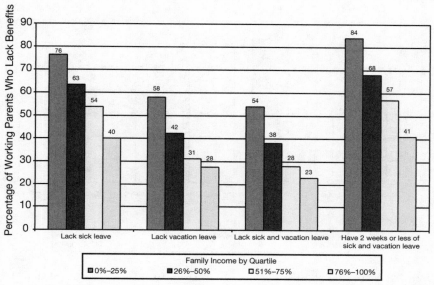

Note: The figure is based on analyses we conducted with data from the National
Longitudinal Survey of Youth. Bars represent parents who lacked benefits some or all of the
time they worked over a six-year period.

Moreover, low-income families faced still worse conditions than did
middle-income ones.

A gradient exists in the need for, as well as the availability of, flexible working conditions. Lower-income working adults have to spend
substantially more time than upper-income adults caring for both
their children and their parents. For example, we found that providing a few hours of care for parents each month was common across
social class, but low-income families were twice as likely to need to
provide more than thirty hours of care each month for parents and
parents-in-law (see Figure 4-7). One of many reasons for this was that
lower-income children and adults were getting sick more often and
had more chronic conditions than upper-income individuals. Yet
fewer lower-income employees had the economic resources to pay for
help, and the government provided little support.

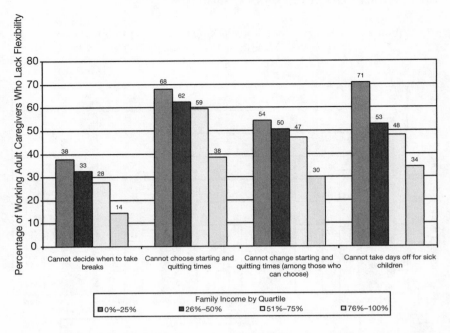

FIGURE 4-6. The Percentage of Working Parents Across Social Class
Who Lack Flexibility at Work

Note: The figure is based on analyses we conducted with data from the National Study of the
Changing Workforce.

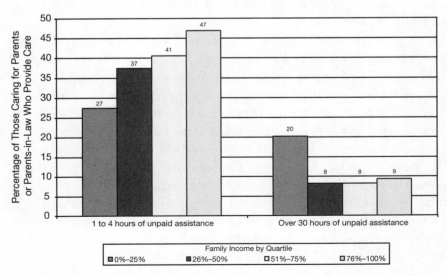

FIGURE 4-7. The Percentage of Working Parents Across Social Class
Who Provide Care for Parents or Parents-in-Law

Note: The figure is based on data we collected in the Survey of Midlife in the United States.

Persistent Gender Inequalities

The profound inequalities that plague families across social class simultaneously create a chasm between women's and men's opportunities in the United States. In the national research we conducted, both working men and women said that women have far more family caretaking and household responsibilities (see Figure 4-8). More specifically, eight out of ten employed mothers and seven out of ten working women caring for their parents said they did far more of the household chores than their spouse or partner. Men agreed: more than five out of six said their wife or partner did most of the household chores. Similarly, women and men reported facing unequal demands from family members. Twice as many mothers as fathers said their family often made demands of them.

Working women were more likely than working men to also be caring for a child, a spouse, or a partner with a disability, or an elderly relative (see Figure 4-9). Those men who did help care for a disabled adult or elderly relative were more likely than women to have spent one day or less a month providing that care. Women were three times

FIGURE 4-8. Balance of Family Responsibilities Among Women and Men

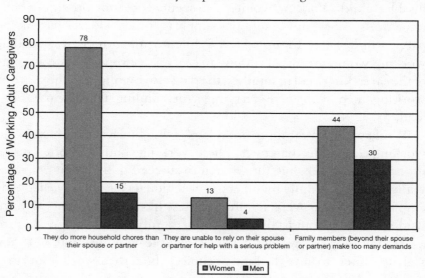

Note: The figure is based on data we collected in the Survey of Midlife in the United States.

FIGURE 4-9. Caregiving Responsibilities of Women and Men

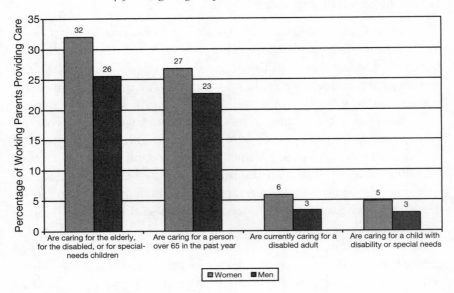

Note: The figure is based on data we collected in the Survey of Midlife in the United States.

as likely as men to have spent forty hours or more a month caring for a disabled child. Working women also spent more time providing both unpaid assistance and emotional support to their elderly parents or parents-in-law (see Figure 4-10). While our data made it clear that working women were continuing to carry a disproportionate amount of the caretaking load in families, the data also highlighted the share of working men who were carrying a demanding family-caretaking load.

While women bear more of the caregiving burden, they face worse working conditions than men. These working conditions often make it difficult or impossible for women to succeed to their full potential while caring for family members. Our national research revealed that employed mothers were significantly less likely than fathers to have paid leave they could take to care for family members (see Figure 4-11). Not only did women have less paid leave in general, but they were less likely to have the kind of choices about their work hours that can make balancing work and caregiving more feasible. Women had less choice both in terms of when to start and end work and when to

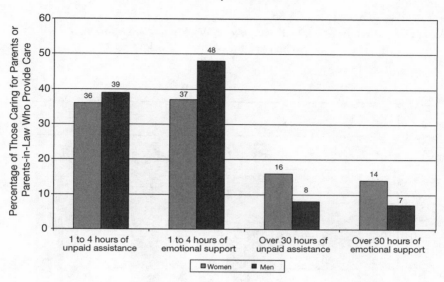

FIGURE 4-10. The Extent of Caregiving for Parents or
Parents-in-Law by Women and Men

Note: The figure is based on data we collected in the Survey of Midlife in the United States.

FIGURE 4-11. The Percentage of Working Women and Men
Who Lack Basic Fringe Benefits

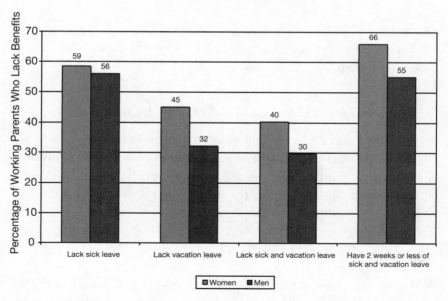

Note: The figure is based on analyses we conducted with data from the National
Longitudinal Survey of Youth. Bars represent parents who lacked benefits some or all of
the time they worked over a six-year period.

FIGURE 4-12. The Percentage of Working Women and Men
Who Lack Flexibility at Work

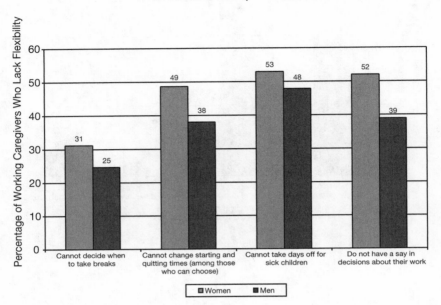

Note: The above figure is based on analyses we conducted with data from the National
Survey of the Changing Workforce and the Survey of Midlife in the United States.

take breaks (see Figure 4-12). In fact, on all measures of job autonomy
(such as having a say on what tasks are to be done), women had less of
a voice than men.

POLICIES THAT CAN MAKE A DIFFERENCE

Having described the widening gaps American families face, it is important to address whether anything can be done about it. A number
of readily achievable advances would dramatically change the prospects of American adults and the children, elderly parents, and disabled family members for whom they care.

Basic Job Benefits

While passage of the 1993 Family and Medical Leave Act (FMLA), the
only federal legislation to directly address any needs of working fami-

lies in the United States, was an important first step, there are as many holes as threads in this safety net. For those who are covered by the FMLA, the act has safeguarded the possibility of returning to their jobs after unpaid leave for a major illness of a limited number of immediate family members. The value of this leave to those able to use it should never be understated. However, the FMLA fails to provide any coverage to nearly half of American workers, including those who work for small employers (those with less than fifty employees) and those who do not meet the minimum hour requirement because they have recently changed jobs or work multiple part-time jobs to make ends meet. Moreover, three-quarters of those who are in theory covered cannot, in fact, afford to take unpaid leave. In practice, they are thus left with no option. Furthermore, the act provides no coverage for common illnesses of young children that nonetheless require an adult present, nor does it provide any coverage for educational needs, no matter how great; together, these make up the vast majority of children's unpredictable problems. Major illnesses, including terminal ones, of brothers and sisters, parents-in-law, and grandparents are among the many adult needs that remain entirely uncovered.

We should support the ability of Americans to care for themselves and for their loved ones in at least two ways. First, short-term paid leave should be available to all working Americans. As documented here, many Americans still have no or only intermittent paid leave. We, as a country, can afford to ensure that all Americans have at least two weeks of paid family leave annually, which they can take to meet their own or their family's health needs. This leave should be available for use to see doctors for preventive, as well as curative, care. It should also be available to meet urgent developmental or educational needs— as when a child is failing in school and parents need to meet with teachers, when a child is diagnosed with a learning disability and meetings with specialists are required, or when elderly parents can no longer care for themselves and need to have essential services arranged. Many companies would not need to increase the leave they already provide. The amount of sick leave they currently provide would be sufficient; the only change would be to officially allow it to be used to meet critical needs of family members as well as of the employee. Even this amount of guaranteed leave would make an enormous difference for those families currently facing the worst problems.

Second, we need to bring the United States up to global standards when it comes to paid parental leave. A review of what other nations offer in terms of the maternity and paternity components of parental leave is instructive. More than 150 countries around the world—countries ranging from high- to low-income ones, countries with a wide range of political, social, and economic systems—all provide paid maternity leave. Throughout the Organisation for Economic Cooperation and Development countries, paid parental leave is also common. We need to catch up to these standards. Paid parental leave could be created through many different options, ranging from legislation requiring businesses to provide minimum levels of parental leave to a public insurance system paralleling unemployment or disability insurance.

Early Educational Opportunities

While many social institutions need to adapt, the most important changes need to occur in our approach to education. In spite of the well-documented importance of early childhood education in how children fare in school, access to early childhood education today looks a lot like access to high school education did in 1949 (see Figure 4–13). In fact, the enrollment rates of children in kindergarten, nursery schools, and other preschools are lower in the United States than in many countries, including, among others, Italy, Luxembourg, and the Netherlands.[32]

We can afford to do more. In the United States, public expenditures for early childhood education are less than similar public expenditures in Finland, Norway, Austria, the United Kingdom, the Czech Republic, Germany, Italy, and Portugal. Our combined public and private expenditures on early childhood education are a smaller percentage of gross domestic product (GDP) than the public and private spending on early childhood education in all the aforementioned countries, as well as in Canada, Denmark, Hungary, Sweden, Spain, Turkey, and the Netherlands.[33] State and federal governments have provided so little funding to preschool that it is a parody of the need. For example, Alabama spent $395 per poor child per year (including the contribution of federal funding), or less than $1.10 per day. California spent $536 per poor child (approximately half state funding and half federal

FIGURE 4-13. High School Graduation and Preschool Enrollment Rates, 1870–1996

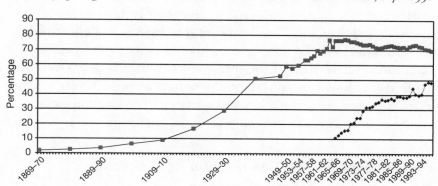

Note: The figure is based on data from National Center for Education Statistics, *Digest of Education Statistics 1997* (Washington, DC: NCES, 1997), Table 6, 15, available at: http://nces.ed.gov/pubs/digest97/d97t006.html (for preschool enrollment); National Center for Education Statistics, *Digest of Education Statistics 1997* (Washington, DC: NCES, 1997), Table 99, 108, available at: http://nces.ed.gov/pubs/digest97/d97t099.html.

funding)—still less than $2 per day.[34] Given the high cost of preschool, the lack of government funding means that too many families simply cannot afford to send their children.

We currently face grave problems in terms of quality as well as affordability. A 1998 study by the Consumer Product Safety Commission found that two-thirds of licensed child care settings had safety hazards. The National Institute of Child Health and Development reported that three out of five preschool settings were either fair or poor in quality.[35] Moreover, while teachers of older children are required to have certification, those caring for our youngest children are commonly not required to have either certification or any training in child development. While school districts have been trying to ensure smaller class sizes for older children, the majority of states still fail to meet the child-to-staff ratios for young children that are recommended by professional organizations, including the National Association for the Education of Young Children and the National Association of Childcare Resource and Referral Agencies.

We need to ensure that children younger than five, who are at critical developmental stages, are taught by teachers as well trained as teachers of elementary school children. We need to ensure that they are adequately paid, so that high-quality educators will continue to work in this area and so that the enormously high rates of staff turnover will decrease. Finally, we need to mandate adequate adult-to-child ratios. We should guarantee high-quality early education for all families, just as many European countries already do.[36] Only with public funding will low-income children have an opportunity to benefit from quality early education, and quality early education is essential for lower-income children to have an equal opportunity in education.

Expanding What Is Available to School-Age Children

We need to expand the opportunities for elementary and secondary school children as well. There is nothing magical about the current short school day and 180-day school year. Over the past 130 years, the length of the school year has been changed to adjust to the needs of families and children, and there is every reason now to extend it to better meet the needs of children (who need to learn enough to compete in a global economy when they are adults) and their working parents.

FIGURE 4-14. Change in School Year in Perspective

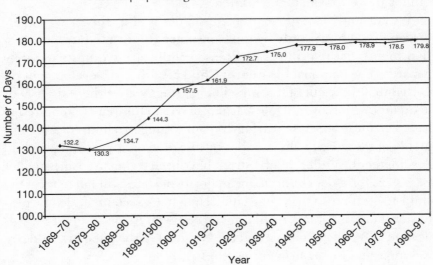

Note: The figure is based on data from National Center for Education Statistics, *Digest of Education Statistics 1997* (Washington, DC: NCES, 1997), Table 39, available at nces.ed.gov/pubs/digest97/d97t039.html.

As what children needed to learn in school for their economic survival increased, so too did the length of the school year. From 1870 to 1930, during a period of rapid industrialization, the length of the school year increased 30 percent, from 132 days to 173 days. Then the expansion of public education stalled; from 1930 to the present, the school term has increased only 7 days, from 173 to 180 days.[37] Leaving the agrarian school calendar behind and extending educational opportunity are long overdue. These changes are important for both children and parents. In fact, a wide range of countries have substantially more school than the United States. Countries with over 200 days per year range from Korea to Chile, Denmark to Brazil, the Philippines to Italy.[38]

The school day is as important as the school year. Few states have invested adequately in extended school programs, in spite of all the evidence regarding their effectiveness. Only in Hawaii do more than half of all public schools have extended days. In more than half of the states, no more than one in five public schools offers after-school programs. Parental demand markedly outstrips spaces nationwide. The federal government's efforts are currently focused on the Twenty-first Century Community Learning Centers initiative, which provides limited funding to communities so they can provide services for children and families during after-school hours, including tutoring, mentoring, homework centers, academic enrichment activities, sports, and arts. The idea is very promising, but the centers touch only a fraction of the need.[39] For the more than fifty-five million school-age children in the United States, the funds amount to less than $15 per child per year— enough to pay for little more than one afternoon.[40] We need to make access to academic extended-day and year-round programs universal. When extended and after-school programs are provided, we need to ensure that they are of high quality. The ability, training, and number of staff are all critical factors in the quality of programs. The relationships the programs have with the children's schools, families, and community are equally crucial.

Extending the educational opportunities for school-age children is not only important to working families but necessary in far more wide-reaching ways. Economists have repeatedly argued that how individuals and families fare in a global economy will increasingly depend on their educational achievement. Political scientists and policy makers go one step further to argue that the welfare of communities and nations will depend on the educational attainment of their citizens. But in international mathematics achievement tests, scores for U.S. students in 1997 placed behind, in rank order, those of students in Singapore, Japan, Korea, Hong Kong, Belgium, the Czech Republic, Austria, Hungary, the Slovak Republic, Switzerland, France, Slovenia, Bulgaria, the Netherlands, Canada, Ireland, Australia, Israel, Thailand, Sweden, Germany, New Zealand, Norway, and England. Furthermore, the eighth-grade science scores of U.S. students ranked behind those of students in twenty-one of the same countries tested.[41]

Extending the school day and the school year by 25 percent would simultaneously provide more educational opportunities for children, who need to be able to compete economically, and help working parents, who need their children to receive enrichment activities and quality supervision in a safe place. The use of existing school buildings would reduce the cost of these programs and increase their accessibility. The educational and productivity gains would bring important long-term economic benefits, further offsetting the costs.

Not only is the U.S. educational system failing to measure up against those of other countries, but it currently fails to measure up against the fundamental American principle of equal opportunity. At present, children from affluent families typically spend their after-school hours and summer days in enrichment activities. At the same time, children from poor families too often spend those hours alone or in the inadequate care of other young children. Teachers commonly observe that over the course of the summer, the skills of marginalized children fall farther behind as they forget some of what they learned during the school year—and that, in contrast, children who have enrichment opportunities move ahead. Providing a public opportunity for enrichment activities during the after-school hours and summer days would narrow the class-based rifts in how American children fare educationally.

Caring About Elderly and Disabled Adults

Caring for families is about more than meeting the needs of children. Between 1870 and 1990, the U.S. population increased sixfold, but the population of Americans sixty-five years old and older increased twenty-seven-fold.[42] While those sixty-five years and older accounted for just over 1 million Americans (3 percent of the population) in 1870, as of 1999 there were more than 34 million older Americans (13 percent of the population). The U.S. Bureau of the Census has estimated that by the year 2030, there will be approximately 70 million people sixty-five and older (20 percent of the population).[43]

Although a great range of experiences and interests exists among older individuals, they are more likely than younger people to have limitations in their activities. While fewer than one in twenty adults younger than sixty-five have limitations in their ability to care for themselves, one in five adults sixty-five years or older have difficulty bathing, dressing, or getting around inside or outside the home.[44] Only a small minority of sixty- and seventy-year-olds have significant limitations, but the probability of having health problems increases with age.

We, as a nation, need to ensure that there are affordable solutions to meeting the routine and urgent needs of the elderly. At first glance, meeting the long-range needs of the elderly appears to be an overwhelming task. In fact, effectively addressing the needs of the elderly and of disabled adults is not as daunting as it first seems, and it is urgent. As society focuses on other needs, the needs of the elderly grow.

The good news is that there are clear steps that can be taken both to decrease the need for long-term care and to improve the quality of life for older and disabled Americans. We need to eliminate age discrimination in the workplace so that older Americans who are interested in and capable of working can do so. We need to ensure that the Americans with Disabilities Act is successfully implemented and enforced so that the same is true for disabled Americans. Not only is income from work the key to self-sufficiency, but work and intellectual and physical stimulation have repeatedly been shown to play a critical role in health and longevity. We should ensure that elderly and disabled Americans who are not in the paid labor force have sufficient opportunities for exercise, social interactions, and stimulation—all essential ingredients for their ability to live as healthy and independent a life as possible.[45] When these opportunities include volunteer work, the elderly and disabled will also be able to contribute to communities. We need to ensure that those who cannot live alone without support but do not need twenty-four-hour care will get the amount of help necessary for them to continue living at home and avoid the far greater social, personal, and economic costs of being unnecessarily institutionalized. The critical question of long-term-care insurance—how to pay for the care of those who need twenty-four-hour nursing home or other care—will remain. But both the need for and the cost of that care will be reduced if, first, we provide elderly and disabled adults with sufficient opportunities and supports for continuing to live independently and, second, we provide their family members with the necessary leave from work to help when urgent needs arise.

Bringing Social Institutions into the Twenty-first Century

Too often left out of any discussion of what needs to change so that both work and families can thrive are outmoded civic and social institutions—that is, ones whose practices are grounded, often for no better reason than habit, in the rhythms of a nineteenth-century agrarian economy or in the mid-twentieth-century moment when most households had only one adult in the paid labor force. A few examples follow.

In the city in which we conducted the Urban Working Families study, a parent needing to register a child for school had to go in person during the workday to the Parent Information Center, which had no evening or weekend hours. Making it possible for working parents to register a child for school by mail—just as they now can register to vote—or offering a wider range of registration times would mean that many parents could accomplish this vital task without missing any work.

Many private institutions have readily changed with the times. Malls are open in the evening, banks have weekend hours, and grocery stores are open seven days a week. But the gatekeepers for public services and supports for families are often available only between 9:00 A.M. and 5:00 P.M., or even for more limited hours, Monday through Friday. As in other cases, the barriers are greatest, ironically, for the lowest-income families who most need child care vouchers, food stamps, WIC, and other public services and supports—and who are also the least likely to have flexible work schedules or paid leave they might use for trips to public offices during the workday.[46]

Public transportation provides another example of an antiquated system. As a result of the inadequacy of public sources of transportation for children, the elderly, or ill and injured adults, one of the most frequent causes of work disruption reported in our national research was to provide transportation for family members. Lack of transportation was also one of the frequent reasons why families could not make use of available services. For example, while public schools provide buses for children to attend during the short school day, even those schools that offer before- and after-school programs commonly fail to provide any transportation to and from these programs. Similarly, the elderly may have health insurance, so they can see a physician, but no way to get to their appointments when they cannot drive or walk.

When services of any kind are designed, we need to think about how children and adults will get to and from those services, given that the majority will come from families in which all working-age adults will be employed outside the home. For some services, this will mean considering distance and location in selecting providers. For other services, we will need to provide public transportation. If we can provide transportation for children to get to and from school, then we can provide transportation for children to get to and from after-school programs. We can no longer ignore transportation issues in the provision of any services for children, the elderly, or the disabled.

MAKING CHANGES NECESSARY FOR EQUALITY

More than improving the lives of families that work in the United States, this set of public policies could dramatically increase equality. By any measure of equity, our nation's employer-based approach to meeting families' needs has failed. Both gender and class disparities are exacerbated by the dramatic disparities in working and social conditions that women and men face all along the different points on the income gradient. Because they currently carry more of the caregiving responsibilities in workplaces that have failed to adapt, women are markedly disadvantaged. Because of our nation's failure to provide public services and set even minimal public standards for working conditions that affect families, lower-income families have a much smaller chance of simultaneously succeeding at work and caring well for family members than do middle-income ones, who, in turn, have a smaller chance than the well-to-do.

While economic factors help create the initial inequities, they are markedly exacerbated by the public policy areas our nation has neglected. These neglected areas include our failure to provide public preschool or early education to parallel public school; our failure to extend the school day and school year, now that our economy is postindustrial and no longer primarily agricultural; our failure to respond to the needs of the rapidly expanding elderly population for care; and our failure to ensure employees basic family-related leaves from work. In most other industrialized nations, working families can count on publicly guaranteed parental leave, and in many, preschool child care or early childhood education is already publicly provided. Furthermore, many nations mandate that employers provide a minimum number of vacation and sick leave days, while others provide public insurance guaranteeing paid leave for all families. These provisions limit what would otherwise be dangerous disparities across the social gradient. The United States does none of these. Consequently, low-income families in the United States face many more obstacles than do their counterparts in most industrialized countries.

Understanding the extreme conditions working-poor families face is critical to our formulation of poverty policy. In 1935, when Aid to Dependent Children (ADC) was established as part of the sweeping New Deal reforms, the country had decided that it was impossible for single mothers living in poverty (most of whom were single because of the death of or abandonment by a spouse) to support themselves economically and still care adequately for their children. By 1996, when Congress passed the Personal Responsibility and Work Opportunity Reconciliation Act and repealed the federal guarantee of income support for parents and children living in poverty, the country made an about-face. A fundamental shift in the public debate had taken place: instead of believing it was impossible for most single parents to care for their children adequately while earning enough money for subsistence, the public contended that nothing other than willpower was stopping single poor parents from working full time and caring for their children well. The argument seemed simple: if middle-class mothers apparently could work and care for their children well, so could poor mothers. Little was said about the fact that it would be difficult or impossible for many parents living in poverty to succeed in the workforce and in caring for their families with the far fewer private and public resources available to them than to middle-income parents.

At the same time as heightening the impact of income inequalities, our failure as a nation to address the obstacles working caregivers face has exacerbated the wide gap in opportunities that women and men have. Even though pregnancy and marriage bars and other forms of public gender discrimination have been made illegal, women—who carry most of the American caregiving burden—remain highly segregated from men in jobs and disadvantaged in wages.

Currently, both women and racial and ethnic minorities remain at a significant disadvantage in wages in comparison to white men. In 1980, women were earning only 60 percent as much as men, while black men were earning 85 percent as much as white men, after educational differences were taken into account.[47] In the 1990s, full-time, full-year-employed women still earned less than 75 percent of what men did.[48] Various people have argued that this gender-related wage gap is not a cause for concern, and they point to the fact that the wage disparities are not so great among young employees. While this is certainly the case, it is unfortunately not a case for optimism. Rather, this largely reflects the fact that young women have not yet experienced the disadvantages associated with becoming caregivers. Among thirty-year-old working women, for example, those who are not mothers earn 95 percent as much as men, whereas mothers earn 75 percent as much as men. Economic studies have shown that a majority of the pay gap between women and men is associated with their differing family responsibilities.[49] The gap is not due merely to differences in years of paid work experienced, to differences in the number of hours worked, or to differences in amount of education. In fact, when adjustments for education are made, the gender-based earnings gap—as compared to that between blacks and whites—grows even worse.[50]

We need policies that make it possible for both women and men to succeed at work while caring for their family members. Making this possible for women will remove many of the current barriers they face in decent wages and professional advancement, as well as some of the greatest obstacles in filling a greater percentage of leadership roles. Making this possible for men is a necessary first step toward increasing the number of men who are willing to share family labor responsibilities equally with women. Even if we were concerned only with women's inequality, it would be essential to implement work-family programs and policies for both men and women. But there are other reasons to implement these programs and policies on a gender-neutral basis: they affect the ability of all workers to balance work and family, and consequently, they affect our society's future.

SOCIETY'S BEST PROSPECT: AN EQUAL CHANCE FOR ALL CHILDREN AND ADULTS

Failing to respond to the past century and a half's change in work means that we are failing to meet the essential needs of children and adults in the United States. Moreover, without addressing this failure, we will not be able to successfully address inequality. The gaps in care-giving do not exist because adults work. The gaps are formed as a result of social conditions that never adapted to the changes in where and how parents work. Our society—like any other—must continually reexamine how best to approach at least three essential issues: what values we will uphold, how the work of our society will get done, and how generations that will lead our country in the future will be raised.

The failure to address how working families' needs are met in the United States is affecting all three of these. As both our national surveys and in-depth urban studies have shown, our failure to address working families' needs is profoundly affecting the health, development, and education of children.[51] It is also severely limiting the support available for adults with special health and daily care needs. Furthermore, anyone who decides to care for children or adults in need faces less of a chance in the workforce, because our country allows workplaces to have unnecessary barriers to meeting both job and family responsibilities. When we discriminate by caregiving status, we diminish the likelihood that adults will take the time to voluntarily provide the care our whole society depends on.

Affordable and Necessary

Much of what we need to do is not so new as to be unimaginable. In the past, we expanded public education for high school; expanding early education is equally important now. We have school days and calendars that matched the agrarian work cycle; we need to update them to match parents' industrial and postindustrial work schedules and children's increasing need for skills. We have social security, which helps older Americans with their income needs; we must pay attention to their need for care from family members as well. We have national unemployment insurance that dates from when a single wage earner's loss of work was the largest threat; we need paid family leave insurance for the current workforce, since loss of work is now as likely to result from an adult's need to be at home providing care for a family member. We have adequate transportation systems for healthy adults; we need equally good ones to link children and adults in need with their caregivers.

Countries with a wide range of economic, political, and social structures have demonstrated the feasibility of meeting the needs of families that work. One case is paid maternity leave: from Brazil to Belgium, from Germany to Gabon, women receive paid maternity leave.[52] Providing paid paternity leave is no less affordable, and it is already done in countries ranging from Iceland to Denmark, from Finland to Canada. Furthermore, public programs for preschool-age and school-age children have already been adopted in a wide range of countries from Mexico to Sweden; the feasibility of and access to a longer school year have already been established in a range of nations from Australia to Korea.[53]

What will making the needed changes on a national level mean to employers? On balance, the changes will make it easier for employers to get their essential work done well. Employees who currently must miss work because they cannot find care for preschool- or school-age children will not need to do so when we have the option of quality early education and extended school days available nationwide. Employees who have had to miss work while registering a child for school or their family for food stamps will not need to do so when public services either increase their hours or expand their registration and reenrollment methods to include mail, phone, fax, or Internet. Employees who now must take off an hour and a half every day to transport a child to an after-school program will no longer need to leave work when adequate transportation services are implemented. While in some cases necessary absences will increase—such as when parents use their newly available leave time to be with sick children they might otherwise have left at home alone—these will be balanced by the drop in preventable absences. Whereas now companies that offer good conditions for working families have to compete with companies that offer none, universal benefits will level the playing field nationally.

Addressing working families' needs will no more threaten our economy than providing public education or ensuring basic safety standards for workers has. In fact, as with the case of providing public education, many of the most necessary steps will strengthen our economy by providing for early and extended education for our nation's children. In the long run, our international competitiveness is determined by the quality of our labor force. Both by making it possible for all Americans—irrespective of their income, gender, or caretaking responsibilities—to contribute in the workplace to their full potential and by improving the educational opportunities and support available to children who will join the labor force in a generation, addressing the needs of working families will strengthen our ability to compete.

We *can* afford these needed changes; what we cannot afford to do is to continue our current practices. Making changes on a national scale is necessary if all American working families are to have a chance. Perhaps most overlooked in the entire debate about addressing the needs of working families is how fundamental this effort is to equal opportunity. Without it as a keystone, the chasm between the opportunities that poor, middle-class, and rich children have will only widen.

Across the political spectrum, both conservatives and progressives have noted that "we cannot tolerate, over the long haul, fundamental and growing gaps in the ways of life that Americans lead and presume that the civic 'glue' will hold."[54] As a nation, we face critical choices. Will poor working parents and their children continue to face far worse odds than other families? What will happen to a sizeable fraction of the middle class—particularly those families in which a child or adult has special needs? Will they all be left behind? Or will we bring our social institutions into the twenty-first century? In order for our nation to live up to the professed goal of ensuring equal opportunity, we will have to address the needs of *all* families that work.

APPENDIX A

Parental Working Conditions and Children's Educational Outcomes

TABLE A-1. Relationship Between Parental Evening Work and
Children's Academic Achievement on Math PIAT

Stepwise Regression Model Controlling For	Odds Ratio for Evening Work
Family income	1.18
Parental education	1.16
Marital status of parents	1.16
Child's gender	1.16
Total number of hours worked by parent	1.17*

Note: The above table is based on multivariate regression analyses we conducted with data
from the National Longitudinal Survey of Youth.

* For every hour a parent works between 6 and 9 P.M., his or her child is 1.17 times as likely
(or 17 percent more likely) to score in the bottom quartile on math tests. This is the case even
after taking into account family income, parental education, marital status of parents, the
child's gender, and the total number of hours the parent worked. This finding was
statistically significant, with $p < 0.03$.

TABLE A-2. Relationship Between Parental Night Work and
Probability Child Is Suspended from School

Stepwise Regression Model Controlling For	Odds Ratio for Night Work
Family income	2.91
Parental education	2.91
Marital status of parents	2.71
Child's gender	2.73
Age of child	2.72*

Note: The above table is based on multivariate regression analyses we conducted with data
from the National Longitudinal Survey of Youth.

* The children of parents who work nights are 2.72 times as likely (172 percent more likely)
to have gotten into trouble and been suspended from school. This is the case even after taking
into account family income, parental education, marital status of parents, the child's gender,
and age of the child. This finding was statistically significant, with $p = 0.007$.

5

When There Is No Time or Money: Work, Family, and Community Lives of Low-Income Families

Lisa Dodson and Ellen Bravo

Most families in the United States today—particularly families with children—face a tough challenge in simultaneously meeting work obligations and caring for loved ones. America exceeds all other industrialized nations in average annual hours on the job, and time for family and community life has been eroded throughout U.S. society.[1] Yet a review of the expanding literature on work and family reveals that, for the most part, the issues that define the field are based on middle-class family life. The harsh time bind, the domestic labor balance of dual-earner couples, gender-based roles that lead to "mommy-tracking," and the career off-ramps associated with marriage and childbearing capture the work-family dilemma as it is known by the American middle class.[2] This same focus is reflected in emerging programs and policies to address the tension between career and family care. Flexible work schedules, job sharing, and telecommuting—approaches to alleviating the work-family crunch—have been used in some workplaces but tend to be available only to higher-wage employees.[3] Above all, most work and family discourse presumes an income sufficient to provide for a family's basic needs.

But the situation is markedly different for the so-called bottom third of the economy—that is, people (in this case, families) whose annual income is less than 200 percent of the federal poverty threshold. Bottom-third families generally fall far below regional self-sufficiency standards, set to describe the cost of essential family needs.[4] The contemporary American challenge of pursuing a career, advancing in one's chosen field, and still having the opportunity for a life that includes engaged caregiving and personal relationships presents considerable tension for most families. Yet these tensions simply do not describe the acute dilemmas lived every day in low-income America.

Considered in a historical context, the general omission of lower-income families from the mainstream work-family discourse is not altogether surprising. National approaches toward addressing poor and near-poor people—a population disproportionately composed of single-parent families and families of color—have different ideological and political roots. Historically and today, policies for poor families are focused on reducing single motherhood, increasing labor force participation, and eliminating dependence on public assistance. The more ambitious goals of economic equity, career development, flexible time to promote rewarding family and kin contact, and individual fulfillment have been largely missing in national debates about managing work and family demands in low-income America, despite the voices of a few notable researchers.[5]

ACROSS THE BOUNDARIES: A STUDY ON WORK AND FAMILY IN LOW-INCOME AMERICA

During 2000 and 2001, a collaborative project known as Across the Boundaries was conducted by the Radcliffe Public Policy Center at Harvard University and 9 to 5, the National Association of Working Women. The research, carried out in Milwaukee, Denver, and Boston, included in-depth qualitative assessments of work, family, and community life in low-income America. In gathering qualitative data from the three respondent groups—parents employed in low-wage jobs, teachers and child care providers working in low-income neighborhoods, and employers who hire and supervise entry-level employees—the study triangulated data from individual interviews, ethnographic observations, and group discussions and analyses. Three key research interests included:

- Gathering information about the tensions families face in meeting job demands while being sufficiently engaged with their children, larger families, and communities
- Uncovering the strategies that job supervisors may be using to help workers hold on to their jobs
- Learning from educators and child care workers how child-focused institutions could help low-income parents participate in their children's development while maintaining employment

Sample

This study gathered data mostly from mothers; only one respondent was a father. The racial/ethnic composition of the sample was 45 percent African American, 29 percent white, 16 percent Latino, 1 percent Native American, and 9 percent who identified as "other." Half of the interviewees had been welfare-reliant recently (within the previous two years), another 30 percent had used welfare at some point, and the remainder had never used Aid to Families with Dependent Children (AFDC) or Temporary Assistance for Needy Families (TANF), though most had been income-eligible for other kinds of public assistance (food stamps, Women, Infants, and Children [WIC], etc.). Most continued to use some kind of public supports based on income eligibility despite employment. The salary range of the respondents varied, with 27 percent earning less than $10,000 per year, 23 percent earning $11,000 to $15,000 per year, 20 percent earning $16,000 to $20,000 annually, 18 percent earning $21,000 to $25,000, and 12 percent earning $26,000 to $30,000, with one respondent who had an income above $30,000. The majority of the respondents worked in retail and service sector employment.

Project Methodology

The Across the Boundaries project gathered information from low-income working mothers with family incomes below 200 percent of the national poverty threshold. The study also gathered information from employers who hired and supervised entry-level employees in industries that employed low-wage workers, as well as from key community informants (mostly teachers, child care workers, and local social service providers) who worked principally with children from low-income families. A total of 342 people took part in the study, with 202 participating in in-depth interviews and 140 participating in focus groups held in all three major study cities. These study sites were chosen because the cities were in different phases of welfare reform and represented a diverse range of living and working conditions.

The researchers met with the respondents in homes, workplaces, schools, neighborhood churches, and community centers. Local contextual data were gathered in the three cities, including the demographic characteristics of welfare leavers and low-income workers, common industries of their employment, and the availability of work support services. Theme-gathering focus groups were used in each city with all three respondent groups. Intensive one-on-one interviews were conducted. Major themes from the initial focus groups and the interviews were identified, and interpretive focus groups subsequently were conducted with respondents from all three groups and in all three cities.[6]

All quantitative data from the interviews and focus groups were analyzed using SPSS. All other data were coded and analyzed using Atlas software (a qualitative theme-coding database software), as well as through manual review. The Atlas analysis allowed the research team to match themes, strategies, and best practices that emerged from the interviews with respondents' demographic data.

MAJOR WORK-FAMILY ISSUES
AMONG LOW-INCOME FAMILIES

Most of the findings presented in this discussion are derived from the Across the Boundaries project, and additional data are drawn from unpublished ethnographic research done in 1998 and 1999 in elementary schools in Boston. Also, relevant findings from other national and statewide studies (also performed by Dodson) are cited, since many of the themes that emerged from this study complement trends identified in other researchers' investigations of low-income families' work-family struggles.

Caring for Families While Trying to Stay Employed

As U.S. parents work an increasing number of hours, trustworthy nonparental care has become requisite for most families. While most child care research once focused on preschool-age children, various researchers have recently explored the care and monitoring of school-age children, preteens, and even adolescents, whose education and development still require consistent adult support.[7] For a growing number of families, care also extends to elderly, fragile, and ill family members.[8] In the absence of national family-care policy, most care is given by family members or through private services, which tend to be expensive.

For families with children, the cost of high-quality market-based child care is of particular concern. In the United States in 2000, the average annual full-time cost for a four-year-old in an urban child care center ranged from $3,640 in Arkansas (Conway and Springdale counties) to $8,121 in Massachusetts (Boston area). For an infant, the same costs were $3,900 in Arkansas and $12,978 in Massachusetts.[9] In one recent study, 40 percent of working poor families with children younger than thirteen reported paying for formal child care. Among these families, the average cost of care was $237 per month for children younger than five and $175 for those ages five to twelve; child care expenses represented almost 20 percent of these families' earnings.[10] Since more than two-thirds of the working parents in this study made less than $20,000 per year, their child care costs were prohibitive.

For precisely such reasons, significant federal money was shifted during the period of welfare reform from income support into funding child care programs, specifically the Childcare and Development Fund (CCDF), a federal block grant intended to support child care for low-income families. Yet now, several years later, these efforts clearly are not meeting the vast majority of low-wage parents' child care needs. Nationally, an estimated 12 percent to 15 percent of eligible children in 1999 and 2000 were served by the CCDF, up from 10 percent in 1998.[11] Research has suggested that relatives and friends are the most common sources of child care.[12] These informal care providers are most often grandparents, siblings, or friends, whose assistance is likely to be more flexible and inexpensive.[13] Various studies of "kith and kin" child care have suggested that such care—particularly by relatives—is based on kinship relationships and less on financial incentives.

But according to a review of several studies, the quality of informal child care may be lower than that of regulated, formal care. Other research, also performed by Dodson, has suggested that many children are spending increasing time home alone and that low-income children may be doing so in neighborhoods that, because of poverty, may expose them to greater risks. And one post-welfare study of 872 families in Arizona who had left the TANF program reported that almost half of the parents with children younger than five and 65 percent with children ages six to twelve had *no* child care—not even arrangements with relatives or neighbors. Other research on the quality of child care has revealed parental concerns about the care that low-income children younger than five receive, and some studies have revealed inadequate care levels. Although extensive research has been undertaken on low-income children and on children in families that have left welfare, the current full-day caretaking arrangements for most low-income children of employed parents remain undocumented.[14]

Patchwork Child Care

Meeting children's care needs emerged as a major theme among all the groups of respondents, parents, teachers, and employers in this inquiry. Parent respondents tended to address the theme of child care largely from the perspective of their immediate worries and circumstances. Teachers and child care providers offered intimate observations about children and families, many of whom they had known over an extended period. Employers, of whom many were parents, were able to understand, and even identify with, some of the conflicts that their employees faced. Yet at the same time, they often spoke of a bottom line and the cost to business of children's need for care and attention during working hours. The employers also identified the large number of children with special care needs (see the next section) as particularly disruptive to employment and, thus, a threat to businesses' economic stability. Further, parents of adolescents and middle and high school teachers emphasized that preteens and adolescents needed as much supervision and attention after school as did young children, yet far fewer resources were available for this age group.

The effort to care for and monitor a child while holding a job is considerable if a parent cannot purchase routine, daily, full-time care. For the parents in this study, such child care was often not available; even if it had been, they could not have afforded it. They described child care as involving a complicated, ever-changing array of age-specific arrangements. The descriptions of the majority of parents revealed that, despite the complexity of their plans and the number of people involved, many families did not have child care that covered the entire working and commuting day. Cost, above all, led many parents to a patchwork of fragmented, inexpensive strategies—the kinds of arrangements that most often tend to unravel.[15]

Parents reported using such strategies as relying on grandmothers to babysit for one or two mornings, sending a child to a youth club one afternoon per week, or working two evenings in order to be able to stay home with a child two afternoons a week. The same families sometimes relied on the oldest child (in some cases, younger than ten) to watch a younger child for two evenings each week. Sometimes they had to send their young children off to school unaccompanied, as with one second grader who had to be alone for almost an hour each morning before walking solo to the corner to catch a bus for school.

A previous study conducted in Boston (mentioned earlier) provided the example of a single father who left his two children at his mother's apartment while he worked a night shift. His mother, who had severe diabetes and could not even walk down her front steps, awakened the children shortly before their father's arrival at 2 A.M. They were then awake until he could get them home about an hour later. He seldom saw them in the mornings. Teachers told him that his children sometimes fell asleep in class.[16]

Common Problems with Child Care Arrangements
Most parents interviewed for this project called their child care arrangements acceptable; that finding corroborated the results from other recent research.[17] However, the in-depth interviews revealed a complex and sometimes contradictory story. Problems with child care were the most common cause of conflicts and anxiety for parents at work and often resulted in some kind of work sanction being taken against the parent. Furthermore, looking closely at the detailed interviews, we often found gaps in much of the daily child care. In addition,

many families indicated that their child care arrangements differed from day to day. Even when parents said they were satisfied with their child care, most also described ongoing problems and reported anxieties about their children's safety and care. In fact, few low-income parents seem to have experienced or expected a secure, routine child care schedule of the type described by the employers who had children.

Fifty-two percent of the parents had no regular access to a car. Therefore, in addition to expense, proximity was a major factor in making child care and work arrangements. For parents who had children in schools or child care locations far from their workplaces, the difficulty of reaching their children in case of an emergency was a major concern; several parents cited this as a reason they might seek a different, more conveniently situated job. We found that many mothers were trying to orchestrate arrangements from afar, calling from work to check and recheck how a given day's version of child care was working out. Parents admitted that this meant making and receiving phone calls during working hours; some described sneaking into offices to find a phone. One employer in Milwaukee remarked with some amusement that at the office she supervised, she "really didn't expect there to be much work done" between 3:00 and 3:30 P.M., when parents phoned their children's babysitters, after-school programs, neighbors, and relatives to find out whether the children had arrived safely. Of course, as several employers from all three sites complained, when these fragile arrangements fell apart, workers often were forced to leave work abruptly or failed to show up at all. Both happened far too often, according to parents and employers.

Parents' degree of trust, or lack of trust, in their child care providers emerged as a deep and abiding concern, which sometimes contradicted their statements of satisfaction with their child care situations. Many of these mothers expressed explicit distrust of public child care or of child care not provided by their own relatives. This distrust came from their own experiences, visits to voucher family day care centers, or stories they had heard about overcrowded or neglectful child care centers or family day care providers to which the state referred families. Several mothers in a focus group discussion expressed deep suspicion about all group care and about child care provided by the state in particular. Describing her experiences with a state-funded service, one Boston mother told us, "I just had to change. . . . The lady there, she wasn't watching him [her baby] too well. . . . One of the kids scratched him in the face." A Denver parent said she did not trust the publicly available care and confided, "I am really, really in a bind but . . . I don't trust anybody with my son. Nobody. If I don't know you, then you can't watch my son." And a Milwaukee mother expressed her own desperation: "I almost had to put up a sign in the local high school. . . . I had to go to that extent." But she added, "[I was] searching for someone who is trustworthy. You should be picky."

The respondents who seemed to have the most successful arrangements were those who co-parented with a spouse or partner or who had several close relatives (most often, grandparents) who provided extensive, flexible, and trustworthy child care. The researchers noted, however, that several mothers recounted stories about neglectful or casual care provided by relatives who felt they had an obligation—but no real desire—to watch their relatives' children.

Employers' Views on Employees' Child Care Practices

Employers reported that the unreliability and complexity of their entry-level employees' child care arrangements sometimes were significant impediments to conducting business. On some days, workers arrived late because of a transportation problem—often in getting a child to her or his destination—or called in sick at the last minute because of a child's illness; sometimes they simply failed to report to work and afterward explained that they had had a child care emergency. Some of the employers acknowledged how difficult it could be for their employees to balance family needs with work demands. Another spoke for many, however, when he said, "These people don't seem to know how to be organized [in their child care arrangements]." But whether an employer blamed unreliable care arrangements on a parent's lack of options or lack of organizational skills, they all agreed that employees' child care issues posed an ongoing problem for themselves and other employers. One employer in a focus group in Denver remarked, "It's like everything is shaky. . . . The car doesn't work in the winter; the buses are late. The kids are sick, first one, then the other. . . . It becomes a real problem for us."

One Denver employer repeatedly expressed sympathy for his employees, 80 percent of whom were parents and many of whom were single mothers. Though he offered flexible work schedules, he referred to the wages as "poverty-level," and he knew that these precluded his employees' use of most market-based child care services.

In a focus group discussion, an employer who supervised office workers and was also the mother of a young child expressed her own conflicted feelings about putting pressure on mothers who faced child care conflicts. She admitted that when she thought "about it in terms of being a mother," she found it extremely difficult to penalize another mother who did not come to work for three days because of her baby's fever. She would never have left her own baby "that sick." But, she said, "when I think about it as a boss," she admitted—as did other employers in this study—that she had fired mothers for staying home with sick children.

Barriers to Parents' Involvement in School Activities

In all three sectors interviewed, all of the respondents who were parents reported believing that participating in children's schools and educational activities is an important part of parenting. Some employers and teachers were openly critical of parents who "don't focus enough on education," as demonstrated, they said, by parental absence from school events. But it was clear from the focus group discussions that few of the low-wage parents who worked full time could attend. Some reported that they worked part time specifically so they could be more available to their children.

The complexity of patchwork child care frustrated everyone. The teachers, of course, had a close-up view of the impact of these arrangements. They generally discussed child care in terms of "appropriate care" and attention, particularly focusing on readiness for preschool-age children and on academic success for children already in school. A fifth-grade teacher from Boston contended that inconsistent care contributed to instability in children's daily lives and to a lack of preparedness for learning. "The kids . . . they come back and say, 'I left my book here or there,'" the teacher explained. "And that can be five different places." The families of her students are generally poor, with parents who work as cooks and janitors. She described a direct connection between the organization of children's lives and their parents' employment. "They don't see much of their parents. A lot of these peo-ple could only get jobs at night . . . [so] kids come in without signed permission slips or homework [done]" and are unprepared for school.

In a group discussion, teachers in Milwaukee focused on the impact of parental involvement (or lack of it) on children's daily lives and on students' academic progress. A second-grade teacher remarked of parental participation at her school in recent years, "[It has] dwindled down to where it hardly exists, [whereas] a few years ago, it was huge." A colleague remarked that parental attendance at evening events had decreased and that it was hard for teachers to adjust their parent-teacher time to parents' nontraditional work schedules. Another teacher said that while 80 percent of all parents in her school attended the parent-teacher conferences, they hardly ever attended the more entertaining events, such as concerts and plays. She said that, other than a required meeting after the first report card was distributed, "pretty much the only contact they have is negative, when their child has done something wrong."

This focus group of teachers discussed how this situation only widened the schism between parents and school staff. One bilingual teacher pointed out, "For some [parents], their own education is not high . . . [and] they may not speak English that well." A teacher in Boston remarked that field trips presented an economic burden on some families who "ha[d] to plan four weeks in advance to pay $2.50" for their child's participation. While she tried to include them as chap-erones so they could enjoy the event with their children, these parents seldom could take time off from work or adjust their schedules, as par-ents with higher-wage, higher-status jobs could more readily do. In a focus group in Denver, one parent described the core of parents who always attended the field trips and school parties and who helped with the annual school play as "more middle-class." Describing a time when she was finally able to attend one event, she said, "I felt like I was not even a part of her [the daughter's] school."

One Boston mother told us why she had left a job she liked: "It was taking this toll on my son. . . . I couldn't take one day off to go on a field trip with him. . . . I wasn't there for him." A mother in Milwau-kee said the only reason she was keeping her job—which paid $7.50 per hour—was that it gave her "some flexibility to be with [her] chil-dren."

In one Boston-based focus group conducted late in the summer of 2001, parents began the session by expressing explosive anger at news that many had just received in the mail. In order to more efficiently use school buses in Boston, a cluster of schools had announced that with the schools' opening in three weeks, the school day would start one hour later, at 9 A.M., rather than 8 A.M. Parents who already had been leaving their children alone for about thirty minutes each morning in order to arrive in time for jobs that started at 8 A.M. were going to have to quit or leave their children alone for more than an hour and half and wonder whether they had made it to school. Employers in all three cities expressed some disgust with the way that public schools instituted schedule changes, schools closings, professional days (when teachers were in training), and shortened days for other activities. Despite employers' common criticism that parents did not have tightly organized child care plans or good child care "contingency plans," as one security guard supervisor put it, most employers were also critical of school departments' apparent lack of regard for parents' work schedules. The researchers noted that several teachers and child care providers spoke to these issues as well but reversed culpability, faulting employers' lack of regard for family obligations and effects on children's overall advancement, particularly in the case of poor children. A Boston after-school teacher commented on the effect such problems were having on the preparation of the future workforce: "They ought to remember they are going to be hiring these kids in about eight years."

Gaps and Challenges During After-School Hours
While some parents said in focus groups that they relied heavily on one of their older children (usually a daughter) to take care of their younger ones, conflicts arose (not surprisingly) when the older siblings, often in middle school or high school, wanted to participate in after-school activities and sports or wanted to get jobs of their own. A school bus driver and hall monitor in Denver described children whose afternoons were unsupervised while their parents worked. Numerous children, she reported, "would talk about how they were supposed to go here or there after school [for example, to a neighbor's or aunt's house or a church group], but they wouldn't go," and no one would really know. She reported talking with young children and

encouraging them to cooperate with their mothers' after-school plans, but, she said, "some were just using it as a chance to hang out where they shouldn't and some . . . were trying to get their mom fired, you know, so she could be home with them."

This comment illustrated another aspect of the child care dilemma noted by all three groups of respondents: the need for parents to spend more time monitoring their children's out-of-school lives. The concern arose not only because parental or adult support was important for routine homework completion and school success but also because adult supervision was seen as critical for general discipline and overall social development. The different respondents observed that growing children and adolescents—who had to make choices about their relationships, peers, and activities—needed interested and firm adults who helped them "stay on the right path." However, a simple review of work schedules revealed that some parents in the study could not spend more than a few waking hours each day with their children. Furthermore, even though many other parents could make it home in the evenings, after long days and long bus rides, they had "just enough [energy] to make dinner and crawl into bed," as one Boston parent explained.

Slightly more than half of the low-wage parents said they had *some* time to assist their children with homework, but, overall, the researchers found that mothers' absences in their children's lives was a topic of considerable discussion and a chronic source of anxiety for mothers. One Milwaukee woman described the difficulty of working at a dry cleaner from 9 A.M. to 1 P.M., doing home health care for an elderly person from 2 P.M. to 8 P.M., arriving home at 9 P.M., and then trying to help her learning-disabled child with his homework. "I can't keep my eyes open," she said.

Strains Associated with Low Economic Status

The low economic status of these ninety-seven families was reflected throughout the material conditions of everyday family life. Of the whole sample, only 2 percent of these parents owned their homes, while 2 percent were homeless. Fifty-two percent had regular access to a car (this did not necessarily mean ownership), and 53 percent were receiving some form of public assistance, such as Medicaid, food stamps, or subsidized child care, at the time of the interviews. Additionally, 37 percent of the sample of low-income families had sought donated food at some time during the previous year.

Beyond these statistics, we found that low wages and low-wage work daily affected families' general well-being. Most parents described ongoing tension between fulfilling the basic demands of their jobs, meeting the basic needs of their children (and, in some cases, of other family members), and living on these annual incomes. As a parent in Boston put it, "It's not making ends meet at all. I'm robbing Peter, promising Pam, and dodging Paul. 'I'll get to you next week.' 'Oops, I forgot about you.' 'You're going to have to wait.' So no, it's not making ends meet at all."

In a focus group in Milwaukee, mothers spoke about the chronic anxiety they and their children lived with every day. These mothers said their children asked whether they were going to become homeless, whether they would have enough to eat, and whether they might get some new sneakers during the year. Parents told of children who would not tell their teachers that homework was unfinished because the electricity had been turned off. Older siblings told teachers they had been ill rather than that they had actually been home with sick younger siblings to prevent their mother from losing wages or even her job. Parents in poverty disliked the dishonesty that seemed necessary in regard to their family lives. But one young mother in Denver said, "They [the children] feel shame, you know. They don't want to go telling that they haven't enough food, or clothes, or what have you."

One employer in Denver described the day a mother of a young child called to say she had to be out because her child was sick. The employer, not convinced the child was ill, probed for more information. She told us the young mother broke down over the phone and explained that she had no money and no disposable diapers to leave with her baby at the child care center. Because this had happened in the past, they would not accept the child. This employer bought some diapers and drove over to the child care center so the baby's mother could go to work. "Unless I had that kind of relationship with her, so that she would trust me to tell what is really going on," the woman said, "I would have just been angry and assumed she was screwing up." The employer admitted that, had she not understood the family situation, she would probably have held this incident against the mother and moved a step toward dismissal. As she noted, "It makes a mother feel bad, you know, [to] not have a diaper, to get turned away from your child care center . . . in front of the other parents. And all because of [a] damned diaper." But she also understood that the child care facility was underfunded. "It's not like they can support the extras, either," she continued. The solution? The employers who listened to this story all agreed that parents should have enough money to buy diapers or whatever they needed to be able to work. But they were reluctant to assign responsibility for ensuring that this basic need was met, perhaps worried that any suggested solutions might affect their own economic interests.

Some parents who participated in the interpretive focus groups acknowledged that their own ongoing economic hardships—even though they had jobs—affected their children's attitudes about work. All the parents who discussed their children's futures said that they emphasized the importance of education and employment. But many also admitted how challenging such lessons could be to communicate when their children had seen that their parents work so hard but remain poor—in some cases, just as poor as they had been before their mothers joined the labor market. Describing how her children perceived her job, one mother in Denver said, "I'm not moving up in society . . . like a person should be. It's just a dead end." And teachers, too, considered the consequences for children of parental employment and adherence to the "work ethic" to be largely negative. A second-grade teacher in Boston said that some children in her class openly admitted trying to sabotage their mothers' efforts to keep a job because their mothers were not there when they arrived home after school, were never able to participate in school activities, and, when at home, often were too tired to pay much attention to their young children. While parents, children, and those who observed them closely recognized how the chronic hardship of poorly paying jobs diminished the effectiveness of "work ethic" lessons, most parents nevertheless reported that they wanted to work. Also, many children, according to their parents, were proud of parental employment, or at least preferred it to depending on welfare.

WHEN CHILDREN HAVE SPECIAL CARE NEEDS

To capture the complexity of care demands that low-income working parents were facing, we took special notice of the health and learning status of these parents' children. Other research has established a higher prevalence of certain health problems among low-income children, and our research certainly reflected those findings as well.[18] The low-income working parents in this study had a total of 237 children. Of these children, the parents interviewed had direct-care responsibility for 187 children, 4 percent of whom were eighteen or older but still living at home. (Most of the other 50 children were older, were living with fathers or other relatives, or were in foster care.) All parents in the study had primary responsibility for at least one child at the time of the interviews and focus groups. Of those 187 children, 23 percent had diagnosed asthma, 11 percent were being treated for attention deficit/hyperactivity disorder (ADHD), and 18 percent had a diagnosed learning disability. Additionally, children had other ongoing health issues such as lead poisoning (3 percent) and emotional problems such as depression (14 percent). Twenty-five percent had experienced conflicts at school, and 7 percent had been emotionally withdrawn.

The Heightened Need for Attentive Care

While few national studies have provided cumulative data on overall childhood health, mental health, and learning conditions, other research has established high rates of asthma among low-income children and among parents of children on welfare.[19] In fact, as many as 30 percent of all children are estimated to have some chronic health condition.[20] While it is important to note that not all chronic illnesses are disabling, families with limited resources and chronically ill children face increased caretaking demands, time pressures, and stress associated with their children's illnesses.

Research has shown that caring for a baby or child with developmental delays or disabilities can be physically and emotionally taxing, particularly for mothers. Raising children with chronic health or learning problems is especially demanding of adult time and patience, as it often requires ongoing care by and frequent visits to doctors and other health professionals, such as respiratory therapists or physical therapists, or education professionals, such as reading specialists.[21] The typical wait in a crowded pediatric office is lengthy. When that wait is combined with a trip to the doctor's office made via public transportation, a doctor's office visit can easily represent a lost day of work for a parent. Depending on the season (as with asthma) and the severity of the illness, such arrangements may be necessary as often as several times a month.

Since the quantity and quality of attention that children with physical or emotional illnesses or learning disabilities receive will likely have lifelong effects on them, parents' and other adult caretakers' ability to carry out their caretaking responsibilities becomes all the more critical. Indeed, recent research has shown that primary caregivers are the individuals with the greatest impact on determining children's outcomes, both at school and in medical institutions, and that they bear the major responsibility for gaining access to the government resources that ill or disabled children depend on.[22]

From a pediatrician's perspective, vigilant care by an adult is mandatory to ensure the well-being of any child, but especially of chronically ill ones. In one study, a pediatrician who provided asthma education to parents in a Boston elementary school told parents, "You can't just go about business as usual when you have a child with asthma. It is simple: this child needs more time, more care, and sometimes you won't be able to do much else." As he spoke, parents in the group glanced at each other and shook their heads. Later he remarked, "I just don't think they get it . . . this is serious, you know. We have pediatric deaths from asthma these days." But a parent confided later, "It's not that we don't get how serious this is, but he doesn't know what we have to do every day just to be sure they have food and a roof. I mean, that's a health problem too, right?"[23] A study participant from Wisconsin was informed she could not use her own sick leave time to care for her kids when they were ill. Although her daughter's asthma caused problems, particularly in the winter, she was told, "No kid gets sick that much." The woman told the researchers, however, that she stayed home with her daughter, "whether they liked it or not." But she was reprimanded for using sick leave time, rather than vacation time.

The Mesh Between Parents' and Caretakers' Responses

Children with a diagnosed learning disability need more support to learn and, depending on their states' regulations, must have special educational plans that include ongoing meetings with parents. Special education teachers, after testing children to ascertain the root of their learning problems, will also arrange for social work home visits, ask the parents to complete assessment forms on the children's developmental and medical histories, summon parents to meetings to discuss their children, and expect parents to attend follow-up meetings throughout the school year. School officials sometimes become frustrated and judgmental when parents do not participate actively in this process. In our study, an educator in Denver had concluded of one family, "[The parents are] just . . . not that interested in how this kid is going to progress." But other teachers in our study expressed more sympathy for working parents whose places of employment would not allow time off for these activities. And many parents remarked that they simply could not attend meetings at school unless those were scheduled in the evening, after 6 P.M., long after teachers and staff had gone home. Some employers admitted their skepticism that parents actually *had* school business to attend to. Even when it was indisputable that a parent needed to attend a school meeting, some employers were less than accommodating. One employer with a temp agency in Boston said repeatedly, "We are not running a social program here . . . those are not our issues."

Children with ADHD particularly need dependable routines, patterns, and caretaking as they learn to build more focus and self-control.[24] Difficulties that arise when these children experience problems, stress, and unanticipated changes in their routines can easily become a problem for their caretakers and, consequently, a work issue for the children's parents. As employed mothers in our study who had special-needs children reported, their children's caretakers—adults in charge of the children when the parents are at work, including teachers, child care providers, school nurses, babysitters, and after-school care providers—were very likely to phone repeatedly during the mothers' work hours. A young mother of a child with ADHD in Denver reported, "I get at least three calls a week." She said that her jobs lasted about as long as her supervisors could tolerate the interruptions.

Children with asthma tend to experience episodic events—for some children, more frequently than others—set off by seasonal and environmental stimuli, exercise, or stress.[25] A child may go for weeks without an incident that requires contacting parents or, if bronchial dilation equipment is on hand, may be attended to by school or child care staff. Yet other children have frequent events, some of which require emergency intervention. Research in Boston revealed that in one school (kindergarten through eighth grade), most children's health insurance covered only one breathing-assistance device.[26] Parents were reluctant to have a young child carry the device to school, where it could be lost and, thereby, unavailable for the many asthma attacks that took place at home in the evenings. At that school, despite a well-trained staff, some children who needed emergency assistance had no equipment on hand, necessitating emergency-room care and, subsequently, parents' absence from work.

Most teachers and child care workers consider parental availability essential to support all children in managing change in their lives.[27] A school nurse working in a K-8 school in Boston reported that when young children were going through routine changes—a new grade, a new school, a new residence, or a change in family life—they were likely to be anxious and come to her office with various complaints that "really mean[t], 'I'm scared and I can't concentrate.' " When she knew parents were home or could be contacted without jeopardizing their jobs, she was likely to contact them. A very involved staff person, this nurse knew that some parents could lose their jobs if she called; "then the child may be in worse shape," she noted. She admitted that she sometimes bent the rules a little and avoided calling a parent even when, "according to the book," she should have. Other nurses, child care providers, and after-school teachers admitted in our focus groups and interviews that they were sometimes risking a mother's job by calling repeatedly when she was at work. "But if this child is acting out and distracting all the other children . . . or the kid is wheezing and his eyes are bulging, I call. I call again and again," said one frustrated Milwaukee schoolteacher. Parents of children with special needs were particularly likely to feel that they were constantly being pulled in two different directions and that, at both ends, the needs were critical.

THE WORK REALM: WORKERS' WAGES, JOBS, ATTITUDES, AND SCHEDULES

Wages and Income

The ninety-seven families of the parent sample in this study had, over-all, a higher hourly wage distribution than those in other research examining the status of families who had left welfare.[28] Because half of the low-income parents participating in this project had either left welfare three or more years earlier or had never received welfare, their income potential was likely to be higher than that of those who had left or lost welfare benefits more recently. Additionally, the median educational level of the parents in this study was higher than that for welfare recipients nationally during the 1990s. Consequently, they were more employable and more likely to have reached a higher hourly wage level. (This variable was analyzed on the basis of all jobs worked. Thus, $n = 110$ because some parents had worked more than one job at a time.) About 40 percent of these parents were making more than $10 per hour, a wage distribution more similar to that in other studies whose samples had combined both welfare leavers and low-wage workers who had not received welfare.[29] Despite the parents' relatively high hourly wage rate, the distribution of annual earnings for low-income families in this study was lower than might have been expected.

In analyzing these data, we explored the reasons why these low-wage working parents, most of whom were single mothers, had a relatively high hourly wage and still had such low annual incomes. We observed two trends that may explain this discrepancy. First, almost 31 percent of these parents worked less than full time (defined in this study as 37.5 hours per week). Second, this group of workers had a high incidence of "churning," or job changing. Both of these trends reduced the total of hours worked annually and consequently reduced yearly incomes, despite the comparatively high hourly wages.

Kinds of Employment and Turnover Rates

Similar to findings from other research on post-welfare and low-wage work, the most prevalent workplace settings for the low-wage working parents in this study were, in order, personal services, clerical, retail, and light manufacturing.[30] Typical jobs included administrative assistant, data entry clerk, day care teacher, factory or light-manufacturing worker, fast-food server, and home health aide. In focus group discussions and interviews, parents spoke about the circumstances of leaving or losing jobs, and about work opportunities they were seeking. Often, they reported being attracted to the possibility of a new job because it seemed to have a more child-friendly work schedule, because it was closer to their homes or to their children's schools or child care centers, or because they had heard through their personal networks that a supervisor was considerate and flexible.

Child care workers, more often than teachers, were likely to be aware of job changes among parents and were sometimes a source of information, passing on good job tips from one parent to another. Also, of course, child care itself was (and is) a notoriously low-wage occupation with a very high turnover rate. One child care provider in Denver, speaking to the researcher after the focus group, told of a colleague at her day care center who had recently left the job, after a tip from a parent, to take a better-paying job in a dog kennel. "We pay worse than they do," she said.

All three sets of respondents returned repeatedly to the issue of job turnover and its effects. The main reason parents worked less than full time *and* the reason that most jobs ended were families' and children's care needs. As explained earlier, unreliable child care was one source of parents' reluctance to work full time, and the high prevalence of families with children who needed some kind of special care intensified the necessity for parental availability. For many parents, full-time (as opposed to part-time) work would have been worthwhile only if their incomes had increased substantially. Because of the consequent opportunity costs associated with leaving needy children for longer periods, the higher child care costs, and the loss of some forms of public assistance, full-time work was not always the best choice.[31]

Job turnover rates (which combine resignations, firings, layoffs, and jobs being eliminated) vary, but they have been as high as 40 percent annually among lower-wage workers in the post-welfare era— and particularly high for women and workers of color.[32] We found that many parents had only recently begun new jobs and that many were considering leaving their current jobs, usually because of family and scheduling reasons. Essentially, they told us, few jobs offered adequate reasons to stay. When jobs paid low wages and offered few benefits, and when job longevity did not provide significant improvement or long-term career ladders, these working parents saw no reason to sacrifice short-term family needs to maintain employment. In addition, some recent research on job turnover patterns among low-skilled workers has suggested that those who voluntarily leave one low-wage job for another may not lose much in the process and a fraction will realize some wage improvement.[33]

Parents' Attitudes Toward Work

Echoing the findings of most other research on post-welfare employment (and on working people in general), the majority of the working parents in this study reported that they liked having a job. They liked "having that paycheck," and they liked working with other adults. Interestingly, several mothers said their jobs sometimes were "stress relievers" that gave them time away from the often entrenched needs of their families. Those parents who described their workplace environments as flexible and friendly were the most likely to speak positively about their jobs and to look forward to going to work. In addition, as reported in other qualitative research, parents discussed maintaining a job and meeting the demands of a regular work schedule as behaviors that provided "good models" they hoped their children would observe and emulate.[34] As one mother of three in Denver said, describing her family's industriousness, "There is no hanging around in our family. . . . We're up and out."

Despite their generally positive attitude toward employment, however, most mothers reported that their jobs failed to provide even minimal economic security. Nor did they envision that the job market—which has worsened since this research was completed—would offer them any real chances to advance economically or socially. Recent research has indicated that this view is largely accurate. Low-skilled workers' incomes have typically increased between 4 percent and 6 percent annually, which is a similar rate to the recent yearly income gains for better-skilled, higher-paid workers. However, because their salaries are so small to begin with, these percentage increases translate into very small real increases in income.[35] For example, a parent working full time at a typical wage of $7 or $8 per hour who receives an annual raise of 4 percent to 6 percent will see her income rise only $600 to $1,000, resulting in a negligible improvement in her family's economic circumstances over time.

Reflecting on her own lack of economic advancement, one working parent in Milwaukee said, "There is no light at the end of this tunnel. . . . It just goes on and on." Several parents discussed the necessity of getting more education if they ever hoped to earn a living wage, but they wondered how they could fit more into their already overcrowded lives. A young mother in Denver explained, "I started to take classes in the late afternoons [after a 7 A.M. to 3 P.M. job], but . . . I had to cut back my hours to get there on time. And then I couldn't pay my babysitter." Consequently, she was forced to drop out of a computer training program that would presumably have improved her chances of finding better employment and stabilizing her children's lives. Parents acknowledged that employers' thoughtfulness and flexibility, as well as friendly co-workers, attracted them to particular jobs. However, in the end, said one parent in Boston, "money is the problem." Another mother from Boston told of leaving a job that she liked for one that paid somewhat better, even though it had meant seeing her son less. "I work and all, but I am not paying my bills, [and] my credit is going bad," she said. "There's no catching up, no chance to advance myself."

Other parents, however, seemed to have made the opposite choice by cutting back their work hours or changing jobs because they considered the cost of working more hours to be greater than the wage gain. There has been some national research supporting this rationale and showing that the first twenty hours per week of employment offer a much greater economic boost to a family than do additional hours, particularly at higher wages, because of çosts associated with more work (such as child care), and because, in some cases, the increase in income will be more than offset by a loss of eligibility for such benefits as food stamps, Medicaid, child care subsidies, and public housing.[36]

Employer concern and flexibility were clearly additional criteria that many parents considered when deciding whether to seek specific jobs or stay in current ones. In a large parents' focus group in Boston, several women described their jobs at a security guard company. They said the previous supervisor had looked the other way when parents had brought children to work with them in the evening. The children had eaten dinner with their mothers, done their homework, and sometimes even curled up in blankets to sleep. However, a new manager had taken over the week before the focus group's discussion. The day that he had declared "no kids on these premises," respondents reported, the entire evening shift had quit. One woman, a grandmother who took her four-year-old grandchild to the job, remarked that the former boss "was no prince but he knew . . . this was like a job benefit. . . . Why else would you take that little money?"

Some women faced other forms of inflexibility. For example, one mother, a security guard working for $7 an hour, was called to her ten-year-old son's school after he had been involved in a fight. (Teachers told us that parents had to be available to help school officials respond to such incidents.) She told her supervisor she would miss a day's work, but her absence resulted in the loss of a week's pay. A young mother in Denver explained that after she had used more than three sick-leave days to care for her child with chicken pox, she had lost her job, which she had been very glad to have. "It was the rule," she said. "They told me, 'No exceptions.' "

Employers' Attitudes About Their Employees' Work-Family Situations

Interestingly, these parents' employers had fairly similar perspectives. In focus groups, some employers acknowledged that entry-level work was largely without any "real future." When asked if the jobs *they* offered would "lead to something more, offer a ladder upward," most employers said that without additional education and the acquisition of more "marketable skills," people working in entry-level positions would have no "career ladders" to climb. While good work histories could have helped workers find new jobs, those jobs were unlikely to have improved the economic status if the workers had not obtained more education or better skills. One employer reflected ruefully, "I suppose the only way [for the workers] to do better is leave [my place of employment] and try to get something better. . . . But really, even if you're a good worker and all . . . without more school they aren't going anywhere." An employer who runs a housecleaning service admitted that he sought non-English-speaking workers precisely because immigrant workers had so few alternative work options that offered them a better wage and because they tended to expect fewer raises.

One notable exception was a Milwaukee-based employer in the health care field. A supervisor in that company reported that the firm paid for coursework to train nurses' aides to become nurses. She acknowledged that an aide would indeed have a "hell of a time" doing his or her job, taking care of children, and attending and passing all the courses. But, she said, a few of her employees had used this program and become nurses, significantly improving their economic status. She acknowledged that these efforts took extraordinary determination and "kids that don't get sick too much." Among all the employers in focus groups (n = 31), this woman's firm offered a unique employment opportunity, and other employers who heard of it during the focus group praised it. One supervisor of an employment agency for temporary workers reflected that if he could offer computer classes as part of his company's employee benefits program, he would have much more success "placing people in jobs. They would have more skills to offer, and those skills would go with them." Clearly, some of the parents and other employers had developed additional creative ways of addressing parents' work-family conflicts, thereby affecting the employees' job histories and future prospects. For instance, some employers attempted to treat the workplace as a source of support beyond the wage relationship. A supervisor at a Milwaukee printing facility described how he bent the rules from time to time. "I'm willing to work with them if there's a problem, give them an excused day," he said. "I might refer them to [human resources] for child care referrals." If workers needed to leave early for something "really important to them," this supervisor tried to accommodate the workers, even when the site was very busy. In return, he said, the employees were willing to come in early or stay late the next day. "You get it back," he explained.

A supervisor at a security company in Boston described his personal efforts to provide some flexibility, often without his superior's knowledge. "I try to work it out if someone is late because she needs to meet with a teacher or another needs overtime," he said. He lamented the lack of understanding on the part of top management. "My boss doesn't want me to be compassionate," he said. "It's a man thing. You have to be there, and if you're a woman, then you just have to adjust to being in a man's environment." This supervisor further commented, "You can't grow your business if people are leaving you" because they aren't getting the flexibility they need. A supervisor for a cable television company in Denver observed that many supervisors "don't present a very flexible picture when dealing with low-wage workers. It's a 'my way or the highway' mentality."

The idea that supervisors should be concerned with workers' lives beyond a simple bottom-line exchange was the single most controversial topic among employers in each of the focus group discussions in all three cities. Employers shared many concerns, frustrations, and strategies, but when some of them suggested that employers needed to take into account workers' and their families' demands, some heartily agreed, while others were ambivalent, and a few flatly rejected this opinion. Of all the issues employers raised and discussed, only this one caused acrimony in the focus groups. In a focus group in Denver, one young manager argued, "We are accountable for how we treat these women because . . . we have a big effect on their families." Another employer was clearly agitated by this comment. "You have a sick kid—that's your problem, not mine," he said, "and I am not going to get dragged into it. Once you start opening the door . . . forget it." The other employer responded, "My door is open because that's part of the job. I see my community service as trying to help these mothers keep their jobs and be able to take care of their children, not some one-day-a-year employee [appreciation] gift."

As noted earlier, some employers described their low-wage employees as disorganized or unable to coordinate their children's needs properly. Cars that broke down, unreliable public transportation, lack of contingency child care, and workers' social and emotional problems frustrated supervisors, and some employers were harsh. One Boston employer said, "These women shouldn't have a child if they can't afford to." She was particularly critical of mothers who asked for time off work to care for sick children, arguing that she did not expect special flexibility when her husband was ill. Even though they may have previously expressed admiration for the tenacity many low-wage parents displayed, some supervisors suggested that "these people" had complicated relationships and home lives that disrupted work routines.

One Milwaukee employer in a focus group, however, recounted her own experience years earlier in a violent relationship and her then-supervisor's help and offer of company support. She had moved and taken over another regional office of that business, and she believed that move had saved her life. Consequently, she explained, "I don't turn my back on people and say, 'Well, this is a job; I am not going to get involved with any of that,' or . . . 'I'll just get rid of her' . . . because I know a lot of times it's not your fault you're in trouble." This employer's remarks illustrated an observation that parents expressed repeatedly in their comments: employers who had experienced some kind of real hardship, who were busy parents or single parents, or who had a child with a chronic illness tended to be much more flexible.

A Different Perspective on Work Flexibility

Recent discussions and research about work design have been capturing a broader idea of work and family integration. Flexibility in scheduling work has been touted as good not only for workers and their families but for employers as well because it can improve the hiring and retention of valuable employees. Recent research also has focused on the effect of decision-making autonomy and greater employee control of work schedules.[37] Generous maternity leave policies have been associated with higher employee retention following childbearing, and flexible scheduling has been found to reduce absenteeism (though its relationship to turnover rates is less clear). The availability of family-friendly policies, particularly when a workplace culture actually promotes their use, has been linked to positive workplace outcomes and attitudes.[38]

For most of the ninety-seven parents in this study, however, *flexibility* had a different meaning than it does in mainstream work-family discourse. For the most part, they did not expect to be able to adjust their work schedules or to participate at all in creating work arrangements that might have made their lives easier. With a few exceptions, these workers saw *adjusting work schedules* as requiring leaving a job and finding another one. The majority of the interviews and discussions about flexibility did not focus on institutionalized policies such as a family or medical leave. All of the parents who discussed such workplace policies—which were unfamiliar to many of them—assumed that any such policies were not accessible to them; their assumptions were often correct.

Many parents in this study interpreted *flexibility* in terms of whether or not their own bosses, because of attitudes and temperaments, would have understood a family or health issue that might have arisen. In focus groups, employers explicitly expressed a preference for work-related flexibility to be at their discretion—that is, they wanted complete control over workers' access to leave time, early release, or schedule adjustments. Perhaps one of this study's most intriguing findings was that among workers, the most common definition of flexibility at work was a mother's ability to take a child or children to the workplace. As noted earlier, some mothers who worked as security guards took their children to work, at least for a while. In some cases, children of mothers who worked in child care centers were integrated into their mothers' classes or, if they were older children, came by after their own school day ended to help out. We listened to accounts of children working alongside mothers at community centers, copying documents or delivering files to colleagues in the office, sleeping while their mothers cleaned offices, and sitting in fast-food restaurants or doughnut shops or shopping malls.

In particular, we heard accounts of children riding around with parents who drove school buses, vans for people with special needs, and camp buses—one mother had two babies in car seats at the front of the camp bus she drove every day. (Other researchers have also reported on bus-driving parents who brought their children to work.)[39] The study's principal investigator was driven to a focus group in Milwaukee by a cab driver whose son slept next to him every night, unbeknownst to the cab company, before being dropped off after his mother's evening shift ended. One elder care worker told us she took her son to the house of her elderly patient, without having discussed this with the patient; the four-year-old stayed quietly downstairs watching television. Domestic workers, Salvation Army staff members, cleaners, custodians, and cooks quietly slipped children into workplaces to avoid leaving them alone. Many supervisors did not know such practices were taking place. When employers either accepted such practices or looked the other way, the affected parents viewed such responses as generous, flexible practices that influenced their decision to stay in their jobs. Very few parents expressed opinions about whether such practices were good for their children. As one mother in Boston said, "She's with me, or she's home alone."

The Special Perspective of Child Care Workers

The single most common way to keep child care for low-income families "affordable" is to keep the cost of labor low; consequently, child care workers in the United States largely fall into the category of the working poor.[40] As noted earlier, most of the interviewed child care workers were parents who earned low wages, changed jobs fairly often, and frequently could not afford to place their own children in the very centers where they worked. (Several child care workers mentioned, after the open discussion, that they would not have enrolled a child in the center where they worked because of the understaffing.)

A group of child care workers at a publicly subsidized center in Denver discussed the struggles that confronted the parents of the children in their care. A senior staff person described a typical morning:

> I watch them come hurrying over . . . telling that little baby, "Hurry up, you got to run, I'll be late again," or "You don't want Mommy to get fired, do you?" . . . I try to meet them, you know, pick the baby up, and say, "Let's wave bye-bye to Mommy." These same parents are . . . struggling to pay their monthly bills. . . . They are behind a lot, and we got to get paid, too.

Describing the economics of child care, she explained that a fee of $150 per week for a ten-hour day worked out to only "$3 an hour [per child] for all we do." But, she added quietly, "I couldn't have afforded it when mine were young—not even close now on the money I make."

The group said that many children were pulled out of a center and put into some kind of kin-care setting when parents could no longer keep up with their payments. Most expressed skepticism about these arrangements, on the reasoning that if good kin care had originally been available, that would have been most parents' first choice. An older child care worker expressed sincere worry about the children who were abruptly removed from child care centers when parents had fallen too far behind in their tuition payments. "They just don't make enough money to afford it," she said, "even as cheap as we try to make it."

Good care, even when subsidized, is still too costly for many families. Of all the low-income families in this study, 58 percent paid $50 or less per week for their child care, and another 22 percent paid between $50 and $100 per week. It is hardly surprising that the jobs available to them and the wages they earned profoundly affected the quality and reliability of the child care systems they could use; these, in turn, profoundly affected parents' ability to hold jobs—any jobs.

FROM FEEDBACK TO POLICY MAKING: INCLUDING LOW-INCOME AMERICANS IN WORK-FAMILY STRATEGIES

To raise children and keep a job is all but impossible for low-income American parents under current conditions, according to the parents, employers, teachers, and community service providers who took part in this study. While these participants represented a range of perspectives and held a variety of sometimes clashing opinions, they almost universally agreed that inflexible job schedules, lack of benefits (from employers or the state), and, especially, low wages directly undermine the nurturing of children and threaten family stability—unless other resources are available. Participants in the Across the Boundaries project consistently pointed to an overwhelming need for serious national and local leadership to address the intractable work and family conflicts that confront low-income working parents. This leadership, respondents said, must come especially from government and business, but also from organized labor, public schools, nongovernmental organizations, and local business networks. As many of our respondents noted, a failure to address the pressing needs of the families in the bottom third of our economy, those who are barely surviving despite valiant efforts, will have repercussions not just for these families but throughout our society.

Policy Recommendations

As the Across the Boundaries findings have shown, families at the bottom third of our economy have complex, multilayered needs.

Addressing the problems we found—patchwork child care, barriers to parental involvement in children's education and health care, economic strain, and job turnover—requires change in three interconnected areas:

- *Time,* not just to care for family emergencies but to be a family, to enjoy and nurture each other, to be involved in children's education and in the community
- *Sufficient income* to support a family and to afford to be able to take time off from work when necessary
- *Access to quality caregiving resources* for those times when one cannot care for family members oneself

In each of these areas, new private (employer-sponsored) and public policies must be created that will benefit low-income families and help ease the work-family conflicts for many other families as well.

Time: Employers' Policies and Public Policies

Employers can help by instituting policies that formalize the behaviors of the sensitive supervisors that parents in this study praised—policies that reduce the tension between work and family responsibilities and that allow time not just for emergencies but also for general family and personal development. These policies include giving workers much more control over their schedules: instituting flexible start and end times, offering choices of shifts, allowing workers to use breaks to check on their families, and offering them time off (which could be made up, before or after school hours) to attend to school issues or children's routine medical needs. Workers also should be able to reduce their hours if necessary without penalty in wage rates or benefits, advancement, or treatment on the job.

When necessary, workers need to be able to take time off to care for minor, as well as serious, personal or family illnesses. Workers also need time for themselves. That would mean having no mandatory overtime and no requirement that vacation be used up and counted as family leave. It is also critical for time off to be accessible for use within a reasonable period after someone begins a new job. In order for these policies to be meaningful, absence control efforts must minimize discipline for legitimate family care needs. Policies should apply to all employees on a formal basis, rather than being dependent on managers' discretion. And, last but not least, managers should be evaluated by their employers on how well they contribute to their employees' balancing of their work and family responsibilities.

Government policy especially needs to recognize the additional time demands faced by those who care for family members with special needs. Changes in TANF policy must be made to allow reduced work hours for those who have a family member with special needs, with no effect on a worker's "clock" (the total amount of time someone may receive benefits over a lifetime). TANF assistance should not be restricted to those without any income, but rather should also be available on a prorated basis to those whose incomes fall below a certain level.

A broader minimum standard is also needed in the Family and Medical Leave Act (FMLA), which currently excludes many low-wage workers. Policymakers need to (1) end the minimum-hours-worked requirement in order to include part-time employees, (2) change the tenure requirement to the job's probation period or three months, whichever comes first, and (3) cover employers with fifteen (rather than fifty) or more employees, as do other federal employment laws. In addition, reasons for taking FMLA leave should include routine school and medical activities, plus all activities and meetings considered essential by teachers and health professionals. And, given the realities of family life in the United States today, the definition of *family* under the law should be broadened to include other family members, such as siblings and same-sex partners. Finally, prohibiting mandatory overtime would be an important addition to minimum labor standards that the government should guarantee to all workers.

Government can help develop model employer policies by directing tax and other public dollars to reward workplaces that meet the family-friendly policies listed here. Built into any such incentive programs should be the provision that dollars go directly to worker benefits, rather than being absorbed into the business's general operating budget.

Wages and Benefits: Employers' Policies and Public Policies

In addition to receiving decent wages, workers need access to affordable benefits and to some form of income during time off from work;

they need sick leave and vacation time, as well as family leave. Employers can also help by providing equal pay rates and at least prorated benefits for part-time work. They can also supply education benefits and make sure employees have the flexibility to use them. Workers need two things most: a higher wage floor and the right to bargain collectively over pay and benefits. However, sometimes a raise means the loss of access to needed income supports. Public policy change is needed for a higher minimum wage, a living wage, a fund for wage replacement during family leave, and income supports. Specifically, workers need an increase in the funding level and eligibility for programs such as the earned income tax credit, food stamps, and child care. In addition, the programs need to have more realistic end points. The public agencies that administer these benefits need to be open on a more family-friendly schedule.

The right to some paid sick leave and vacation time should fall among minimum labor standards. The unemployment insurance system also needs to be changed in most states to include part-time workers and those who turn down jobs for family care reasons. In order for low-wage workers to benefit, unemployment insurance calculations should include the latest quarter of earnings. Finally, TANF policies need to place more emphasis on education and training as a means for increasing long-term earning capacity.

Access to Resources: Employers' Policies and Public Policies

Employers can help by providing information about care, as well as access to affordable care. These efforts could include subsidies, on-site care with sliding-scale fees, or access to child care for sick children (although employers need to recognize that sick children sometimes most need their parents' care). We need to increase the supply of affordable, quality care in areas close to where people live. In addition, we must provide more training for "kith-and-kin" caretakers and make it easier for families to use public subsidies to pay these workers. Public support for child care means investing more funds in improving the quality of care and providing higher wages for child care workers.

Greater resources need to be allocated for school-age care programs, both those after school and those on days when schools are not in session. In addition, these programs should include homework and academic support so that children and parents could spend time at home together without hours of homework looming over their heads. School policies should be made more flexible, with alternatives devised for handling suspensions and illness if parents cannot take time off from work. (For example, some schools have developed in-school supervision of suspended students.) While the supply of child care needs to be increased, including during nonstandard shifts, public funds should especially be directed toward development of family-supporting jobs close to where low-income families live and with schedules that recognize family care responsibilities.[41]

None of these recommended changes alone will make the system work—the previously mentioned list leaves out several key areas, including housing, transportation, and health care. But most importantly for policy alterations, the approach taken must address the whole family, and policies and services must fit together so that they work in those times and situations where parents are attempting daily to reconcile the competing demands of work and family. Also, in order to understand the complicated whole of low-income work and family life, working parents must be part of the process of designing and critiquing the programs and policies that circumscribe their lives. One suggestion from a focus group was that policy makers should establish work and family advisory groups with a genuine, and not simply symbolic, role in evaluating and recommending public policy. Decision makers of all kinds should take into account the well-being of families in the bottom third, as well as that of higher-income families. Thus, each policy should be evaluated by asking two key questions: How will this affect children's health and well-being and communities' social stability? Will this policy help people achieve genuine self-sufficiency? We can make great strides at reducing job turnover and poverty for workers in the bottom third of the economy. When we do, employers and society will also benefit because of the greater stability in the workforce, within families, and in the larger community.

6

Addressing the Time Crunch of High Earners

Sylvia Ann Hewlett

In February 2001, I conducted an informal focus group with eight young professionals who worked at three firms in Cambridge, Massachusetts—an Internet consulting firm, a venture capital firm, and an advertising agency. The session was held in the offices of Global IT Strategies, where three of the people worked. Just down the road from MIT, this small firm has a fast-growing list of blue-chip clients and has attracted some of the best talent in the Boston area. The offices of Global IT Strategies were predictably edgy and hip. The whole place smacked of youthful energy.

We holed up in the conference room for an entire morning, myself and these six women and two men who ranged in age from twenty-six to thirty-four. Glamorous, smart, sharp, and irreverent, they came from all over—Boston, Australia, England, California, and Texas—and all held demanding, fast-track jobs. One was married, one was living with a partner, and the others were single. None had children, although five of the women spoke wistfully about having children as being a short-term goal.

Much of our discussion centered on time—or the lack of it. It reverberated throughout the conversation like a drumbeat.

JENNIFER: This career of mine is eating me alive. I mean, it's stimulating and challenging and I love working for this particular firm, but the time demands are awesome.

When I'm working in Cambridge it's not too bad. I get in about 8:30 A.M. and leave at 7:30 P.M. Now, I do check my e-mail twice during the course of an evening, but we're still talking about a pretty decent workweek—fifty-eight hours or so. It's when I'm working with a client at a project site that the hours get insane. Since I'm on the road four days a week for two-thirds of the year, this is a big chunk of my reality.

On the road, here's what happens: I work at the client's office 8:00 A.M. to 7:30 P.M., I then have a team meeting over dinner—to coordinate and strategize—and then around 9:30 P.M. I go back to my hotel room and check my e-mail to see what else I have to do.

PAULA: Don't forget voice mail. We all have voice mail at the office and voice mail on our cell phone, both of which we check on a daily basis. Between e-mail and voice mail you can count on an additional three items of work at the end of the day. So at 10 P.M., there you are in your hotel room, working on your laptop, responding to a question from some other client.

ANNABEL: And the phone rings, and it's the new boyfriend back in Boston, who's fuming because he's been calling all evening and hasn't been able to reach you. You try explaining that you've just finished a two-and-a-half-hour team dinner with colleagues (yes, some of these colleagues are male), and although you sound a little tipsy (yes, I did have wine with dinner), you actually have to get back to work. And by the way, you'll be back Friday but won't have much time this weekend because you need to leave Sunday evening for a four-day trip to Albuquerque (yes, this is a business trip).

RACHEL: It's hard on boyfriends. I had a date with this guy last month. At the end of the evening he said, "When can I see you? How about next week?" I said, "I'm sorry, but I'm going to be out of town working with a client next week." And he said, "Well, how about the following week?" And I said, "You're not going to believe this, but I won't know my travel schedule until closer to the time, [so] I can't make any plans yet." At that point he threw up his hands and, in an annoyed tone of voice, said, "How d'you expect a relationship to get off the ground?"

DAN: It's just hard on relationships—period. I moved in with my girlfriend a year ago and we're really trying to make it work. But two weeks of every month I'm not even in the country. My company is very active in Eastern Europe, which means that each month I have an extended business trip to either Prague or Warsaw. She just gets very lonely. I mean, it's not that we spend a lot of time together when I'm in town—she's in real estate and works very long hours, too—but at least we have dinner together. There's this precious time between 9:00 P.M. and 10:30 P.M. that we can plan on spending together.

NATALIE: You know, I really love this work. It's draining and demanding, but it's also exhilarating. You get to work with an extraordinary range of clients and issues. In my book, there's no better feeling than sinking your teeth into a complex, multilayered problem and solving it.

But I don't know whether I can survive in this business over the long haul. This is the third consulting firm I've worked for, and I've yet to see an older, more senior woman whose life I would actually want.

RACHEL [clearly shocked]: What do you mean?

NATALIE: I know a few hard-driving women who are climbing the ladder at consulting firms, but they are single—or divorced—and seem pretty isolated. And I know a handful of working mothers who are trying to do the half-time thing or the two-thirds-time thing. They work reduced hours so that they can see their kids, but they don't get the good projects, they don't get the bonuses, and they also get whispered about behind their back. You know, comments like, "If she's not prepared to work the client's hours, she has no business being in the profession."

SONIA: I hear those same whispers, and quite frankly, they scare me. I just turned twenty-eight and have been married a year. I'm terrified of having children. To me, it's synonymous with waving good-bye to being taken seriously, waving good-bye to first-class citizenship.

ANNABEL: It's not true elsewhere. I've worked for European companies where professionals who opt for a reduced workweek are not marginalized. I mean, they're used on the high-profile projects and treated with respect. But in the U.S. it's different. Here, the "inside team" is made up of the people who bump into each other in the hallway at 11:00 at night. But how does a woman with children work until 11:00 P.M. on a regular basis?

SONIA: At my last job, part-timers got stigmatized so badly I often thought they might as well be walking around with a scarlet letter emblazoned on their chests.

But I don't think it had a whole lot to do with performance or efficiency. I see no reason why a professional at an advertising agency can't go half time and deal with half as many clients. In my view, what it really comes down to is attitudes and mindsets.

Colleagues are simply jealous. Advertising is a profession that creates a famine on the time front. Therefore anyone who gets a break is seen as avoiding paying his or her dues and is resented. If you take a two-thirds workweek, you can expect to take a lot of heat—to be punished in some way. The only way around this is for everyone to get a better deal. I mean, why should anyone have to work a seventy-hour week?

JEFF: I'll second that. One thing that gets me riled up is the assumption that the only people entitled to a life outside of work are women with children. But how does a man become a halfway decent partner if he has to work every waking hour?

RACHEL: That's a good point. But I guess at least you guys aren't dealing with a biological clock and have the option of having children later in life when you're more established.

I used to be so critical of women who got married and had their children young. It seemed so wrongheaded—raising kids on very little money before you've seen the world or worked out your own identity. But now I think they may have been on to something. At least they have their children.

When I look into the future, I don't know how I'm going to do it all. I'm twenty-nine now and know I need to go back to school and get an MBA. After that there will be a big push to take my career to the next level. And yet these are also the years I would like to get married and have children. How do I reconcile these goals? I haven't a clue.

JENNIFER: Part of my problem is that I come from this picture-book family. My mom ran a beautiful home and looked after my dad, but she also proofread my history papers and drove me to swim team practice at 7:00 A.M. Saturday morning. I once added it up: she spent seventeen hours a week supporting me in a variety of activities. If I have a family, I'm going to be faced with those impossible standards.

PAULA: Time is just a huge issue. You just can't get around it. Expectations are so high. We have these high-powered careers that sit in the center of our lives. But we also want an emotionally nourishing relationship with a man—someone who's not just a stuffed shirt. Relationships take time. No two ways around it. And a little ways down the road, we also want a child or two—children we fully intend to spend all kinds of quality time with.

From where I sit, it doesn't seem possible to do all three things—they just won't fit into a life—at least not simultaneously.[1]

As free-floating anxiety around time—how to get enough of it, how to gain control over it—ricocheted around the conference room that morning, I was reminded of the women who participated in our 2001 national survey of high-earning women.[2] They too were deeply aware of the time famine in their lives, and many in the older age group had wrestled with this problem for years.

WOMEN SPEAK OUT ON WORK-FAMILY ISSUES

As we discovered in the national survey, across occupation and sector, high-earning women are dealing with long and lengthening work-weeks. Twenty-nine percent of high earners (ages twenty-eight to forty and earning more than $55,000, or ages forty-one to fifty-five and earning more than $65,000) and 34 percent of ultra-high earners (those earning more than $100,000) are at work more than fifty hours a week, and a significant proportion of these women are on the job ten to twenty more hours a week than five years ago (see Figures 6-1 and 6-2). It is also true that few of these women can count on much help at home. Whether you're talking about doing the laundry or driving the children to Little League practice, only 3 to 12 percent of husbands take prime responsibility for house-related or child-related tasks (see Figure 6-3).[3]

FIGURE 6-1. High-Earning Women and Working Hours by Employment Realm

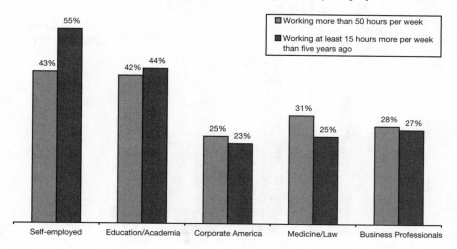

"High earners" are those women who are either twenty-eight to forty years of age and earning more than $55,000 or forty-one to fifty-five years of age and earning more than $65,000. In the employment realms, "corporate America" includes firms with five thousand or more employees. Data from High-Achieving Women 2001 survey.

FIGURE 6-2. High-Earning Women Working More than 50 Hours per Week, by Employment Realm

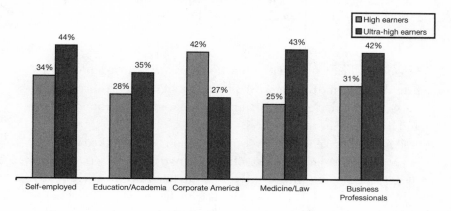

"High earners" are those women who are either twenty-eight to forty years of age and earning more than $55,000 or forty-one to fifty-five years of age and earning more than $65,000. "Ultra-high earners" are those women earning more than $100,000. In the employment realms, "corporate America" includes firms with five thousand or more employees. Data from High-Achieving Women 2001 survey.

FIGURE 6-3. Among High-Earning Women and Men, Primary Person
Handling Child Care and Household Responsibilities

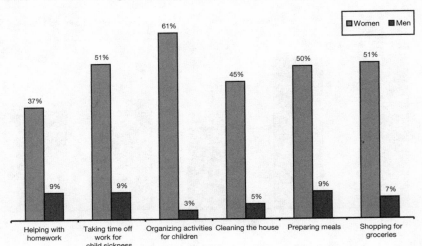

Data from High-Achieving Women 2001 survey.

These high-earning women tend to look to their workplaces for relief. And at least some of them are finding relief, as shown in the following examples.

Barbara, age forty-five, is a part-time partner at a Boston law firm.[4]
She works four days a week and could not be more pleased with her
schedule:

> I thank my lucky stars that I came up for partnership in a progressive
> firm that gave me the chance to prove I could make a reduced sched-
> ule work over the long haul. And I've produced! My clients are happy
> and I've pulled in new business.
>
> My salary is obviously lower than it would be if I worked full time,
> but for me that's an easy trade-off. I have two children ages nine and
> twelve, and I have turned Fridays into this magical day where I catch
> up with myself and do special projects with the children. Sure, I stay in
> touch with the office—I take my Blackberry [a handheld wireless
> communications device] everywhere—but last Friday Sophie and I
> planted a garden after school, and this Friday I'm taking Jonathan to
> the science museum.

According to our national survey of high-earning women, some firms provide significant time relief: 12 percent offer career breaks, and 31 percent offer job sharing. However, many more provide various kinds of flexibility: 69 percent offer staggered hours, and 48 percent offer work-at-home options. These less ambitious policies seem to be of limited use to the time-pressed, high-earning women.

For the past five years, thirty-nine-year-old Joanna had worked as an account executive at a headhunting firm in Chicago. She had always thought that her firm had great work-life policies—until eleven months ago, when she adopted a child.

> I don't mean to sound ungrateful, but this company has a whole slew of benefits—flextime, telecommuting, compressed workweeks, emergency child care, and concierge services—but they don't add up to a whole lot. In my opinion, they're chicken feed.
>
> My main problem—the one that keeps me awake at night—is the number of hours I am expected to put in. I work sixty hours a week fifty weeks of the year, which leaves precious little time for anything else. How am I supposed to bond with my baby if I don't finish my last assignment until after she goes to bed at night? Telecommuting and emergency child care don't give me time with my child.
>
> What I crave is a reduced schedule—three-fifths time sounds good. I know this should cost me, and I'm prepared to take a salary cut. But it's no go. I asked my boss and was told that the firm doesn't want to establish a precedent. I almost told him that maybe this is a precedent worth establishing, but I stopped myself. I hit the job market last month and don't want to tell my colleagues yet. I'm out there looking for either a part-time job or a job share. So far I've gotten two nibbles. We'll see.

The Time Crunch and Career Trajectories

Two themes reverberated through the e-mails and interviews that constituted the follow-up to the 2001 national survey of high-earning women: the severity of the time crunch and the women's inability to see their way around this time crunch without major adjustments in conventional career trajectories. At the heart of the matter was the respondents' sense that a long-hours culture had become so oppressive that tinkering around at the margin would no longer do the trick—at least not if you were interested in having a family. Flextime, telecommuting, and even on-site child care simply do not do enough to rein in the workday and workyear. A delayed start Monday morning, permission to telecommute Saturday morning, or even the ability to put baby Lucy in the company crèche just doesn't cut the mustard in a world where the "normal" workload, week in and week out, is fifty or sixty hours and the normal vacation is eleven days a year. The kinds of relationships these high-earning women are interested in—with significant others and with children—seem to require something more substantial than the energy left over after a thirteen-hour day.

Think of what a fifty-five-hour workweek translates into in terms of work-life balance. Assuming an hour for lunch and a forty-five-minute round-trip commute (the national average), the workday stretches to almost thirteen hours—7:30 A.M. to 8:15 P.M. or 8:30 A.M. to 9:15 P.M. Even assuming no "extras" (out-of-town business trips, client dinners, power breakfasts, and so on), this kind of schedule makes it extremely difficult for a professional to jump-start a relationship—or be a "good-enough" parent.[5] A mother of a five- or eight-year-old working a fifty-hour week would not make it home in time to eat dinner with her child and would have only a slight chance of getting home in time to read a bedtime story and kiss her child goodnight.

Policies and Programs to Help with the Time Crunch

In the survey, and again in the follow-up interviews, high-earning women with children made it abundantly clear that what they prize most are work-life policies that confer on them what one woman called "the gift of time."

Amy, forty-one, works as a marketing executive at the IBM facility in Austin, Texas. Her son, Kevin, just turned three, and Amy is newly back at work. She explains:

> People don't believe me when I tell them that my company offers a three-year personal leave of absence. Some people take it to look after a child or an elderly parent; others take it to go back to school. Now, this leave is unpaid, so you do need to have an employed spouse, but the company provides benefits and job-back guarantees.

I can't tell you how grateful I am to have had this kind of time-out. Because of infertility problems, it took us five years to conceive Kevin, and he is likely to be our only child, so I was particularly eager to savor his babyhood. I breast-fed him until he was eighteen months old, signed us both up for "Music Together," and made friends in the neighborhood. Most of all, I avoided splitting myself in two. I know so many new mothers who are tugged and pulled in all directions when they go back to work too soon.

This three-year leave enabled Kevin and me to establish a bond so strong that I feel we can withstand anything that comes down the pike. IBM gave me this gift, and I will always be grateful.

The high-earning women who participated in our 2001 national survey were asked to identify policies that would help them achieve balance in their lives over the long run. Overwhelmingly, they endorsed a cluster of work-life policies that would make it much more possible to get off conventional career ladders and then get back on again. The following list reflects what these women said they wanted. (Throughout the list, the first figure represents high-earning career women; the figures in parentheses represent high-potential women currently not in careers.)

- *A time bank of paid parenting leave.* Eighty-eight percent (86 percent) of respondents support the creation of a time bank to allow for three months of paid parenting leave, portions of which could be taken by a parent until a child was eighteen years old.
- *Alternative retirement plans.* Eighty-seven percent (91 percent) of respondents would like to restructure retirement plans so as to reduce the penalties attached to career interruptions.
- *Career breaks.* Eighty-five percent (87 percent) of respondents would like the option of an official "career break" involving two or three years of unpaid, job-protected leave.
- *Reduced-hour careers.* Eighty-five percent (91 percent) of respondents support the creation of part-time career tracks—high-level positions featuring reduced hours and reduced workloads on an ongoing basis and allowing for the possibility of promotion.

- *Part-time job listings.* Eighty-five percent (90 percent) of respondents support the notion of separate job listings for part-time/flexible-schedule positions in newspapers, trade publications, and Web sites.
- *Tax breaks for reentry.* Eighty-one percent (88 percent) of respondents would like to see tax breaks or subsidies for reentry programs that would enable professionals to get back up to speed in their jobs or transition to a new career.
- *Alumni status.* Seventy-four percent (79 percent) of respondents advocate the creation of something called "alumni status" for former employees. Alumni would continue to provide counsel, and the company would pay dues and certification fees to maintain alumni's professional standing. Analogous to active retirement, alumni status would help professional women currently at home to stay in the loop with their careers.

What does this wish list tell us? Whether age twenty-eight or fifty-five, whether they are currently in careers or currently at home, these high-earning women understand that a worsening time famine is at the heart of their struggle to lead more balanced lives, and they would like employers and the government to be much more creative in designing work-life policies that would provide the "gift of time." By huge margins (eight or nine to one) these high-earning women want imaginative versions of paid and unpaid leave, as well as part-time career options. They also want institutional changes ranging from a redesign of job listings to pension plan reform.

All of which brings us to a critical question: How realistic is this wish list? Are companies (and other employers of high-earning women) beginning to offer a rich array of time-enhancing work-life policies? If not, what are the chances that companies can be induced to offer such policies? Before answering these questions, we need to back up and create a little historical perspective.

FACTORS SHAPING U.S. WORK SCHEDULES

Concern about the time crunch has been with us for about a decade. In the early 1990s, Juliet Schor, in *The Overworked American,* and other scholars contended that Americans were working more hours—per week and per year—than at any time since World War II.[6] In subsequent studies, researchers have refined the analysis of these issues.[7] It seems that workweeks have not expanded across the board; rather, there is a growing bifurcation in working hours, with a large increase in the number of people who work long hours (fifty hours or more per week), coexisting with a large increase in the number who work part time.[8] These sharply divergent trends are linked to education and occupation. Short and shrinking workweeks are typical of jobs requiring less education at the low end of the labor market, whereas long and lengthening workweeks are typical of managerial jobs requiring college degrees at the high end of the labor market. As we know from the data contained in our national survey, some of the more dramatic trendlines involve women. Indeed, according to the sociologists Jerry A. Jacobs and Kathleen Gerson, the percentage of women working fifty hours per week or more is now higher in the United States than in any other country.[9]

Why do so many professionals—women and men—feel constrained to work longer and longer hours? A number of powerful structural and cultural factors help explain the increased incidence of long workweeks in America.

Senior managers in most companies are under intense pressure to use their professional workforce for as many hours a week as possible, since there are no marginal costs attached to high-echelon workers. The reasons behind this go back to 1938, when Congress passed the Fair Labor Standards Act, which institutionalized the forty-hour workweek and required that employers pay overtime for additional hours worked. A provision of this act was to exempt managers and professionals. This might not have produced overload in 1938, when only 15 percent of employees were in the exempt category and most of these employees were husbands with stay-at-home wives. However, it may have helped produce significant overload currently, when close to 30 percent of employees are in the exempt category and many of these are parents who do not have an at-home partner.[10]

The reality is that when managers and professionals do not qualify for extra pay for additional hours spent on the job, the marginal cost of labor falls to zero—a fact that undoubtedly encourages long workweeks. In this circumstance, employers have a strong incentive to squeeze as many hours as possible out of professional employees, because this reduces unit labor costs. Professionals have no option but to fall into line, because employers use the number of hours worked as the basis for promotion and future compensation. The size and structure of benefits packages also contribute to long and lengthening workweeks. The costs associated with providing employment benefits such as health insurance and pensions have climbed steadily in recent years and now account for about 25 percent of total compensation. Since the costs of most benefits are fixed for a full-time employee, no matter how many hours he or she works, the real hourly cost of such benefits declines as a professional spends more hours on the job. So again, an employer has a strong incentive to wring as many hours as possible out of professional employees.

Obviously, there is a limit to how hard an employer can press and squeeze. At some point, a professional employee will decide it is not worth the struggle and will either get off the career ladder or go to work for some other company that has more work-life options. This kind of "professional flight" becomes much more likely when labor markets are tight and highly skilled employees can choose between alternative employment opportunities—all of which spells trouble, since professional flight can be extremely expensive for companies because of the costs inherent in labor turnover.

THE TIME CRUNCH:
COMPANIES' DILEMMAS AND RESPONSES

The fact of the matter is that there is enormous expense wrapped up in failing to retain skilled personnel. When an employee departs, leaving a slot that needs to be filled, a company faces significant costs. There are direct costs tied up in the search process—advertising charges, headhunter fees, and the opportunity cost of time spent selecting and interviewing candidates. In addition, there are significant indirect costs—the former employee's lost leads and contacts, the new employee's depressed productivity while getting up to speed, and the time co-workers spend guiding and training the new person.

According to a 1999 survey by *Fortune* magazine that polled human resources executives, the cost of replacing a professional employee, when all factors were considered, approximated 150 percent of the departing person's salary. A recent study by the Work-Family Task Force at the University of Texas reported that turnover costs ranged from 93 percent to 200 percent of the departing employee's salary.[11] The rule of thumb seems to be that the more senior the departing person is, the higher the cost of replacing him or her will be. Turnover costs can be even higher in hot sectors of the labor market. In the late 1990s Integral Training Systems Search Inc., a national consulting and training firm, found that the cost of turnover in California's Silicon Valley averaged $150,000 to $200,000 per employee.[12] Also, in a recent American Management Association survey, 76 percent of human resource managers reported that it was more difficult and more expensive to recruit high-echelon workers than had been true three or five years earlier.[13]

Efforts to Retain Highly Skilled Employees

The labor market for professionals has undoubtedly tightened in recent years, and this fact has made companies much more aware of the costs of turnover and the need to develop strategies that both attract and retain highly skilled workers. As a result, work-life policies have become much more widespread. Lisa Benenson, the former editor in chief of *Working Mother* and *Working Woman* magazines, points to the fact that *Working Mother* has a growing pool of companies to choose from when the magazine compiles its annual list of the hundred best companies to work for.[14] Indeed, a recent survey of a thousand large companies found that 87 percent provided child care assistance, up from 78 percent in 1993, while 77 percent provided flextime, up from 60 percent in 1993.[15] A select few offer elaborate work-life policy packages. Ernst and Young, IBM, and Merck are among the best.

Ernst and Young's Work-Life Policy Package
The accounting firm Ernst and Young (21,842 employees) has a state-of-the-art approach to flexibility. In the mid-1990s, in response to high turnover rates among its women professionals, this company established an Office of Retention (currently called the Center for the New Workforce), and it now offers a particularly rich array of flexible

work arrangements. Options available to employees include flexible hours, which allow employees to work irregular hours, compressed workweeks, or reduced days during less busy times, balanced by longer days during busier times; reduced schedules, which allow employees to work fewer days per week or fewer hours per day; and seasonal long-term arrangements, which allow employees to work a normal work schedule for most of the year, followed by a period of time off that can last from two weeks to three months.[16]

At Ernst and Young, these new work-life options are reinforced by measures designed to embed these options in the culture of the firm. For example, the company has developed something called the Life Balance Matrix—a collection of best practices that is made available to managers responsible for staffing and planning. Flexible work arrangements are already affecting turnover rates at Ernst and Young. According to Deborah Holmes, the Americas director with the Center for the New Workforce, "Two-thirds of the people using flexible work arrangements tell us that they would have left—or would not have joined us in the first place—if it had not been for their flexible work arrangement."[17]

IBM's Work-Life Policy Package

IBM (143,399 employees) has a particularly impressive set of policies regarding paid and unpaid leave. Since 1991 the company has offered a three-year personal leave of absence for full-time employees. This leave is unpaid, but benefits are continued and there are job-back guarantees. Since 1997, unpaid leave has been supplemented by part-time, paid leave—an option that IBM calls flexible leave of absence. Employees taking this leave work a minimum of sixteen hours a week for up to three years, and they receive prorated pay and vacation, full benefits, and the opportunity to earn pay increases and bonuses.

IBM is aiming to be the premier employer of women worldwide, and senior managers feel that creative work-life policies have helped attract and retain high-caliber women workers. Twenty-one percent of executive employees at IBM are now women, up from 12 percent in 1995. "Our motivation is not to be generous, but to be astute in the management of our human resource talent pool," said Ted Childs, vice president of global workforce diversity at IBM. "If you operate from the premise that you hire the best people—and we do—you want to send them the message they're valued and cause them to stay." [18]

Merck's Work-Life Policy Package
The pharmaceutical firm Merck and Company (32,722 employees), sometimes known as "Mother Merck," is particularly proud of its child care and family leave policies. Merck offers twenty-six weeks of family leave with partial pay and phase-back options for new mothers. The company also contributes to the operating costs of three on-site child care centers and provides subsidies and discounts for use at community child care centers. In addition, Merck serves as its employees' concierge, counselor, personal trainer, caterer, banker, and recreation director. An employee who works at Merck's headquarters in Whitehouse Station, New Jersey, can drop off a car for an oil change, pick up laundered shirts, order a birthday cake, rent a video, and pick up dinner—complete with freshly baked baguette—with the help of these services.

Support for these elaborate perks emanates from the top of the company. The CEO, Raymond Gilmartin, claims that balancing work and family is "the most important human resource issue facing Merck today." In recent years he has personally led a charge to develop additional work-life options. They seem to be paying off. Women now account for half of Merck's research scientists and 36 percent of top earners in the company—much higher figures than for the pharmaceutical industry as a whole. [19]

THE SURVEY RESPONDENTS' EXPERIENCES WITH COMPANY WORK-LIFE POLICIES

Our national survey data provide concrete proof that companies offering a rich array of work-life policies are much more likely to hang on to their professional women than companies that lag behind. According to our survey, high-earning women who stayed in their careers tended to work for organizations that offered substantial help on the work-life front. Flextime, telecommuting, paid parenting leave, job sharing, and help with child care are all very likely to be part of the benefits package at these organizations. In sharp contrast,

SYLVIA ANN HEWLETT · 172

TABLE 6-1. Access to Work-Life Policies

	Percent of high-earning career women who have access to work-life policies in their current job	Percent of high-potential women not currently employed who had access to work-life policies in their last job
	N = 1,168	N = 344
Flexibility to take time off from work to attend children's school or child care function	77	56
Flexible changes in starting and quitting times	69	49
Gradual return to work after childbirth or adoption	56	39
Regular at-home or off-site work	48	28
Paid time off for female employees who give birth to a child	46	37
Compressed workweek	42	28
Shared jobs	31	28
Paid time off for male employees whose partners give birth to a child	29	19
Child care facility at or near work	20	14
"Career breaks"	12	8

Data from High-Achieving Women 2001 survey.

high-potential women not in careers at the time of the survey had left organizations with extremely inadequate work-life policies (see Table 6-1).

Furthermore, it is not just a question of a better benefits package, it is also a question of better attitudes. High-earning women who had stayed in their careers felt strongly not only that their companies offered generous policies but also that their managers supported employees' use of these policies. Indeed, almost 90 percent said they had made personal use of at least one such policy. Again, high-potential women not in careers at the time of the survey felt differently. These women reported that at their last job, managers had not supported employees' use of the rather inadequate policies that had been in place.

OFFICIAL AND UNOFFICIAL WORKPLACE RULES

It seems that companies these days are buffeted by two antagonistic sets of demands. Long-standing cost-cutting pressures to squeeze professional employees so that they spend as many hours as possible on the job are juxtaposed with much more recent cost-cutting pressures to bring turnover rates down by work-life policies that reduce hours spent on the job. In any given workplace these pressures can clash and collide, which helps explain why employees often feel that there are two sets of rules: one up-front and official, the other unwritten and unofficial.

The official rules are those set out in company handbooks and manuals that technically define the conditions of employment. They tend to highlight recently instituted work-life policies. The unofficial rules are unwritten but are embedded in the corporate culture and need to be taken extremely seriously by an employee wanting to be tapped for promotion. These unwritten rules emphasize the need to put in "face time" twelve- to fourteen-hour workdays in the office. As the sociologist Jessica DeGroot has noted, generally speaking, the more face time an employee puts in, the more points he or she gets, but some forms of face time are more valuable than others in the corporate culture. "The face time ritual deducts points for the woman who comes in at 7:00 A.M. so she can pick up her child at the day care center by 6:00 P.M. It adds points for the man who comes in at 9:00 A.M. and stays at his desk until 8:00 P.M. This is because 'after hours' face time yields the highest points of all."[20]

The pressures to cut costs by squeezing professionals have, in fact, been with us a long time—much longer than the pressure to cut costs by lowering turnover rates. Over the past several decades, corporate America has developed an extremely unforgiving long-hours culture that is hard to shake, even though another logic—one that centers on lowering turnover rates—may well be more powerful on the cost-cutting front. According to Jacobs and Gerson, "Long workweeks persist—and spread—not because they are, necessarily, the most efficient way of organizing work, but because a long hours culture has succeeded in 'stigmatizing' those who work less."[21] As the participants in my young professionals focus group pointed out, refusing to work long hours can brand a professional employee with the modern-day equivalent of a scarlet letter. According to group respondents, such a person is seen as a "deviant" or an "outcast," unworthy of serious consideration for advancement.

It takes an extremely gutsy professional to ignore the unwritten, unofficial rule book, break ranks, and take at face value what is written in the official rule book. In fact, professionals are increasingly seeking help from people such as Ellen Ostrow, a new breed of psychologist who provides personal and career coaching for lawyers. Specifically, she focuses on young attorneys—most often women, but sometimes men—seeking to buck brutal billable-hours requirements and seventy- to eighty-hour workweeks and take advantage of work-life policies newly on the books. The following example is described in one of Ostrow's newsletters. A mother of two and seventh-year associate had "been working a reduced hour schedule for several years. . . . Although her firm allowed part-time schedules, she felt they were regarded as a special accommodation to the family-challenged, for people ostensibly not tough enough to do everything. She felt completely marginalized. 'I can't talk to anyone,' she confided to me. 'How can I go into work on Monday morning and say to the people in my practice group, who bill 3,000 hours and worked straight through the weekend, that I spent my weekend taking my children to an amusement park?' "[22]

According to Ostrow and others such as DeGroot, we, as a society, still have a long way to go. Having a raft of work-life policies on the books is one thing; changing the culture of the firm and managers' mind-sets so that these policies are freely available to individual professionals is something else entirely.[23]

TOWARD A COMPREHENSIVE U.S. WORK-LIFE POLICY PACKAGE

So where do we go from here? Can we, in fact, craft workplace and government policies that succeed on both the official and unofficial fronts? Can we institute policies that both formalize a set of work-life options and transform mind-sets and attitudes regarding our long-hours culture?

Private Sector Initiatives

Three initiatives in particular would expand U.S. work-life options. The first involves giving every working parent a time bank of three months of paid leave, portions of which could be taken by a parent until a child is eighteen years old. This would be in addition to paid parenting leave granted around the time of childbirth. As any mother or father knows, the demands of a newborn are urgent but not unique, and a child can be extremely needy at four, fourteen, or any other age. If a child flunks fourth grade or plunges into depression at puberty, a parent may well want to take some time off from work in order to find the right help and be more available.

Spreading paid parenting leave over an eighteen-year period has the additional attraction of undercutting discrimination. Once it is clear that paid parenting leave can be taken by both men and women at any time over an eighteen-year span, discriminating against married women in the childbearing years becomes much less likely. It is also true that when paid parenting leave is flexible and generous, sexual stereotypes begin to break down. The Swedish experience is relevant here. In 1974, when parenting leave was introduced in Sweden, only 3 percent of fathers took advantage of it. But by the late 1990s, 80 percent of fathers were taking at least part of this leave.[24]

A second initiative would involve creating high-level jobs that would provide reduced hours and a reduced workload on an ongoing basis. As we have seen, various professional service firms are experimenting with part-time partnerships. Flexibility seems to be a key. Even with a reduced client load, a part-time professional needs to bend with the needs of clients. The challenge in this case would be to ensure that these reduced-hours jobs would allow for the possibility of promotion, rather than being dead-end positions (though it obviously would take workers longer to accumulate the necessary experience).

Ironically, this proposal is a gender-neutral version of one put forth by Felice Schwartz twelve years ago[25] that provoked a storm of opposition based on concerns that the policy would "shunt female employees off on a slow road to nowhere."[26] The galloping time crunch has made this proposal more appealing to professional women in the United States. European professionals currently have access to a variety of reduced-hours options. In Sweden, mothers and fathers are entitled to limit their workday to six hours until a child is eight years old.[27] In the Netherlands, the official workweek is thirty-six hours, and in France the official workweek has recently been reduced to thirty-five hours. Indeed, Europeans now work a staggering 350 fewer hours a year than Americans, and the gap is particularly wide for professional employees.[28]

A third initiative involves developing career "off-ramps" and "on-ramps." For many long-hours professionals, achieving work-life balance means interrupting conventional career trajectories. Such interruptions exact a huge toll—in terms of both earnings and promotions—because careers have many exit points but very few entry points. In a recent article, the policy analyst Nancy Rankin developed the idea of the career highway and made the very useful point that we need to develop at least as many "on-ramps" as "off-ramps."[29] In this regard, the following options (as described earlier) would be helpful: career breaks which would maintain continuity through the device of unpaid, job-protected leave; alumni status, which would preserve a worker's ties to her or his company and profession; separate job listings, which would make reduced-hours jobs easier to find; and alternative retirement plans, which would reduce the long-run penalties attached to taking time out.

Government Initiatives

Needed changes can also be shaped through government initiatives such as the following three. The first involves extending the Family and Medical Leave Act (FMLA) to workers in small companies and turning it into paid leave. Available since 1993 for the purpose of looking after a new child, an elderly parent, or a seriously ill family member, the FMLA is of central importance to families. For example, childbirth is not only a joyous event but also a life-bending one. For most parents, it is a time of profound vulnerability. If a family can successfully negotiate the magical first months of life, all kinds of good things will happen; a newborn will bond with his or her parents, a family will cohere, and a child will get off to a good start in life. At the moment, however, the leave mandated by the FMLA is unpaid and is limited to workers in companies with more than fifty employees. The coverage needs to be universally available.

A second initiative involves providing tax incentives to companies that offer employees the "gift of time." The list of eligible benefits should include reduced-hours jobs, job sharing, paid parenting leave, telecommuting, and compressed workweeks.

A third initiative involves promoting new legislation to eliminate incentives for long-hours workweeks. The goal in this case is to remove the perverse incentives that lie behind our long-hours culture. A reduction in the number of employees who are considered exempt and the adoption of a proportional benefits plan are measures that would increase the marginal cost of professional labor. This would cause employers to insist on fifty- or sixty-hour workweeks only when long workweeks ensured an efficient solution to production problems, not simply because long workweeks might reduce unit labor costs. Thus, government should extend the Fair Labor Standards Act to many more professional and managerial employees so that a large proportion of high-echelon workers are eligible for overtime. Government should also require mandatory benefits that accrue in proportion to the number of hours worked. This would entitle employees who work very long hours to receive additional benefits (such as retirement contributions, life insurance, or cash bonuses) and would protect part-time workers.

Advancing Key Work-Life Principles

The policy package just described embodies some powerful principles. First and foremost, these policies respond to the needs and desires of many professional women (and probably men as well). As we can see from the results of our survey, high-earning women want work-life options that give them the gift of time. This is in sharp contrast to conventional work-life packages, which all too often focus on policies that enhance work rather than on those that enhance time. Sick-child care is an example of a benefit that reduces the impediments to work by providing for a needy child and making sure that a mother or father can continue working. However, even if the child's needs are being well attended to, a parent may well prefer to be home with a sick child.[30]

Reduced-hours jobs, paid parenting leave, extended career breaks, prorated benefits—these are the kinds of policies that enable a professional to permanently shift the boundary between work and life and, thereby, to achieve long-term balance. These options might even allow a professional couple to contemplate what the child psychologist Stanley Greenspan has called "the four-thirds solution"—an arrangement whereby each partner allocates two-thirds time to career and one-third time to family, and together they provide four-thirds of a single income. Greenspan has described this solution as "an optimal framework" for child development and adult well-being.[31]

Second, these policies recognize the need to tackle head on the long-hours culture by removing the perverse incentives that underpin fifty- and sixty-hour workweeks. If employers were hit with overtime charges and fringe benefit charges every time they squeezed an extra five or ten hours out of a professional employee, they might think twice about requiring long workweeks. Most probably, the top stratum of senior managers should remain exempt—CEOs, for example, should not expect to work forty hours a week or be paid overtime—but fully 30 percent of all employees are now in the exempt category, and many would be treated better if they were included in the provisions of a revamped FLSA.[32]

Third, this policy package has enormous potential for helping advance gender equity. Curbing our long-hours culture will go some distance toward leveling the playing field between men and women. As long as large numbers of professional workers continue to put in fifty, sixty, and even seventy hours a week, individuals who choose to take advantage of extended leave or reduced-hours workweeks will pay an extremely high price in terms of career advancement and earning power. Mothers are likely to pay this price disproportionately because, on average, they earn less than their husbands, which creates an incentive to have mothers, rather than fathers, take time off work.[33] These factors combine to set in motion a vicious circle: lower earnings increase the likelihood of career interruptions for mothers, which, in turn, lead to even lower earnings down the road.

Thus, reining in our long-hours culture is central to gender equity. Once we have narrowed the definition of what constitutes exempt labor, few professionals would work long workweeks, there would be greatly reduced penalties attached to taking time off, and perhaps many more men would feel free to take time out for family-related reasons. In such a world, many more couples might choose Greenspan's four-thirds solution.

Finally, these policies would go some distance toward healing the perceived rift between parents and the "child-free." In our national survey, fully 54 percent of high-earning women without children said that people without children were unfairly expected to pick up the slack for those with children; indeed, 45 percent of these women said that people with children had altogether too many options or benefits. In our survey, for example, Anna, a fifty-two-year-old managing editor of a San Francisco–based publishing company, expressed these views:

> If anyone else walks into my office and tells me she's pregnant, I will have a hard time being polite, let alone congratulatory. I have eleven women on my staff and two are expecting in the fall, which means that they will be out for our busiest season—leaving the rest of us to do their work. One of the women had the gall to ask for some additional unpaid leave. She told me six weeks wasn't long enough. I don't know whether that's true or not—I've never had children. But I don't believe in featherbedding. It strikes me [that] in the real world, grown-ups have hard choices.

Similarly, as Sonia pointed out in the young professionals focus group, being generous toward co-workers is difficult when someone is working extremely long hours in high-pressure professions. To repeat her words, "Anyone who gets a break . . . is resented. So if you take reduced hours, you can expect to take a lot of heat. The only way around this is for everyone to get a better deal." The policy package I have described would produce such a deal. Compensating young professionals for extra hours spent on the job and creating an imaginative package of work-life options that enhance time would help everyone—employees who have children and those who do not—have a shot at more balanced lives.

7

The National Story: How Americans Spend Their Time on Work, Family, and Community

David M. Almeida and Daniel A. McDonald

"Sorry, I have too much on my plate right now." "Too busy." "Not enough time." While recruiting volunteers for a Parent-Teacher Association fund-raiser, one of the authors of this chapter heard these common explanations for people not having the time to participate. The finite nature of hours, minutes, and seconds in the course of a day suggests a zero-sum equation: time spent in one pursuit necessarily detracts from time spent in another. Adding up the hours spent working for pay, engaging in leisure activities, caring for others, and sleeping can total no more than twenty-four. Whether we have time to savor the moment or are constantly on the run depends on the degree of discretion we have in determining how we use our time. How Americans spend the limited resource of time is of great interest to working parents, elected officials, volunteer organizations, and employers—especially as the topic concerns the changing nature of time spent at the workplace, plus time devoted to family, social relationships, and civic affiliations. For the purposes of this study, we have chosen to broaden the scope of what is considered socially responsible behavior to include activities that reach beyond civic involvement to capture the more familial and informal endeavors that constitute everyday contributions to society.[1] Specifically, we examine how time in paid employment is associated with the time devoted to family, friends, and community on a day-to-day basis over time.

BALANCING THE DEMANDS OF WORK, FAMILY, AND COMMUNITY

The extent to which we can choose how and with whom we spend our time may be influenced by several factors, including gender, socioeconomic resources, and social roles.[2] For instance, Barnett found that men have greater discretion than women do in how they spend their time outside of work with family and in leisure.[3] According to Rossi, people with fewer resources, such as less education and income, are more likely to provide practical support to their families than to make financial contributions, whereas those with higher levels of education and income tend to give more of both time and money to the community.

In our analyses, we focus primarily on education. This strategy was chosen because it captures the well-established gradient of socioeconomic disadvantage and the primary educational benchmarks that provide the foundation for subsequent stratification of occupation and earnings. Moreover, educational attainment has been the primary proxy for socioeconomic status used in previous studies, thereby allowing comparability with other studies; it is less prone to exhibiting missing data values; it is relatively stable across the life course after early adulthood; it is more comparable across men and women than occupation, and more comparable across single and married people than income. Most importantly, education is less prone to endogeneity bias from reverse causality (e.g., work hours affecting the socioeconomic status or SES measure) than measures such as income and occupation. Of course, it is important to note that any association between level of education and time use does not mean that individuals "learn" in college how to spend their time. Rather, education is a marker for social advantage. To illustrate this point we will present some findings assessing the association between income and time spent giving to others.

Age may also play a role in the propensity to engage in socially responsible behaviors, such that providing for the welfare of others apparently evolves over the life span.[4] Findings from the present sample (as described in the next section) showed that older people, who presumably have more discretionary time due to retirement, give informal assistance to others more frequently and volunteer their time more often and for longer periods of time than younger people. In addition, our research highlighted the temporal rhythms of giving by showing that individuals are more likely to contribute time to family and community on the weekends and during the summer months.[5]

Previous research has also suggested that the amount of discretionary time available to attend to others' welfare should be associated with participation in paid employment. Direct evidence for this contention, however, has been equivocal. Robinson and Godbey estimated that for each additional hour of work (for those working less than fifty hours per week), there is approximately half an hour less in free time.[6] Yet Putnam found work hours to be positively associated with civic activity.[7] It appears that busy and highly involved individuals make time for civic engagement by reducing time spent in other activities such as eating, sleeping, and watching television, although, on average, women employed full time spend less time volunteering. After careful consideration of the possibilities, Putnam concluded that those most likely to be involved in their communities are women who choose to work part time, as opposed to those who work out of necessity.

Putnam also suggested that the manner in which discretionary time is distributed across the day and throughout the week is essential to the understanding of civic engagement.[8] While some may have morsels of time scattered throughout the day, others possess a few large chunks of available time. Such diverse patterns of discretionary time may account for the decrease in participation among Americans in formal social activities over the past several decades.

Perhaps Americans have devised other ways to balance the often conflicting demands of work, family, and community by weaving the threads—or patches, as the case may be—of discretionary time into the fabric of their daily lives. Perhaps the mode and delivery of our social involvement has changed such that we fulfill our social obligations in less structured settings, yet just as meaningful and important ones. Rather than view this social phenomenon as a zero-sum one, we may see it as synergistic, that is, one aspect of life enhancing another. For example, work may enhance the role of men as fathers by enabling them to fulfill their obligations and provide for their families.[9] Furthermore, becoming a father often points men in the direction of broader community service, such as participation in parent and sporting associations.[10] Likewise, possessing multiple roles appears to enhance women's overall psychological well-being by enabling them to use all of their talents.[11] Women, more often than men, choose occupations that enable them to nurture and care for others while in the work setting.[12]

The zero-sum perspective does not explain Putnam's finding that the busiest among us are more likely than others to be involved in socially responsible activities.[13] Contrary to what the zero-sum perspective might suggest, Rossi found that the number of hours worked by employed women was not the determining factor in time allocated to volunteering. Rather, the lack of gratification from the job propelled women to seek volunteer opportunities that provided them with a sense of appreciation for their efforts.[14]

Approaches to Studying Daily Time Use

One way to examine this interweaving of work, family, and community is to study the day-to-day linkages among these overlapping spheres of adult life. The use of innovative research tools such as time diaries and event sampling methodology has permitted researchers to obtain detailed accounts of how people spend their time. This daily approach to examining the work-family-community interweave affords the researcher benefits that cannot be easily achieved through the use of standard designs. Daily measurement helps resolve recall problems by allowing respondents to report about experiences in various domains of life much nearer to the time when they occur.[15] Daily designs are especially useful in capturing information about the dynamics of daily experiences that appear static in traditional cross-sectional designs. The amount of time individuals spend contributing to others is likely to vary day to day.[16] By following individuals intensively over time, researchers can compute estimates of time based on several days, rather than relying on a single report about one day or subjective estimates of time use over several days.

THE NATIONAL STUDY OF DAILY EXPERIENCES

The chief aim of our daily telephone interview study, the focus of this chapter, has been to add to our understanding of how Americans use their time. More specifically, we have been examining the quantity of time adults spend giving of themselves daily for the welfare of others, including their children, other relatives, friends, neighbors, co-workers, and community. We also have assessed the quality or type of giving performed, such as providing emotional support, lending informal assistance, spending time with children, or volunteering for an organization. The data are from a U.S. national study of daily experiences, the overarching goal of which was to chart the day-to-day stressors and challenges that individuals face during middle adulthood.

From a wide-angle perspective, how much time do American adults spend giving to family members (parents, siblings, children, and other relatives) and to their communities (friends, neighbors, co-workers, and organizations)? The first step toward answering this question was to capture a wide array of giving experiences that encompassed both the quantity and quality of daily giving activities. During daily interviews, we asked respondents how much time they spent in the following activities: (1) providing anyone with informal assistance such as shopping or free babysitting; (2) providing anyone with emotional support such as comforting him or her, listening to personal problems, or giving advice; (3) doing things with their children, such as helping with homework, playing, eating meals, or watching television; and (4) volunteering at a community organization such as a church, hospital, or senior center.

Looking more closely at the individual differences in giving, we asked: What is the social demography of those who give to family and community? Our analysis allowed us to assess the extent to which sociodemographic factors such as gender, education, and marital status predicted how much time people contributed to a variety of family and community activities. Given the theme of this volume, we now take a close look at the impact of employment status and daily giving. We do this by first assessing the gross associations between employment and each type of giving. We then conduct more fine-grained descriptive analyses of individuals' profiles, based on a combination of their socioeconomic characteristics, in order to determine who is giving most in specific areas and in the total amount of time across all areas.

Methodology

Data for the present analyses came from the National Study of Daily Experiences (NSDE), one of the in-depth studies that are part of the National Survey of Midlife in the United States (MIDUS) carried out under the auspices of the John D. and Catherine T. MacArthur Foundation Research Network on Successful Midlife. Respondents in the NSDE were randomly selected from the MIDUS sample and received $20 for their participation in the project. Of the 1,242 MIDUS respondents we attempted to contact, 1,031 agreed to participate, yielding a response rate of 83 percent. Respondents completed an average of seven of the eight interviews, resulting in a total of 7,221 daily interviews.

A comparison of the characteristics of the NSDE subsample and the MIDUS parent sample from which it was drawn revealed that the two samples were very similar in terms of age, marital status, and parenting status. The NSDE sample contained fewer minority respondents than were in the MIDUS sample, 9.7 percent and 12.2 percent, respectively. Individuals in the NSDE sample were on average slightly better educated than those in the MIDUS sample, with 62.3 percent of NSDE respondents and 60.8 percent of the MIDUS sample having thirteen or more years of education. Respondents for the present analysis were, on average, forty-seven years old; men were slightly older than women, but they had similar levels of education. Seventy-seven percent of the women and 85 percent of the men were married at the time of the study. Forty-seven percent of the households reported having at least one child present. The average family income was between $50,000 and $55,000.

Study Design

Over the course of eight consecutive evenings, respondents completed short telephone interviews about their daily experiences. On the final evening, respondents also answered several questions about their previous week. Data collection spanned an entire year (March 1996 to March 1997) and consisted of forty separate flights of interviews, with each flight representing the eight-day sequence of interviews. The initiation of interview flights was staggered across the days of the week to control for the possible confounding between day of study and day of week.

Measures

The daily telephone interview included questions about daily experiences in the previous twenty-four hours concerning time use, mood, physical symptoms, productivity, and daily stressors. Table 7-1 describes the measures of daily giving behaviors in family and community domains. Because respondents were interviewed over eight days,

TABLE 7-1. Domains and Dimensions Tapped by Daily Giving Measures

Domains		Descriptive Detail
FAMILY		
	Time with Children	Summed number of hours and minutes per week spent doing things with children such as helping them with homework, playing with them, taking them places, or doing other things with them
	Informal Help	Summed number of hours and minutes per week providing unpaid assistance such as free babysitting or help with shopping for family members (outside of the household)
	Emotional Support	Summed number of hours and minutes per week providing emotional support such as comforting, listening to, or advising family members
COMMUNITY		
	Volunteer Help	Summed number of hours and minutes per week doing formal volunteer work at a church, hospital, senior center, or any other organization
	Informal Help	Summed number of hours and minutes per week providing unpaid assistance such as free babysitting or help with shopping for friends, neighbors, co-workers, or others outside of the family
	Emotional Support	Summed number of hours and minutes per week providing emotional support such as comforting, listening to, or advising friends, neighbors, co-workers, or others outside of the family

we averaged the first and last days of the interviews before computing the mean across the rest of the interviews. We did so to eliminate day-of-week bias in the average daily estimate. The actual quantity of weekly giving was estimated by summing the total amount of time each respondent gave each day across the entire week.

Results

The goal of our initial set of analyses was to present a broad description of the pattern of time our respondents contributed to several family and community domains. We analyzed how much time the entire sample spent per week in each of these domains, the percentage of the sample who spent *any* time in each of these domains, and how much time this subset of respondents contributed. On average, the entire sample reported spending 13.3 hours per week with their children, with close to 74 percent of the sample spending any time with children; 50 percent spent at least 7.3 hours, and 10 percent of the sample spent 40 hours during the week with their children. Respondents who reported *any* time with children spent close to 18 hours per week taking care of or interacting with children. These figures are based on the entire sample. Not surprisingly, the most important factor in spending time with children is whether there are children in the house. We will discuss this topic later in the chapter.

It is important to note that these estimates were much higher than estimates obtained from time budget studies in which respondents kept a log of all of their activities over a twenty-four-hour period. However, they were similar to results from studies that used average workday and nonworkday estimates of time use.[17] We believe that the discrepancy between these telephone diary estimates and results from time budget studies had to do with our less restrictive estimate of time with children. Whereas time diary estimates count only time spent providing child care as the primary activity, our estimate included many secondary activities with children, such as eating meals and watching television together.

Our estimates of time spent providing informal help and emotional support to family members show that on average, respondents spent approximately 1.5 hours per week helping and supporting family members, with 10 percent of the sample spending at least 10 hours supporting family members. However, fewer respondents gave informal help than gave emotional support. Among respondents who gave any support, they spent 8 hours per week contributing informal help and 3.3 hours giving emotional support.

Our findings regarding the amount of time respondents gave to the community show that on average, the entire sample spent between 45 minutes and 1 hour 45 minutes per week contributing to the community across these three domains, with 40 percent of the sample giving at least 1 hour and 10 percent of the sample giving 5.4 hours of their time to fellow workers and community members. Respondents were much more likely to have given emotional support to others than to have given informal and volunteer help. Among those who gave to their community, each week they spent an average of 3.6 hours volunteering for organizations, 3.4 hours providing informal help, and 2.5 hours giving emotional support to community members.

Across all of the categories of giving, our participants reported spending 22.04 (*SD* = 24.13) hours during the study week giving of themselves to their families and communities. Only 4 percent reported giving no time in any of the areas of giving, and 50 percent of the sample gave at least 14.35 hours, while 10 percent gave at least 50.75 hours of their time to others during the study week.

Sociodemographic Assessment of Contributing to Family and Community
The next set of analyses addresses who was most likely to have contributed *any* time to family and community. Table 7-2 brings together several sociodemographic characteristics as simultaneous predictors of whether respondents spent any time in each of the giving domains. The first row of odds ratios (that is, the likelihood of contributing any time) shows that respondents with higher levels of education were less likely to have given any informal help to family members, but they were more likely to have given emotional support to family members and to have contributed time to all three community domains. Married individuals were more likely to have spent time with children and to have engaged in volunteer work, but they were less likely to have contributed any informal help and emotional support to community members. Not surprisingly, respondents with more children in the home were more likely to have spent time with children, but they were also more likely to have contributed volunteer hours. The findings for

TABLE 7-2. Logistic Regressions of the Social Demography of People
Who Give to Family and Community (Odds Ratios)

Predictor Variables	Family Domain			Community Domain		
	Any Time with Children	Any Informal Help	Any Emotional Support	Any Volunteer Help	Any Informal Help	Any Emotional Support
Education	1.05	.82*	1.25*	1.53*	1.24*	1.69*
Married (no = 0, yes = 1)	3.33*	1.26	1.06	1.61*	.74*	.62*
Number of Children at Home	9.16*	1.02	1.15	1.42*	1.17	.94
Gender (male = 0, female =1)	1.62*	1.57*	1.36*	.89	.84*	2.12*
Employment Hours	.85*	.88*	.93	.96	.92	.98

$N = 608$

*$p < .01$

gender indicate that women were more likely not only to have spent some time in each of the family domains but also to have provided emotional support to community members. Men were more likely to have provided informal assistance to community members. Finally, respondents with more paid work hours were less likely to have spent any time taking care of children and providing informal help to family members.

Amount of Time Contributing to Specific Areas

Next we explored whether these demographic categories made a difference in how much time people gave of themselves. Results of these analyses are portrayed in Figures 7-1 through 7-4. The bars display the average amount of time across the study week that participants spent in each type of giving. Across all of the demographic categories, gender made the biggest difference. Figure 7-1 shows that women spent 12.44 more hours per week than men giving care, support, and assistance to family and community. Compared to men, women spent more time in each category of giving. Marital status also made a big difference in how much time people gave to others, as shown in Figure 7-2. Married individuals gave 8 hours more per week than individuals

FIGURE 7-1. Weekly Hours of Giving to Others by Gender

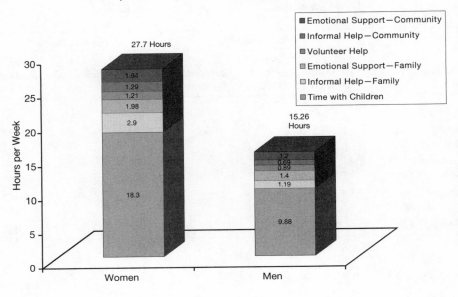

FIGURE 7-2. Weekly Hours of Giving to Others by Marital Status

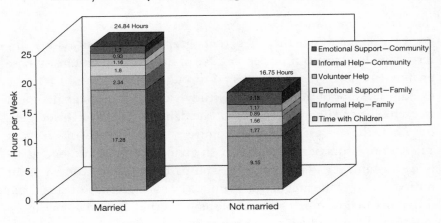

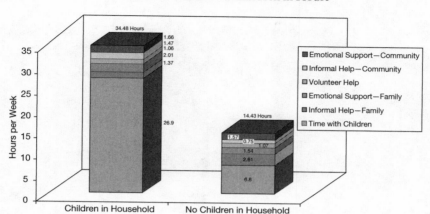

FIGURE 7-3. Weekly Hours of Giving to Others Spent by
Those with and Without Children in House

who were not married. The main difference was almost entirely due to time with children, whom married individuals were more likely to have had in their households. Interestingly, single respondents reported having given more emotional and informal assistance to co-workers and community members than married respondents.

Figure 7-3 compares respondents with children (i.e., less than 18 years) in the household with respondents without children in the home. Respondents with children at home spent 20 more hours per week providing for others than respondents without children; time spent with children actually accounts for this difference. One interesting difference was that respondents without children at home spent more time providing informal assistance to family members.

With regard to educational status, Figure 7-4 shows no difference between the total time that college-educated and non-college-educated respondents gave to others. However, college-educated participants contributed more time to their community, while non-college-educated participants gave more time to family members. The same pattern was observed when we divided the respondents by household income (above the national average and below the national average; see Figure 7-5). Those with higher income may have been able to pay for more assistance in caring for family members and thus provided less themselves while spending more time in the community. However,

FIGURE 7-4. Weekly Hours of Giving to Others by Education

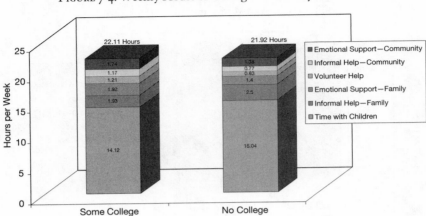

resulting differences in income are only one of the several potentially important mechanisms for how education may determine how people contribute their time. For example, higher education is also associated with better and more flexible working conditions. This may translate into more availability to participate in community activities. Indeed, future research should assess the multiple modes of social advantage that foster how individuals spend their time. Finally, Figure 7-6 shows differences in giving by employment status. Employed participants

FIGURE 7-5. Weekly Hours of Giving to Others by Household Income

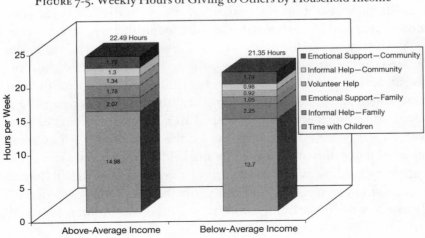

FIGURE 7-6. Weekly Hours of Giving to Others by Employment

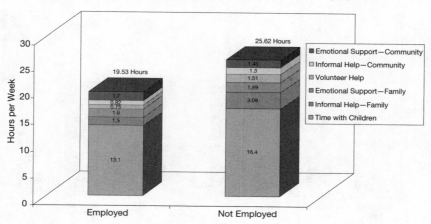

spent 6.09 fewer hours during the week giving to others than did non-employed respondents. Much of the difference was due to differences in child care, informal family assistance, and formal volunteer time.

While these analyses provide an initial picture of the American social demography of giving, they do not provide a very detailed account of who was most likely to have given in specific areas. To refine our description, we investigated various participant profiles based on a combination of their social demographic characteristics. The results of these analyses are presented in Figures 7-7 through 7-13. Because one of our main goals for this chapter was to examine the interconnections between paid work and time spent contributing to family and community, the bars in the figures highlight differences in employment status. Our initial analyses showed that work hours played a role in whether or not people contributed to the family. The next set of analyses addressed how employment status might have affected the amount of time individuals contributed to family and community. For the following analyses, the sample was divided into sixteen mutually exclusive profiles based on employment status (employed, not employed), gender (male, female), level of education (no college, some college), and marital status (single, married). It is important to note that, due to limited sample size, we grouped divorced and widowed respondents into the single group and limited assessment of socioeconomic advantage to education. A series of analyses of variance (ANOVAs) were

FIGURE 7-7. Time with Children

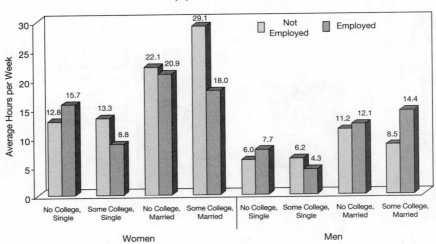

conducted to detect differences between groups for each category of giving as well as the total for all giving.

Figure 7-7 shows the average amount of time respondents were engaged in some activity with their children throughout the week. As compared with other groups, married women outside of the workforce, regardless of their level of education, spent more time on average engaging in activities with their children. In contrast, married employed men with some college education spent more time on average in activities with their children than did single employed men with similar levels of education, who spent the least amount of time with children during the study week.

Figure 7-8 shows the average amount of time respondents spent providing practical assistance to other family members during the week. Among women, employment status made a large difference in this category of giving. College-educated women outside the paid workforce spent an average of 2.5 more hours per week providing assistance to family members than did their employed counterparts. Single employed men with no college education provided the least amount of time in helping family, averaging 23 minutes per week, and married nonemployed men provided the most time assisting family members.

Figure 7-9 shows the results for the average amount of time respon-

FIGURE 7-8. Providing Practical Assistance to Other Family Members

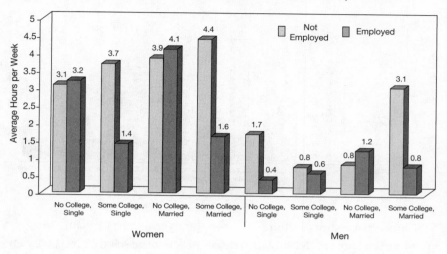

FIGURE 7-9. Providing Emotional Support to Family Members

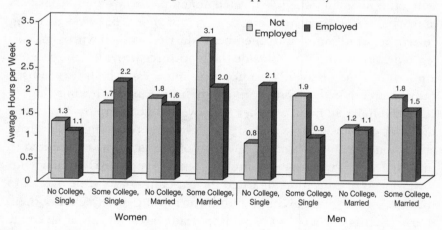

dents spent providing emotional support to family members. Again, married women with higher levels of education who were not participating in the paid workforce provided the greatest amount of emotional support to family members (3 hours per week, on average). This provision of emotional support was approximately 1 to 2 hours more than that provided by all other groups. In contrast, among men, single employed respondents with no college education provided the most emotional support.

FIGURE 7-10. Providing Practical Assistance to Their Communities

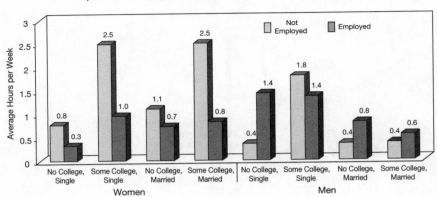

Figure 7-10 shows the results for the average amount of time respondents reported having provided practical assistance to those in their communities such as friends and co-workers. In comparison with other women, college-educated nonemployed women, regardless of marital status, spent an average of 1.5 more hours per week assisting co-workers and community members. Married women with some college education who were outside the workforce provided the greatest amount of time on average (2 hours 30 minutes), which was statistically greater than the average amount of time provided by more highly educated married men, whether employed or not (employed, 33 minutes; not employed, 23 minutes). Single women with higher levels of education were a close second in terms of average time committed to informal help (2 hours 29 minutes). Single employed women with lower levels of education allocated the least amount of time overall to this category of giving, with just under 20 minutes per week. For men, marital status appeared to be an important factor in this area: single men (with the exception of nonemployed non-college-educated ones) contributed almost twice as much time to assisting others than did married men.

Figure 7-11 shows the results for the average amount of time respondents spent each week providing emotional support to others in their communities. Compared to other groups, single women with some college education, regardless of their employment status, provided the greatest amount of emotional support to co-workers and

FIGURE 7-11. Providing Emotional Support to Their Community

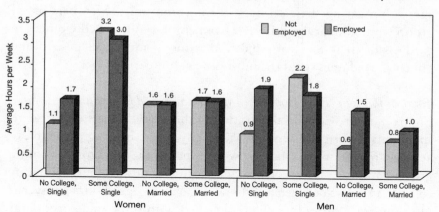

community members. These women spent significantly more time giving emotional support than did most of the married male groups. Single nonemployed men with some college education provided the third largest amount of time for the provision of emotional support to others in their communities, averaging 2 hours 12 minutes.

Figure 7-12 shows the results for the average amount of time respondents reported volunteering at community organizations. For men and women, employment status made a consistent difference in the amount of volunteer time. Nonemployed married women with

FIGURE 7-12. Volunteering in the Community

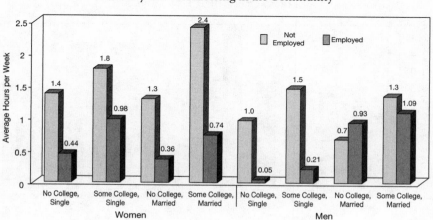

higher levels of education spent the greatest amount of time, on average, volunteering their services in the community. Members of this group were statistically different from employed married women, regardless of their level of education. Among men, college-educated nonemployed men spent the most time volunteering.

Total Amount of Time Contributing to Family and Community
Figure 7-13 provides an illustration of the overall amount of time respondents reported having provided any of the helping activities, on average, for the week. Married women not in the workforce spent the greatest amount of time, on average, caring for others (those with some college, 43 hours per week; those with no college, 32 hours per week). No significant differences were detected within the male groupings. When we excluded the amount of time spent providing child care (not shown in this figure), which accounted for most of the overall giving time, we found that nonemployed married women with higher levels of education still provided the greatest amount of care to others (on average, 14 hours per week), as compared to other groups. Among males, the groups that provided the least amount of time to overall giving were those who were married, were not employed, and had high levels of education. Other male groups were fairly similar in their overall giving patterns. The least amount of time, on average, for women

FIGURE 7-13. Total Time Giving

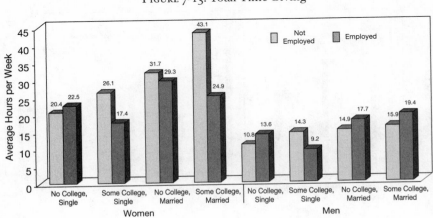

(6 hours 42 minutes) was provided by employed single individuals who had no college education.

CONCLUSION

The results presented in this chapter shed some light on who is spending the most time attending to the welfare of family, friends, and members of their communities. By focusing our social science microscope on giving experiences within the domains of family and community, we can begin to understand the sociodemographic patterns of their work, family, and community lives. Consistent with previous research, these findings showed giving behaviors to be multidimensional, weaving an intricate tapestry of work life, family life, and community life.[18] Furthermore, by widening the angle of our lens, we were able to capture the more familial aspects of giving and to provide what we believe to be a broader and more refined perspective on what it means to contribute to society. Finally, we showed that the availability of time on a daily basis and throughout the week was clearly associated with patterns of giving.[19] Our findings supported Robinson and Godbey's contention that the degree of discretion people have in regard to socially responsible behavior is associated with certain social and temporal factors.[20]

By examining the demographic evidence, we can create a composite of who is most likely to provide *any* care within the respective domains of family and community. Based on the results from Table 7-2, the person most likely to provide practical help to family members is a woman who works fewer hours and has a lower level of education. On the other hand, the typical person providing practical help to those in the workplace and community domains appears to be a single man with a higher level of education. Furthermore, more highly educated women are most likely to provide emotional support to relatives, and those who are single are most likely to provide that support to members of the community. The person most likely to volunteer in the community is a more highly educated married woman with children. Finally, our findings confirmed those of previous research and suggested that married mothers who work fewer hours are most likely to spend time with their children.

A slightly different pattern emerges when we consider the *amount of time* people spend in each of these caring domains (see Figures 7-5 through 7-11). Women are clearly likely to spend far more time than men in providing care. In addition, employment status appears to play an important role in individuals who provide care. However, the association between employment status and provision of care depends on the domain of care, level of education, and gender. Among college-educated women, those who are not employed are likely to spend more time than their employed counterparts in caring for family members and community. For women with no college education, employment status was less of a factor. Among men, those who are employed tended to provide more care than their nonemployed counterparts. Finally, our sixteen sociodemographic profiles suggest that nonemployed, college-educated, married women are likely to provide the most care, while employed, college-educated, single men are likely to provide the least care. The difference between these two profiles is almost 34 hours per week.

This pattern of findings indicates that social roles and the social connections arising from those roles shape how people will be able to provide for others. Those with fewer resources and fewer social connections outside of the family provide care and comfort to their family members. Those with greater resources and more expansive social networks, through work and their children's activities, are more outwardly focused in their provision of care. But, as Rossi has pointed out, caution must be taken in how we interpret family-focused versus community-focused socially responsible behaviors.[21] There is a tendency in American society to place greater value on socially responsible activities that are more publicly visible, such as participating in the political process or making large financial contributions. However, we must not underestimate the value to society of the woman who cares for an elderly parent or the man in the neighborhood who is always there to jump-start a car or help change a flat tire. These are the Good Samaritans of our communities who work silently, providing for others with little acclaim or public recognition. Furthermore, we must bear in mind that those with fewer resources must work all the harder to have extra to give. Those with fewer resources must spend a greater portion of their time trying to make ends meet.[22] Therefore, like the poor widow who casts but a farthing into the treasury (Luke 21:2;

Mark 12:42), those with less are giving not from an abundance, but from a limited amount of time, money, and energy left over after meeting their families' basic needs.

Spending more hours in the workplace detracts from the number of hours we have available to spend with our children, provide care to our families, and contribute to our communities. However, we can and do make the most of the time available to us. The question then arises: How does public and organizational policy support working families presently? And would policy changes alter the findings of this chapter? Clearly there is a wide range of workplace policies that could facilitate the ability to care for others, including flexible work schedules, sick-child care, and support for workers who need to take time to care for other family members. Less common are explicit policies that allow for nonmedical care for families and contributions to community. An evaluation of the Family and Medical Leave Act of 1993 (FMLA) provides some evidence concerning the impact of public policy on caring behaviors.[23]

The FMLA covers a portion of the U.S. workforce by requiring certain employers to provide up to twelve weeks of unpaid leave, full or intermittent, to employees in cases of personal illness or when caring for a family member. The Department of Labor compared usage of the FMLA between 1995 and 2000 and found that the percentage of employees taking advantage of the leave provisions increased over that time period (1.2 percent in 1995 to 1.9 percent in 2000) and that those reporting a need to take leave but the inability to afford one had decreased from 3.1 percent in 1995 to 2.4 percent in 2000. Respondents who took leave indicated positive effects on their ability to care for family members (78.7 percent) and to attend to their own well-being or that of another family member (70.1 percent). Furthermore, the study shows that employers not covered under the FMLA requirements have gradually increased leave benefits to their employees, perhaps as a means of being competitive in the labor market.

However, there are gaps in the utilization of leave benefits, according to the authors of the FMLA study. The reason most commonly cited for not taking advantage of leave policies was the inability to afford the unpaid leave (77.6 percent). In the 2000 survey, 87.8 percent of respondents who needed to take a leave but did not indicated that they "would have taken leave if some/additional pay had been received."

Nearly two-thirds of those taking a leave (65.8 percent) received at least partial pay during the leave period. In addition, there were other important reasons provided for not taking a leave, including fear of losing their job (31.9 percent), concern about a leave being detrimental to advancement (42.6 percent), and concern over losing seniority (15.1 percent).

A gender gap is also apparent among those who have utilized the leave provisions, with 58.1 percent of leave-takers being female. Of those with young children, there was a significant difference between women taking a leave (75.8 percent) and men taking a leave (45.1 percent). Levine and Pittinsky suggest that it is often the corporate or organizational culture that covertly discourages men from utilizing leave opportunities.[24] However, Pleck contends that men take advantage of "informal" leaves, in the form of sick or vacation time, to a greater extent than is typically reported.[25] Finally, those who are covered and eligible to take a leave under the FMLA provisions tended to be more highly educated as compared to those not covered, with 60.2 percent having graduated from college. Those covered also have significantly more household income as compared with those not covered.[26]

Clearly, the FMLA report demonstrates that public policies providing for leaves to care for ill family members can help to ease the burden of balancing work and family during a crisis. However, the FMLA is only a beginning in terms of the policies needed for working Americans to address family needs. Even with the FMLA, employees fear losing their jobs or jeopardizing opportunities for advancement if they take a leave. Many cannot afford the reduction in wages, and men are less likely to take advantage of such leave policies. For public and organizational policies to be effective in supporting family care, there needs to be a simultaneous change in organizational environments to better reflect an acceptance of leave utilization. Employees, especially men, must alter their attitudes to reflect a willingness to use leave opportunities for care of children and other relatives. Moreover, policies need to be developed so that working Americans can contribute to their communities.

Postscript: After numerous e-mails, faxes, messages on answering machines from work and home, and more than a few cups of coffee during Saturday morning meetings, the PTA fund-raiser mentioned at the beginning of this chapter went off without a hitch. Many contributed to the event's success in their own way. The students provided the entertainment. Various parents baked desserts. Those who were able moved tables and chairs and cleaned up afterward. Some people wrote out checks, and others gave of themselves. The end result, of course, totaled more than the funds raised.

Section III

Challenges to Moving Forward

8

Challenges to Change: The Invasion of the Money World

Christopher Beem

The Work, Family and Democracy Project contends that while the daily lives of working Americans have changed radically, our social institutions have done little to keep up with the pace of change. In this chapter, I offer one account of the challenges to change presented by our society, culture, and politics.

THREE NARRATIVES

Let me start by presenting brief definitions of the three value narratives that I think are most relevant to our American circumstance: the economic narrative, the civic narrative, and the public religion narrative. The descriptions that follow are idealized summaries in that they abstract from the stories to outline the values conveyed. This is not meant to be an exhaustive description—either of the narratives themselves or of the value narratives operative within American social history.[1]

The Economic Narrative

Economic rationality is the pursuit of self-interest, defined in material terms. Individuals act in the market in order to maximize profit, and they do that in order to increase their ability to acquire material goods. Entailed in that pursuit is the constant demand for efficiency (that is, producing as much as possible for as little cost as possible) and growth (expanding into new markets and expanding one's market share).

In terms that echo throughout American history from Benjamin Franklin to Horatio Alger to Bill Gates, these market goods have been seen as laudable social goods. The same goals that drive the entrepreneur—creativity, innovation, initiative, self-reliance, and cooperation—are described as benefiting society at large. The market narrative argues for freedom from governmental restraint in order to foster and reward these personal attributes. Limits to the pursuit of efficiency and growth are to come from the entrepreneur's own conscience, and from social constraints that operate within the market's own logic.

The Civic Narrative

The civic narrative, by contrast, concerns the values that are constitutive of a democratic society. Though the notion of what it means for the people to rule is complicated, contested, and never fully realized, democracy inevitably entails and lauds equality among the citizenry. Wrapped up within this commitment to equality and popular sovereignty is some notion of shared responsibility and concern for the commonweal. Inaugural speeches by Lincoln and Kennedy have become iconic precisely because they give voice to these ideals. So, too, do the stories of patriotism, duty, and sacrifice that American culture is replete with, from Molly Pitcher to Rosa Parks, from Sergeant York to the soldiers raising the flag at Iwo Jima. All of these are commonly associated with the civic narrative as well.

In his book *Democracy's Discontent,* political theorist Michael Sandel referred to implications of political equality this way:

> Sharing in self-rule involves . . . deliberating with fellow citizens about the common good and helping to shape the destiny of the political community. . . . It requires a knowledge of public affairs and also a sense of belonging, a concern for the whole, a moral bond with the community whose fate is at stake.[2]

The interest in children as future citizens and, accordingly, the desire to inculcate these concerns in children are part of the destiny to which Sandel refers, and are therefore also commonly associated with the civic narrative.

The Public Religion Narrative

The third relevant narrative is American public theology. Typically, nations derive norms and values from a complex amalgam of ethnicity, religion, history, and tradition. In doing this, American society has depended more heavily on a value system that is tied to a shared public religion.[3] By downplaying the idiosyncrasies of specific Christian denominations, and later of Judaism and other religions, American public religion functions as a kind of lowest-common-denominator faith, sanctifying the social order, informing public discourse, and buttressing cultural norms and values.[4]

This religious narrative echoes and reinforces basic features of democratic life—"that all men are created equal, [and] that they are endowed by their Creator with certain unalienable Rights." Drawing from its Puritan roots, American public theology has also been occupied with personal sin, viewing it as an ineradicable element of every human life. It has likewise celebrated stories of sacrifice, giving, and concern for others. Here, too, the moral upbringing of children features prominently, as does the desire to preserve the family.[5] Finally, analysts have frequently noted that public religion in America moderates but does not condemn the materialist bent within American society, decrying only the single-minded pursuit of consumption and acquisition.[6]

The Interplay of Narratives

The content and application of these narratives have changed throughout American history. Americans' understanding of the proper restraint of the economic sphere, for example, was dramatically different in the Gilded Age, the Progressive Era, and the Reagan administration. Consensus surrounding these narratives has likewise waxed and waned. Before and during the Civil War, it was virtually destroyed; in the 1950s, by contrast, historians acknowledge that consensus was particularly strong. Yet despite radical changes in every aspect of the American experience, these narratives and the values and beliefs contained therein are perennial within American culture. This notion of constancy within change is captured in the words of Henry Steele Commager:

To Crèvecoeur's famous question, "What, then, is an American?" Crèvecoeur himself, Tocqueville, and Bryce, each separated by half a century, returned much the same answer. It required almost a new vocabulary to do justice to the changes in material circumstances which each successive generation of interpreters discerned, but for the analysis of character, the old vocabulary sufficed.[7]

What is more, American society has also been characterized by the interplay between these narratives. Public religion, civic associations, and the market checked each other's influence, creating a balance that was itself uniquely American. This balance, in turn, helped to account for many of the civic innovations in American history. In the words of Theda Skocpol:

American democracy flourished within a unique matrix of state and society. Not only was America the world's first manhood democracy and the first nation in the world to establish mass public education, it also had a uniquely balanced civic life, in which markets expanded but could not subsume civil society, in which governments at multiple levels deliberately and indirectly encouraged federated voluntary associations.[8]

DOMINANCE OF THE ECONOMIC NARRATIVE

Assuming this is a fair characterization of American culture, the operative question, of course, is: What is the condition of these narratives and that balance in contemporary American society? In 1992, sociologist Robert Bellah (the principal author of *The Habits of the Heart*) wrote an article titled "The Invasion of the Money World." Applying terms coined by German philosopher Jürgen Habermas, Bellah argued that the problems associated with contemporary American families resulted from the fact that the "systems" ("the market economy and the administrative state") have invaded the "lifeworld" ("the family, the church and the public").

I think Bellah is correct to argue that our society is currently plagued by an imbalance between these narratives—that is, by the invasion of market thinking into what were once inaccessible social domains. More importantly, I think he is correct to argue that this imbalance stems from the fact that American narratives that express a different set of values have declined and are unable (or at least significantly less able) to prevent the expansion of economic rationality.

In this chapter, I want to argue that our society's apparent inability to address the problems associated with work and family stems from this invasion. To make this argument, I describe four recent and rapid changes in American society. I use these changes as examples of what I take to be a broad and deep shift in the American social fabric—namely, the invasion of economic rationality into social realms formerly dominated by civic or public religious narratives. What follows is by no means a systematic account; indeed, I have tried to choose examples that are not well known or obviously related to the subject at hand. My objective is to show that our society has undergone a broad, rapid, and dramatic change, and that this change forms the broader social context in which we must address problems of work, family, and democracy.

Legal Advertising

Upon being admitted to the state bar, lawyers take an oath to uphold the Constitution and the laws of the state. Along with judges, they are at that point understood to be "officers of the court." This ritual oath taking is meant to underscore the point that lawyers occupy a unique civic role and that they are duty-bound to fulfill it.

This same understanding accounts for the fact that in 1908, the American Bar Association (ABA) forbade lawyers from advertising their services. This rule—which had its roots in English common law and which already existed in many state bar associations—reflected the ABA's desire "to preserve the dignity . . . of the profession by promoting its altruistic 'service' aspects while downplaying the practical profit motives that would equalize law with characteristics of businesses in the 'goods' market."[9] To be sure, this ban had not been transmitted continuously from the days of English common law. Throughout much of American history, and especially in nineteenth-century frontier areas, lawyers routinely advertised their services.[10] Nevertheless, the idea appears repeatedly in American jurisprudence that the legal profession occupies a unique position within society and performs an essential public service—a service over and above providing direct legal counsel—that requires its members to concern themselves with more than simply the profit motive.[11]

In 1977, the Supreme Court ruled in *Bates v. State of Arizona* that the ABA prohibition violated First Amendment rights regarding commercial speech. Citing their earlier ruling allowing advertising by pharmacists (*Virginia State Board of Pharmacy v. Virginia Citizens Consumer Council*), the Court concluded that professions could advertise and still maintain their distinctive professional status.[12] They also noted that "the belief that lawyers are somehow 'above' trade ha[d] become an anachronism."[13] Decades later, questions persist about whether the profession can develop effective standards for advertising, and what the effects of increased adverting are on the public's perception of the legal profession. But there is no doubt that legal advertising is now well established. In the mid-1990s (the last period for which data are available), "lawyers spen[t] over half a billion dollars per year on advertising in the Yellow Pages and on television alone."[14]

Naming Rights for Stadiums

From their inception, professional sports teams in America were identified with specific municipalities or regions, and venues for those teams were commonly given names referencing the organizations that had paid for their construction. Thus, stadium names reflected team identity (as with Tiger Stadium and Yankee Stadium), ownership (as with Comiskey Park and Wrigley Field), or history (as with Lambeau Field).

Many such venues were constructed primarily or exclusively with the use of public funds. These venues received names that, at minimum, acknowledged the public ownership (such as County Stadium in Milwaukee and Municipal Stadium in Cleveland), and many received names that reflected civic pride or lauded some civic virtue. Others were named after some unique and celebrated geographical feature of their host cities, such as Three Rivers Stadium in Pittsburgh, Riverfront Stadium in Cincinnati, Candlestick Park in San Francisco, and Mile High Stadium in Denver.[15] Many stadiums were given names that commemorated the service and sacrifice of veterans, such as Soldier Field, Memorial Stadium, and Veterans' Stadium. Some were named after a civic figure. For instance, Shea Stadium was named after William A. Shea, an attorney who helped New York acquire a new baseball franchise after the Giants and the Dodgers moved to California. D.C. Stadium, in the nation's capital, was renamed the Robert F. Kennedy Memorial Stadium after Kennedy's assassination. War Memorial Stadium (Buffalo), so named from 1960 to 1972, was one venue that reflected all three possibilities, in that its previous names had been Grover Cleveland Stadium (the original) and Civic Stadium.[16]

The connection between public financing for sports venues and the naming of those venues for public purposes effectively ended in 1985. In that year, the Atlantic Richfield Corporation paid $7.5 million to the Sacramento Kings for the right to name the Kings' new basketball arena ARCO Arena.[17] That transaction began a trend that is now ubiquitous within American professional sports.[18]

Sports franchises continue to routinely negotiate substantial public financing to allay the costs of construction for a new stadium (and many leverage their financing deals with threats to move the franchise).[19] On average, more than two-thirds of the construction costs for new baseball and football stadiums are paid for with public money. But now, upon completion of the stadiums, the teams routinely sell the naming rights for the buildings to private corporations and then divide that revenue with the host cities. The corporation sees the rights as a creative and cost-effective way of building brand identity, prestige, and brand loyalty within a community. The cities use their share to reduce the public cost of the construction. It should be noted that these transactions are frequently approved in advance through public referendums, thus demonstrating that the public would rather have a marginally lower tax increase than stadium names that reflect public investment or civic pride.[20]

Marketing in Public Schools

Throughout American history, educators have argued that public education is the preeminent means by which our society realizes equality of opportunity. In the work of Horace Mann, John Dewey, and others, public education was understood as an essential means for inculcating a common American identity and democratic ethos, and curricula were developed in service of this larger social desideratum. For well over 100 years, public schools have cultivated an identity as a place devoted to both enlightenment and democracy.

In 1989, Channel One began providing an innovative service for school districts struggling with budget cuts and dwindling revenue. In exchange for the right to deliver ten minutes of news (broadly construed) and two minutes of ads each day to junior high and high school students, Channel One provided the district with VCRs and television sets. Advertisers were quick to take advantage of this unique marketing opportunity. In part, they responded to claims such as this one, made in 1994 by the then-president of Channel One:

> The biggest selling point to advertisers [is that] we are forcing kids to watch two minutes of commercials. . . . The advertiser gets a group of kids who cannot go to the bathroom, who cannot change the station, who cannot listen to their mother yell in the background, who cannot be playing Nintendo, who cannot have their headsets on.[21]

The notion of "forcing" children is not overstated. According to Naomi Klein, "Turning off the cheerful ad patter is not an option. Not only is the programming mandatory for viewing for students, but teachers are unable to adjust the volume of the broadcast, especially during commercials."[22]

Educators and parents responded to this new initiative with outrage, insisting that schools should remain free of advertising. Russ Baker noted that initially,

> [t]he service faced heavy criticism from liberal groups and from educational powerhouses such as the national Parent-Teacher Association, the American Federation of Teachers (AFT), the National Education Association (NEA), and various principals' associations; even the American Academy of Pediatrics frowned upon for-profit classroom television.[23]

But as budgeting woes continued (and frequently, during the 1990s, worsened) more and more local school systems rejected such arguments. For many districts, signing up for Channel One service has proven the only way—or at any rate, the only viable way—to procure long-sought technology. In addition (though the point is contested), they also have noted that Channel One has provided many students with their only exposure to national news. Finally, many parents concluded that they were fighting a losing battle. In Naomi Klein's words, "Many parents and educators could not see anything to be gained by resistance; kids today are so bombarded by brand names that it seemed as if protecting education spaces from commercialization was less important than the immediate benefits of finding new funding sources." [24]

Though the disputes about Channel One are continuing, the product undeniably has become an established feature in many public schools. As of 2000, the programming was beamed into twelve thousand schools every school day. In that same year, a Government Accounting Office (GAO) report estimated that 25 percent of the nation's junior high and high schools were showing Channel One. [25] The report also noted that Channel One was only one of a number of innovative marketing strategies developed within public schools during the 1980s and 1990s. Over the past decade, two hundred school districts around the nation have established exclusive agreements with soft drink manufacturers, and many more have accepted corporation-sponsored educational materials to supplement established curricula. [26]

The GAO report acknowledged that this trend had raised concerns, and it concluded that "often the values of school board members, district officials, and parents determine whether an activity is controversial or not, rather than the nature of the activity itself." [27] The contemporary state of affairs may well reveal a declining consensus on those values and their relative status, and in their absence, parents and educators are ill equipped to argue against a well-financed company that appears to save school districts much-needed money.

State-Sponsored Gambling: Lotteries

Lotteries have appeared frequently in American history. In fact, "lotteries were frequently used in colonial-era America to finance public works projects such as paving streets, constructing wharves, and even building churches." [28] Over time, other lotteries have been state-sponsored; some have been illegal, such as the inner-city policy games of the late nineteenth and early twentieth centuries; and some have been quasi-legal, such as the Irish Sweepstakes. Nevertheless, from 1894 to 1964, lotteries were effectively outlawed in the United States.

The arguments against gambling have been almost exclusively moral and religious ones. Gambling, some have claimed, encourages indolence and vice, and causes workers to squander their paychecks, often resulting in mothers and children being left without needed resources.[29] However, the move against lotteries that began in the 1870s was not fundamentally an argument about sin; rather, it stemmed from a political scandal involving the Louisiana state lottery. After uncovering massive corruption involving kickbacks and prizes that were never awarded, the public asserted that neither the state nor its citizens should be involved in such a corrupting business. Thus, until about forty years ago, there were no government-sponsored U.S. lotteries—indeed, there were effectively no legal lotteries anywhere in the United States.[30]

In 1963, according to David Nibert, New Hampshire had one of the least well funded public school systems in the United States. With its long libertarian, antitax tradition, New Hampshire also had no state property or income taxes.[31] A state-run lottery seemed to offer a way to fill state coffers without raising taxes, and voters approved it in 1963. On March 3, 1964, the governor bought the first ticket. While many states in the Northeast followed suit in the seventies, it was not until New Hampshire's problem spread that the solution did likewise. During the 1980s, states faced a four-sided dilemma: first, the Reagan administration cut many federal programs; second, citizens were not willing to accept a decline in levels of governmental service; third, most states could not, by law, run a budget deficit; and fourth, there was strong popular resistance to any tax increase. It was in response to this crisis that lotteries became an ever more common solution. By 1988, twenty-three states had established lotteries. By 1999, thirty-eight states had state-run lotteries, and every state except Utah and Hawaii had some form of legalized gambling.[32]

Nibert acknowledged that during the 1980s, "ethical and moral arguments against the revival of lotteries were abundant." Many citizen groups struggled mightily to keep their states out of the gambling business. But he concluded that those "ethical issues about appropriate ways to raise public revenue were largely eclipsed by economic pressures."[33] Thus, while this abrupt change did not mean that Americans were unconcerned with questions about state-sponsored gambling, those concerns did not carry the day.[34] Indeed, many states instituted lotteries only after putting the matter before a public vote.

THE TIPPING OF THE SCALES

I am not trying to argue that each of these changes is universally bad. Still less am I arguing for a return to some kind of moral status quo ante. Rather, I use these examples to demonstrate a more fundamental proposition: that in an astonishingly brief period of time, the previous social understanding of the limits within which the market was supposed to operate has changed radically. Over the course of a little more than a decade, our society changed its mind about the balance between the values of the marketplace and other values. In every instance recounted thus far, the pursuit of profit or (in what amounts to the same thing) the unwillingness to expend added resources has proven sufficient to swamp the concerns more closely associated with the civic and public religion narratives. As a result, the notion of who advertises, where, and for what purposes has expanded dramatically, and the market and market values intrude into our social lives in ways that would not have been contemplated, let alone tolerated, even a generation ago.

The broad notion that there has been a dramatic change in the moral condition of American society is not controversial. To be sure, the idea that our problems are related to the expansion of market thinking is not a common refrain, but public opinion polls have demonstrated a long-standing and widespread belief that morals have declined in our society. It is also fair to say that the relative status of the civic narrative and the role of religion in opposing the economic narrative have declined in American society since, say, the end of World War II.[35] In what remains, I want to focus on what this change means for the relationship between work, family, and democracy.

WORK, FAMILY, AND DEMOCRACY

The Time Crunch

Workers report that they are working longer hours, sleeping less, and participating in social and leisure activities less than they did even five years ago.[36] What is more, 80 percent of parents have reported that their biggest worry is that they do not spend enough time with their children. To be sure, the question of whether and how much working hours have increased is a contentious one, and the data are difficult to sort out. Nevertheless, there is good reason to believe that these feelings reflect reality. Robert Putnam has attributed as much as 10 percent of the decline in civic participation to longer commutes and lengthening of the workday.[37] Juliet Schor reports that in the last decades of the twentieth century, overtime hours increased, as did rates of second-job holding, and working hours among suburban high school students rose.[38] And in perhaps the most famous study, Schor contended that in 1987 "the average employed person [was] on the job an additional 163 hours, or the equivalent of one extra month a year."[39] Regarding the effects of these changes on families, a study by Victor Fuchs showed that "between 1960 and 1986 household time available for children went down sharply."[40] On the contrary, a recent University of Michigan study concluded that working married women in 1997 spent just as much time with their children as nonworking mothers did in 1981. However, it noted that time women spent for themselves and time they spent sleeping had both declined.[41] The differences between these studies are important, but both point to the larger issue: increased work means less time for other things, and those other things—whether family time or time devoted to social and civic pursuits—have had to give.

Importantly, Americans appear not only to be working more hours but also to be working more often during nontraditional hours. According to the Bureau of Labor Statistics, "almost 30 percent of the nation's workforce worked outside the 9 A.M. to 5 P.M. time frame in 1997, up from 15 percent of the workforce in 1991; and 17 percent worked hours that fell outside of the 6 A.M. to 6 P.M. period."[42] The point is that if parents are working during evening or weekend hours, the possibility for meaningful interaction with children or other family members declines regardless of how many hours they are on the job. Yet, most of those who work evening and night hours do so out of necessity, not choice. Furthermore, while work hours may be interchangeable for a corporation, they are not for a family. A study by Jody Heymann and Alison Earle showed that parental evening work was "associated with a negative impact on the capacity of the home environment to support children's development."[43]

The Limits of Market Solutions

Just as the invasion of money has exacerbated the tension between work and family life, so too has it affected the climate within which the needed changes must be addressed. Solutions to the problems of work and family are not hard to come by, and the felicitous effects of paid parental leave, universal preschool, and after-school centers are well established. The problem is that we cannot muster the civic will to address these problems in the political arena, because those alternative expressions of value have declined in public discourse and public understanding. Because the market is ascendant, we have only the market to turn to for solutions. Because civic and governmental solutions cannot at this point garner sufficient public support, we are left to pursue accommodations within the corporation and, hence, within economic rationality. When that strategy fails, every family is left to shift for itself.

It must be said that accommodations with the marketplace are possible. Employers who provide perks such as flextime or on-site day care are more likely to have satisfied employees, and employee satisfaction is tied to higher productivity and job retention rates. As long as a corporation is willing to evaluate profitability over the long term (something that is increasingly difficult for publicly traded corporations), prospects for work-family accommodations are real and important. But while these arguments are surely worth pursuing, they can never adequately address the problems we face.

In the first place, there is the problem of scale. Not all of these solutions can be adequately accommodated by every employer. For example, most small employers are not large enough to justify the expense of an on-site day care center, no matter how much their employees would appreciate it. Furthermore, because the Family and Medical Leave Act exempts businesses that employ fewer than fifty workers, even the minimal benefits of that law are frequently unavailable to fully half of all American workers.

Second, as Heymann has demonstrated, market-based solutions are far more likely to be available to those at the high end of the labor market.[44] As a result, the more financially burdened a family is, the less likely it is that the family is going to be able to accommodate the realities of both work and care. The not-so-tender mercies of the labor market are turning the ability to balance work and family responsibilities into a perquisite.

But the larger problem is more fundamental: even those employers who can introduce these innovations are constrained by the market. They can offer solutions only insofar as they are cost-effective, that is, insofar as they help employers achieve a profit. But the profit motive cannot always accommodate problems that revolve around different—and in some cases competing—concerns. As one example, many large corporations offer on-site child care services, which are often great success stories for everyone involved. But what do parents do when their child is sick? Some employers provide special on-site child care even if the child is sick with a cold or the flu. Others subsidize a service whereby qualified professionals go to the family home to care for the child. These innovations address the basic needs of the child, even as they reveal the limits of marketplace accommodation. The question is not whether the facility or the caregiver is good enough (though these are not always adequate); rather, it is whether these options can possibly respond adequately to the child's needs.

The idea of packing up a sick child and driving him or her to a child care center or leaving that child in the care of a stranger simply cannot be understood to be in the best interest of the child. Rather, corporations pursue these and similar accommodations because they address the problem in the most cost-effective manner—that is, they enable working parents to keep working.[45] According to the National Association of Sick Child Daycare, parents who take time off from work to care for their sick children cost businesses between $2 billion and $12 billion annually.[46] Yet the most frequently used alternatives, which may well be the best available within the confines of the profit motive and which are surely better than a parent losing his or her job, do not begin to accommodate the demands of sick children's care. Sylvia Ann Hewlett and Cornel West are correct when they say that parenting (and, by extension, all care) is "the ultimate nonmarket activity."[47] And because it is, we Americans cannot expect that such an activity could be addressed adequately within market rationality.

WHAT TO DO?

Clearly, we face an extremely difficult problem. The issues associated with work and family transcend the limits of the employer-employee relationship, and yet, because of the invasion of the money world, any other moral resource by which we might deal with them appears inadequate, if not wholly moribund. But how, then, are we to proceed? The next two sections of the book will seek to address this question. While their suggestions are critically important, they are unlikely to succeed without restoring cultural limits to the money world. And that restoration, in turn, may not be possible without a more robust civic narrative and a narrative of public religion arguing for the limits on the monetary one. Strategies for such a cultural reclamation are beyond the scope of this chapter. More to the point, in the short term, the problem is a political one: how can our society develop the constituencies that can face up to the market and effect political change?

Resist the Money World's Invasion

If work and family issues are caught up with the invasion of the money world, then it will not do for advocates to ignore the broader set of concerns. The specific problems associated with work and family manifest a broader social condition. They can therefore best—and, perhaps, only—be addressed if the broader framework changes, which means that advocates should pursue any opportunity to push back the invasion. Many parents have committed themselves to resisting the new consumerism in their own lives. Web sites such as retroparents.com, adbusters.com, and familylife1st.com offer ideas and support to families trying to place limits on the demands of the marketplace. These include curtailing or at least limiting television, helping children deconstruct the advertising they do watch, and restoring family meals and family evenings. But this resistance must become broader and more explicitly political. Those concerned about work and family issues should look at advertising in the public schools, for example, as a work and family issue. They must also frame a range of other issues in broader terms. For example, work-family advocates should help others (such as policy makers) understand after-school programs not merely as child care but as a necessary innovation that enables our ever-changing society to better meet children's needs for moral, civic, and social formation. Finally, in service to these broader political ends, advocates should be willing to explore unlikely political alliances. The invasion of the money world is most clearly demonstrated in the power of money in politics. In light of that political dynamic, advocates must be willing to find allies wherever they may be. To note one example, both Ralph Nader and the Southern Baptists have denounced Channel One.

Make Civic and Political Life Family-Friendly

As noted thus far, work and family problems are exacerbated by the invasion of the money world. We are left without the resources to resist demands that we work more than we want to, and our family, social, and civic commitments suffer as a result. In order to reinvigorate forces for political change, we therefore must find ways for people to be political and civic without worsening their time bind. In short, we must find ways to make civic and political life family-friendly. That does not mean simply providing child care at a union meeting, for example (though, of course, that should be done). It also means, as Theda Skocpol has noted, that we should engage families through the organizations and activities in which they are already involved—day care, schools, sports leagues, and congregations. Finally (and this is also similar to a point that Skocpol has made), it means that parents and other caregivers cannot devote time to civic life unless they can do so in ways that involve their family as a family. We must therefore develop or rediscover activities that combine civic and political engagement with recreation. In short, we must make politics fun for the whole family. In generations past, settlement houses, ethnic societies, and fraternal organizations were very good at making the connection between the social and the political and thereby involving the whole family. How might we find a connection that works in our time and place?

Here are three ideas: Naomi Klein refers to the Reclaim the Street movement, in which young people use the Internet to take over a busy intersection with a spontaneous party. Klein calls this effort to create, however briefly, a public, uncommercialized space "the most vibrant and fastest-growing movement since Paris '68."[48] To be sure, she also acknowledges that these events sometimes degenerate into "some jerk demanding the right to sit in the middle of the street for a loony reason known only to him."[49] But at its best, the Reclaim the Street movement parodies consumer culture in a way that is vibrant, social, and fun, as well as political. More conventionally, Howard Dean's campaign also used the Internet to arrange "meet-ups" between supporters. Indeed, these events were one of the principal means by which the campaign rallied the troops, and at least some were explicitly designed to attract the whole family, including picnics, Halloween parties, and the like. Rodolfo de la Garza, of Columbia University, has proposed that neighborhood associations in Latino communities host neighborhood parties on the evening of Election Day: entrance would be free, but adults would have to show a ballot stub to get in. All these ideas are new and have met with varying degrees of success (in fact, de la Garza's has not even been tried), but all suggest a new kind of politics where the families can be welcome as families. Even in their nascent form, they provide hope for future innovation.

As limited as such suggestions are, they at least point to the fact that developing a broad understanding of our social circumstance is prerequisite to understanding the specific problems of work and family. Just so, they might help to demonstrate that expanding our concept of work and family issues offers perhaps the best strategy we have for addressing them.

9

The Paradox of Corporate Solutions: Accomplishments, Limitations, and New Opportunities

Marcie Pitt-Catsouphes and Bradley K. Googins

The contemporary concept of the family-friendly workplace emerged in the 1980s and matured during the 1990s, a time when increasing percentages of women, particularly the mothers of young children, were entering the labor market. Just twenty years ago, there was a 27 percentage point difference in the labor force participation rates for men and women. In 1980, only 51.2 percent of women (sixteen years and older) were in the labor force, compared to 78.2 percent of men. The U.S. Bureau of Labor Statistics anticipates this difference will be reduced to 13 percentage points by 2008, with estimates that 61.5 percent of women and 74.5 percent of men will be in the labor force at that time. One of the most dramatic changes in U.S. labor force demographics has been the labor force participation of married women: in 1970, 40.5 percent were in the civilian labor force; in 2000, 61.3 percent.[1]

This shift in women's employment patterns has been a global phenomenon, but countries have responded in different ways to the new realities of working families.[2] Some nations have promulgated public policies that offer security and services to families, especially those with dependent-care responsibilities. For example, the 1993 Maastricht Agreement and subsequent agreements adopted by the European Union have established protections for particular employee groups, such as working parents, in an effort to promote social inclusion and equity at the workplace. In the United States, the emphasis has been placed *not* on the promulgation of public sector policies but rather on the development of family-friendly workplaces as the first line of defense against potentially serious work-family conflicts.

FACING REALITIES:
WORKPLACE WORK-FAMILY INITIATIVES

Although there is no single, operational definition of the family-friendly workplace, many people have suggested that it has four important dimensions.[3] First, there are numerous policies, services, and benefits that can fall under the rubric of work-family policies and programs (often designated as "work-life" by employers).[4] Employer-supported policies and programs are sometimes categorized into five basic groups: dependent-care supports (for example, information and referral, subsidies, and on-site caregiving programs such as child development centers), flexible work and alternative work options (such as flexible scheduling, part-time work, and home-based work), family and career leaves (such as paid parental leaves and sabbaticals), financial assistance (for example, subsidies for specific family expenses such as college tuition), and quality-of-life benefits (such as health insurance and long-term care insurance). Many work-family champions have noted that these programs and policies are "necessary, but not sufficient" for the establishment of a family-friendly workplace.[5]

Second, studies have suggested that employees' perceptions of the supportiveness of workplace cultures are related to employee and family outcomes such as work-family balance and life satisfaction. Analysis of the data from a 1997 *Business Week* study, which had nearly twelve thousand employee respondents, revealed strong relationships between employees' perceptions of workplace culture, the quality of their work experiences, their work-family balance, and their life satisfaction. For example, 51.4 percent of the respondents who reported that the culture of their workplaces was supportive (as measured by the Workplace Culture Index) felt they had "very good" work-family balance, whereas only 1.8 percent of those in workplaces with unsupportive cultures felt that their work-family balance was good.[6] Workplace values and expectations may also affect the use of work-family supports, such as an employee's gradual return to work after a leave. As Fried noted in her study of employees' use of parental leave options, workers may be hesitant to use particular work-family programs and policies if they are concerned that they could jeopardize their careers or their workplaces by doing so.[7]

Third, studies of the supportiveness of workplace relationships have suggested that employees' relationships with supervisors and co-workers may affect employees' work-family outcomes.[8] In the 1997 National Study of the Changing Workforce conducted by the Families and Work Institute, which gathered information from a nationally representative sample of 2,788 employees, most employees felt that their immediate supervisors were supportive of their work-family experiences. For instance, 91 percent of the respondents agreed with the statement "My supervisor is understanding when I talk about personal or family issues that affect my work," and 76 percent agreed with the statement "I feel comfortable bringing up personal or family issues with my supervisor."[9] Clearly, the absence of such supportive relationships constrains the possibility of a workplace being perceived as family-friendly.

The fourth dimension of the family-friendly company—family-sensitive work systems, processes, and job design—is tied to the work itself. Rapoport and her colleagues conducted a groundbreaking study linking work-family experiences to work processes. The results of their study, and subsequent work conducted by Bailyn and colleagues, suggest that improvements in ineffective and inefficient work systems can affect employees' work-family outcomes.[10]

Public interest in the family-friendly workplace was sustained during the 1980s and 1990s, a time of unprecedented economic growth. However, the twenty-first century—which began with a pronounced recession—may lead to different work and family priorities and concerns. Therefore, the emphasis on developing family-friendly workplaces may no longer fit with current challenges and opportunities. Since work-family conundrums continue to challenge working families and their employers, we, as a nation, must carefully consider how much emphasis to place on the strategy of creating family-friendly workplaces. It is time for work-family leaders to grapple with questions such as the following:

- Do we anticipate that the current level of employer interest in family-friendly workplaces will be sustained, despite the vicissitudes in our economy and the increasing demands that employers will be placing on employees?

- Can we expect the number of family-friendly workplaces to continue growing to the point where a majority of U.S. workplaces will eventually offer their employees comprehensive work-family supports?
- Is there sufficient evidence that the policies and benefits associated with the family-friendly workplace can, by themselves, appreciably improve the quality of life for working families?
- Is it realistic to assume that organizations currently at the forefront of the family-friendly workplace movement will be willing to do even more on behalf of working families?
- What are the societal consequences if our country continues to rely on the voluntary provision of comprehensive workplace-based policies and programs?

In this chapter, we outline three approaches to the framing of work-family issues. Then we examine the accomplishments, limitations, and new opportunities for employer-supported work-family initiatives. We hope this chapter can contribute to public discussions about the need for new ways to promote the quality of life for working families.

THE MULTIPLE REALITIES OF WORK-FAMILY ISSUES: THREE KEY PARADIGMS

As has been long observed, the paradigms we use to think about our ideas and experiences do, in fact, influence the observations we make and the conclusions we accept about social phenomena.[11] To date, three paradigms have dominated the American conceptualization of work-family issues. These models are not mutually exclusive, however, and each has become increasingly nuanced over the decades. Table 9-1, which highlights the three paradigms' roots, reflects both the contrasts and the overlaps in these approaches.

According to the first paradigm, work-family issues are principally women's issues because women tend to assume the majority of family dependent-care responsibilities and because they tend to face more

TABLE 9-1. Roots of Work-Family Paradigms

Historical Framing of Issue	What Was the Problem Perceived to Be?	What Were the Priority Concerns?	Who Was Seen as Being Primarily Responsible?
Paradigm 1: In the 1960s and 1970s, work and family discussions emerged as part of the discourse around the women's movement. At that time, work-family issues were seen as affecting a small percentage of the population. These families, such as single-parent families, were sometimes seen as "families at risk."	Work-family conflicts were often perceived to be the consequence of nontraditional family roles and structures.	There was concern that maternal employment might be deleterious to children's development and families' well-being.	The resolution of work-family conflicts was seen as a private matter for women who chose or had to work. There was sentiment that mothers who chose to work were putting their personal needs above the needs of their children and families.
Paradigm 2: In the late 1970s and the 1980s, trends such as increases in the number of dual-earner families resulted in work-family issues being perceived more as normative experiences and affecting a range of families. Since the structures of and roles within families had begun to shift, work-family issues became less stigmatized. The focus was placed on developing supports and services that could minimize negative outcomes.	The entry of mothers into the workforce created a dependent care crisis for many working families.	It was anticipated that work-family conflicts could largely be resolved once a sufficient level of quality resources was developed (particularly dependent care services).	Although working women often continued to shoulder the bulk of home life responsibilities, there was growing acknowledgment that the shifts in family structure affected all family members, including men. Families were seen as being primarily responsible for securing the resources they needed to ensure that family and work responsibilities could be met.
Paradigm 3: In the 1980s and 1990s, work-family conflicts began to spill more visibly over into the workplace. Work-family champions advocated recognizing these issues as relevant workplace concerns.	There was growing recognition that work-family conflicts could be problematic for the workplace, as well as the family. Discussions began about the characteristics of family and workplace systems that contributed to the challenges confronting working families.	Leaders advocated changes in family systems (e.g., reconsideration of fathers' role), as well as in workplace systems (e.g., flexibility, work hours, workplace culture, the design of work itself), so that work-family concerns could be adequately addressed.	It was increasingly seen as appropriate for workplaces to share the responsibilities for addressing problems with employees/families.

barriers than men in the workplace. Some of the challenges that women encounter at the workplace are connected to their caregiving responsibilities. There is a rich tradition in feminist discourse that focuses on the discriminatory impact of gender on the constraints and opportunities related to people's work-family situations.[12]

Proponents of the second paradigm contend that appreciably improving working families' quality of life necessitates viewing work-family issues as relevant to, and owned by, men as well as women.[13] By expanding the focus from women to dual-career families, this paradigm's supporters have increased the recognition that many working men, as well as women, are affected by work-family experiences, conflicts, and priorities.[14]

The third paradigm's adherents see work-family issues as being relevant to the contexts of both home and work, in that employers, as well as families, have a stake in addressing work-family conflicts. Thus, work-family issues are framed as legitimate business concerns.[15] This paradigm began to gain more widespread acceptance in the 1990s, particularly during those years when the robust economy triggered heavy competition for talent among employers in particular industries. Furthermore, as the numbers of employees with dependent-care responsibilities and those in dual-income families continued to rise,[16] a small but increasing number of employers began to acknowledge that unresolved work-family conflicts were spilling over into the workplace, with the potential for negative consequences for the workplace.[17] One of the powerful conclusions that has emerged from the third paradigm is that employers could and *should* respond to at least some of the most pressing work-family conflicts.

Interest in the third approach to work-family issues increased during the 1990s. That decade witnessed the creation of several professional associations for work-family practitioners such as the Association of Work/Life Professionals, the establishment of the work-family feature column in the *Wall Street Journal,* and the publication of *The Corporate Reference Guide to Work-Family Programs* by the Families and Work Institute,[18] which provided employers with a developmental assessment for evaluating their progress toward providing a family-friendly workplace.[19] These are some of the early benchmarks of the interest in the family-friendly work environment. Where are we today?

ACCOMPLISHMENTS OF THE
FAMILY-FRIENDLY WORKPLACE STRATEGY

By some accounts, substantial progress has been made in the work-family arena. As a society, we are still interested in and intrigued by work-family issues, both as social trends and as personal experiences. Public awareness about today's work and family dilemmas is high, in part due to continued media attention, such as the 2001 Public Broadcasting Service production *Juggling Work and Family*.[20] A steady stream of articles about work and family experiences continues to appear in newspapers, magazines, and academic journals. Furthermore, the phenomenal growth in the number of work-family studies has resulted in a much more sophisticated understanding of these issues.[21]

The number of workplaces offering at least some family-supportive policies and programs has increased steadily, if slowly, and employer-supported information and referral services, alternative work schedules, flexible benefits, and other supports for family life and household management have become more widely available, especially at large corporations.[22] The U.S. Department of Labor tracks the availability of some work-family benefits. Data from the department's Employee Benefits Survey have indicated that in 1988 only 12 percent of employees in medium and large businesses were provided reimbursement accounts (for business-related expenses), whereas 32 percent were in 1997. Child care was available to 4 percent of employees in 1988 and to 7 percent in 1993 (the last year when this statistic was reported).[23]

The 1998 Business Work-Life Study conducted by Galinsky and Bond, of the Families and Work Institute, collected information from a national sample of U.S. firms with one hundred or more employees. This study is currently the only comprehensive research on U.S. companies' work-family policies and programs.[24] As indicated in Table 9-2, a majority of the employers offered some work-family policies and programs to their employees, such as leaves to attend their children's school functions. However, only a small percentage of employers had established other types of work-family supports, such as subsidies to help defray the costs of child care.

This study and others have suggested that four sets of factors affect if, when, and how firms respond to work-family issues. First, a num-

TABLE 9-2. Percentage of Workplaces with 100+ Employees Offering
Work-Family Policies and Programs (*n* = 1,057 workplace respondents)

Type of Policy/Program	Percentage Offering
Flexible Work Arrangements—Allow Employees To:	
Take time off for school/child care functions	88
Return to work gradually after childbirth or adoption	81
Periodically change starting and quitting times	68
Move from full time to part time and back again while remaining in the same position or level	57
Work at home occasionally	55
Share jobs	37.5
Work at home or off-site on a regular basis	33
Change starting and quitting times on a daily basis	24
Leaves—Allow Employees To:	
Take less than 12 weeks of maternity leave	9
Take 12 weeks of maternity leave	58
Take 13–26 weeks of maternity leave	25
Take more than 26 weeks of maternity leave[a]	8
Take less than 12 weeks of paternity leave	10
Take 12 weeks of paternity leave	74
Take 13–26 weeks of paternity leave	13
Take more than 26 weeks of paternity leave[b]	3
Take less than 12 weeks of adoption/foster care leave	10
Take 12 weeks of adoption/foster care leave	74.5
Take 13–26 weeks of adoption/foster care leave	13
Take more than 26 weeks of adoption/foster care leave[c]	3
Take less than 12 weeks of leave to care for seriously ill children	7
Take 12 weeks of leave to care for seriously ill children	78
Take 13–26 weeks of leave to care for seriously ill children	11
Take more than 26 weeks of leave to care for seriously ill children[d]	4
Leaves—Some Pay Offered During:	
Maternity leave	53
Paternity leave	13
Adoption/foster care leave	12.5
Child Care Assistance	
Dependent care assistance plans (DCAPs) that help employees pay for childcare with pretax dollars	50
Access to information to help locate child care in the community	36
Child care at the worksite	9
Financial support of local child care through a fund or corporate contributions beyond United Way	9
Reimbursement of child care costs when employees travel for business	6
Child care for school-age children on vacation	6
Payment for child care with vouchers or other subsidies that have direct costs to the company	5

(continued on page 232)

Type of Policy/Program	Percentage Offering
Child Care Assistance *(continued)*	
Sick care for children of employees	5
Private-public partnership in child care	5
Backup or emergency care when regular child care arrangements fall apart	4
Reimbursements of child care costs when employees work late	4
Elder Care Assistance	
Elder care resource and referral services	23
Long-term care insurance for family members	9
Direct financial support for local elder care programs	5
Family Services	
Employee assistance program	56
Workshops or seminars on parenting, child development, care of the elderly, or work-family problems	25
Programs for Teenagers	
Any program	12
Health Care Benefits	
Personal health insurance for full-time employees	97
Health insurance for part-time employees on a full or prorated basis	33
Health insurance that includes coverage for family members	95
Full or part payment of premium for family members	87
Health insurance coverage for unmarried partners who live together	14
Wellness program for employees and their families	50.5
Space/storage facilities for nursing mothers	37
Benefits to Enhance Economic Security	
Temporary disability insurance	70
Defined/guaranteed benefit pension plan	48
401(k) or 403(b) individual retirement plan	90
Company contribution to individual retirement plan	91
Scholarships or other educational assistance for employees' children	24
Public-Private Partnerships	
All types	11

[a] Median maternity leave = 12 weeks; mean = 17 weeks
[b] Median paternity leave = 12 weeks; mean = 14 weeks
[c] Median adoption/foster-care leave = 12 weeks; mean = 14 weeks
[d] Median leave to care for seriously ill child = 12 weeks; mean = 14 weeks

Source: E. Galinksy and J.T. Bond, *The 1998 Business Work-Life Study: A Sourcebook* (New York: Families and Work Institute, 1998), iii–xvi.

ber of investigations have documented that firm characteristics, such as firm size and industry, are related to the profile of work-family initiatives established by particular companies.[25] In general, larger companies and firms in specific industries, such as pharmaceutical, telecommunications, and the high-tech sector have been more likely to develop more comprehensive work-life initiatives. Second, the Business Work-Life Study revealed that the following characteristics of a company's workforce were related to the development of particular types of family-supportive policies and programs: higher percentages of women in leadership positions, higher percentages of employees affiliated with unions (for benefits but not for flexible work arrangements), and higher percentages of people of color in leadership positions.[26] Third, organizational support at various levels can influence work-life programs. It has frequently been noted in the practitioner literature that top management's support is important for the successful development and implementation of work-life initiatives. However, work-life managers typically want to develop support and commitment to their policies and programs throughout their organizations, rather than only at the top. One exploratory investigation found evidence that work-family change efforts at different companies have, in fact, started at virtually all levels of the corporate hierarchies.[27] Fourth, characteristics of the business environment—namely, the economic, social, and political environments in which businesses operate—exert pressures that affect the development of work-family initiatives. These pressures range from public sector mandates (such as the Family and Medical Leave Act)[28] to media coverage (such as being included in *Working Mother* magazine's list of the most family-friendly companies) to public expectations and the attitudes of business and industry groups toward work and family issues.[29]

The Benefits of Work-Family Initiatives

Work-family initiatives are commonly perceived as having the potential to benefit organizations, as well as employees and their families. In recent years, various researchers have examined the outcomes associated with the work-family initiatives established at U.S. workplaces.

Organizational Benefits

In 1995, managers of work-family programs at ninety-three firms regarded as family-friendly were asked about their perceptions of the organizational benefits of their companies' work-family programs. Of the respondents, 61 percent felt that these initiatives had contributed to an enhanced image of the company; 26 percent, that they had improved employee morale; 19 percent, that they had reduced unwanted turnover; and 19 percent, that they had resulted in improved productivity. In addition, 15 percent of the respondents reported that tardiness and absenteeism had been reduced, and 12 percent thought that employees' stress had been reduced by a "great" or "very great" extent.[30]

Four different approaches to documenting the organizational outcomes of work-family initiatives have been identified:[31]

- The *human cost approach* focuses on the resultant reductions in personnel costs, such as absenteeism and turnover. Several researchers have used this approach to examine the outcomes of flexible work arrangements. For example, Baltes and associates conducted a metanalysis of studies of flexible work arrangements and compressed workweeks; they found that flexible work arrangements, but not compressed workweeks, were associated with decreased absenteeism.[32]

- The *human investment approach* to measuring organizational outcomes frames work-family initiatives as investments in the organization's human capital, which can result in long-term payoffs including improved morale, increased organizational commitment, and improved performance and productivity. In a now-classic study, Lambert and colleagues at Fel-Pro found that the establishment of work-family initiatives could result in employees' willingness to "go the extra mile," even if they did not use the programs or policies.[33] In another study, researchers analyzed the data collected as part of a 1990 survey with 849 respondent workplaces and found relationships between the establishment of work-family initiatives and firms' productivity.[34]

- The *stakeholder approach* considers the impacts of work-family initiatives on different stakeholder groups, including

(but not limited to) employees and their families. For instance, researchers in one study examined flexible work
arrangements and found that 22.6 percent of the managers
reported that their workloads had increased as a result of
needing to supervise employees with flexible work arrangements.[35] In another study, focused on part-time work arrangements, researchers found that, in general, the majority
of supervisors felt that their own workloads were affected either positively or neutrally by having part-time employees as
part of their work teams. However, one of every five of these
supervisors did report that their own workloads had increased as a result of supervising part-time employees.[36]

- The *strategy approach* assesses the outcomes of work-family
initiatives according to the extent to which they contribute to
a core business strategy of the organization. Workplaces that
have placed a priority on strategies such as quality, globaliza-
tion, or customer relations, for example, might look at the relationships between work-family initiatives and these overall
strategies.[37] Despite interest in describing these complex relationships between organizational strategies and work-family
initiatives, there has been no published research documenting
when and to what extent work-family policies and programs
have contributed to particular business strategies.

Benefits for Employees and Their Families

Researchers have also examined the outcomes that work-family initiatives have for employees and their families using a variety of methods,
including case studies of different family-friendly workplaces and
their employees' experiences in them.[38] To date, the research has been
focused on the interface between work and family, as measured by the
extent of work-family conflict or of work-family balance. The results
of these studies have been less than conclusive.

Early research suggested that certain policies and programs might
address the work-family priorities of particular groups of employees.
For example, Bohen and Viveros-Long found that the use of flexible
work schedules did reduce work-family conflict for some groups of
employees; however, the positive outcomes were experienced more
often by employees without children, rather than by working par-

ents.[39] The findings of other studies have also suggested that the use of flexible work arrangements, by themselves, may not result in reduced work-family conflicts.[40] In contrast, however, studies of part-time workers have indicated that reduced hours can enhance work-family balance if the reduced hours are desired by the employees and if the part-time schedule does not jeopardize career opportunities.[41]

Studies documenting the outcomes associated with on-site child care centers have often found that employees who were satisfied with employer-sponsored child care also tended to report positive changes in their work-family balance. Research was recently conducted at a large pharmaceutical company to compare the experiences of employees who had enrolled their children at the company's new on-site child care centers with parents employed by the same firm at another work location that did not have on-site child care (the control group). Information was gathered from the parents before and after the opening of the child care centers, measuring parents' perceptions of the impact of their use of the child care center on work-related variables (such as absenteeism), the supportiveness of the company culture, their commitment to the organization, and their own work-life balance. Parents with children enrolled in the centers were significantly more likely to have reported a better balance between their work and personal issues, as measured by statements such as "It is usually easy for me to balance the demands of work and personal life" and "Worrying about my job makes it hard for me to enjoy myself outside of work."[42]

Despite the increase in the number of work-family studies that have been implemented, questions remain about the efficacy and outcomes associated with the implementation of specific work-family policies and programs. Kossek and Ozeki reviewed twenty-seven studies for their metanalysis to examine the relationships between work-family initiatives and indicators of outcomes at the workplace. They concluded that it will be necessary to implement more rigorous studies with more complex research designs before we can have a sophisticated understanding of which work-family policies and programs result in what types of outcomes for which types of employees under what types of circumstances.[43]

LIMITATIONS OF THE FAMILY-FRIENDLY
WORKPLACE APPROACH

Despite evidence of progress, there are many compelling reasons why it is both critical and timely to reexamine the efficacy of the current model of the family-friendly workplace. If the creation of family-friendly workplaces is America's primary strategy for supporting the well-being of working families, we need to consider whether it will be enough. Critics of the U.S. reliance on the family-friendly workplace strategy have noted several limitations to this approach.

Access to and Use of Work-Family Policies and Programs

The most disconcerting problem associated with the family-friendly workplace approach is that most working families have limited or no access to employer-supported work-family policies and programs. The 1997 National Study of the Changing Workforce, conducted by the Families and Work Institute, found that employees were less likely to have access to some core work-family benefits, such as dependent-care supports, than to traditional benefits, such as health insurance. As reported in Table 9-3, only a minority of employees reported that they had access to even the most modest of work-family supports, such as child care information and referral (only 20 percent of the respondents) or pretax dependent-care assistance plans (29 percent of the respondents).[44]

The variability in employees' access to work-family policies and programs is related to organizational characteristics, occupational characteristics, and characteristics of employment contract.[45] Employees who work for large organizations are more likely to have access to a greater number of employer-provided supports to families than those who work for small or medium-sized workplaces. According to the U.S. Bureau of the Census, however, nearly four-fifths of today's labor force works for businesses that employ fewer than 500 people.[46] Unfortunately, small workplaces are less likely not only to offer traditional benefits but also to provide comprehensive work-family initiatives to their employees. A study comparing small (fewer than fifty employees) and medium or large firms found that small businesses were less likely to offer a comprehensive set of work-family benefits (as

TABLE 9-3. Availability of Traditional Benefits and
Work-Family Policies and Programs in the United States

	Percentage of Employees with Access
Personal health insurance	84
Retirement plans	75
Paid vacation days	82
Paid holidays (any)	80.5
Paid time off for personal illness (at least some)	74
Child care resource and referral services	20
Child care services operated or sponsored by the employer	11
Direct financial assistance for purchasing child care services	13
Dependent care assistance plan	29
Elder care resource and referral	25
Able to choose starting and quitting times	45
Able to change starting and quitting times on a daily basis	25
Able to take time off to address family/personal matters	66
Report women can take an unspecified amount of time off after childbirth	94
Report men can take an unspecified amount of time off after becoming a father	80
If working part time, can switch to full time	58
If working full time, can switch to part time	38
Would work from home at least for some of the regularly scheduled hours	19

Source: T. Bond, E. Galinsky, and J. Swanberg, *The 1997 National Study of the Changing Workforce* (New York: Families and Work Institute, 1997).

well as some specific policies and programs), whether on a case-by-case basis, to a portion of their employees, or to all of their employees.[47] As indicated by the data in Table 9-4, small businesses are particularly unlikely to offer the more costly supports that provide income security to working families, such as paid leave to care for sick family members.

The National Study of the Changing Workforce, which sampled employees rather than workplaces, found that employees working for

TABLE 9-4. Policies and Programs at Small and Medium or Large Businesses, by Percentage

	Small Firms (n = 188)				Medium/Large Firms (n = 88)				
	To No One	Case by Case	To Some Groups	To All	To No One	Case by Case	To Some	To All Groups	X^2
Adoption assistance	96.8	2.1	0.0	1.1	94.3	0.0	0.0	5.7	7.0*
After-school care	96.3	2.1	0.0	1.6	98.9	1.1	0.0	0.0	1.8
Backup child care for sick kids	94.7	3.7	0.5	1.1	95.5	2.3	0.0	2.3	1.5
Breaks: used for personal/home	27.8	24.6	2.7	44.9	13.6	27.3	8.0	51.1	9.6*
Career counseling	87.8	8.5	1.1	2.7	67.0	12.5	3.4	17.0	23.1***
Dental insurance	54.8	2.7	14.9	27.7	18.2	1.1	27.3	53.4	35.2***
Disability insurance	40.5	4.9	13.5	41.1	19.8	0.0	25.6	54.7	19.0***
EAP/counseling	66.8	14.1	2.7	16.3	48.9	12.5	2.3	36.4	13.8**
Employee support groups	83.9	7.0	1.6	7.5	85.2	6.8	2.3	5.7	0.5
Financial assistance for child care	92.5	3.8	0.5	3.2	92.0	3.4	1.1	3.4	0.3
Health insurance	24.1	5.9	25.1	44.9	2.3	2.3	28.7	66.7	23.7***
Help finding child/elder care	93.0	2.7	0.5	3.7	84.1	10.2	0.0	5.7	8.2*
Information on community programs	66.5	15.1	0.5	17.8	47.1	19.5	0.0	33.3	11.1**
Long-term care insurance	74.7	2.7	8.8	13.7	50.0	2.3	18.2	29.5	17.8***
Mentoring	73.4	12.2	2.1	12.2	58.0	17.0	5.7	19.3	7.5
On-the-job training	6.9	7.4	4.8	80.9	5.7	10.2	15.9	68.2	10.8**

(continued on page 240)

	Small Firms (n = 188)				Medium/Large Firms (n = 88)				
	To No One	Case by Case	To Some Groups	To All	To No One	Case by Case	To Some	To All Groups	X²
Paid sick days	35.8	7.0	25.1	32.1	19.3	3.4	29.5	47.7	11.0***
Paid time off for chronic medical problems/disabilities	53.8	21.1	7.6	17.4	26.4	28.7	10.3	34.5	19.3***
Paid time off: family care	58.6	18.3	4.8	18.3	33.3	26.4	10.3	29.9	15.7***
Periodic adjustment of work hours	19.9	39.2	7.0	33.9	17.0	43.2	18.2	21.6	10.6**
Pretax dependent care accounts	89.1	3.8	1.6	5.5	60.2	0.0	11.4	28.4	45.5***
School vacation care for kids	95.7	2.7	0.0	1.6	97.7	1.1	0.0	1.1	.75
Tuition assistance: employees	70.6	11.2	6.4	11.8	29.5	15.9	14.8	39.8	45.8***
Tuition assistance: employees' family members	97.9	1.1	0.5	0.5	96.6	3.4	0.0	0.0	2.8
Unpaid leave: sick-family care[a]	27.7	22.7	3.8	46.5	6.8	15.9	4.5	72.7	20.8***
Work from home	81.8	13.9	3.7	0.5	60.2	29.5	9.1	1.1	14.9***
Work part time	12.3	41.2	15.1	31.0	8.0	45.5	31.8	14.8	15.1***

Source: M. Pitt-Catsouphes and L. Litchfield, "How Are Small Businesses Responding to Work and Family Issues?" in R. Hertz and N. Marshall, eds., *Working Families: The Transformation of the American Home* (Berkeley: University of California Press, 2001).

Note: The table reflects the percentage of respondent organizations reporting availability either "to no employees," "on a case-by-case basis only," "to some groups of employees," or "to all employees."

[a] Most of the small workplaces that participated in this survey would be exempt from the FMLA provisions; however, the FMLA provisions would have applied to most of the medium and large organizations that responded.

* $p < .05$; ** $p < .01$; *** $p < .001$

larger organizations were more likely to have access to a greater number of dependent-care benefits than those working for small or medium companies. However, on the positive side, this research also found that employees working at small firms were more likely to work at home for part of the workweek than were employees working at medium or large organizations. Work-at-home practices were reported by 30 percent of the employees working at small firms (fewer than 25 employees), 25 percent of those at medium-sized firms (25 to 249 employees), and 22 percent of those at large companies (250 or more employees).[48]

Part-time and temporary employees are also less privileged with regard to conventional benefits and work-family supports. The National Study of the Changing Workforce revealed that 15 percent of the workforce had part-time jobs as their primary or main employment. Whereas 21 percent of women in the labor force held part-time jobs as their main jobs, 8 percent of men did so. In this study, only 51 percent of employees who worked part time at their main jobs had access to personal health coverage, in comparison to 90 percent of full-time employees. Furthermore, only 48 percent of the part-time employees, compared with 88 percent of the full-time employees, had paid vacation and paid holidays. Significantly, whereas 50 percent of part-time workers received paid time off for their own illnesses, 78 percent of full-time workers did.[49] Clearly, the absence of these basic supports would make workplaces family-unfriendly to part-time employees, even if these workplaces were family-friendly to their full-time colleagues.

In 1995, Christensen surveyed members of the Work and Family Roundtable, firms that had made commitments to work-family initiatives. Despite the availability of some innovative policies and programs at these companies, Christensen found that the work-family supports were virtually unavailable to the temporary and contingent employees, who in some cases worked alongside the permanent staff.[50]

Some critics of the family-friendly workplace model have observed that this approach further disadvantages low-income employees, as compared to middle- and upper-income employees. Three concerns have been raised. First, large percentages of low-wage workers are employed at workplaces that offer limited traditional benefits and few, if any, work-family-specific policies and programs. Second, some types of work-family policies and programs, such as fee-for-service concierge or errand services, seem to reflect the lifestyle preferences of professional and managerial workers more than those of hourly workers. Third, even when low-wage employees work at family-friendly workplaces, they may not be able to take advantage of these supports because the costs (oftentimes shared by the employer and the employee), such as the fees for on-site child care or the economic costs of taking unpaid family leave, may not be affordable.

The National Study of the Changing Workforce found that low-wage workers have less access to benefits, policies, and services that can contribute to family well-being. Only 65 percent of those in the bottom quartile of wage earners had access to personal health care insurance, in comparison to 90 percent of all other workers. Only two-thirds of the low-wage workers had paid vacation time, in comparison to 86 percent of all other workers. Whereas only 58 percent of the low-wage employees received paid sick leave, 79 percent of other workers did.[51] Other studies have also indicated that wage-earning employees tend to have less access to flexible schedules and alternative work arrangements. Glass and Fujumoto found that professional and managerial workers had more access to leave and work-at-home options.[52] Similarly, the National Study of the Changing Workforce reported that 62 percent of management and professional employees stated that they could take time off to care for a sick child without losing pay, forfeiting vacation time, or having to resort to "making up an excuse," in comparison to 43 percent of the respondents who indicated that their jobs were not managerial or professional.[53]

One of the constraints associated with the family-friendly workplace model is that availability, by itself, may not be enough. Clearly, if work-family initiatives are going to result in any positive outcomes, employees who might benefit from them must actually use them. Many work-family champions have noted that use may be limited if the workplace culture does not encourage employees to take steps (such as requesting reduced work hours) that might help them improve their work-family balance.[54] There is ample evidence that workplace culture and inflexible policies have limited the effectiveness of work-family initiatives, in some cases even when the workplace has attempted to create a family-responsive work environment.[55]

Short-Term Employer-Employee Relationships and Long-Term Implications of Policies

The nature of the contemporary social contract between employers and employees introduces an additional concern about the family-friendly workplace model. It is no longer assumed that the employer-employee relationship will necessarily be a long-term one; the concept of lifelong employment is a thing of the past. Even if employees do work for family-friendly employers at one point, they cannot be sure that they will have access to specific types of plans (such as mental health services for family members) in the future, since those employer-supported programs are available to them only if they are employees at the same organizations (or other family-friendly ones). The vulnerability of working families may be heightened if they depend on employers not only for income but also for services and programs that support their family members' well-being.[56] For some time, it has been clear that unwanted unemployment puts family well-being at risk. The negative impacts of layoffs on families may well be magnified if other important supports, such as dependent-care subsidies or tuition assistance for employees' children, are eliminated at the same time that their earnings are reduced.[57]

Finally, it is important to consider whether the use of work-family policies and programs—even when they alleviate work-family conflicts in the short term—might be associated with negative outcomes that may not become apparent for some months, or even years. For example, Judiesch and Lyness found that the use of leaves negatively affected the subsequent promotion of managers.[58] Similarly, Pruchno and associates found that telecommuters, as well as their co-workers, felt that the use of work-at-home options would negatively affect employees' careers, in part because they would be less likely to receive the types of challenging work assignments that could lead to promotions.[59]

Our society should step back and take a critical look at the family-friendly workplace model, if only because businesses may not continue to be interested in offering these supports. Employers' long-term commitment to work-family initiatives may vacillate, depending on overall economic trends and the extent to which these initiatives are viewed as being vital to core business strategies. Traditionally, the business case for the family-friendly workplace has been tied to three business priorities: recruitment, retention, and productivity issues such as absenteeism.[60] Recruitment and retention are compelling motivators during periods of labor market shortages, but they become less urgent during times of rising unemployment. If the economic slowdown continues, it is unclear whether employers will rely on their work-family initiatives as a cornerstone of human resource strategy.

Ultimately, ensuring the quality of life of working families is a challenge that extends beyond the capacity of any single employer. Although it is appropriate to expect that employers should be accountable for the quality of their employees' work lives, there are many factors outside of work that impinge on the overall well-being of working families. The complex needs and priorities of contemporary working families require a new paradigm: promoting the family-friendly workplace within the context of the family-friendly society.

NEW VISIONS FOR THE FAMILY-FRIENDLY WORKPLACE

Given the limitations discussed thus far, should we conclude that the family-friendly workplace is an obsolete response to the needs of today's working families? If only a limited percentage of working families can actually access these employer-provided supports, should we decide that it is not worth the effort to increase the responsiveness of workplaces across the country? Worse still, is it possible that the creation of a few family-friendly workplaces reduces pressure on employers just enough that they can avoid examining whether they should make fundamental changes to enhance working families' well-being? Clearly, the family-friendly workplace approach is not perfect. If our society is, indeed, at a crossroads with respect to the family-friendly workplace model, we have three basic choices.

Option 1: Adapt and Improve the Model of the Family-Friendly Workplace

There are many work-family champions who are steadfast in their efforts to improve and expand the family-friendly workplace approach. From their perspective, there are several key goals and objectives that could be achieved, such as increasing the number of companies that strive to become family-friendly workplaces, updating the meaning of a family-friendly company in the context of today's economy (which is, of course, radically different from the economy of the 1980s, when the original model emerged), and raising the bar for the standards of excellence that characterize a family-friendly company.

In 1996, the Work and Family Roundtable adopted the Principles of Excellence in Work and Family.[61] These principles outline new expectations for family-friendly employers such as working with external stakeholders in the community and partnering with the public sector in order to strengthen the well-being of working families. The four key principles are:

- The employer recognizes the strategic value of addressing work and personal life issues.
- The work environment supports individuals' personal life effectiveness.
- The management of work and personal life effectiveness is a shared responsibility between employer and employee.
- The employer develops relationships to enhance external work and personal resources.

If embraced, the Principles of Excellence could expand the model of the family-friendly workplace.

Option 2: Advocate a Greater Role for the Public Sector in Providing for the Well-being of Working Families

Some observers have strongly criticized the family-friendly workplace and have concluded that there are basic flaws in this approach. They have proposed that public sector alternatives, such as government-sponsored services and mandated policies, be pursued.[62] From this point of view, the voluntary establishment of family-responsive work environments will inevitably result in small percentages of workplaces actually becoming family-friendly. Indeed, Kelley and Dobbin concluded that employers' responsiveness to work-family issues may remain limited unless employers anticipate that legislative or court mandates will require them to become more family-friendly.[63]

Although there are many cogent arguments associated with this perspective, the public sector model probably would not facilitate cross-sector collaborations. At present, work-family champions closely allied with the business sector are providing significant leadership and commitment. If we attempt to establish supports for working families without the continued engagement of those workplaces that have striven to become family-friendly, we might well lose key supporters and jeopardize effective planning for other possibilities.

Option 3: Create a New Paradigm of the Family-Friendly Society

If we, as a nation, want to catalyze change, we must determine the best place to intervene and shape systemic change.[64] It is *not* our contention that work-family leaders in the United States should abandon the quest for the creation of more family-friendly workplaces. However, we feel that the work-family movement may become stalled unless we recast our visions for change. In our estimation, the family-friendly workplace model—by itself—will not result in a sufficient level of policy, service, and cultural supports for working families. However, a reconfigured family-friendly workplace model could become an agent for the adoption of a new model of the family-friendly society. The three paradigms discussed earlier in this chapter essentially frame family issues as private concerns relevant to individuals, families, and employers. In contrast, the paradigm of the family-friendly society frames work-family issues as priorities that are in the common good. We recommend that our society continue to put efforts into the establishment of family-friendly workplaces within the context of building a family-friendly society.

The family-friendly society paradigm will challenge business leaders, elected officials, and community advocates to accept new roles and responsibilities. In particular, the new approach may prompt employers to think about promoting quality-of-life issues for working families through a corporate citizenship lens where businesses invest time and resources in strengthening the well-being of working families in a specified community (or in the society at large), rather than limiting their focus to a human resource perspective. The family-friendly paradigm will create new opportunities for business involvement in the building of a family-friendly society.[65] The family-friendly society model would also encourage employers to develop new types of relationships with the public sector that would result in more universal sets of supports. One such effort, called Corporate Voices for Working Families, was recently initiated by Marriott International. Corporate Voices is "a non-partisan, non-profit corporate membership organization created to bring the private sector voice into the public dialogue on issues affecting working families."[66] This mission begins to frame a new role for corporations and suggests the importance of articulating a vision of a family-friendly society.

In the United States, we do not yet have a vision of a family-friendly society, but this concept has become familiar in some Western European countries. As conceived by some of the members of the European Union, a family-friendly society is one that acknowledges the family as one of the most critical social institutions, creates a range of policies and supports designed to enhance the well-being of families, and holds the society at large responsible for the well-being of families.[67]

In preparation for writing this chapter, we interviewed nearly fifty individuals and asked them to help us visualize a family-friendly society.[68] It was their collective wisdom that a family-friendly society would adopt explicit strategies for enhancing the quality of life of all families, including the many different types of working families. Although these individuals expressed a range of opinions (many of which conflicted with one another), Table 9-5 highlights their thoughts about some of the key characteristics of a family-friendly society.

CONCLUSION

Julia Brannen, professor of sociology at the Thomas Coram Research Institute at the London School of Economics, has suggested that the intense focus on employers' responsiveness is outdated and that the familiar model of the family-friendly workplace is part of the "old order." Furthermore, she has contended that the current paradigm of the responsive workplace is too narrow.[69] Indeed, despite the accomplishments that have been made with respect to work and family issues over the past two decades, there are disconcerting indications that the work-family movement might, in reality, be stuck. It is ironic that our fascination with the possibilities associated with the family-friendly

TABLE 9–5. Ten Dimensions of a Family-Friendly Society

Ensure universal availability of basic work-family supports	In the United States, we have established two universal supports that reflect the family/personal life cycle: public education and social security. As a society, we could consider whether we need other types of universal supports or services, such as year-round school schedules, as a way to support healthy families.
Offer service and program choices to working families	A family-friendly society would develop different types of services for working families that could meet the needs of diverse populations and the range of family structures across the life course. These supports might be offered and/or supported by the business sector, the voluntary sector, the public sector, or cross-sector collaborations.
Encourage multisector leadership relative to work-family issues	The public, business, and voluntary sectors would all be perceived as stakeholders in the creation of a family-friendly society. As a consequence, corporate decision makers, elected officials, and civic leaders would articulate their visions for a family-friendly society and would outline action agendas for promoting the well-being of employees, citizens, and their families.
Position work-family responsiveness as strategic social and economic investments	A family-friendly society would view the supports offered to working families as strategies for enhancing the country's human, social, and monetary capital.
Expect families to contribute to society as citizens of their communities and their workplaces	Working families would be seen as important beneficiaries of a family-friendly society. Therefore, it would be expected that they would make contributions back to the society, as citizens of both their neighborhoods and their workplaces. Citizenship behaviors would be encouraged in the community and at work to ensure a good fit between the responsiveness of the society, on one hand, and the priorities of working families, on the other.
Measure societal progress according to work-family indicators	A family-friendly society would adopt indicators to benchmark its progress over time. These indicators would include measures of the impact of economic/employment policies on family well-being, as well as measures of the impact of family policies on labor force participation.

Support families' efforts to fulfill work responsibilities

A family-friendly society would recognize that paid employment is important for most adults, because it not only provides the income that their families need but also offers them opportunities to be productive contributors to our market-based society. A family-friendly society would attempt to reduce the barriers experienced by some adults, such as those caring for elders, so that they could pursue employment options without having to compromise the well-being of their families.

Support families' efforts to fulfill caregiving responsibilities

A family-friendly society would recognize that many adults—whether or not they have dependents at a particular point in their lives—want to be responsible family members. A family-friendly society would create policies and programs that would make it easier for working adults to provide support, care, and nurturance to their family members and close friends. A family-friendly society would view caregiving as an important role that contributes to our social infrastructure.

Encourage a common-ground perspective about work-family by promoting cross-sector collaborations

Organizations in the business, public, and voluntary sectors would identify strategic links between their organizational missions and the creation of a family-friendly society. Multiorganizational partnerships (e.g., work-family programs sponsored by several employers) and cross-sector collaborations would be established to ensure the long-term quality of life of working families.

Create sustainable strategies

A family-friendly society would purposefully design its policies and programs so that they would offer benefits for employees and their families today, as well as tomorrow.

workplace may have contributed to the stalling of the work-family movement, in part because we have been reluctant to examine the inherent limitations of this approach.

While we can celebrate the fact that some employers have made commitments to and investments in their work-life initiatives, it is abundantly clear that many people struggle on a daily basis to meet both the expectations of their employers and the needs of their families. Although the family-friendly workplace approach might seem congruent with the prevailing optimism regarding market-driven solutions to social problems, we may have settled too quickly on an exclusive corporate approach rather than an inclusive and comprehensive societal approach.

10

Public Opinion on Work and Family Policy: The Role of Changing Demographics and Unionization

Henry E. Brady and Laurel Elms

merican workplaces and families have changed dramatically in the past thirty years. Women constitute a much larger share of the workforce, and there are many more single mothers. In two-parent families, fathers are now expected to be more involved with their children, and workplaces are expected to accommodate these efforts. At the same time, to make ends meet, many Americans work odd hours and in multiple part-time jobs that have minimal benefits. These changes have strained both the American family and the American workplace. Public policies on family try to ameliorate the adverse consequences of these changes while simultaneously supporting the good outcomes of these transformations. *Family policy* is a very broad term encompassing all governmental actions that impinge on families, including the legal framework for marriage and family, the regulation of those aspects of work that affect family life, and the provision of family and work-related public services such as health, education, welfare, and public safety.

In this chapter we focus on government policies that are at the intersection of work and family. These policies include family leave, which allows employees to take time off from work to deal with infants or sick family members; child care, which makes it possible for parents with young children to work; and health care, which provides families with the resources to deal with sickness and to remain productive as workers. Our primary focus is the mobilization from 1986 to 1993 of public opinion on family leave, which culminated in the Family and Medical Leave Act of 1993. The mobilization of public support for new government policies can encourage legislators to act and to vote for bills that have the vocal support of their constituents. While public opinion clearly does not always determine the actions of political leaders, it can influence the direction and speed of changes in public policy. We use our findings on family leave as a springboard for discussing public opinion about other family policies.

PUBLIC OPINION AND POLICY

Family policies are especially contentious because they appeal to fundamental values about work and family. In America, it is widely believed that people should work and not get "handouts." It is also widely believed that family and children are of ultimate importance. But what happens when work and family interfere with each other? What happens when single parents are required to work *and* to take care of young children? What happens when workers must balance their jobs against caring for sick family members or infants? What happens when families cannot afford health care and their illnesses make them unable to work?

Problems arise because there are different views about the responsibilities of families, businesses, and government. Some people believe, for example, that all families should have a father and mother joined through marriage, and that the father should work and the mother should stay at home with the children or sick family members. This division of responsibility solves the problems addressed by family leave and by child care policies, but it flies in the face of the increasing number of single-adult families and two-parent families where both of these parents work. Others want to come to terms with the changes in the structure of work and family in America by asking businesses or government to provide child care, family leave, and health care. But such proposals run up against beliefs that businesses should not be required to bear the costs of these programs and that governments should not raise taxes to fund them. Some opponents also raise questions about whether these policies might discourage two-parent families in which mothers stay at home. Not surprisingly, it is hard to design family policies that everyone agrees reduce the adverse results of changes in American life and yet facilitate the good ones. This problem is particularly difficult because there are profound disagreements about what is good and bad about the changes in American work and family structure.

Data from Public Opinion Surveys

To fashion public policies that garner the widest possible support, we must know more about the nature of current work-family disagreements and the kinds of policies that can be used to overcome them. Public opinion surveys provide an excellent way to find out what Americans think about issues in general. Public opinion questions specifically about family policies are scattered across different surveys, so to obtain adequate coverage and some perspective on changes over time, we have drawn on a large number of questions from surveys completed by ABC News/*Washington Post,* CBS News/*New York Times,* Gallup, the National Election Studies, the General Social Survey, and Roper. To complete a more in-depth analysis, we have used three sets of surveys that include questions that have been asked over several decades: the Roper Social and Political Trends data set, the American National Election Studies (NES), and the General Social Survey (GSS).[1]

In order to interpret public opinion, we need to break the public into distinct groups within which people are likely to hold similar opinions and across which there might be significant variation in support for policy proposals. For family policies involving the workplace, it seems likely that support varies by personal characteristics such as people's occupation, size of family, and sex, although the exact way in which support would vary might depend crucially on the details of the programs. For example, occupational groups with lower and middle incomes and with fewer benefits might gain significantly from family policies that provide funding or services such as child care or paid family leave. Those at the upper end of the socioeconomic ladder might benefit more from family policies that make options available on an unfunded basis, such as a requirement for businesses to provide unpaid family leave guaranteeing reemployment after a worker returns from the absence.

It makes sense, therefore, to examine how public opinion about family leave differs across groups defined by occupation, family size, and sex. Because opinions on family policies are typically shaped by partisan identification and by membership in interest groups, it also makes sense to explore how public attitudes toward family leave varies by party identification and by membership in the most important employment-related group—labor unions. We now examine the history of support for family leave and consider in detail the related results from our analyses of public opinion surveys. In discussing our findings, we begin by assessing public support for family leave and then examine workers' views on other key topics related to family policy. We conclude with a summary of our findings and an assessment of their implications for policy making.

PUBLIC OPINION TOWARD FAMILY LEAVE

The Family Leave Movement

The major push for a national family leave policy began in 1984 soon after a federal district court struck down a California maternity leave law, ruling that the law represented the state's unconstitutional discrimination against men.[2] Two Democratic representatives from California, Howard Berman and Barbara Boxer, later joined by Patricia Schroeder of Colorado, collaborated with women's groups to draft the first national legislation requiring employers to provide unpaid family leave.[3] At the early stages of drafting the proposal, proponents of family leave debated over whether to try to include paid leave, but they soon chose to focus on the less controversial goal of ensuring unpaid leave. They also considered how expansive the coverage should be. Expanding traditional maternity leave to include new fathers was important for the early sponsors, in part to avoid the legal challenges raised against some states' women-only maternity leave programs.[4] Making the legislation more inclusive also helped draw support from organized labor, since many union contracts already included maternity leave but not paternity or medical leave. Removing any abortion-related coverage helped the family leave bills gain support from some pro-life members of Congress and from church groups,[5] leaving business groups as the main opposition to the legislation.[6] The various congressional bills introduced between 1985 and 1993 differed in terms of the length of leave and the size of businesses that would be covered, but each proposal required unpaid leave for both women and men to care for their own serious medical problems and for newborns, newly adopted children, and ill children.[7]

The first family leave bill was introduced by Schroeder in the House in April 1985. This effort, as well as separate 1986 and 1987 bills, failed to reach a vote. In 1990, the renamed Family and Medical Leave Act (FMLA) passed in both the House and the Senate for the first time, only to be vetoed by George H.W. Bush. Bill Clinton made parental leave one of the major issues of the 1992 presidential campaign after Bush again vetoed a bill passed by the Democratic Congress in September 1992, less than two months before Election Day. Once in office, Clinton pushed for and, on February 5, 1993, signed the Family and Medical Leave Act of 1993—the first major piece of legislation he signed as president. This act entitled employees to take up to twelve weeks of unpaid, job-protected leave within a twelve-month period to care for a newborn or adopted child or to care for an immediate family member with a serious health condition.

Although labor groups were early supporters of a national family leave policy, the lead role in the coalition for national legislation initially came from women's groups, especially the Women's Legal Defense Fund.[8] The earliest union supporting the legislation was the Service Employees International Union (SEIU), led by John Sweeney (now the head of the American Federation of Labor–Congress of Industrial Organizations [AFL-CIO]). Throughout the 1980s, more and more labor unions, including the American Federation of State, County, and Municipal Employees, the International Ladies' Garment Workers' Union, and the United Auto Workers, joined the SEIU in supporting family and medical leave for working people.[9] Starting in 1987, the AFL-CIO joined the coalition in earnest.[10] Along with the American Association of Retired Persons (AARP), labor unions were the main financial supporters of the long legislative battle over family leave rights.[11]

Features of Family Leave

There are four important features of family leave policy that might affect public opinion:

- *Purpose of family leave.* Is it for employees with new babies or for employees to take care of sick family members? There are many important details within these two major distinctions, such as whether both fathers and mothers get to take leave, how *father* and *mother* are defined, whether both adopted children and biological children are included, and whether sick family members must be part of the immediate nuclear family (that is, one's spouse and children) or whether extended family members, especially parents, are included in the definition as well. The survey questions we are considering in this chapter (discussed later) referred to "parents" or "employees" with "new babies" without being more specific about the relationship to the child and without singling out the mother or father. They also referred to a "sick family member," "immediate family," and sometimes a "sick child or other sick family member, such as a parent or spouse."

- *Duration of the family leave.* Some of the survey questions we consider asked about a specific number of weeks, but others referred to a "minimum period" or avoided mentioning any specific period at all. The periods mentioned run from twelve weeks (three months) to six months.

- *Unpaid or paid nature of the leave.* Unpaid family leave merely protects a person's job and benefits without providing any replacement income during the time when the person takes leave. Paid family leave provides some replacement income.

- *Employers' optional or mandatory provision of family leave.* In the debate over family leave, lobbyists for business argued that the provision of family leave should be left to the employer's discretion and should not be mandated by government. This argument appeals to a powerful pro-business, laissez-faire strain in American public policy.

The Lability of Attitudes Toward Family Leave

We collected twenty-five items that were asked on various public opinion surveys from 1986 to 1996. Eighteen of them were comparable enough to include in Table 10-1. The remainder had some idiosyncratic features that made them hard to compare with others, although we later mention some of the more interesting ones. Table 10-1 organizes the questions in rows. Those that elicited the highest level of support for family leave are in the first row, and those that elicited the lowest level of support are in the last row.

More than three-quarters of the public supported unpaid family leave for a "minimum period" for care of a sick family member or for an unstated period for care of a new baby (see the top two rows of Table 10-1). For those who supported family leave for care of a new baby, the Gallup organization asked (using varying formats on all four surveys) how long employers should guarantee reemployment. The median answer among the three-quarters who supported some unpaid family leave was two to three months (eight to twelve weeks). The median among the entire sample was about two months (eight weeks), and the average was about three months (twelve weeks). About one-third of all respondents either opposed family leave or proposed durations of less than a month. About 5 percent proposed more than nine months.

Not surprisingly, adding a specific duration (twelve weeks) to the initial question and combining both forms of family leave—that is, to care for a new baby and to care for a sick family member—reduced support somewhat, to an average of 70 percent, but there was still overwhelming support for family leave. There was also substantial support for continuing health and other benefits while people are on unpaid family leave, and there was support for applying family leave for a new baby's care equally to men and women.[12] Even when asked about making the family leave paid (albeit for an indetermine length of time), the majority (53 percent) were still in favor of it. When those favoring paid leave were asked (on the November 1989 Gallup poll) about a proper duration, they responded with a median answer of "a little over one month"—substantially shorter than the recommended length for unpaid family leave.

None of these considerations—the purpose of the leave, its duration, or whether or not it is paid—led to less than majority support for family leave. In fact, the only consideration that seemed to show dramatically reduced support for family leave was whether or not government should interfere with business by mandating they provide it for their employees. Indeed, whether or not government should regulate business is one of the most contentious issues in American politics.

Table 10-1. American Opinion on Family Leave: Items from 1986 to 1993

RESULTS—PERCENTAGE FOR FAMILY LEAVE
(Letters Indicate Survey Organization—See Below)

DESCRIPTION OF SURVEY ITEM

For What	Duration	Paid or Unpaid	Required of Employer	# of Surveys	Mean of All	86: 1-6	...	89: 7-12	90: 1-6	90: 7-12	91: 1-6	91: 7-12	92: 1-6	92: 7-12	93: 1-6
New baby	Not stated	Unpaid	Required	4	78%			81% G		77% G		76% G		76% G	
Sick family	* = "minimum period" ** = not stated	Unpaid	Required	3	76%			81% G *		76% G *				71% G **	
New baby Sick family	12 weeks	Unpaid	Required	6	70%				69% G			67% A	83% G		76% G 65% C 67% A
New baby	Not stated	Paid	Required	1	53%			53% G							
New baby or "certain circumstances"	12–24 weeks	Unpaid	Required; also asks about "leaving to employer"	4	33%	31% R					32% C			31% N 38% R	

Six-Month Time Periods for 1989–1993 (Year: Months)

Survey Organizations: A—ABC/*Washington Post*
  C—CBS/*New York Times*
  G—Gallup
  N—National Election Studies
  R—Roper

From the passage of child labor laws almost a hundred years ago to the passage of environmental laws in the last quarter century, debate has raged over whether business should be required to limit workers' hours or to clean up effluents. It is not surprising, therefore, that the questions receiving the least support were those that gave respondents the explicit option of allowing employers to make their own decisions about providing family leave.

It is surprising, however, to see how much allowing for employer discretion on family leave, no matter how it was described, affected the responses. For example, a fall 1992 NES question (and a very similar one from the June 1991 CBS News/*New York Times* poll) asked: "Do you think the government should require companies to allow up to six months unpaid leave for parents to spend time with their newborn or newly adopted children, or is this something that should be left up to the individual employer?" Unlike the other questions reported in first four rows of Table 10-1, this question primed respondents to think about whether family leave is "something that should be left up to the individual employer." The result was that only 31 to 32 percent of respondents in these two surveys supported family leave. Two Roper questions from December 1986 and December 1992 asked, "Do you think granting such leaves is something companies should be required to do, or something that would be nice for them to do but not required, or something that they should not be expected to do?" Only 31 percent of respondents in 1986 and 38 percent in 1992 thought that companies should be "required" to provide family leave when they were also given the option of merely expressing their hope that companies would provide family leave on their own. The average of 33 percent support for family leave for these four questions was much lower than for all the others reported in Table 10-1, because here respondents were given the option of relegating family leave to the employer's discretion. All the other questions reported in Table 10-1 simply asked some variant of whether people "supported or opposed" laws that "required" businesses to provide some form of family leave.

Public opinion on family leave is very labile—it varies substantially when described in different ways. This lability of opinion suggests that family leave is an issue on which leadership and political cues could make a difference. Two very similar questions asked around the time that Bush vetoed the 1992 Family and Medical Leave Act revealed the balance of policy considerations and partisan forces. Both Gallup and CBS/*New York Times* poll respondents were told, in separate surveys in early October 1992, that Congress had passed a bill requiring companies to provide up to twelve weeks of unpaid leave for employees to care for a new baby or a sick family member. The Gallup respondents were then told that "President Bush has said he opposes the bill because it might hurt the economy and create too much government interference in business." The CBS/*New York Times* respondents were told that "George Bush refused to sign the bill, saying the federal government should not mandate employee benefits." In each case, the respondents were then asked if Bush should have signed the bill. Majorities of each poll's respondents—53 percent for Gallup and 57 percent for CBS/*NYT*—said he should have signed it. Predictably, the CBS/*NYT* poll revealed a partisan split, with 71 percent of Democrats and only 36 percent of Republicans saying he should have signed the bill. However, a majority of independents, 59 percent, said he should have signed it, and even conservatives were almost evenly split over the bill.

Changes in Support for Family Leave from 1986 to 1992

By 1992, therefore, the American public expressed its newly developed support for family leave. Consider the two previously described Roper items that gave respondents several options regarding family leave.[13] In 1986, 30.5 percent of the public supported required family leave, but by December 1992, 38 percent supported it, even when asked a question that would likely minimize support by providing several answer options. Clearly, important changes in public opinion had occurred in this six-year period.

To understand these changes, we divided the public into four simple occupational groups that allowed us to make comparisons across data sets with relative ease.[14] These four occupations are:

Managerial and professional workers, such as administrators, middle- and upper-level managers, lawyers and doctors, and teachers

White-collar workers, including technicians, clerical workers, and sales workers

Service and protective workers, such as food service and child
care workers, police officers, and firefighters
Blue-collar workers, including skilled, semiskilled, and unskilled laborers.[15]

In addition, we divided those not employed into three categories:

Unemployed people and students
Retired people
Homemakers (who are almost all women)

Support for unpaid family leave was at only 30.5 percent among
Americans in 1986 when the campaign for it began. Blue-collar workers, women, people with children, Democrats, and union members
were somewhat more supportive than others, but their support was
typically only 5 to 8 percent higher than that of other groups on the
Roper question. Although union members were more supportive of
family leave, the effect was not consistent across occupations. Blue-
collar workers were more supportive of family leave. Union members
in the managerial and professional and the blue-collar occupations
were more supportive than their nonunionized counterparts, but
unionized white-collar and service and protective workers were not
more supportive than their fellow nonunion workers. Finally, retired
people seemed much less supportive of family leave.

Overall support for family leave increased by about 8 percentage
points on this Roper question by December 1992, just before the family
leave bill was passed and signed into law by Clinton. Support for family leave grew substantially from 1986 to 1992 among all groups, but
especially among service workers and union members. In 1986, service
workers were no more likely to support unpaid family leave than an
average respondent, but by 1992, they had increased their support by
17 percentage points to 46 percent support, putting them well above
the average. Only 38 percent of union workers supported unpaid family leave in 1986, but this figure increased to nearly 53 percent in
1992—a 15 percentage point increase. Figures 10-1 and 10-2 summarize the changes from 1986 to 1992 for nonunionized and unionized
groups. Among nonunionized groups, there was an increase in support of between 3 to 15 percentage points, with the largest gains

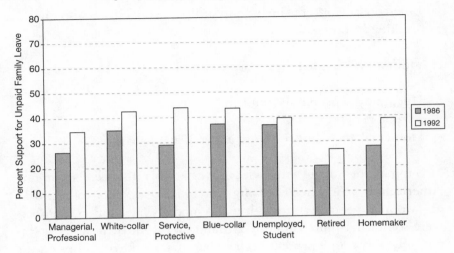

FIGURE 10-1. Nonunion Workers' Support from 1986 to 1992 for
Unpaid Family Leave by Occupation Type (Roper)

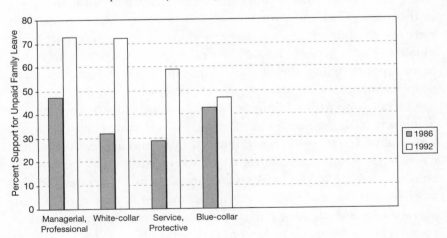

FIGURE 10-2. Union Members' Support from 1986 to 1992 for
Unpaid Family Leave by Occupation Type (Roper)

among service and protective workers (15 percentage points) and
homemakers (11 percentage points). But among unionized groups,
there were stunning gains of between 25 and 40 percentage points for
all groups, except for blue-collar workers, who increased by only 4 percentage points from a relatively high level of support in 1986.

Women's support for family leave also grew in comparison to that of men. In 1986, 28 percent of men and 33 percent of women supported required family leave, but by 1992, these figures had grown to 34 percent for men and 42 percent for women. Support among those with children also increased from 34 percent to 43 percent. Through further analysis of these data we located the exact groups among which increases occurred. The average gain among male union members from 1986 to 1992 was 15 percent, and the average gain among female union members was 19 percent. The most startling gains were among male union members with children (from 35 percent to 69 percent), female union members with children (from 46 percent to 68 percent), and female union members without children (from 45 percent to 69 percent).

SOCIOECONOMIC STATUS, OCCUPATIONAL GROUPS, AND PARTY AFFILIATIONS

The preceding results suggest that we need to know more about occupation and how it is related to individual well-being, union membership, and politics. We begin this exploration by creating a measure of socioeconomic status defined by using information on income and education for each respondent. This measure allowed us to define socioeconomic status quintiles.[16] The income measure is for the household, and the education measure is for the respondent.[17] Each respondent is scored from one to five, reflecting the quintile he or she was in.[18]

Our strategy is to rank the respondents in each survey by their socioeconomic status and divide them into five hierarchical socioeconomic status groups of equal size. This approach requires a number of discretionary decisions that merit elaboration. For two reasons, we combine measures of education and income into a composite socioeconomic status index. First, in the Roper surveys, income levels and, to a lesser extent, educational attainment were measured only in ranges.[19] In some cases these ranges had as few as four categories. It is obviously impossible to create quintiles from a measure with only four categories. By combining two measures, we can substantially increase the possible number of distinct rankings.[20] In addition, there are good reasons to expect uncorrelated errors of classification across the two measures, so the summary index will be less error-prone and will produce a better ranking.[21]

The Roper data show that the five quintiles differ dramatically in their demographic characteristics and partisan commitments. The top quintile is composed disproportionately of males, almost entirely white, and largely of thirty- to sixty-year-olds.[22] Those in the top quintile are disproportionately likely to be married and to be employed.[23] Although a bare majority are Protestant, they are, in fact, somewhat less Protestant than the entire population.[24] Although roughly the same percentages profess Democratic and Republican affiliations, the upper quintile is markedly more Republican than the other quintiles.[25] The bottom quintile is disproportionately female and African American. Those in the bottom quintile are most distinctive when it comes to age and employment: compared with those at the top, they are four times as likely to be sixty or older and less than half as likely to have a job.[26] They are also somewhat less likely to be married or unionized.[27] In addition, those in the bottom quintile are both more Protestant and more Democratic than the population at large.[28]

Figure 10-3 shows the mean socioeconomic status quintile score for those in each occupation. There is a clear ranking of occupations by this measure, with managerial and professional workers at the top at about 4.4, white-collar workers at 3.6, service and protective workers

FIGURE 10-3. Mean Socioeconomic Status by Occupation Type: 1973–1994 (Roper)

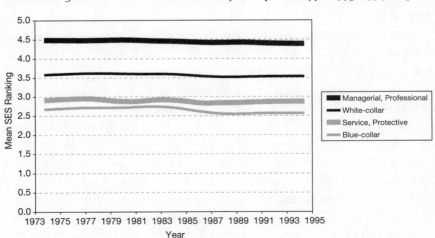

at 2.9, and blue-collar workers at 2.7.[29] The figure suggests that this ranking remained quite stable over the previous thirty years, except for some indication that blue-collar workers' socioeconomic status fell from about 2.75 to just above 2.5. Although this ranking demonstrated clear socioeconomic status differences among the occupations, it also shows that the average service and protective or blue-collar worker is nearly in the middle quintile. As will be discussed later, this finding has implications for the opinions of these occupational groups.

Changes in Occupational Groups and Unionization

Over the past thirty years, economic and demographic changes have significantly altered the number of Americans employed in different occupations and the composition of the labor force. Figure 10-4 displays the proportion of Roper survey respondents who were working in each of the four main job types. While the fraction of blue-collar workers dropped from slightly more than 40 percent in the early 1970s to less than 35 percent in the mid-1990s, the number of managerial and professional workers rose from slightly less than 20 percent to nearly 25 percent. The number of Roper respondents working in white-collar (30 percent) and in service and protective occupations (10 per-

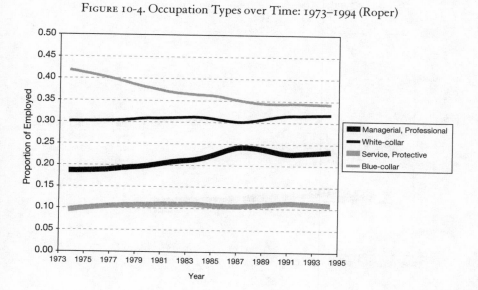

FIGURE 10-4. Occupation Types over Time: 1973–1994 (Roper)

cent) remained stable over the same twenty-year period. The greatest change was the increase in the proportion of managerial and professional employees and the decline in blue-collar workers.

Unionization rates varied in inverse order of status of occupation, with the highest levels of unionization among blue-collar and service and protective workers and the lowest levels among white-collar and managerial and professional workers. Figure 10-5 displays the proportion of union members in each occupation in the Roper surveys. The unionization levels for all four occupational groups had fallen since the early 1970s, with sharp drops among the two most unionized groups—blue-collar and service and protective workers—and much smaller dips among the less unionized white-collar and managerial and professional workers. Union membership plunged among blue-collar workers, with a drop from over 40 percent in the mid-1970s to less than 20 percent twenty years later. This traditional base of the labor movement not only became a smaller share of the labor force but also became dramatically less unionized. As a whole, service and protective workers also became less unionized. However, service workers were considerably less likely to be union members than protective workers. (Protective workers, as a separate category, are now the most

FIGURE 10-5. Unionization by Occupation Type: 1973–1994 (Roper)

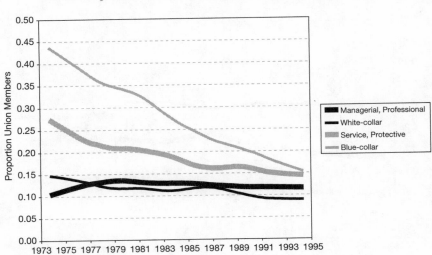

unionized occupational category, according to the Bureau of Labor Statistics.) [30]

Each of the four occupation categories has a different demographic composition, sometimes varying by union membership within a category. For example, while the proportion of men among union members and nonunion workers of managerial and professional occupations was nearly equal, men are far more likely to be unionized than women among the other three occupational categories. The representation of women in all occupation types has increased, but they are least likely to be working in blue-collar jobs, followed by professional and managerial ones; they are most likely to be working in white-collar and service and protective jobs.

The rate of unionization varies by socioeconomic status. Overall, rates are lowest in the bottom quintile but highest in the third and fourth quintiles. Levels of unionization for the bottom socioeconomic status quintiles also plunged over the twenty years of the Roper studies, but the proportion of union members among the top quintile remained nearly constant, with only a slight decline. Among respondents in the bottom three quintiles, the rate of unionization was cut in half over the two decades. While roughly 20 percent of the third and fourth quintiles were union members in the mid-1970s, by the mid-1990s only 10 percent or fewer were. For respondents with the lowest levels of income and education, the rate of unionization dropped from more than 10 percent to less than 5 percent.

The partisan identification of the four basic occupational groups varies, and the differences among the groups also changes with time. For simplicity, we consider a summary measure, macropartisanship, that is, the Democratic proportion of major party identifiers (Democrats and Republicans).[31] Managerial and professional employees were the least likely to be Democrats and the most likely to be Republicans (see Figure 10-6). While all occupational types became less Democratic over the preceding twenty years, the decline was quite large for the blue-collar and service workers and quite small for the managerial and professional group. Occupational differences in Democratic identification narrowed over time. The four occupation types also become more similar in the level of independent identification (a volunteered response in the Roper surveys) and less similar in the proportion classified as having chosen no particular party (also a volunteered response).

FIGURE 10-6. Macropartisanship by Occupation Type: 1973–1994 (Roper)

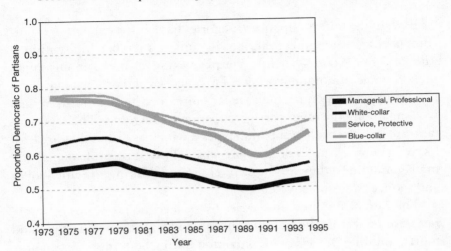

Within each occupational classification, union workers were more likely to be Democrats than were nonunion workers. The gap was particularly wide for the managerial and professional category, which included heavily unionized primary and secondary schoolteachers, and was a bit larger for white-collar than for blue-collar workers. The gap was narrowest for the service and protective workers. Thus, we found shifts away from the Democratic Party for all groups, but the greatest movement was for service and protective workers. (This trend suggests that for service and protective workers we might have found some growth in conservative attitudes during the 1990s.)

Clearly, partisanship in the United States still varies considerably by socioeconomic status. The bottom quintile remained by far the most Democratic-leaning stratum, while the other quintiles moved in a pro-Republican direction. The highest socioeconomic fifth was the least Democratic, hovering around parity between the parties, while at least 75 percent of major party identifiers among the bottom fifth were Democrats.

These facts about the changes in the occupational structure of the American workplace, in American families' socioeconomic structure, and in the partisan distribution within politics suggest that other factors might affect attitudes toward family policies. In the next section we explore whether these factors can account for changes in attitudes toward family leave and what they portend for the future of public opinion toward family policies.

PUBLIC OPINION TOWARD FAMILY LEAVE AND OTHER FAMILY POLICY ISSUES

Unpaid Family Leave

Based on tabular analysis of the 1986 and 1992 Roper questions, we argued that through the family leave campaign, unions activated the self-interest of women and men with children. Thorough analysis, however, would require that we rule out the existence of some other confounding factor, such as socioeconomic status, age, party identification, or ideology, that might also explain this result. In this section, we report on a regression analysis that shows that even after controlling for the factors described in the preceding section, the basic pattern in changes in attitude toward family leave policy remains.

Table 10-2 presents the results of regressions for 1986 and 1992 in which the dependent variable is whether or not unpaid family leave should be required of businesses. The independent variables, except for party identification and ideology, are all dummy variables or interactions of one dummy variable with another. Using a binary system, we assign a value of 1 to the subjects who fit into the category in question (for example, union members, occupational category, women, income quintile, age group, children younger than eighteen, union members who were women, union members with children younger than eighteen) and 0 otherwise.[32] The party identification variable is a three-unit measure with *Republican* coded as 1; *independent, no particular party,* and *don't know* as 2; and *Democrat* as 3. The ideology variable is a five-unit measure with *very conservative* coded as 1, *moderately conservative* as 2, *middle of the road* and *don't know* as 3, *moderately liberal* as 4, and *very liberal* as 5.

Before discussing these groups, it is important to note that the coefficients in Table 10-2 for both the occupational and socioeconomic status quintiles present no clear patterns. The age variables, however, indicate that older people were less likely to support family leave, although this effect was attenuated by about 40 percent by 1992. Finally, both party identification and ideology had highly significant and sub-

TABLE 10-2: Determinants of Support for Family Leave in 1986 and 1992

	1986		1992	
Variable Name	Regression Coefficient	Standard Error	Regression Coefficient	Standard Error
Occupation				
Baseline: nonworking	.000	xxx	.000	xxx
Managerial/professional	−.028	.043	−.004	.048
White-collar	.032	.036	.060	.040
Service and protective	−.029	.052	.057	.053
Blue-collar	.061	.036	.046	.030
Income Quintile				
Lowest fifth	.027	.042	−.033	.046
Second fifth	−.018	.041	−.056	.045
Third fifth	.044	.040	.020	.044
Fourth fifth	−.038	.038	.044	.042
Baseline: highest fifth	.000	xxx	.000	xxx
Age Group				
Baseline: 18–29	.000	xxx	.000	xxx
Ages 30–44	−.081**	.031	.013	.036
Ages 45–59	−.114**	.036	−.040	.041
Age 60 and up	−.167***	.039	−.112*	.045
Group Memberships				
Union membership	.066	.058	.036	.074
Female	.050*	.026	.075**	.028
Children under 18	.036	.029	.031	.032
Union and female	.088	.074	.030	.110
Union and children under 18	−.062	.071	.204*	.101
Political Identities				
Party identification	.035*	.014	.037*	.017
Ideology	.033**	.012	.060***	.014
Constant	.176*	.061	.102	.070
Sample Size/R²	1,588	.055	1,398	.076

* Significant at .05 level

** Significant at .01 level

*** Significant at .001 level

stantial impacts in 1986 and 1992, with greater support for family leave coming from Democrats and liberals. These results are unsurprising. The regression coefficients can be interpreted as probabilities. Each coefficient indicates how much a one-unit change in the independent variable increases the probability of supporting family leave. For the dummy variables, a one-unit change occurs as we move from one category to another.

Table 10-3 presents the more intriguing effects that involve groups defined by union membership, sex, and having children younger than eighteen. Here, we used the coefficients from Table 10-2 to compare the support from a group with the given description (such as union women with children younger than eighteen) with the support of the baseline group of union men without children younger than eighteen. Since we care only about increments in support above that baseline case, we assign it 0 percent. Thus, the entries tell us how much the changes from this baseline group increased the support for unpaid family leave. For example, nonunion women with children were 8.6 percent more supportive of family leave in 1986 than nonunion men without children.

Only five of these groups were (statistically) significantly different from the baseline. Female union members with no children and female union members with children were substantially more likely to have supported unpaid family leave than nonunion males without children in both 1986 and 1992. Male union members with children were substantially more likely in 1992 (but not in 1986) to have supported family leave than nonunion males without children. In fact, they were much more likely to have supported family leave than any other group of males in 1992. These results show the power of the interaction between union membership and having children or being a traditional caregiver.

This interaction was intensified by the family leave campaign from 1986 to 1992, as indicated by the last column, in which we took the difference between the 1992 figure and the 1986 figure. An increase between these two years is presumably the result of the family leave campaign. Only two of these differences are statistically significant, and each of them involves union membership and children—for both men and women, there is an increase of 20 percent or more in support for family leave from 1986 to 1992.

TABLE 10-3. Support for Unpaid Family Leave by Groups after Controlling for Other Factors

Characteristics of Composite Group			Year of Survey and Increment Above Baseline Case		Difference of 1992 and 1986
Male/Female	Union/Nonunion	Children/No Children	1986	1992	1992–1986
Male	Nonunion	No children	0.0%	0.0%	0.0%
Male	Nonunion	Children	3.6%	3.1%	-0.5%
Male	Union	No children	6.6%	3.6%	-3.0%
Male	Union	Children	4.0%	27.1%**	23.1%**
Female	Nonunion	No children	5.0%	7.5%	2.5%
Female	Nonunion	Children	8.6%	10.6%	2.0%
Female	Union	No children	20.4%**	14.1%**	-6.3%
Female	Union	Children	17.8%**	37.6%**	19.8%**

** Statistically significant, compared to the baseline case, at the .01 level

Note: The entries are computed from the regression coefficients in Table 10-2.

SURVEY RESULTS ON THREE FAMILY POLICY ISSUES: CHILD CARE, PAID FAMILY LEAVE, AND HEALTH CARE

What does this analysis mean for family policy in general? Is the weak relationship between policy position and occupation or unionization that we found in 1986 for unpaid family leave repeated for other issues? What is the likelihood that voters could be mobilized in these issue areas?

When reviewing the surveys, we found it hard to find questions directly related to family policy. Our review of the NES, GSS, and Roper studies uncovered only about twenty items, five of which we focus on here.

Child Care Policy

We begin with two questions from the NES about child care funding. The more general of the two asked whether respondents wanted spending increased or decreased for child care. Another asked whether government should provide child care to low- and middle-income working parents.[33] Figure 10-7 depicts the percentage of people, by occupation and union membership or nonunion status, who supported increased government spending for child care. The results are similar for government provision of child care to low- and middle-income working parents. These data provide no evidence for the hypothesis that support for child care would differ by occupational group or by unionization. Some possible explanations for this are the following. First, on both questions, women were about 9 percentage points more likely than men to support child care funding. This difference could help explain the low level of support for this policy among blue-collar workers, who were predominantly male, and the higher level of support among service and protective workers, a much higher proportion of whom were women. Second, the party identification difference in support was very large—amounting to about a 33 percentage point difference between Democrats and Republicans. Nevertheless, it is astonishing to see that the blue-collar workers, who might have benefited from child care funding for low- and middle-income working parents, showed the least support for it, and it is surprising that unionism seemed to have had no impact.

FIGURE 10-7. Support for Increased Government Spending on Child Care by
Union Membership and Occupation Type: 1988, 1990, 1992, 1994, 1996, 2000 (NES)

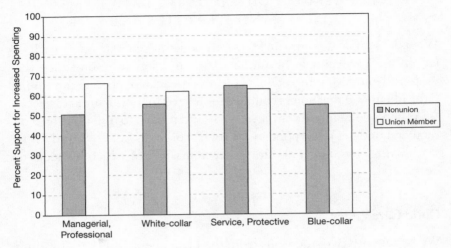

Paid Family Leave Policy

What about support for *paid* family leave? In 1996, the GSS asked how
people felt about paid leave that would be voluntarily provided by employers.[34] The results are depicted in Figure 10-8. On this issue there
was significantly more support among union members (12 percentage
points more) than among nonunion workers, but there was virtually
no difference across occupational groups, except for unionized service
workers. This number was two to three times larger than the additional support among union members for all other policies that we
considered.[35] It seems likely that the greater support among union
members in 1996 was a legacy of the campaign for unpaid family leave.

Health Care Policy

We also examined two items on health care policy, one from the NES
and the other from the GSS. The NES item asked whether there
should be a government insurance plan that would cover all medical
and hospital expenses for everyone. The GSS item similarly asked
whether the federal government should help people pay for doctor and
hospital bills.[36]

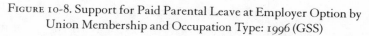

FIGURE 10-8. Support for Paid Parental Leave at Employer Option by
Union Membership and Occupation Type: 1996 (GSS)

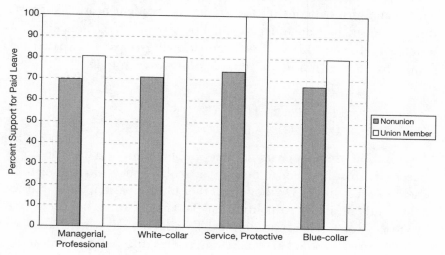

The results for both the NES question and the GSS question are alike. While support for paid family leave was uniformly higher among union members across all occupation types, the relationship between union membership and support for government health care insurance varied by occupational group, as observed with union support and paid leave policy.[37] For both health insurance questions, nonunion members in the two lower occupational groups were more supportive of government-subsidized health care than those in the two upper occupational groups. Among union members there were similar attitudes across the occupational groups for the GSS question, but the results for the NES question suggest that union members in the two lower occupational groups, especially those who were service and protective workers, were significantly less supportive of government-subsidized health care. This conclusion is based on relatively small numbers (seventy-one unionized service and protective workers, so the standard error is 6 percent, which produces a confidence interval of about 37 percent ± 12 percent), but the figure is still notable. Furthermore, although union members in the two upper occupational groups were more likely to support government-subsidized health insurance than nonunion members, those in the two lower ones were either less likely to support it (service and protective workers) or were no differ-ent from their nonunion counterparts (blue-collar workers). A multi-variate analysis that controls for sex and party identification suggests that unionism had an independent liberalizing effect, but only for union members in the top two occupational groups. This pattern is similar to what we found for unpaid family leave in 1986.

PARTICIPATION BY OCCUPATIONAL GROUPS OVER TIME

Unionization, then, appears to affect public opinion when there is a concerted effort by labor to push a particular policy. Do unions have other impacts as well? Do they affect the political participation that ac-tually sends messages to politicians? To answer these questions, we turn to the Roper Social and Political Trends data set, which has a bat-tery of questions about participation in twelve different political activ-ities.[38] In order to get an overall index, we simply sum the total number of activities of each person.

Figure 10-9 displays the number of activities by occupational group. This figure has three notable features, none of which is surpris-ing, given what is known about the socioeconomic characteristics of

FIGURE 10-9. Number of Political Activities by
Occupational Type: 1973–1994 (Roper)

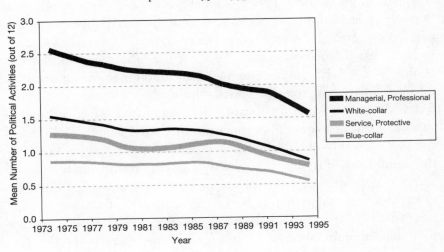

members of each of these occupations. First, all the lines decline, providing evidence for Robert Putnam's argument that people now participate less in American life.[39] Second, there is a clear ordering of managerial and professional, white-collar, service and protective, and blue-collar workers. The four lines never cross, and there are significant differences among them. Third, the political participation of the managerial and professional group is considerably higher than that for any other occupational group.

Figures 10-10 and 10-11 break out the participation levels for each occupational group by union and nonunion respondents. In every case, there is a significantly greater level of participation for those in unions, but the sizes of these impacts differ across the occupations. The biggest impact, percentagewise, is for blue-collar workers and for service and protective workers. Roughly speaking, unions increase participation from .7 to 1.0 acts for blue-collar workers (about 42 percent), but they increase activity from 2.0 to 2.4 acts for managerial and professional workers (about 20 percent). The corresponding figures for white-collar workers are 1.25 to 1.5 acts (about 20 percent); for service and protective workers, from 1.0 to 1.3 acts (about 30 percent). Hence, the progression from blue-collar to managerial and professional workers is approximately 42 percent, 30 percent, 20 percent, and 20 percent,

FIGURE 10-10. Number of Political Activities by Union Membership, Managerial, Professional, and White-collar Workers: 1973–1994 (Roper)

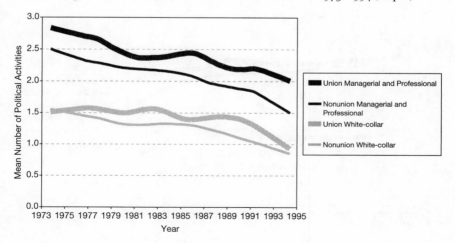

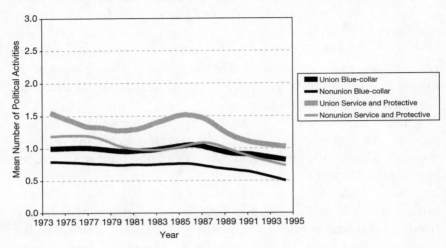

FIGURE 10-11. Number of Political Activities by Union Membership, Service, Protective, and Blue-collar Workers: 1973–1994 (Roper)

showing that unions can have a substantial impact on the political participation of those in the lower occupational groups.

The results for the socioeconomic status quintiles are even more impressive. Figure 10-12 shows that the largest percentage impact is for the lowest quintile: the increase is from about .4 to .6 acts, which is

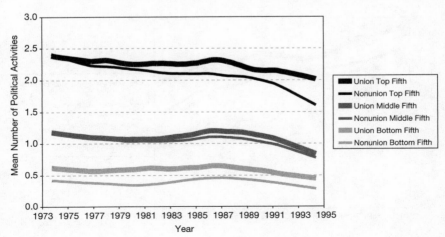

FIGURE 10-12. Number of Political Activities by Socioeconomic Status and Union Membership: 1973–1994 (Roper)

a 50 percent increase. For the third (middle) quintile, the change is from 1.0 to 1.1 (about 10 percent); for the fifth (top) quintile, it is from 2.0 to 2.2 (about 10 percent). When this finding is combined with the earlier result that the degree of unionization has fallen most dramatically in the bottom quintile, it seems obvious that changes in unionization have important implications for those at the bottom of the socioeconomic status ladder.

SUMMARY AND ASSESSMENT OF POLICY IMPLICATIONS

We found that support for family leave was weak and labile in 1986 before the family leave campaign for public support began in earnest. Support was greater among women, people with children younger than eighteen, union members, and Democrats, but it was only somewhat larger among these groups than among others. Between 1986 and 1992, support for family leave changed significantly after an energetic campaign that used people's union affiliations to define and arouse their self-interest. Male and female union members with children younger than eighteen dramatically increased their support for family leave from 1986 to 1992. As we have demonstrated through our analyses of survey results, attitudes toward family leave varied greatly from survey to survey (and even within a survey) in the late 1980s and early 1990s because of the highly variable wording of questions that emphasized competing values. Our results showed that attitudes toward family leave were labile and could be affected by a campaign that framed the policy one way or another in addition to the wording of the questions.

The campaign for family leave during the late 1980s and early 1990s mobilized the support of union members, certain occupational groups, and women. To make this case, we showed that support for unpaid family leave was not exceptionally strong in 1986 when the campaign began for it. Blue-collar workers, women, people with children, Democrats, and union members were somewhat more supportive than others, but their support was typically only 5 to 8 percent more than other groups' on a Roper survey question that asked whether granting family leave "is something companies should be required to do, or something that would be nice for them to do but not required, or something that they should not be expected to do." However, overall support for family leave increased by about 8 percentage points on this Roper question by December 1992, just before the family leave bill was passed by Congress and signed into law by President Clinton. Our evidence strongly suggests that the campaign for family leave significantly increased support for the policy between December 1986 and December 1992, particularly among union members who were women or men with children younger than eighteen.

We examined the argument that the family leave campaign mobilized people from important social groups by first assessing how occupational groups differed on a measure of socioeconomic status based on income and education. Our findings reproduced the familiar result that occupational groups can be arranged in a hierarchy of income and status, with managerial and professional workers at the top, white-collar workers next, then service and protective workers, and, finally, blue-collar workers at the bottom. Not surprisingly, unionization—an organizational device for overcoming the deficits in power and influence resulting from these socioeconomic status differences—is highest in the bottom, blue-collar group and decreases as we go up in the hierarchy.

Recognizing that changes in the workforce and in unionization have significant implications for family policy, we described the well-known drop over the past thirty years in the blue-collar proportion of the workforce and the somewhat less well-known increase in the proportion of managers and professionals. We looked at the secular drop in unionization across all four occupational groups, especially the precipitous drop in blue-collar unionization. In addition, we showed that the levels of unionization for the bottom socioeconomic quintiles plunged over the twenty years of the Roper studies, but the proportion of union members among the top quintile remained nearly constant, with only a small decline. Among respondents in the bottom three quintiles, the rate of unionization was cut in half over two decades. These facts mean that those with the greatest needs for paid family leave, child care funding, and better health care have become decreasingly represented by organized labor. These changes in the workforce and unionization have been accompanied by other changes in the social and political characteristics of occupational and socioeconomic status groups. The increase in the female labor force over the past thirty years has affected all occupations, but women still constitute only about 34 percent of the blue-collar workforce and 45 percent of managers and professionals. They are close to 60 percent of the white-collar and service and protective workers.

As expected, we found that members of the lower-status occupational groups and the bottom socioeconomic status quintiles were more likely to be Democratic in their party identification, and union members were even more likely to be Democrats. However, all occupational groups and socioeconomic status quintiles became less Democratic from the 1970s to the 1990s. Furthermore, there were especially large declines in the Democratic party identification of service and protective workers and of blue-collar workers, and members of these two occupational groups increasingly indicated that they did not identify with any particular party.

Implications for Family Policy

The changes in the occupational structure of the workplace and the partisan structure of American politics have had major implications for public opinion toward family policy. We found that women (especially working women), Democrats, and union members were the most supportive of family policies such as family leave, child care funding, and mandatory or government-provided health care plans— although the support among Democrats and women was greater than that among union members. But the declines in union membership and partisan support for the Democrats have reduced the size of the coalition that might support family policies. The greatest impacts come from the decline in partisan support for the Democrats among blue-collar and service and protective workers, and from the decline in unionization among blue-collar and even service workers. One of the consequences of changing partisanship and declining unionization is that support for family policies among people in blue-collar and service and protective jobs is not much different than the support for these policies among people in white-collar and managerial and professional positions.

Yet we found one instance—unpaid family leave—where labor

unions made a concerted attempt to put an issue on the public agenda, and their efforts seem to have paid off in dramatically greater support among labor union members. This finding suggests that labor unions can engage in successful agenda setting and that their activities, or the activities of other broad interest groups, may be a major way in which family policy will be pushed forward.

Favorable public opinion, however, is not all that is needed to develop new policy. Getting legislation passed requires active political participation by those groups who favor it, and we explored how political participation for occupation groups, SES quintiles, and union members has changed over time. By combining this information about participation with information about public opinion, we can say something about the likely sources of support for efforts to promote family policy. We demonstrated that union membership can have a significant impact on political participation, although it must overcome the very low rates of political participation among workers at the bottom of the occupational and socioeconomic status hierarchies. According to our research, political participation among people in lower-status occupations and lower quintiles is one-fifth to one-third that for those in higher-status occupations or the upper socioeconomic status quintiles. Unions can and do help compensate for these lower rates, especially in the lower quintiles, by increasing participation by as much as 40 percent. Nevertheless, the decline of unionism and the decline of Democratic party identification among people in these groups mean that the development of support for family policy faces a long, hard road.

Key Questions for the Future of a Family Policy Movement

Where do people concerned with advancing family policy go from here? We believe that a great deal more can be done to flesh out the argument we have begun to develop. For one thing, additional data sources might reveal more relevant questions that could be used to provide a better sense of which family policies might be successful. The resulting data might also allow us to pin down some important causal questions considered only briefly in this paper. For example, is it true that the labor unions' support for family leave led union members to be more supportive? Is it true that labor unions cause their members to participate more in politics? Our evidence suggests that unions can be effective in both ways, but more work is needed to confirm this.

Another important need for research would be to determine the rhetorical force of the phrase *family policy*. The Christian right and conservative Republicans have made great strides by emphasizing that they are "pro-family." It is clear that this claim gains succor from its linkage to conservative moral values and Christian fundamentalism. Does family policy—or *can* family policy—gain similar sustenance from its connection to traditional cultural values? Or is family policy inevitably problematic for even Republican moderates because it typically involves government action and an implicit, if not explicit, support for working women? These questions can probably be answered only by studying people's responses to thoughtful formulations of different descriptions of *family policy* on surveys. Studies with such features would be well worth undertaking because they would get at one of the basic questions about American politics: the relationship between economic policies and social/cultural concerns.

Finally, upper- and middle-class Democrats and liberals are obviously an important source of support for family policy, even though many of them might benefit much less from these policies than Americans in the lower occupational groups. Do they have the desire to promote it, given other, competing demands such as their traditional commitment to environmental policy? Do they need to bring others into their coalition in order to gain enough support and to assemble a core of people for whom the policies are vital?

Sources of Support for a Family Policy Movement

The major sources of differences in support for family policies were partisan identification, sex, and union membership, with Democrats, women, and union members being more supportive. However, the support by union members varied substantially across occupational groups and the effects were not always large. But we also found that in one instance, family leave, where labor unions worked hard to put an item on the policy agenda, the result was significantly more support for the policy among union members than among other workers. Finally, we found that unions are capable of increasing lower-class political participation by as much as 40 percent.

Our conclusions, therefore, are mixed. The decline of unionism and the decline of Democratic Party identification among those in blue collar and service-protective jobs mean that the development of support for family policy faces many challenges ahead. But unions can be effective under the right circumstances because they can place issues on the national agenda and they can mobilize their members, especially those with the lowest income and status.

I I

Work, Family, and Children's Consumer Culture

Juliet Schor

For the most part, work and family have been theorized as either conflictual or complementary. Themes in the conflict literature include, for example, the idea that the temporal demands of jobs are too great,[1] that the stresses of jobs have "spillover" effects in the family,[2] that family tensions result in excessive work schedules,[3] and that requirements for occupational success are incompatible with family responsibilities and therefore are discriminatory.[4] The complementarity perspective stresses the benefits of multiple roles and the combination of work and family. (For an explanation that reconciles these two strands, see the accompanying note.)[5]

What these two perspectives share, along with virtually all of the work-family literature to date, is that they theorize two places—the workplace and the household. While such a focus has been useful in the early stages of this research, it is ultimately inadequate, as it fails to recognize the effects of other spheres of society. For example, a rapidly growing literature on civic engagement developed in the 1990s, with important connections to work and family. Admirably, the Work, Family, and Democracy initiative incorporates a third arena, democracy, which includes both civil society and the public sphere. But the public sphere does not exhaust the set of additional social spaces that are relevant to the work-family nexus. In this chapter, I propose the incorporation of an additional sphere—the consumer economy or consumer culture. I argue that we cannot fully understand the ways in which changing patterns of work and family life are affecting well-being, particularly for children, without considering the role of consumer expenditure, consumer values, and consumer dynamics. In the case of children, this is because childhood is increasingly commercialized. By this I mean that children's life experiences are increasingly constituted and influenced by products and consumer culture, that products are increasingly mediating child-parent relations, and that identity is increasingly constituted through or in relation to products and the status of consumers. American children lead active and highly engrossing consumer lives, they spend enormous amounts of time immersed in commercial media, and even from an early age they are very aware of brand names.[6]

My purpose in this chapter is not to put forward definitive propositions but to raise questions and hypotheses concerning the relationship between the commercialization of childhood and work-family trends. I begin with a brief summary of the trend toward commercialized childhood. I then discuss some possible relationships that I believe are fruitful areas for future study. One is the idea that parents are using media as a babysitter and that exposure to consumer culture is positively related to parental working hours. A second is that consumer expenditures operate as a substitute for parental input and that the substitution effect is positively correlated to parental working hours. A third is that children's consumer desires are growing and that they are positively correlated to parental working hours. My hope is that by raising these questions, other work-family researchers will consider the consumer sphere and its impact on children's well-being.

CHILDREN AND CONSUMER CULTURE: A SUMMARY OF RECENT TRENDS

Child Consumption

In the past decade, children's consumption of both media and products has increased dramatically. After modest increases from 1960 to the mid-1980s, it was estimated that direct expenditures by children four to twelve years old rose nearly sixfold to $23.4 billion in 1997, and those were expected to be $35 billion in 2001.[7] Children are also believed to be indirectly responsible, through their influence on parental purchases, for $550 billion more in 2000, an increase from $50 billion in expenditures in 1984 and $188 billion in 1997.[8] The teen market is even larger, with $155 billion in direct expenditures.[9]

Behaviorally, children are becoming more like adult consumers. They have more of their own money (through allowances, work effort, and gifts), and they are spending more. They are also shopping, often alone. By the age of five, half of all children are reported to have made solo visits to stores and to have gone an average of twice per week. By age ten, they are making an average of 5.2 visits per week, a rate comparable to that for adults.[10] Finally, children, like adults, have developed a strong orientation to the symbolic meanings that are constructed through branding, rather than relating purely to the utilitarian aspects of goods. Children display considerable awareness of brands, and a variety of market research has suggested strong preferences for particular brands. (See Table 11-1, question 6, for data on the age at which brand requests begin.)

Not surprisingly, the growth of this market has led to a dramatic increase in advertising to children. In 1998, an industry source estimated that direct advertising to children was approximately $2 billion, a twentyfold increase from 1990.[11] Exposure to ads is partly driven by high levels of media usage. According to the 1999 Kaiser Family Foundation study "Kids and Media at the New Millennium," the average U.S. child, ages two to eighteen, spent 5 hours 29 minutes per day with media (television, video games, computers, radio, CD players, and print media). Of that total, the most significant medium was television, which accounted for 2 hours and 57 minutes of the total. Other screen-oriented media (videotapes, movies, and video games) accounted for 1 hour 22 minutes. Use of print media (excluding school reading) averaged 44 minutes.[12]

Advertising and the Commercialization of Childhood

Corporate efforts directed at children have become increasingly aggressive and have turned the former backwater of children's marketing into one of the industry's most dynamic and sophisticated submarkets. Children are a special target audience for marketing, both because of their growing influence over parental purchases (referred to as the "influence market") and because they represent the

TABLE 11-1. Parental Attitudes Toward Commercialism

	All	Fathers	Mothers
1. Which of the following statements comes closer to your view:			
Marketing and advertising puts too much pressure on children to buy things that are too expensive, unhealthy, or unnecessary OR			
Advertising is a good way for children to get accurate information about products			
Puts too much pressure	78	75	80
It's a good way for kids to get info	15	15	14
Both (volunteered)	5	7	3
Neither (volunteered)	2	2	2
Don't know	1	1	1
2. Advertising and marketing aimed at kids has a negative effect on their values and worldview OR			
Children today are very sophisticated about advertising and are not really influenced by them all that much			
Negative effect	70	67	74
Not really influenced	23	28	19
Both	3	3	4
Neither	3	2	3
Don't know	1	1	1
Do you strongly agree, agree, disagree, or strongly disagree with the following statements?			
3. Advertising and marketing aimed at kids today make children and teenagers too materialistic.			
Strongly agree	54	54	55
Agree	33	34	32
Disagree	9	8	11
Strongly disagree	3	3	2
Don't know	1	2	0

4. Buying and spending is a good thing. It is the American way.

Strongly agree	19	23	16
Agree	39	39	39
Disagree	28	26	30
Strongly disagree	12	11	13
Don't know	3	3	3

5. My child defines his or her self-worth in terms of the things he or she owns and wears more than I did when I was that age.

Strongly agree	40	44	36
Agree	23	20	26
Disagree	21	21	21
Strongly disagree	11	10	13
Don't know	2	3	3
Does not apply (child too young)	3	3	2

6. At what age did your children start asking for brand-name products?

2–3	22	18	26
4–5	22	24	20
6–10	41	44	37
11–14	13	12	14
15–17	2	2	2

7. Have you ever bought something for your child that you knew was too expensive, unhealthy, or just junk because your child wanted the product to fit in with his or her friends?

Yes	55	53	57
No	44	45	42
Don't know	1	1	1

(continued on page 290)

	All	Fathers	Mothers

8. Which of the following best describes how you feel when your child pressures you to buy something as a result of an advertisement?

	All	Fathers	Mothers
Angry	20	18	22
Pressured	38	37	40
Ready to please	6	5	7
Happy I have the money to buy it	17	21	13
Doesn't apply (volunteered)	15	17	14
Don't know	4	3	5

9. Are you or your spouse working longer hours than you would like in order to pay for the things your children feel they need?

	All	Fathers	Mothers
Yes	31	36	27
No	68	63	71
Don't know	1	1	2

10. Which of the following statements comes closer to your view:

It is getting harder and harder to set limits with kids because so much advertising is aimed at making kids feel they need all of these products in order to fit it OR

Blaming advertisers is just an excuse parents give because they do not know how to say no

	All	Fathers	Mothers
Harder	41	44	39
Excuse	43	41	45
Both (volunteered)	12	12	11
Neither (volunteered)	3	3	3
Don't know	1	0	2

11. Do you think Internet providers are doing enough to protect kids from the undue influence of online advertising?

Yes	15	20	15
No	64	59	64
Don't know	21	22	21

Do you strongly approve, approve, disapprove or strongly disapprove of the following practices or do you not care one way or the other?

12. Showing commercials for brand-name products in school

Strongly approve	4	6	2
Approve	10	11	9
Disapprove	34	39	29
Strongly disapprove	44	36	52
Do not care	7	7	6
Do not know	2	1	2

13. Requiring TV networks to reduce the amount of product advertisements aimed at kids, especially during Saturday morning cartoons, when children watch TV the most

Strongly approve	41	37	45
Approve	24	26	22
Disapprove	18	19	17
Strongly disapprove	7	6	7
Do not care	9	12	6
Do not know	2	0	4

Note: Poll conducted by EDK Associates, New York City, July 20–21, 1999. Nationwide poll of four hundred parents of children two to seventeen years of age who were selected by random digit dialing. Margin of error = +/–4.9 percent.

potential for early brand loyalties. Marketers now describe their goal as gaining "share of mind," rather than the older notion of gaining share of market. Adults are relatively fixed in their brand preferences, leaving children and teens as an increasingly desirable audience for brand marketing.

Eager to discover the strategies that will capture children's attention and desires, marketers are involved in an intensive data-gathering effort. In addition to traditional methods such as focus groups, surveys, and consumer panels, market research and advertising firms are sending cultural anthropologists into homes, stationing "coolhunters" in stores and on the streets to watch and talk to children, videotaping children, tracking their movements on the Internet, and analyzing child-parent interactions.[13] Marketers are hiring psychologists to give expert advice, conduct experiments, and do market research. Some schools have joined these efforts. In exchange for a fee, they allow market research firms to conduct focus groups and surveys during school hours, and even create data-collection exercises in the guise of "homework assignments."[14]

Marketers are also finding new venues for promoting their products, as standard television advertising has come to represent only a small fraction of total marketing expenditures. The development that has gained the most attention is the use of public schools as marketing institutions. Schools are appealing because they are able to deliver captive audiences in an environment relatively free of advertising clutter. An estimated 40 percent of the nation's public-school children in grades six through twelve are now subjected to mandatory viewing of Channel One's commercial broadcast.[15] Direct advertising is also growing: students are provided with free textbook covers covered with ads, soft drink companies have entered into sponsorship agreements with schools, many companies provide incentive programs for the purchase of equipment, and schools have rented out advertising space on buses and within buildings.[16]

These developments have spawned an increasing lively debate about the commercialization of childhood. The "family values" movement, childhood experts and advocates, progressive media critics, and members of the anticonsumerism movement have criticized both the content of media and the very practice of marketing to children.[17] For example, within the American Psychological Association, there has been criticism of psychologists' role in marketing to children, and a task force has been set up to study the issue.[18] Similarly, the American Academy of Pediatrics has weighed in on children's television exposure.[19] The 2001 Children's Defense Fund conference devoted an entire day to the impacts of commercialism and marketing on children. On Mother's Day 2001, the Motherhood Project of the conservative Institute for American Values issued a statement critical of media and marketing efforts directed toward children, which garnered support across the political spectrum.[20] Finally, a group of children's advocates has come together in the coalition Stop the Commercial Exploitation of Children (www.commercialexploitation.com).

A 1999 poll by the Center for a New American Dream (CNAD), on which I collaborated, explored parental attitudes about these issues and provided evidence that parents were aware of and critical of the impacts that advertising and marketing were having on their children.[21] Parents believed marketing puts pressure on children to buy things they do not need, negatively affects their values and worldviews, and makes them too materialistic. When asked, "Which of the following best describes how you feel when your child pressures you to buy something as a result of an advertisement?" 20 percent said "angry" and 38 percent said "pressured." By contrast, only 6 percent reported themselves "ready to please" and 17 percent "happy I have the money to buy it."[22] The CNAD poll also found that a large fraction of parents (78 percent) were opposed or strongly opposed to showing commercials for brand-name products in school, 64 percent believed Internet providers were not doing enough to protect children from online advertising, and 65 percent believed TV networks should be required to reduce the amount they advertise to children. However, the poll also revealed that parents held complicated attitudes about these issues (for example, 58 percent of parents agreed that "buying and spending is a good thing; it is the American way") and were by no means homogeneous in their opinions. Large majorities preferred more protection for children from advertising, supported the notion of spaces (such as schools) free from commercial messages, and understood that marketers often peddle products detrimental to children's health and well-being.[23]

Others are less concerned about children's relationship to media and consumer culture. The standard approach from economists and businesses has emphasized "consumer sovereignty," contending that the growth of expenditures is occurring because parents and children derive utility from spending, that marketing sustains the growth of expenditure, and that in any case parents have the right to limit their children's exposure to commercial culture.[24] Similarly, media and cultural studies research has recently contended that children are sophisticated viewers and consumers of commercials and other media, far less in need of protection than liberal maternalist advocates have realized. And finally, a conservative historicist view has stressed continuities with the past, arguing that children's lives have been commercialized for more than a century and that the trend of growing commercialization is itself more than a century old.

Creation and Destruction of Childhood

It is difficult to assess the contemporary debates without a historical perspective on childhood. This is partly because much of the criticism of current practices is rooted in an ahistorical and nostalgic view of what childhood has been and should be. Indeed, adults have had a long history of worrying about moral decay and excessive consumerism among youth. Furthermore, much of the child development literature is universalist and essentialist—that is, it assumes that children are all "essentially" the same, regardless of their culture of origin, class, race, and so on. These cultural or social differences tend to be minimized in favor of a biologically determined, "essence of what it means to be a child" approach.[25] A critical perspective on current trends of commercialization needs to be self-conscious about its assumptions of child development and adult-child relationships; it needs to understand adults' own relationship to consumer culture, and it needs to be aware of how childhood has changed over time.

Perhaps it is best to start with the recognition that childhood (as a set of ideas and practices) is a historically and socially constructed category, rather than solely a biological or evolutionary imperative. Indeed, as Philippe Ariès argued in his pioneering work, childhood, as a social category, only arose in the West in the sixteenth and seventeenth centuries.[26] Prevailing ideas and social practices about children—for example, whether they are inherently depraved and sinful, whether they are blank slates in need of socialization, whether they are capable of representing their own interests—have changed radically over time.

Not long after a historical literature on childhood appeared, so too did the concern that children and childhood itself were in jeopardy. By the 1980s, this view was being strongly articulated. Prominent examples include Neil Postman's *The Disappearance of Childhood* (1984)[27] and Viviana Zelizer's *Pricing the Priceless Child* (1985).[28] Postman argued that the contemporary idea of childhood, conceptualized as a stage in which children should be separated from the adult world and treated distinctly, arose only with the decline of an oral culture and a shift to a literate one. Postman argued that social isolation (in schools) was necessary because reading and writing are difficult skills to learn and are acquired only over a number of years. This long learning process also resulted in a lengthening of the period of childhood.[29] If childhood developed or was lengthened by the transition from an oral culture to a literary one, then in Postman's view, the disappearance of childhood is attributable to the shift from a literate culture to one based on television. Because television requires no special skills to understand and develops no skills itself, it undermined the hierarchical relation between child and adult. Furthermore, its confessional and graphic orientation exposed children indiscriminately to the adult worlds of sex, violence, illness, and so forth.[30]

Zelizer also argued that childhood changed between 1870 and 1930 as social attitudes toward children underwent a profound change that she described as a "sacralization" of childhood. She contends that by the beginning of the twentieth century, childhood had come to be culturally inscribed as an almost idyllic, play-filled, carefree period that every human being had a right to. Evidence can be found in the declining tolerance of infant death, the increased concern for children's physical safety, the opposition to placing monetary valuations on children in court cases, the decreased public tolerance of child labor, and the growth of a market for infant adoption. Zelizer showed that children were increasingly considered to be priceless, as well as irreplaceable in sentimental terms, at the same time that they were being excluded from productive work and the commercial sphere and thus being rendered "useless" economically. Childhood became a special extra-*commercium* social space, even as the larger world became increasingly commercialized.[31]

The image of childhood as extra-*commercium* has great resonance for contemporary critics of commercialization. Today's practices are contrasted with a previous era in which children were excluded from the market and commercial influences: play was unstructured and involved fewer toys, and children were less materialistic and less oriented toward marketed commodities.[32] While there is much that is correct in this view, it is important not to overstate it. Children have had a long-standing relationship to commodities and consumer culture. Today's children are not the first to have been swept up in toy fads, to care about their possessions, or to have intense desires for new things.[33]

Indeed, the description of childhood as extra-*commercium* applies only partially. The social construction of childhood has occurred in significant part *through* consumer objects. In the late sixteenth century, special children's clothing emerged; in the mid-eighteenth century, the first children's books appeared. To be a child meant to be someone who played with toys, read particular books, preferred certain kinds of food, and wore certain clothes. As Daniel Cook's work shows, the very stages of childhood arose out of marketing practices.[34] For example, Cook has argued that the "toddler" stage emerged as a result of apparel marketing by department stores in the 1920s. Commodities were salient in constructing childhood because children were part of the system of conspicous consumption that drove middle- and upper-class spending patterns.[35] However, this salience is also attributable to the fact that consumer goods and experiences have long been a major constituent of Western culture.

These caveats aside, there are important parallels between the "commercialization" of childhood and its "disappearance." Commercialization can be understood as one component of both the erosion of a protected space for children and their incorporation into the adult consumer world. Current trends also represent a desacralization; for example, children are now legitimate targets for commercial exploitation, through Internet data tracking, the use of psychologists, and the bypassing of parental consent in market research. In contrast to the thinking in the 1970s, when activists were able to garner widespread support for the idea that children need to be protected from advertising, in the current mood, almost anything goes.

Bypassing Parents

Why is the commercialization of childhood a component of its disappearance? The answer lies in the argument that at the core of commercialization is a restructuring of the relationships among children, mothers, and marketers. To put it (too) crudely, childhood was previously constructed *for* children, by an alliance of mothers and marketers. Today, marketers and children are allied, as the architects of childhood, either in place of or, in some versions, *against* mothers (and to a certain extent fathers). In the previous alliance, mothers protected children's interests; now they are excluded since marketers interact directly with children, but do so in order to sell products and not for the purpose of enhancing children's well-being. The earlier, maternalist approach was a subset of a larger alliance between women and merchants or manufacturers, all of whom jointly promoted the emergent consumer culture in the late nineteenth and early twentieth centuries in the United States and England. Consumers were mainly women, and opposition to consumer society came from men, who worried that it threatened sobriety and self-control, as well as patriarchal and religious values (such as chastity and male authority). The success of commercial retail establishments, including department stores, is partly attributable to a range of practices that allowed women to purchase goods on credit without their husbands' consent (and even in the face of their opposition) and to shoplift goods without effective detection or sanctions.[36] I argue, however, that there was a second relationship: marketers allied *with* mothers, *for* children. Companies attempting to sell products for children's use advertised to mothers (not directly to children), and a common message was that the product would improve the child's welfare.[37] The industry's notion of parents as gatekeepers continued in the post–World War II era, and it has not completely disappeared today.

What *is* new in the relationship between children and consumer culture is that the old alliance is being supplanted by a direct relationship between children and marketers, to the exclusion of, and even against, parents. Recent strategies in children's marketing have exhibited this change.[38] Ads now bypass the parent and appeal directly to children. These messages often undermine parental and other adult authority, portray parents as "uncool" or out of touch, or ridicule them.[39] Corporations position themselves as the sole adult actor who understands, relates to, cares about, and empathizes with children.

In research on advertising agencies, I found a systematic differentiation in strategic approaches to children and parents, as well as extensive direct targeting of children. To begin with, in cereal marketing, cereals that are especially high in sugar or that have other negative nutritional qualities are targeted exclusively at children. Also, many toys are exclusively targeted at children. For some products (such as shoes and backpacks), sophisticated "dual-messaging" strategies are used in which the parent-directed marketing highlights certain features and hides others. By contrast, the children's version of the ad emphasizes the jazzy features parents disapprove of or prefer not to pay for.[40]

Bypassing parents and marketing directly to children is now far more feasible than in the early days of television, when adult programming dominated. Now, in addition to Saturday morning cartoons, there are children's television networks such as Nickelodeon, the Disney Channel, and the Cartoon Network. Nickelodeon has been especially aggressive and successful in establishing itself as the representative of the child's point of view, which it has partly done through what I could term a pervasive anti-adult bias in its programming.[41] Direct marketing is also taking place in schools, on the Internet, in movies (with product tie-ins), through kids' clubs, and in other cultural institutions such as museums and amusement parks. Indeed, these are the cutting-edge venues.

A second trend is that advertisers are intentionally attempting to enlist children to influence parental purchasing behavior, for both children's and adults' products.[42] This is known in the industry as the "nag factor"—children's requests for products. As noted previously, the influence market is enormous, currently estimated at more than half a trillion dollars.[43]

Third, advertisers are redefining age appropriateness by reducing target ages and creating a more adultlike relationship earlier, or what the industry terms "age compression." One example is what is known as the "tweening" of the six- to twelve-year-old market, that is, advertising products and messages that were previously intended for teens. There is also a trend toward aiming nominally adult advertising at children, through the use of children's themes such as animals or play scenes.[44] Tobacco and alcohol ads in this genre have attracted attention (such as Joe Camel or the Budweiser frogs, which in 1998 were the most popular commercials of the year among children).[45] These practices are occurring, in part, to create early brand loyalties in children.[46] Indeed, the drive to create brand preferences at early ages has led to cradle-to-grave marketing, and the emergence of direct advertising to children in the zero-to-three age range through television programming (as with Teletubbies, designed for one-year-olds), infant Internet sites, and advertising for preschoolers.

Although children's marketing has existed for at least a century, the past ten years have witnessed fundamental changes in the strategies, intensity, direction, and effectiveness of advertisers' efforts. The volume and scope of these efforts, the sophistication of the psychological messages, and the quantity of research are unprecedented. (For example, individual episodes of certain Nickelodeon programs go through repeated focus-group testing with children.) Finally, the extent to which marketers have aligned themselves with children and against adults is historically novel.

HOW TRENDS IN WORK AFFECT CHILDREN'S RELATIONSHIP TO CONSUMER CULTURE: HYPOTHESES FOR FUTURE RESEARCH

Research on children's relationship to consumer culture is relatively undeveloped, with the exception of an extensive literature on the impacts of television. As I argued in the introduction, I believe that work-family researchers need to incorporate the foregoing trends into their understanding of household dynamics. In particular, the extent to which parental work patterns have interacted with the commercialization of childhood is an interesting question. To that end, I offer two areas for future research.

Parental Substitution

The restructuring of the relationship between children, parents, and marketers has been made possible, in significant measure, by changes in parental attitudes and behaviors. For example, the growth of direct expenditures is largely due to parental transfers of income to children. And the growth of an influence market has occurred because today's parents are willing to give their children a voice in family purchases. This is a significant change from more authoritarian, less consensual parenting styles.

I hypothesize that more than a change in parenting style is at work, however, and that parental labor force behavior has facilitated the shift toward a direct child-marketer relationship. The rates of labor force participation among mothers have increased steadily, and average annual hours of work for mothers have risen substantially.[47] Data from the Current Population Survey revealed that between 1969 and 1999, single parents' work hours rose by 297 per year, married parents' by 497, and married mothers' by 576.[48] Trends in fathers' hours were less dramatic. For instance, Leete and Schor found increases in fathers' hours, although other sources have not.[49] Importantly, the substantial increases in work hours that have been associated with women's entrance into career jobs and greater gender equality have not been matched by equivalent declines among men, which might then provide an opportunity for increased male domestic labor in household and childrearing tasks. For example, Leete and Schor's estimates from 1969 to 1989 suggest that the amount of parental time available for children is estimated to have declined twenty-two hours (or 14 percent) per week.[50] According to time diary studies, mothers have worked hard to protect their time with children. More research on this topic is needed.[51]

Parents' Time Pressures and Media as Babysitters

What is the impact of rising parental work time on children's connection to consumer culture? Two hypotheses suggest themselves. First, the rise of time pressure outside the workplace may lead parents to use television and other electronic media as babysitters in order to make time for household labor or other activities. Increased rates of media use among children are consistent with this hypothesis (although there are certainly other explanations for the rise in media use). So, too, is the finding that children living in single-parent households watch nearly an additional hour a day of television, movies, and videos than children in two-parent households.[52] Another pertinent finding is that relatively low rates of parental co-viewing occur during children's programming. Children older than seven almost never watch television with their parents, and among two- to seven-year-olds, parents are "doing something else" during 81 percent of their children's viewing time.[53] Twenty-four percent of children younger than six have a television set in their bedroom, as do 41 percent of children ages six to eleven.[54] Research evidence of relatively modest parental limitations and restrictions on children's media usage is also consistent with this view. For example, Kaiser found that 49 percent of parents had no rules about television viewing.[55] Direct testing of this hypothesis would be straightforward and useful.

Of course, the relationship between parental working hours and children's television watching is also mediated by other factors, such as after-school care, school hours, and the availability of quality child care. The hypothesis that television watching is a substitute for parental supervision should be tested in the context of the larger social environment. The pressure to use media as babysitters comes about as a combination of longer hours of work and a dearth of social provision of nonparental adult supervision.

Why should we care about the relationship between media use and parental work? A major reason is that there is increasing evidence that television, commercial movies, and video games have a range of negative outcomes for children. These include aggressive behavior, obesity, willingness to smoke and drink, lower reading scores, and more materialistic attitudes and behaviors. There is now an extensive literature on these effects.[56] The American Academy of Pediatrics has stated that children younger than two should not watch television at all, yet there are now programs for one-year-olds. Furthermore, the academy guidelines about levels of media use are considerably below current average viewing times.[57]

Parents' Discretionary Spending on Media for Children

A second hypothesis is that parents use media and commercial products as substitutes for themselves. This effect has been predicted by neoclassical economic models in which children are produced by a combination of parental time and capital goods (such as toys and media). If the opportunity cost of parental time rises, it is predicted that parents will shift toward more capital-intensive child-rearing methods. (Other models with imperfections in the market for hours can also yield these effects.)[58] The "parental substitution" hypothesis was tested by Karen Greve with two types of data. The first was the Consumer Expenditure Survey, in which she hypothesized that discretionary spending on children (for toys, videos, books, and so on) was positively correlated with parental work effort (controlling for income and other household characteristics). Greve found that for every increased hour of work by mothers, discretionary spending rose by $1.76 per month. Mean monthly discretionary expenditures were $155, mothers' mean work hours were thirteen, and fathers' mean work hours were sixty-five. Among high-income families (those with more than $50,000 in after-tax income), spending rose by $2.76. Fathers' work effort had a smaller impact, as one might expect, accounting for an additional $0.67 among all families and $1.54 among those of high-income.[59]

A portion of parents' discretionary spending goes toward the purchase of toys, and we would expect toy-related spending to exhibit a higher responsiveness to parental work time than other discretionary spending, since one of the most important functions of toys, according to play theory, is that they facilitate solitary activity by children.[60] This was the case in Greve's research. Among all families, toy expenditures rose by $2.59 for every additional work hour by mothers and $1.26 for each additional one by fathers. Mean monthly toy expenditures were $79.00. A questionnaire administered to working mothers from affluent families yielded similar results. Mothers who worked longer hours did more discretionary spending on their children (controlling for income). Conversely, mothers who spent more time with their children spent less on them.

Of course, the implications of this finding are complex and need far more investigation. We know a fair amount about the impacts of higher media usage. But other kinds of expenditures remain unexplored. Does the *quantity* of toys that children have affect their well-being? Does frequent purchasing affect their values or levels of materialism? Recent research on materialism and children suggested that materialist values are negatively correlated with well-being.[61] This analysis took toys as an aggregate category, but different types of toys clearly affect children differently. While analysis of aggregate expenditure patterns is a first research step, far more disaggregation is ultimately required.

Children's Consumer Desires and Parental Work Effort

To date, there has been too little research on how marketing, spending, and exposure to consumer culture influence children's materialist values and desires. An important recent study was the randomized, controlled experiment of Robinson and associates, who found that reductions in viewing time reduced children's product requests.[62] Earlier studies had found a positive relationship between exposure, product requests, purchases, and the consumption of foods.[63] An international analysis found that U.S. children made the most product requests.[64]

Survey data have suggested heightened levels of materialism among children. A recent Roper poll reported that "being rich" had become the number one aspiration of American children and teens.[65] In a recent poll by Teen Research Unlimited (www.teenresearch.com), 13 percent of respondents reported that they "believe they will pocket their first million by age 30." Furthermore, adults appear to believe that children are highly materialistic and becoming more so although, as noted earlier, it is possible that the adults hold a distorted picture of the past. A large majority of parents agrees that television "increases materialism" in children.[66] In the CNAD poll, 67 percent of fathers and 74 percent of mothers agreed with the statement "Advertising and marketing aimed at kids has a negative effect on their values and world view." By contrast, 23 percent felt "children today are very sophisticated about advertising and are not really influenced by advertising all that much." Fifty-four percent of parents strongly agreed and 33 percent agreed that "advertising and marketing aimed at kids today make children and teenagers too materialistic." Also, 63 percent of parents agreed or strongly agreed with the statement "My child defines his or her self-worth in terms of things they own and wear more than I did when I was that age."[67]

Are Parents Feeling Increased Pressure to Earn and Spend?

If children are becoming more materialistic, what impact, if any, is this having on parental labor force participation and hours of work? For example, do parents feel increased pressure to provide consumer goods for their children, and if so, are they working longer hours to do so? In the CNAD poll we asked, "Are you or your spouse working longer hours than you would like in order to pay for the things your children feel they need?" Thirty-one percent answered affirmatively. In this context, the findings of Ellen Galinsky, regarding children of working parents, are intriguing. Galinsky reported: "When we asked the children to make a wish that would change the way that their parents' work affects their lives, the most frequently mentioned wish was that their parents make more money."[68] The relatively high levels of satisfaction that Galinsky found among these children of working parents may have been due, in part, to the fact that they were increasingly willing to trade off time with their parents for higher consumer expenditures.

If the foregoing is correct, it suggests that the standard formulation—in which parental labor force participation is modeled on adult preferences for income and consumer goods—may no longer be sufficient. Children's desires for income and goods may well be playing a much larger role than previously. Clearly, more research on this question would be useful. Finally, we should also consider a more complex causal relationship than is standard in the economic literature on labor force participation (in which desires for income are exogenous). Causality may also be operating in the reverse direction. Higher incomes (as a result of greater parental labor effort) may lead to higher expenditures for children, which in turn may increase children's desires for consumer goods and parental work effort to sustain them.

CONCLUSION

When confronted with critics, media industry executives and marketing professionals offer a standard reply: that their efforts are justifiable because parents have the right and duty to limit their children's exposure to media or consumer products they find objectionable. But the ubiquity of advertising, media, and consumer products in the lives of today's youth makes this defense less compelling than in the past.[69] Many parents find they are able to limit their children's exposure less and less, because the social and practical obstacles are growing. For example, the CNAD poll found that parents are evenly divided between the views that "it is getting harder and harder to set limits with kids because so much advertising is aimed at making kids feel they need all these products" and that "blaming advertisers is just an excuse parents give because they do not know how to say no."

Furthermore, long parental working hours required to support families in today's environment may undermine parents' ability to limit or control their children's exposure. A traditional family model with a full-time homemaker available to supervise not only children's media and leisure time but also their purchasing behavior is an increasing rarity and a declining social ideal. Therefore, new approaches to the ways in which children are exposed to and interact with media and consumer culture are necessary. Indeed, if marketers and media producers continue their attempts to directly target children, and if parents find themselves increasingly powerless, then the regulation of content, advertising, and marketing becomes increasingly necessary. The emerging coalition of right and left, as well as growing attention to this issue over the past year, suggests it may become a more pressing public policy concern. For example, possible policy issues include the banning of advertising to children younger than twelve, restrictions on school-based marketing, the incorporation of children's history of exposure to media into annual physical examinations, school-based media literacy efforts, and so on. A less traditional formulation of policy issues would also include connections to parental working hours and patterns. The relevant policy issues would then include questions of after-school supervision and the role of media use in after-school activities, workplace reforms around scheduling and the temporal demands of jobs, and increased provisions for employees to work short hours. These are just some of the possible policy issues that arise from incorporating an analysis of consumer culture into the work-family field.

Section IV

Seeking Solutions

12

Europe Advanced While the United States Lagged

Sheila B. Kamerman

A repeated theme in the media and in public discussion is that families changed in the last half of the twentieth century or that the pace of changes begun earlier accelerated during these years. The changes that have been highlighted include declining birth rates and family size, deferred age of marriage and declining marriage rates, increased rates of divorce, more single-parent families, more out-of-wedlock births, increased cohabitation, and, perhaps most importantly, increased labor force participation of women, especially married women with young children. To a greater or lesser extent, these changes characterize families in all the advanced industrialized countries. Increasingly, the dominant family type in many of these countries is a family headed by one or two working parents.[1] However, the public statutory policies developed either as precursors of these changes or in response to these changes vary across countries.

A second repeated theme in this discussion is that in the face of these changes, the United States has been a laggard in its social policies toward children and their families. It has lagged behind most other advanced industrialized countries—in particular, the Western European countries—with respect to the full complement of "family policies."[2] More specifically, it has lagged behind with regard to the development of policies that support working parents or facilitate the reconciliation of work and family life, in particular income transfers and wage supplements, health care, early childhood education and care, and maternity and parental leaves.

In what follows, I begin with the European developments, describing the evolution of three critical policy regimes: (1) child or family allowances as income or wage supplements, (2) maternity and parental leave policies as guarantors of health protection, economic security, and time for parenting and the promotion of children's well-being, and (3) early childhood care and education as child protection, care, socialization, and education. I suggest why the European countries have enacted such supportive policy and program responses to the growing numbers of working families. Next, I comment briefly on why the United States has lagged behind Europe in its development of family policies generally. I conclude with some comments about possible lessons from the comparisons for the United States.

HISTORICAL PERSPECTIVES

Three policy regimes are at the heart of the European child and family policies: (1) income transfers, both cash benefits and tax benefits, designed to compensate families for the economic costs of child rearing and to supplement wages that do not take account of family needs; (2) maternity, paternity, and parental leave policies designed to ensure women time to recover from childbirth and to adapt to a new baby and a new parenting role without undue economic penalty; and (3) early childhood education and care services that ensure young children good care while parents work outside the home and early education and socialization as they are prepared for subsequent schooling. All had their roots in the mid- to late nineteenth century, but their major expansion and development occurred in the second half of the twentieth century.

Family or Child Allowances:
From Wage Supplement to Child Benefit

Family or child allowances are cash benefits that the government provides monthly (or, occasionally, more or less frequently) to parents, based on the presence and the number of children in the family. In addition, sometimes the benefits depend on the ordinal position and age of each child and, occasionally, on whether the family is headed by one or two parents. The benefits are modest, provided at a flat rate, and, for the most part, equal to 5 to 10 percent of average wages. However, they are an important supplement to low wages and may be a significant component of family income for low-income families, mother-only families, and large families. Unlike pensions, they are usually not indexed but may be adjusted periodically to reflect changes in wages or the cost of living, or for other reasons. They usually last until a specific age (for example, sixteen or eighteen) or when the child leaves secondary school, but in several countries the allowance may continue to be provided until the child completes a university education. The allowances are usually funded out of general tax revenue but may include employers' contributions. They are usually tax-free. Sometimes they are integrated with or replaced by tax provisions, such as child tax credits, especially when these are refundable. At the beginning of the twenty-first century, eighty-eight countries worldwide, including almost all the Organisation for Economic Co-operation and Development (OECD) countries[3] and all the European Union (EU) countries, provide such benefits.[4] They are popular wherever they are provided, and all qualifying parents and guardians take advantage of their availability.

From the outset, the benefits were designed to help with the costs of rearing children.[5] "To equalize the financial burdens borne by those who have children and those who do not" is a repeated theme in relevant legislation and documents. They are usually a universal entitlement, provided to all families regardless of income; but in some countries, even in the EU, eligibility is limited to families with a working parent (or a pensioner).[6] In very few countries the benefit is means-tested, and in France these allowances are limited to second and subsequent children.

Family allowances are at the heart of family policies as they have developed internationally. They constitute the first policies explicitly directed toward families, and their roots may be found in the late nineteenth and early twentieth centuries in France and Sweden. They reflect a concern for several family demographic and economic developments, particularly the problems of low birth rates and low wages. Family or child allowances were the primary policy instrument used to respond to these problems. They were first provided by employers as a supplement to employees' low wages, in recognition of the fact that wages did not take account of family needs. Designed as a way of

TABLE 12-1. Legal Governance, Structure, Financing, and Administration of Family and Child Allowance Programs, 1999

	Governing Laws	Type of Program	Source of Funds	Administrative Organization
Australia	*First law:* 1941 (family allowances) *Current laws:* 1991 (orphan's pension), 1996 (family tax payment), 1997 (parenting payment, maternity immunization allowance), 1998 (family allowance)	Means-tested	*Insured person:* None. *Employer:* None. *Government:* Entire cost from general revenue.	Department of Family and Community Services, general supervision. Administration of programs through local government offices.
Austria	*First law:* 1948 *Current law:* 1967	Universal	*Insured person:* None. *Employer:* 4.5% of payroll. *Government:* Grants by municipalities. Portion of federal income tax receipts transferred to Family Allowances Equalization Fund.	Federal Ministry of Environment, Youth and Family, administration of program through Family Allowances Equalization Fund attached to Ministry. Employers (social insurance institutions or finance offices) pay allowances directly to recipients.
Belgium	*First law:* 1930 *Current laws:* 1967, 1969, 1971 (means-tested allowances for those ineligible for basic benefit)	Employment-related system	*Insured person:* None. *Employer:* None. Distribution of social security resources according to the needs of family allowance scheme. *Government:* Subsidies to employee and self-employed programs covering any deficits.	Ministry of Social Affairs, Public Health and the Environment, general supervision. National Social Security Office, collection of contributions. National Family Allowances Office, distribution of funds.
Canada	*First law:* 1944 *Current law:* 1998 (income tax act)	Universal and tax credit	*Insured person:* None. *Employer:* None. *Government:* Whole cost.	Department of National Revenue determines eligibility of child tax benefits and administers the program.

Country	Law	Coverage	Source of Funds	Administrative Organization
Czech Republic	First law: 1945 Current law: 1995	Universal	Insured person: None. Employer: None. Government: Whole cost.	Ministry of Labor and Social Affairs, general supervision. District social security offices for administration of benefits.
Denmark	First law: 1952 Current law: 1986	Universal	Insured person: None. Employer: None. Government: Whole cost.	Ministry of Social Affairs, general supervision and national administration. Local (municipal) governments, administration of program.
Finland	First law: 1948 Current law: 1992 and 1996 (Child Home Care Allowance)	Universal	Insured person: None. Employer: None. Government: Whole cost.	Ministry of Social Affairs, general supervision; Social Insurance Institution, national administration of Family Allowance Program.
France	First law: 1932 Current law: 1946	Universal	Insured person: None, except for self-employed and farmers. Employer: 5.4% of payroll. Government: 1.1% of total revenues used to finance family allowances, as well as tax of 1% on heritage income.	Ministry of Labor and Social Affairs, general supervision. National Family Allowances Fund, coordination of funds by tripartite governing body composed of employer, employee, and family or family organization representatives.
Germany	First law: 1954 Current law: 1996	Universal	Insured person: None. Employer: None. Government: Whole cost.	Federal Finance Office, administration of benefits through the Federal Institute for Labor (through regional and local labor offices) under the title Family Fund. Separate administration of schemes for public employees.

(continued on page 314)

	Governing Laws	Type of Program	Source of Funds	Administrative Organization
Greece	*First and current law:* 1958	Employment-related	*Insured person:* 1% of earnings. *Employer:* 1% of payroll. *Government:* None. Maximum earnings for contribution of benefit purposes is 7,612,500 drachmas/year.	Ministry of Labor, general supervision. Administration of allowances through local offices. Social Insurance Institute, collection of contributions.
Iceland	*First law:* 1946 *Current law:* 1981[1]	Universal	*Insured person:* None. *Employed person:* None. *Government:* Total cost.	Ministry of Finance, general supervision; tax authorities.
Ireland	*First law:* 1944 (child benefit), 1984 (family income support), 1990 (lone-parent's allowance) *Current law:* 1993 (consolidates all previous laws related to social welfare).	Universal child benefit and income-tested single-parent benefit	*Insured person:* None. *Employer:* None. *Government:* Whole cost.	Department of Social, Community and Family Affairs, administration of allowances. Payments made at post offices on behalf of the department.
Italy	*First law:* 1937 *Current laws:* 1961, 1965, 1970, 1974, 1980, 1983, 1988 (reform of family benefits scheme)	Employment-related	*Insured person:* None. *Employer:* 2.48% of payroll. *Government:* Various subsidies. Minimum earnings for contribution purposes: 67,474 lires/day or, if higher, minimum wage.	Ministry of Labor and Social Welfare, and Treasury, general supervision. National Social Insurance Institute, administration of program through Central Family Allowances Fund. Individual employers pay allowances directly to own employees (except in agriculture).

Japan	Dual employer liability and assistance	First law: 1971 (children's allowance). Current laws: 1981, 1985, 1991, 1994	Insured person: None. Employer: 70% of cost (about 11% of wages). Government: With respect to employees—national treasury, 20% of cost, prefecture 5%, city or town 5%. With respect to self-employed and unemployed—national treasury 66.6%, prefecture about 16.7%, city or town about 16.7%.	Ministry of Health and Welfare, supervision through Children and Families Bureau. City or town grants allowances.
Luxembourg	Universal	First law: 1947 (employed persons) and 1959 Universal (self-employed persons) Current laws: 1977 (birth allowances), 1980 (maternity allowances), 1985 (family allowances), 1986 (beginning of school-year allowances), 1988 (education allowances).	Insured person: Employee, none. Self-employed, 0.7% of income. Employer: None. Government: Entire cost.	Ministry of Family, general supervision. National Family Allowance Fund distributes allowances.
Netherlands	Universal	First law: 1939 Current law: 1980	Insured person: None. Employer: None. Government: Whole cost.	Board of Supervision of Social Insurance, general supervision. Social Insurance Bank, administration of allowances.
New Zealand	Dual universal and social assistance	First law: 1926 Current laws: 1964 (family benefit, discontinued from April 1, 1991), 1973 (domestic purposes benefits), 1978 (disabled child's allowance, 1985 (family support), 1986 (guaranteed minimum family income), 1996 (Ind. Family Tax Credit	Insured person: None. Employer: None. Government: Entire cost financed from general revenues.	Department of Work and Income, administration of allowances through branch and district offices. Department of Inland Revenue, administration of family support, independent family tax credit, and guaranteed minimum family income programs.

(continued on page 316)

	Governing Laws	Type of Program	Source of Funds	Administrative Organization
Norway	*First and current law:* 1946	Universal	*Insured person:* None. *Employer:* None. *Government:* Whole cost.	Ministry of Health and Social Affairs, general supervision. National Insurance Administration, national administration of program and supervision of local offices. National Insurance county offices, administration of county program and supervision of local offices. Local insurance offices, local allowance administration.
Portugal	*First law:* 1942 *Current laws:* 1980, 1997	Employment-related	*Insured person:* 11% of earnings. *Employer:* 23.75% of payroll. *Government:* Family allowances are allocated 2.8% of social pensions and health care revenues.	Ministry of Labor and Solidarity, general supervision through the State Secretariat for Social Security and Work Relations. Regional Social Security Centers, administration of program.
Spain	*First law:* 1938 *Current law:* 1994	Employment-related	*Insured person:* Portion of social pension contributions. *Employer:* Portion of social pension contributions. *Government:* Pays for noncontributory pensions from general revenues.	Ministry of Labor and Social Affairs, general supervision. National Institute of Social Security, Treasurer General of Social Security, payment of claims.

	First and current law:			
Sweden	First and current law: 1947	Universal	Insured person: None. Employer: None. Government: Whole cost.	National Social Insurance Board, central administration and supervision. Regional and local social insurance offices, administration of program.
Switzerland	First and current federal law: 1952 (agricultural only) Cantonal law: All cantons have laws enacted during or after 1943	Employment-related	Insured person: None. Employer: Contributions vary by sector. Government: Federal and cantonal governments share residual costs.	Cantonal (local government) programs: Administered by numerous public and approved private family allowance funds, supervised by cantonal governments. Employers usually pay allowances with wages.
United Kingdom	First laws: 1945 (child benefit), 1987 (family credit) Current law: 1992 (consolidated law)	Universal and refundable tax credit	Insured person: None. Employer: None. Government: Whole cost.	Department of Social Security, administration of allowances centrally through the benefits agency.

Source: Social Security Administration, Social Security Programs Throughout the World, 1999. Available at: http://www.ssa.gov/policy/docs/progdesc/ssptw/1999/. Columbia University Clearinghouse on International Developments in Child, Youth, and Family Policy, information available at: http://www.childpolicyintl.org.

[1] Program transferred from social security to the tax system.

TABLE 12-2. Child and Family Allowances, 1997

	As % of GDP	As % of Social Protection Expenditures
Belgium	2.4	8.8
Denmark	3.9	12.6
Germany	2.9	10.1
Greece	1.9	8.2
Spain	0.4	2.0
France	2.9	10.0
Ireland	2.2	13.2
Italy	0.9	3.5
Luxembourg	3.2	13.2
Netherlands	1.1	3.7
Austria	2.9	10.5
Portugal	1.1	5.3
Finland	3.7	12.6
Sweden	3.6	10.8
United Kingdom	2.4	9.1
European Union 15	2.2	8.4
Iceland	2.3	12.5
Norway	3.4	13.7

Source: European Union, Eurostat, ESSPROS, 2000.

avoiding more general wage increases, family allowances also began by the 1930s to be viewed as a pro-natalist strategy, designed to provide an incentive for parents to have more children.

By the beginning of World War II, seven countries (Belgium, France, Hungary, Italy, the Netherlands, New Zealand, and Spain) had adopted family allowance legislation, and another seven (Australia, Canada, Finland, Ireland, Romania, the Soviet Union, and most of the Swiss cantons) adopted these benefits during the war.[7] The period of major growth in family allowances followed World War II. Family allowances—whether a response to the devastation that children and their families experienced during the war, a conviction about the need for social solidarity that emerged immediately after the war, or a child-related part of welfare state developments following the war—were established throughout all of Europe by 1960.[8] In some countries, child-conditioned housing allowances were introduced as well. In many countries, the 1950s were the golden age of family allowances.[9]

Family allowances in these years were limited initially to working families—that is, those with at least one wage earner. Nonetheless, they achieved their initial goals. Economic pressures on families with children were eased slightly as a result of these benefits, while the post-war baby boom relieved the concerns of those worried about low birth rates. Although fertility rates declined again beginning in the 1960s, and although some people remain concerned about the trend toward one-child families in several countries, public policies in these countries no longer appear to reflect pro-natalist objectives—at least not overtly. Government officials in France, the country with the most explicit pro-natalist concerns, now insist that birth rates and family size are private family matters no longer of concern to the government, but that if people have children, they must be helped with the costs of rearing them. This view is also held in Germany. In the 1960s, a decade of strong economic growth, family allowances were raised, and several countries moved to make the system universal by eliminating the link to employment as a criterion for receipt. In the 1970s, with the economic downturn, the concern for financially vulnerable families increased. In several countries, supplementary family benefits were targeted to poor families, to mother-only families, and later to working families (those with two employed parents). In some countries, this meant introducing income testing into benefits (as for several of the various family benefits in France), while in other countries (but including France) a policy of government-guaranteed child support benefits (advanced maintenance payments) was introduced to protect the situation of mother-only families.[10] A package of family allowances, housing allowances, and advanced maintenance payments, coupled with even half an average wage, was sufficient to protect these vulnerable families against poverty.[11]

Family allowances were never viewed as an alternative to earnings, nor was it ever assumed that they would cover the real economic costs of rearing a child. The assumption, whether explicit or implicit, was that family economic well-being would depend, first and foremost, on employment, earnings, and employment-linked benefits. Family allowances were intended to function as a modest, child-related supplement to wages. In some countries they did this very successfully; in others, less so.[12]

According to historian Susan Pedersen, the French family allowance system redistributed the wage bill in accordance with family needs, "thus effectively distributing the cost of children among the population."[13] In contrast, when faced with the same problem of the lack of fit between wages and family needs, the British tried to protect the superiority of men's wages. While both countries eventually established universal child benefits, these early preferences did affect future developments. Family policy and the family allowance system remained at the heart of French social policy, while only in the late 1970s did a true child benefit emerge in Britain. It did cover the first child, in contrast to France's policy, and single mothers received an extra benefit, but it was never as generous overall as the French policy package and never as central to the British income transfer system.

Tax Benefits

An alternative to a family and child allowance is a benefit provided through the tax system, such as a refundable (sometimes called nonwasteable) tax credit. The use of this device has been growing in recent years and now exists in the United States, Britain, Canada, and Israel, among other countries. Examples of the approach include the U.S. earned income tax credit and the British family credit, working families tax credit, and (more recently) child tax credit. These refundable tax credits are child-conditioned tax benefits that provide for a reduction in the income tax liability of working families. In addition, families with incomes below the tax threshold receive the equivalent amount as a cash benefit.

Gender issues have also affected family allowance policies. Initially, the benefit was provided to fathers, but over time it either became a child benefit, with either parent qualifying as a recipient, or was directed toward the mother, as a modest "mother's wage." The issue became particularly heated in the late 1970s in Britain, when the country debated whether the tax exemptions for children should be increased (viewed as an approach likely to benefit fathers) or whether the child allowance should be raised (likely to benefit mothers, as the recipients of the benefits).[14] Although family income would have been increased overall if either measure had been adopted, the debate underscored the question of how family resources were shared within families. Few discussions about the use of tax benefits versus direct cash benefits appeared to address this issue.

Thus, to summarize, family or child allowances were designed initially as wage supplements to compensate for the absence of a family wage and the fact that market wages did not reflect family needs.[15] Developed at a time when this approach seemed a benign alternative to raising wages across the board, it reflected a concern with promoting children's well-being and with raising birth rates. It certainly did raise the incomes of families with children, but it had no significant impact on fertility rates, and the latter has largely disappeared as an explicit goal of these policies.[16] Although modest, family allowances, when packaged with other categorical benefits (single-parent allowances, housing allowances, advanced maintenance payments) and coupled with earnings (even if modest), have played an important role in reducing child poverty.[17] Their real growth occurred in the post–World War II period, when countries were especially concerned about the consequences of war on children, and in the 1960s, a decade of strong economic growth, when there was concern about child poverty and a strong desire to improve the situation of children.

Family and child allowances have been popular benefits, as shown by the fact that not only do all who have qualified for these benefits claim them, but also that these benefits have had strong support across the political spectrum. There may have been debates over specific provisions (for example, what the maximum age of covered children should be, whether the first child should qualify for benefits, whether the benefit should be income-tested) but not in recent years regarding *whether* there should be a family allowance, which has become an integral part of social policy and of child and family policy almost everywhere.

Maternity, Paternity, and Parental Leave Policies: Health Protection, Economic Security, Gender Equity, Time for Parenting, and Child Well-being

Maternity leaves are employment-related policies that were first enacted more than a century ago to protect the physical health of working women and their babies.[18] They were enacted well before women constituted a significant component of the paid workforce in any of the countries discussed here.[19]

The Link Between Leave Time and Health Concerns

Linked to provisions for sick leaves (non-job-related disabilities), maternity leaves were established on the assumption that relieving women of workplace pressures briefly before and after childbirth while protecting their economic situation would protect and promote their own and their babies' physical well-being. Initially, such leaves lasted from four to twelve weeks and were paid as a lump sum or a flat-rate benefit. By World War I, twenty-one countries had established a maternity leave, and of these, thirteen were paid.[20] By the beginning of World War II, eight more European countries had enacted a paid leave, including all of the major Western European countries; among the major industrialized countries, only the United States and Canada did not have such legislation in place.[21] Provided to employed parents, these statutory leaves protected the parents' jobs during the leaves and

TABLE 12-3. First Maternity Leave Legislation (Unpaid Scheme), Pre-1945

Period	Country	Year of Introduction	Duration of Leave
Pre-1905	Switzerland	1877	8 weeks
	Germany	1878	3 weeks
	Austria	1884	6 weeks
	Portugal	1891	4 weeks
	United Kingdom	1895	4 weeks
	Belgium	1899	4 weeks
	Spain	1900	4 weeks
	Sweden	1900	4 weeks
	Ireland	1901	4 weeks
1905–1918	Italy	1907	4 weeks
	New Zealand	1908	4 weeks
	France	1909	8 weeks
	Netherlands	1910	4 weeks
	Japan	1911	5 weeks
	Australia	1912	4 weeks
	United States	1912	4 weeks
	Greece	1912	8 weeks
	Denmark	1913	4 weeks
	Norway	1915	4 weeks
	Finland	1917	4 weeks
1919–1944	Canada	1921	12 weeks
	Luxembourg	1925	8 weeks

Source: A.H. Gauthier, *The State and the Family* (Oxford: Oxford University Press, 1996).

until they returned to work.[22] Initially, the leaves applied only to certain categories of workers, but now in some countries such leaves also apply to the unemployed and to people with no labor force attachment.

Most countries provide a paid leave that replaces all or some portion of workers' prior wages. This leave may be supplemented by a longer unpaid leave or one paid at a lower level. Among the OECD countries, only the United States, Australia, New Zealand, and Switzerland have no paid, universal, non-means-tested leave. (It is generally recognized that unless the leave is paid, most working parents cannot take advantage of it, since their families' standard of living depends on their wages, and if it is only means-tested, a large group will remain uncovered.) The leave policy is usually part of employment policy, while the cash benefit that replaces forgone wages is usually paid for through the social insurance (social security) system—linked to sickness benefits,

TABLE 12-4. Maternity Leave Benefits (Paid Schemes), Pre-1945

Period	Country	Year of Introduction	Duration of Leave	Type of Benefit[1]
Pre-1900	Germany	1883	6 weeks	c/50%
	Belgium	1894	6 weeks	v/FR
1900–1915	Italy	1910	4 weeks	c/LS
	Austria	1911	4 weeks	c/60%
	Switzerland	1911	6 weeks	v/FR
	United Kingdom	1911	4 weeks	c/LS
	Australia	1912	4 weeks	m/LS
	France	1913	8 weeks	c/FR
	Ireland	1913	4 weeks	c/LS
	Netherlands	1913	12 weeks	c/100%
	Denmark	1915	2 weeks	v/FR
	Norway	1915	8 weeks	v/FR
1916–1944	Japan	1922	10 weeks	c/60%
	Portugal	1922	10 weeks	c/100%
	Luxembourg	1925	8 weeks	c/50%
	New Zealand	1926	4 weeks	v/LS
	Spain	1929	10 weeks	c/FR
	Sweden	1931	8 weeks	v/LS
	Greece	1934	12 weeks	c/33%
	Finland	1937	6 weeks	m/LS

Source: A.H. Gauthier, *The State and the Family* (Oxford: Oxford University Press, 1996).

[1] Designations are as follows: c = compulsory, v = voluntary, m = means-tested, LS = lump sum, FR = flat-rate benefit, % = portion of wage replaced.

primarily, but sometimes to unemployment benefits (as in Canada) or to freestanding parent insurance benefits (as in Sweden).

Paid maternity leaves, an essential support for employed mothers, were established by Prince Otto von Bismarck, the first chancellor of the German Empire, as part of the 1880s German invention and enactment of social insurance. Concerned about rising social unrest linked to rapid industrialization, and threatened by not only the new German state's fragility but also three international movements (Catholicism and the spreading influence of the pro-labor policies supported in the encyclicals of Pope Leo XIII, socialism, and the growing public concern with the problem of low-wage workers), Bismarck turned to the enactment of social insurance as a device for binding workers and other groups to the state, "not only through bonds of loyalty but also through common self interest."[23] In 1883 the first national social insurance law was enacted, providing for health insurance through a large number of independent funds for paid sick leaves and for paid maternity leaves. Germany launched the new policy of providing a six-week leave with payment of 50 percent of a worker's prior wages; France followed soon after.[24] From 1893 on, French women were entitled to medical care and hospitalization at the time of maternity, and after 1913, working women were entitled to an eight-week maternity leave, paid at a flat rate.[25]

The Key Role of the International Labour Organization

In the early development of these leaves, the International Labour Organization (ILO) played an important role in setting international norms.[26] In 1919, the ILO adopted its first convention dealing with maternity protection, which was significantly extended in 1952 and then again in 2000. The first convention applied to all women working in industry and commerce, and it specified that they should be entitled to a maternity leave of twelve weeks in two equal parts preceding and following childbirth, with the part following birth being compulsory.[27] The convention stated that while on leave, women should receive a cash benefit that would be at least two-thirds of their prior earnings. The second, a revised Maternity Protection Convention, was adopted in 1952 and extended the twelve-week leave to fourteen weeks (six before and eight after giving birth) at 100 percent of prior wages. Despite the slowness of formal endorsements, by 1960 the ILO was reporting that fifty-nine countries provided paid maternity leaves; by 1980, seventy-two; and by the end of the 1980s, more than a hundred.[28] The revised convention, adopted in June 2000, strengthens protection over previous ILO instruments in many areas and broadens the scope of coverage.[29] For example, the new convention applies to all women, including those working in the informal sector, whereas the previous convention did not, and it recommends a minimum leave of fourteen weeks, including at least six weeks after giving birth. It also says that "additional leave shall be provided before or after the maternity leave period in the case of illness, complications or risk of complications arising out of pregnancy or childbirth." With regard to maternity cash benefits, the new convention says that they should be provided "at a level which ensures that the woman can maintain herself and her child in proper conditions of health and with a suitable standard of living." On employment protection, the convention states that "it shall be unlawful for an employer to terminate the employment of a woman during her pregnancy or absence on leave or during a period following her return to work."

This convention represents not only the conditions that have, in fact, been adopted in many nations but also the new world standard. Worldwide, for example, 128 countries of the 172 responding to the International Social Security Association in 1999 provided at least some maternity leave.[30] Among countries providing any leave, the average period for basic paid leave was sixteen weeks, which typically included a maternity leave encompassing six to eight weeks before and after childbirth. In almost half the countries, the cash benefit replaced the full wage (or the maximum covered under social insurance). Except for some variations in the benefit level, this was the standard for maternity policies in the EU countries as well. Moreover, in ninety-five of the countries (and all the European countries) both health and medical care were provided also. (Increasingly, in Europe, adoption has been covered as well.) The maternity leave benefits either were linked to sickness (short-term disability) benefits or were a free-standing social insurance benefit.[31] A few additional countries (for example, Austria and Canada) provided these benefits as part of unemployment insurance. All such policies fit with the ILO's intentions, as made explicit since the first ILO convention: "The principal object of these measures is to protect the health of the future mother and child and to guarantee a continuing source of income and security of employ-ment."[32]

Labor Market Policy

In reviewing the history of maternity, paternity, and parental leave policies, the second most important factor driving European develop-ments—after health protection—was labor market policy, often linked with concern about gender equity. During the 1960s and 1970s, labor force participation rates of women began to rise dramatically in many of the advanced industrialized Western countries. The trend in the OECD countries turned toward longer and more generous mater-nity leaves, with benefits replacing all or most of prior wages.

In addition, two significant innovations in maternity leave policies were initiated at the end of the 1960s and the beginning of the 1970s: first, the development of paid child-rearing leaves in the Eastern and Central European countries, and second, the development of paid parental leaves in the Nordic countries. In 1967, Hungary established a child-rearing leave for women to take after the end of the fully paid twenty-four-week maternity leave, in part because it was cheaper than providing decent infant and toddler care, and in part because it per-mitted some manipulation of the unskilled labor supply as needed, both in and out of the workforce.[33] The policy was designed (and, as necessary, modified) to encourage low-skilled women to withdraw from the labor force during periods of high unemployment, since sub-sidizing these women at home with a low, flat-rate benefit was less costly than providing them with decent out-of-home child care (which was provided for those women who remained in the labor force). The policy was soon copied in other Central European countries, such as Czechoslovakia and Poland, and some version of this was enacted by Finland and Germany in the 1980s and, recently, by Austria.

Paralleling this, and for different reasons, parental leave policies were developed first in Sweden in 1974 and, subsequently, in the other Nordic countries. For the most part, these benefits were linked to em-ployment and earnings and replaced all or most of a worker's prior wages. The purpose of this development was to promote gender eq-uity in countries that needed women in the labor force and wanted to encourage their participation, perhaps as an alternative to bringing in

guest workers from other countries. In effect, the objective was to simultaneously facilitate female labor force participation, enhance gender equity, and ensure adequate care of children. There emerged a
growing recognition that these leaves constituted an important component of child care policies, particularly policies regarding infant
care.

Other international bodies entered the policy arena and once again
helped raise norms. An EU directive mandating parental leaves was
proposed in 1983, but Britain refused to support it and so it was not
adopted. However, a directive on a paid fourteen-week maternity
leave was adopted as a health and safety measure in 1992, and a directive mandating a three-month, gender-neutral, job-protected, but unpaid parental leave was enacted in 1998.[34] Britain did adopt this one at
the end of 1999. These EU directives launched new parental leave
policies in several EU countries.

As the preceding discussion has shown, the maternity and parental
leave policies in the EU member countries remain diverse, despite a
general trend toward convergence within the EU.[35] The policies range
from the EU minimum (fourteen weeks of maternity leave, plus fourteen weeks of parental leave) in Ireland to a maximum of three years of
parental leave in Finland, and they include fully paid, partly paid, and
unpaid components.[36] They are popular benefits, and where wages are
fully or almost fully replaced by the benefits, usage rates, particularly
among mothers, are very high.[37] A key issue in recent years has been
recognition of the need to "fit" postpartum leave policies to those associated with early childhood care and education (ECEC) (see discussion
below), making the former the strategy for infant care and the latter
preparation for school.

Early Childhood Care and Education:
Integrating Care and Education

Early childhood education and care (ECEC) programs encompass
services for children younger than compulsory school-entry age and
involve elements of both physical care and education (that is, socialization as well as cognitive stimulation).[38] Apart from their critical
contribution to child development and socialization, they are essential

services for employed parents. Before- and after-school programs may also be provided for primary-school-age children. (The data concerning these programs are far less available, however.) ECEC programs include a wide range of part-day, full-schoolday, and full-workday programs under education, health, and social welfare auspices, funded and delivered in a variety of ways in both the public and private sectors. (See Table 12-5.) ECEC programs may be publicly funded and delivered (the predominant pattern in the Nordic countries, for example) or publicly funded and privately delivered (as in the Netherlands, for instance), or they may include a combination of publicly funded and delivered, publicly funded and privately delivered, and privately funded and delivered programs (as in France and Italy, for example). They may be free, as is particularly true of programs delivered under educational auspices, or they may charge income-related fees, but in almost all cases, they are heavily subsidized. The services are voluntary, and use of them is high wherever the programs are free or fees are modest. Some countries have guaranteed a place for all children by the time they reach a certain age (for example, age one in Sweden, Denmark, and Finland, and age three in France and Germany).[39]

The major cross-national differences have to do with such variables as:

- the locus of policy-making authority (national or local)
- the administrative auspices (education, health, social welfare, or a combination)
- the scale of coverage
- the age group served (infants and toddlers, preschoolers, or primary school–age children)
- other eligibility criteria (poor, with a single parent, with employed parents, and so on)
- the funding strategies (government, employer, parents' fees, or a combination)
- the delivery strategies (supply or demand)
- the locus of care (preprimary schools, centers, caregivers' homes, or in-home care)
- the primary caregiver (a professional, a paraprofessional, a relative, or a parent)
- the program philosophy, as relevant[40]

TABLE 12-5. Early Childhood Education and Care Policy Dimensions and Programs in Selected Countries

Country	Locus of Policy Making— National or Local	Admin. Auspices— Education, Health, Welfare	Age Group Served 0–3; 3–6; 0–6	Eligibility Criteria— Universal, Poor, with Special Needs, Working Parents	Funding Strategies— Government, Employer, Parent Fees, Combination	Delivery Strategies— Supply, Demand	Locus of Care— Centers, Family Day Care Homes, Preschool	Quality	Access/ Coverage (%)[a]
Austria	State/local	Welfare	3–6	Working parents	State and local government and parent fees	Supply	Preschool	No national standards; vary by state: Staff-child ratios 3:20	80%
			0–3				Centers	1.7:14 family day care home, max. 7 staff	3%
Belgium	State	Education	2½–6	Universal	Government—free to parents	Supply	Preschool	1:19; 1.5:20–25	97%
		Welfare (Center and family day care)	Under 3	With working parents, with special needs, poor	Multiple including government, employer, parent fees (income-related)	Mixed		2.5:7 (incl. .5 nurse) in centers; 3–4 ch. max in family day care homes	30%

(continued on page 330)

Country	Locus of Policy Making—National or Local	Admin. Auspices—Education, Health, Welfare	Age Group Served 0–3; 3–6; 0–6	Eligibility Criteria—Universal, Poor, with Special Needs, Working Parents	Funding Strategies—Government, Employer, Parent Fees, Combination	Delivery Strategies—Supply, Demand	Locus of Care—Centers, Family Day Care Homes, Preschool	Quality	Access/Coverage (%)[a]
Canada	State	Education	5–6	Universal	Government—free	Mixed	Preschool	Set by province	50%
		Welfare	Under 5	With special needs, poor, working parents	Mixed, largely parent fees		Centers and family day care homes		45%
Denmark	National and local (primarily)	Education	5–7	Universal	Government	Supply	Preschool	Set locally, generally 1:5.5, 3–6	3–6: 83 %
		Welfare	6 mos.–6 years	Working parents	Government (local) Parent fees income-related—max. 20–30% of costs.		Centers and family day care homes (esp. for under-3s)	1:2.7, under 3	1–3: 58 %
Finland	National and local	Education	6	Universal government	National and local government	Mixed	Centers and family day care homes (also for under-3s)	1:7, 3–7-years old	3–6: 73%[b]
		Welfare	1–7	Universal—priority for working parents	Parent fees income related covering 10% of costs			1:4, under-3s family day care homes, max. 4 pre-schoolers	1–3: 48%

Country									
France	National (primarily) and local	Education	2–6	Universal	Government—free to parents	Supply	Preschool	National health, safety, and staffing standards.	3–6: 99%
		Health/welfare	3 mos.–3 years	Working parents, parents with special needs	Mixed local government, family allowance funds, and parent fees income related, max. 25% of costs	Mixed	Preschool, centers and family day care homes	1:10 2-year-olds 1:27 others staff—teachers 1:8 toddlers; 1:5 infants 1:3 family day care	2–3: 35% 0–3: 29%
Germany	State	Education	3–6	Universal	State and local government + parent fees (income-related, max. 16–20% of costs)	Supply	Preschool	1:10–14	85% [b]
		Welfare	under 3	With special needs, poor, working parents			Center and family day care (largely)	1:5–7.5	5% (West German states) 50% (East German states)

(continued on page 332)

Country	Locus of Policy Making—National or Local	Admin. Auspices—Education, Health, Welfare	Age Group Served 0–3; 3–6; 0–6	Eligibility Criteria—Universal, Poor, with Special Needs, Working Parents	Funding Strategies—Government, Employer, Parent Fees, Combination	Delivery Strategies—Supply, Demand	Locus of Care—Centers, Family Day Care Homes, Preschool	Quality	Access/Coverage (%)[a]
Israel[c]	State/voluntary	Welfare	0–3	Universal—priority is working parents	Combination	Demand + supply +	Centers	No national standard	Age 2: 49.7% 3: 69.7% 4 5
	State/local	Education	4–6	Universal	Parents and government subsidy	Supply	Preschool	National supervision	
Italy	National	Education	3–6	Universal	National government—free	Supply	Preschool	3:25	95%
	Local	Health/welfare	Under 3	Working parents	Local government and parent fees, income related, average 12% of costs, max. 20%	Supply	center	No national standards 1:3 for under-3s is customary in most regions	6%
New Zealand	National	Education	Under 5	Universal	National government and parent fees	Supply	Center	No national standards	56% 3–4: 95% 0–2: 31%

Spain	State/local	Education	0–6	Universal (3–6)	Government—free	Supply	Preschool	National standards 1:25 3–6 years old	3–6: 84%
			Under 3		Government and parent fees, income-related; max. 20% of costs	Modest tax benefit for low-income parents for under-3s.	Center	1:18 2–3 years old 1:10 toddlers 1:7 infants ½ staff "trained"	0–3: 5%
Sweden	National and local (primarily)	Education	0–6	Universal, Working parents, parents with special needs	National and local government Parent fees, income related; about 13% of costs	Supply	Center	No national standards; local government sets standards.	3–6: 79%
							Centers and family day care homes	2:3½ children 3–6 1:3–5 under-3s family day care: 1:4–8	1–3: 48% [a]
U.K.	National/local	Education	3–4		Government, free	Supply and demand	Preschool	2:26	3–4: 60%
		Welfare	0–4	With special needs, poor	Free or income-related fees		Centers and family day care homes	National standards 1:4 for 2–3s 1:3 for under-2s	

(continued on page 334)

Country	Locus of Policy Making— National or Local	Admin. Auspices— Education, Health, Welfare	Age Group Served 0–3; 3–6; 0–6	Eligibility Criteria— Universal, Poor, with Special Needs, Working Parents	Funding Strategies— Government, Employer, Parent Fees, Combination	Delivery Strategies— Supply, Demand	Locus of Care— Centers, Family Day Care Homes, Preschool	Quality	Access/ Coverage (%)[a]
U.S.	National/local	Education	5	Universal	State and local government	Largely demand, but also some supply		32 states require 1:4 ratios for infants	95% of 5-year-olds & 50% of 3–4-year-olds in either preschool or center care; 0–3: 26%
		Education and welfare	0–4	With special needs, poor, welfare, working parents	Federal/state/local government Parent fees cover 76% of costs			Half the states have 1:5 or lower ratios for toddlers	

Source: Adapted from S.B. Kamerman, *Early Childhood Education and Care: An International Overview* (Paris: OECD, 2000).

[a] The age of entry and the access or coverage need to be seen in the context of the duration of the maternity or parental leave.

[b] Coverage in kindergarten for all children age three to six is the goal.

[c] Source: Center for Research and Public Education at the National Council for the Child, Israel, 2000.

The History of Selected Nations' Child Care Programs

ECEC policies and programs in Europe evolved out of remarkably similar historical streams: child protection, early childhood education, services for children with special needs, and services to facilitate mothers' labor force participation. In all the countries, one overarching theme has been the movement from private charity, beginning in the early and mid-nineteenth century, to public responsibility, evolving largely after World War II. The extent of public responsibility does vary, however, across the countries. The relative emphasis given in public policy to custodial care of poor and disadvantaged children of working mothers, on one hand, and education and socialization of all children, on the other, appears to be the most distinguishing variation among countries.[41] Some illustrations of the historical roots of the countries' child care policies follow.

In Britain, day nurseries and infant schools stressing education were established in the early nineteenth century. The former were not very extensive, but the latter expanded rapidly, only then to largely disappear and be replaced later by part-day kindergartens. The infant schools provided the children of poor working women with an "inferior" form of care and education. As of 1851, these schools covered 20 percent of three-year-olds and 40 percent of four-year-olds. By 1901, 43 percent of two- to five-year-olds were attending these schools, and England seemed well on the way to providing a voluntary but free educational service for all children from the age of two or three until five, when compulsory education began. Scholars state that the main need appeared to be improvement of the quality.[42] In contrast, as noted earlier, middle- and upper-class children were cared for at home, by nannies or their equivalent. This care was supplemented increasingly, beginning in the last quarter of the nineteenth century, by part-day kindergartens organized on the German model developed by Friedrich Froebel. The failure to improve the quality of infant schools for working-class children or to integrate these programs with the new educational philosophy of the kindergarten, coupled with the inclusion of five-year-olds in primary schools, contributed to the decline in popularity of nursery education in twentieth-century England. One other result was a continued pattern of fragmentation between early education as an enrichment program and day care as a protective service. Only recently has there been a significant increase in coverage and a renewed effort at integrating the two parallel streams.

In France and Italy, the developments began with nineteenth-century charitable institutions for poor, deprived, often abandoned children.[43] In France, the programs serving three- to five-year-olds were taken over by the Ministry of Education in 1836 and integrated into the public school system in 1886. Since World War II, and especially since the mid-1950s, growing pressure from middle-class families to broaden the programs to include their children as well led to a substantial expansion. The objective was largely to provide a socialization and educational experience for children from age two or three to the compulsory school-entry age of six, and to prepare them for primary school. Provision for younger children emerged later, under the auspices of the health ministry, and grew more slowly. These latter services for the very young were designed initially for protective purposes, to minimize the spread of contagious diseases, and thus with no attention to education. Subsequently, the focus was on providing care to the children of working parents, and the goals broadened. However, the supply of places and the scale of provision have never reached the level of the universal preschool, which now covers all three- to five-year-olds and almost half the two-year-olds.

The Italian developments were similar to the French ones but were totally dominated by the Roman Catholic Church until national legislation was enacted in the late 1960s and early 1970s, dramatically increasing the role of government. After beginning as institutions for poor, abandoned children, ECEC programs emerged as reflections of educational and socialization purposes only after World War II. In 1968, legislation was enacted assigning the national government and the Ministry of Education the major role in financing the establishment and operation of preschools for all three- to six-year-olds and greatly expanding the supply. In 1971, a law was passed that required the national government to contribute also to the funding of child care services for children younger than three but that required regional and local governments to assume responsibility for their operation. (Working mothers have priority for places in these facilities.) The 1968 legislation, with its national funding, led to a rapid and extensive expansion of preschool programs throughout the country, establishing a universal, largely public, and secular program for all. By now, about 95 percent of the three- to five-year-olds are enrolled. In contrast, with very little national government financial support, the 1971 law resulted in only modest growth of the centers for the very young, and regional investment differences led to wide variations in the supply of services for the very young.

As in the countries described thus far, Sweden's ECEC programs were rooted in the nineteenth century, in protective services and private charity. In 1854, the first day care center—funded by private charities—was opened, primarily to provide care for poor working mothers' children. Paralleling this development was the establishment of infant schools (the first in 1836) and kindergartens (the first, following the Froebel model, in 1890). In 1944, when there was limited public support for the day care centers, they were placed under the aegis of the National Board of Health and Welfare, as with the French and Italian day care centers for the very young.[44] In the early years, the major purpose of these centers was to provide care (as an alternative to foster care) for the newborns to six-year-olds of poor, single, working mothers. A separate system of early education, often on part-day schedules, continued for middle-class children.

In 1968, a National Commission on Child Care was established by the government and instructed to develop proposals for a child care system that would integrate both streams—day care and education— and would respond to the growing demands of employed mothers. In 1972, the commission issued its report, recommending that "the old views of care as poverty relief and pedagogical activity as stimulation for children of better off parents should be brought together into a single form to provide education and care for all children. This would be called 'preschool care' irrespective of whether it was provided full-time or part-time."[45] In 1975, the National Preschool Act was passed, incorporating that recommendation and laying down the framework for subsequent child care policy, with programs offering full-workday services (but with parents able to enroll their children for part of the day if they preferred). The children of employed mothers were given priority in admission, and ECEC was defined as a societal responsibility for all children. In 1985, the parliament passed a law stating that by 1991 all children ages eighteen months to six years would have a right to a place in public child care; by 1995, a subsequent law required municipalities to provide places for children ages one to twelve. The guarantee was to cover children from the time that the fully paid parental leave ended and overlapped with the additional six months of partially paid and unpaid parental leave. By the close of the 1990s, the responsibility for preschool had been transferred to the Ministry of Education.

To summarize, then, the roots of European ECEC policies and programs can be found in two mid-nineteenth-century developments: first, protective services for neglected children and the children of poor working mothers, and second, preschool education focused on enhancing or enriching middle-class children's development. Subsequently, during and after World War II, a third component began to shape these policies, namely, that of responding to the needs of the growing number of women in the labor force who wanted decent, affordable care for their children. Fourth and more recently, preparing young children for school has been an added factor.

Changes in Women's Needs and in an Educational Focus for Children

In some countries (such as Belgium, France, and Italy) the educational component became dominant earlier than the rise in women's labor force participation and provided the core of an early education system for children age two and a half or three to the age for compulsory school entry, usually six. As more women entered the labor force in the 1970s, this system began to be used to provide care and to adapt to working mothers'—and fathers'—needs. By now, this model has emerged as dominant in continental Europe. In contrast, in countries where female labor force participation rates increased early (such as the Nordic countries in the 1970s), a child care or day care model designed to respond to the needs of working parents and thus covering a full workday and workyear was dominant from the beginning. Gradually, education seems to be emerging as the frame for these countries as well. Sweden has shifted policy responsibility for its child care programs to the Ministry of Education, and Spain and Italy are moving toward including their programs of care for children younger than three, as well as for three- to six-year-olds, within the educational system.

For younger children, in some countries and over time, leave policies have begun to cover infant, and sometimes infant and toddler, care. Nonetheless, toddler care remains scarce in all countries, and it remains caught in the tension between those who want to promote parental care and those who want to support women's desire to enter paid employment, but not at the cost of their children. This tension has been addressed best in Denmark and Sweden, where the leave covers a maximum of one and a half years; eligibility is linked to prior employment and thus creates a strong incentive for obtaining prior employment, and the benefit levels are wage-related and replace almost all of each worker's prior wages. Moreover, women and men have the right to phase in their return to work on a part-time basis. In contrast, policies that encourage poorly educated, unskilled women to take long, low-paid leaves create a work disincentive for these women and may also deprive their children of valuable group experiences.

In contrast, in the Anglo-American countries, the two parallel streams continued, partly because of the early absence of national policy supporting education and partly, perhaps, because of the continued ambivalence about where primary responsibility for child rearing and socialization should lie.[46] Child care and education still have not been integrated in the United States and Canada, and the two streams (sometimes three: compensatory education, care, and education/socialization) have remained separate. In short, child protection continued to be a factor in the development of ECEC, just as it was in the development of maternity and parenting policies. But more important in this later period were working women's needs, children's need for care while mothers—and fathers—worked, and the emphasis on preparing children for formal education. These were the primary factors driving the ECEC developments in the 1970s, 1980s, and 1990s in Europe. Of some interest, the major legislative initiatives that drove these developments occurred from the late 1960s through the mid-1970s in Europe. These initiatives provided the impetus for the expansion of ECEC programs, the responsiveness to the needs of working parents, and the growing stress on education as the strategy for framing the policy debate.

WHY THE UNITED STATES LAGGED BEHIND EUROPE

Why did the United States not develop policies similar to Europe's? In accounting for the status of U.S. family policies, we concluded more than a decade ago that the United States lagged behind Europe for three main reasons.[47]

Belated Development of a Social Protection System

The United States began developing its national income transfer programs much later than European countries did. The foundation of the social protection system in several countries was firmly in place at the end of the nineteenth and early twentieth centuries, well before the United States was even considering such programs. By World War I, many of the European countries had already established statutory pension schemes, survivor and disability benefits, workers' compensation, some form of national health insurance, and statutory paid sick leave benefits covering non-job-related short-term disabilities, including maternity.[48] Family benefits in the form of child or family allowances became the norm in much of Europe during the immediate post–World War II period, while the United States was still struggling to implement the most basic social benefits (including old age, survivor, and disability benefits, as well as unemployment benefits); disability insurance, for example, was not added to the social security system until 1956.

While Europe was expanding government's social role immediately after World War II, the United States was expanding the social role of employers, developing employer-provided "fringe benefits," albeit for a favored and limited group of workers. In the 1960s, when the European countries were focusing on enhanced equality, the United States was attempting a "war on poverty." The European countries were stressing social "solidarity" through expanded and new universal policies, while the United States was concentrating on community action and social services, as well as continuing the use of means-tested benefits to target existing policies on the poor. Some people have argued that U.S. federalism created still another barrier and that most of the European countries have had unitary governments smaller than the U.S. one. (However, the U.S. readiness to federalize major programs for the elderly but not for children remains an anomaly.)

The Challenges of Complex Pluralism

U.S. progress on national child or family policies also was slower because of the constraints created by the country's complex pluralism. Of all the advanced industrialized countries, the United States has the most racially, ethnically, and religiously heterogeneous population. One result is the difficulty in developing a political consensus regarding policies affecting the intimate realms of parenting and child rearing. Although most of the European countries are far more diverse today than earlier, their family policies were established when their populations were more homogeneous and consensus was easier to achieve. In the late 1960s and 1970s, when much of Europe was beginning to be concerned (again) about declining birth rates, the United States reopened its doors to immigrants, increasing still further the diversity of its population even as its birth rate declined.

The Urgent Need to Address Civil Rights Issues

Another major factor in the inhibited rate of U.S. policy development was the need to deal first with the problem of racial prejudice and blacks' unequal access to social benefits. While the Europeans were searching for social solidarity in an effort to do better by children—after a devastating war that had revealed widespread deprivation and killed many children and young people—the United States was embroiled in a fight for civil rights, attempting to ensure the rights of blacks and other minorities. To the extent that considerations of social equity had an impact on reducing cleavages within the United States, it was the issue of race that demanded and received attention first—not class, income, or the presence of children.

Other Possible Factors

Others have offered additional explanations for U.S. exceptionalism. Thus, for example, the sociologist and welfare state scholar Gøsta Esping-Andersen has written that the public/private mix in social protection is the principal analytic axis undergirding his tripartite regime typology of liberal (Anglo-American), conservative (continental European), and social democratic (Nordic) policy regimes. In his most recent work, he argues for the centrality of family policy to any discussion of welfare state regimes, stressing the centrality of gender equity, responsiveness to family change, the reconciliation of work and family life, and the need to minimize child poverty as key components. He stresses that the varied emphasis on the family, the market, civil society, and government in these countries reflects the different historical, cultural, and ideological themes that frame his analysis and characterize the three family policy regimes, as well as his three welfare state regimes.[49]

ANY LESSONS FOR THE UNITED STATES?

Some years ago we concluded that countries with an explicit family policy were more likely to be generous in the family benefits they provided, the scale of coverage, and the tendency toward universal eligibility than countries with no such policy.[50] Moreover, the economic situation of vulnerable families (single parents, large families, and ethnic and racial minorities) was more likely to be protected in such countries. That conclusion still holds true. The Nordic countries and France remain at the forefront of promoting children's well-being, with France lagging, primarily because it still does not provide a family allowance for the first child. (This is no longer a matter of policy but rather one of resources.) Having said that, what can the United States learn from these countries with regard to specific policy domains?

Clearly, we cannot change history. The United States did not establish a social policy infrastructure in the late nineteenth and early twentieth centuries. A national family allowance system was not established in the immediate post–World War II period. Nor, given U.S. demographic trends, has there been any concern with fertility, and in light of both current fertility rates (which sustain the population size) and a high rate of immigration, concern with fertility seems unlikely.[51] And female labor force participation rates rose later in the United States than in the Nordic countries (albeit earlier than in Britain and the continental European countries). What, then, can we learn from Europe, either to adopt or to adapt?

National Health Coverage

First, all three policy regimes discussed underscore the importance of a fourth policy regime, not necessarily limited to working families: the importance of national health insurance (or health service). Economic security cannot exist without assurance of access to health care. Health protection and promotion cannot be carried out without universal access to affordable health care. Head Start was invented to compensate for cognitive deficits among poor children, but its program components were designed to compensate for inadequate access to health and mental health care, social services, and parent participation, as well as early childhood education. If there is a lesson for the United States here, it is the urgent need to close the gaps in health insurance coverage and in access to health care if we are to ensure adequate support for working families.

Child-Conditioned Tax Benefits

Second, family allowances were invented as a child-conditioned wage supplement, and offering such allowances is an essential policy unless a country has established a family wage. The United States has begun to move in this direction by making available two child-conditioned tax credits. The earned income tax credit, offered to low-income working families with children, is a refundable tax credit that provides both a credit against income tax liability to those with incomes above the tax threshold and a direct cash benefit to those with lower incomes. The maximum credit was worth about $2,300 in 1999 for a working family with one child and slightly more for families with two or more children. More than 18 million families received this tax credit in 1999 out of a total of about 38 million families with children; in effect, about half of all families with children received this benefit. The cost of the tax credit was about $30 billion in 1999, and almost 90 percent of this was refunded to those families claiming the credit, because their income was below the income tax threshold.[52] In addition, the United States provided a $500 annual child tax credit beginning in 1999, which has since been raised to $1,000. This is only partly refundable, however, and thus is of no value to many of those with incomes below the income tax threshold. Integrating the two into a universal, refundable child tax credit could become a U.S. child or family allowance provided through the tax system, a preferred device in the United States.

Parental Leave

Third, the development of maternity, paternity, and parental leaves is critical. These policies remind us of the loss of a historic window of opportunity. By the time the United States was ready to pay attention to this issue in the 1970s, not only had the policy become firmly entrenched in Europe after a history of almost a hundred years, but it was relatively easy to advocate and obtain a gender-neutral supplement in the form of a parental leave benefit. In contrast, the women's movement in the United States was unwilling to accept a maternity policy, and thus the United States lost the first-tier benefit; the movement attempted, instead, to begin at the second tier of a family benefit (and even that took a fifteen-year fight). Consequently, we have ended up with a very brief leave policy—and one involving unpaid leave at that.

Maternal and child health protection remains a powerful factor, as does the need to protect working families' economic security. Given the increasingly high rates of labor force participation of women with very young babies, the theme of maternal and child health protection should convey an urgent message. Recent research has pointed not only to the low cost of extending coverage to all working parents and of providing a paid leave, but also to the value of such a leave.[53] Temporary disability insurance, a parallel to the European sickness benefits program currently available in five states, remains the best device for paying for this leave. Unemployment insurance could be an alternative, and this was actively explored in the United States in the late 1990s, with the encouragement of President Bill Clinton. Canada's reform of its unemployment insurance law in 1971 specifically included coverage for sickness benefits and maternity benefits. Although the benefit level is not especially generous, Canada did manage to supplement its initial maternity leave and benefit package with an additional parental leave and benefit. Together, these cover one year at the time of childbirth or adoption. (All this was achieved in the context of a federal system of government.)

Universal, Publicly Subsidized, and Integrated Child Care and Education Programs

Fourth, ECEC had the same early history in the United States as in Europe. However, without federal responsibility for education or an early and dramatic rise in women's labor force participation, as in the Nordic countries, the United States remained ambivalent about who should receive ECEC, who should pay for it, and who should deliver it. As a result, preschool did not become universal, as occurred in Belgium, France, and Italy. Nor did it emerge as an essential response to the rise in women's employment. The initial pressure for expanding publicly subsidized child care came from the welfare policy side during the 1960s, as assistance rolls increased and the reality of poor women needing child care in order to work and support themselves entered into the policy debate. It took until the mid- and late-1970s before pressure emerged from middle-class families for services to meet their needs; the response was a modest tax credit plus subsequent efforts at encouraging employers to do more. By responding with a series of categorical and targeted programs, the United States missed the opportunity to develop a universal program. The series of early 1970s legislative initiatives enacted in several of the continental European countries is a reminder of the consequences of the failed 1971 U.S. initiative.[54]

The European experience suggests the need for a universal initiative if the United States is to have full coverage in a decent, affordable program. The problems in the public schools also suggest the need for a federal role—and federal incentives—if there is to be any chance at geographic equity. Thus far, two states, Georgia and New York, have established statewide universal preschool programs for four-year-olds. Several other states have launched initiatives (Oklahoma and Connecticut, for example), and many other local jurisdictions have made some beginnings.

Apart from the value of a universal policy and program including all children (not only those of working mothers, let alone those of only poor working mothers), other lessons from Europe underscore the importance of the fifth lesson: stressing education and school readiness is vital. The widespread public interest in ensuring that young children enter primary school ready to learn, the public support for education reform, and the increased federal role in education during the second Bush administration suggest the value of framing ECEC policy in terms of education.

A sixth lesson has to do with the need to understand and acknowledge the link between family leaves and ECEC services. In several Nordic countries, a publicly subsidized place in child care is guaranteed when the parental leave ends. Everywhere, it is clear that the supply of ECEC infant and toddler care services is affected by the duration of the leave. Given the ongoing shortage of infant care services, the continued concern regarding maternal employment during a baby's first year of life, and the existence of a brief and unpaid family leave, it would appear that there is need for more discussion of a longer paid family leave and of a one-year exemption from work requirements for new mothers claiming welfare benefits.

Political Support of Work-Family Policies and Recognition of Children's Claims

Of particular importance is a seventh lesson: perhaps the greatest progress in advancing these benefits in other countries has been achieved when strong political support has come from both the left and the right or when the party supporting these benefits has had a long history of entrenched power. In France and Sweden, for example, parties across the political spectrum have almost always favored doing more for children, even if they have disagreed on the specifics. In France, the right may have stressed pro-natalism while the left may have pressed for vertical redistribution (from the more to the less affluent), but both have agreed on the importance of horizontal redistribution (from those with no children to those with children) as an essential component. In Sweden, the political debate has been not over whether to support family benefits but over which of the parties would be the most generous. Even in West Germany, where there was a debate about child allowances and maternity legislation in the 1950s, basic support has come from a combination of the left wanting to do more for low-income and single-parent families and the right (including strong support from the Catholic Church) wanting to do more for traditional families. In the United States, in contrast, children have not been high on the public agenda of either major party since the beginning of the twentieth century.

Finally, European social and family policy has always been far more child-centered than similar U.S. policy. If there is any other lesson to be learned from Europe, it is the need for greater recognition of children's claims. From the left and from the right, a recent U.S. slogan initiated by advocates and adopted by the Bush administration has been "leave no child behind." It is time to make this slogan real. We need to move beyond the rhetoric and implement this message in our child and family policies if we are to be responsive to the dynamic nature of our social and family changes.

13

Eliminating Economic Penalties on Caregivers

Nancy Folbre

O nce upon a time, some very powerful goddesses decided to sponsor a competition, a kind of Olympics, among the nations of the world. They agreed to award a wonderful prize—health and prosperity for all—to the nation that could collectively run the greatest distance in a set period of time. This was not an ordinary race in which the distance was determined and the winner was the runner who took the least time, but rather a contest to see which society, acting as a team, could move all its members forward. Each nation that decided to compete had a giant scoreboard placed in the sky to count up all the miles traveled per person. But the goddesses did not tell them how long the race would last—the participants were required to guess. When the starting gun went off, one nation assumed that the race would not last long. Its leaders urged all citizens to start running as quickly as possible. It was every person for her- or himself. Very soon, of course, the young children and the elderly fell behind, but none of the front-runners stopped to help them; that would have slowed them down.

At first, those who were out in front were exhilarated by their success. As the race continued, however, some of them became tired or hurt and fell by the wayside. Gradually, all the runners grew exhausted or sick and, with no one to replace them, began to realize that they would lose. Attention turned to a second nation, one that had adopted a slightly different strategy. The leaders of this nation sent all their young men, the fastest runners, out ahead to compete but required all the women to stay behind, carrying the children, the sick, and the elderly, and caring for any runners who needed help. They explained to the women that this was a natural and efficient arrangement from which everyone would benefit. Oh, yes: one incentive offered to men for running fast was the reward of authority and power over the women.

At first, this seemed to work. But then the women found out that they could run just as fast as the men, provided they were not burdened with extra responsibilities. They began to argue that the work they were doing—caring for the runners—was every bit as important as the running itself and that they deserved equal rights. The men (whose brains may have been impaired by the stress of mindless running) found this claim ridiculous. "What incentive," they asked, "would men have to run if they couldn't stay in charge?" The women looked at one another and then went out on strike. Chaos ensued. Eventually it became clear that this nation, too, was losing the race.

Attention turned to a third nation, which, like the tortoise in competition with the hare, had made slow but persistent progress. Its strategy was different: everyone was required both to run and to take care of those who could not run. Both men and women were urged to compete, to run as fast as possible, but the rules required them to carry equal shares of the weight of care. Jogging with a heavy load, these citizens became strong and fast. Their freedom and equality fostered their solidarity. Of course, they won the race. What did you expect? It was a race that goddesses designed. The real world, however, looks rather different.

CARE AS A PUBLIC GOOD

What exactly is the weight of care, and why does its distribution have significant consequences for society? Economists define a *public good* as one that has diffuse benefits or is nonexcludable in consumption. Public goods create externalities, or spillover effects. They cannot be efficiently produced by a market system, because enjoyment of them cannot be restricted to those who pay their price. Provision of national defense, highways, or clean air is physically difficult or inefficient to assign to individuals, which is why all are provided or protected by the government. Public benefits can be, and often are, accompanied by private benefits. Education, for instance, offers a high payoff to those who acquire it, but it also benefits society as a whole in the form of greater creativity and higher productivity. Vaccination not only protects those who receive it from disease but also reduces the spread of disease to others.

Conventional economic analysis tends to assume that both public and private goods are produced for pecuniary gain, something that can be easily measured in dollars. Indeed, it is the inability to privately capture financial gain that creates the need for public provision. What the conventional analysis tends to underestimate is the extent to which goods and services of significant value to society are produced for nonpecuniary reasons. Much of the work performed in families and communities is motivated by altruism, a sense of moral obligation, or simply intrinsic pleasure. This is also true of many paid jobs, which people choose for reasons other than the wages offered. Even if family members expect or indeed receive some reciprocity and wage earners demand a paycheck, the pecuniary reward they enjoy often falls short of the social benefits that their work creates.

Intrinsic motivation leads to the production of many goods and services that are nonexcludable in consumption. Consider a woman who takes pleasure in growing flowers in her front yard. She may not intentionally desire to benefit passers-by, but if they enjoy the flowers, she creates a public good. A more telling example is a person who enjoys being honest, kind, and caring. He may derive intrinsic pleasure from satisfaction of these preferences, but he is also more likely to generate more spillover benefits for others than a person who enjoys being dishonest, mean, and selfish. We describe many norms and preferences as virtuous partly because they create social benefits. One of the few eminent economists to acknowledge this point, Joseph Stiglitz, put it this way:

> The Golden Rule can be thought of as an attempt to deal with externalities:
>
> "Do unto others as you would have them do unto you." ... This may be roughly translated into the language of economics as "Do cause positive externalities" and "Do not cause negative externalities."[1]

Research on so-called social capital has sometimes made a similar point. The networks and personal relationships that people form with one another contribute to levels of trust and reciprocity that improve economic efficiency.[2]

Yet for the most part, research on social capital has avoided explicitly considering the provision of care to family and community. Economists, in particular, have a distinct tendency to assume that the intrinsic motivation underlying the provision of care is exogenously given, perhaps even biologically determined.[3] This motivation is treated as though it were simply a gift of nature, like the water that flows in a river. If we can depend on it to keep flowing, no matter what we do, there is no need to study it, much less worry about it. But even natural flows can be dammed up, impeded, overused, or dried up. Much of the urge to provide care to others probably is part of our biological makeup.[4] That does not mean, however, that it remains unaffected by changes in our social and economic environment.

Indeed, there are good reasons to believe that the supply of care is affected by the costs imposed on those who provide it, as well as by the level of moral and social value that we collectively place on it. Also, the consequences of changes in the motivation to provide care are far-reaching, precisely because this motivation helps create public goods. Economists have argued that it does not matter what we want, as long as we are free to choose.[5] This holds true only if no one depends on us to care for them. For much of our history, the altruistic and moral incentives to care for others have been reinforced by social structures of constraint—laws, rules, property rights—and social norms that have shaped individual decisions. The development of our capitalist economy has weakened these constraints, with some positive consequences, as well as some negative ones.

CAPITALISM AND THE WEAKENING OF PATRIARCHAL CONSTRAINTS

For many centuries, the relationship between the family and the economy in Western European countries conformed to a patriarchal model not unlike the second scenario in the race previously described. Women had little choice but to specialize in providing care. Their opportunities for economic independence outside of marriage were limited. Within marriage, they had few property rights and relatively little bargaining power. Furthermore, both men and women had economic incentives to raise large numbers of children. Mortality rates were high. Children could begin productive work at a relatively early age. Once mature, children were expected to provide support for their parents in old age, an implicit contract that was reinforced by parental control over rights to the use of land or other assets. The family was a basic unit of both production and reproduction.[6]

A number of factors contributed to the early destabilization of this patriarchal system within Western Europe and its colonies. For instance, the growing scarcity of land in the seventeenth and eighteenth centuries reduced the benefits of high fertility. Possibilities for migration to the New World eased that problem but created a new one, as many members of the younger generation left their elders behind. Even within the United States, the opportunities available on the expanding frontier disrupted family ties. The growth of labor markets also increased the scope for individual choice. Young adults could choose to work for someone else, rather than continuing to be part of a family enterprise. Technological change increased the demand for female labor in factories, giving young women new options.[7]

But the direct effects of technological change were probably less important than its indirect effects on the relative power of men and women, the old and the young, the rich and the poor. Many forms of collective action, based on many dimensions of group identity, contributed to changes in social and political institutions. For instance, in the nineteenth century a well-organized U.S. feminist movement won legal guarantees that married women could have control over their property and wages. Other examples include trade union–supported efforts to establish limits on child labor, mandatory state-supported education, and restrictions on the length of the workday. The elderly, as a group, supported the development of pensions for veterans of the Civil War, which represented a precursor to state-financed old age support and, later, the social security system.

By the early twentieth century, fertility rates in the United States had declined to an average of about three children per woman, and a large proportion of unmarried women were engaged in wage employment. However, strong legal and cultural sanctions made it difficult for married women to combine family work with employment. For instance, many individual firms and government agencies (including schools) required women to resign when they married or became pregnant.[8] Women were often tracked into less skilled and less demanding jobs on the presumption that they would not (and should not) remain within the labor force. They were discouraged from obtaining advanced degrees in business, medicine, or law.

During the Great Depression years of the 1930s, both high levels of unemployment and extreme levels of poverty among the elderly prompted the passage of major welfare-state legislation: the Social Security Act of 1935. The retirement provisions of this act taxed working-age adults to provide support for the older generation, with the level of support determined by past wages. In a sense, this provision socialized the traditional intergenerational transfers of the patriarchal family. The basic provisions of the Social Security Act of 1935 also embodied a breadwinner/homemaker ideal: a married woman was eligible for retirement support based on her husband's earnings. Thus, a married man was guaranteed family benefits significantly higher than those accorded to a single man who had paid the same taxes. A married woman who worked for pay could choose benefits based either on her husband's earning history or her own. Since husbands tended to earn significantly more than wives, most wives opted for the former. Thus, they received the same benefits they would have if they had not worked for pay and contributed taxes to the social security system. All of these basic provisions of social security remain in effect today.

Yet the economic and demographic changes that have taken place since 1935 have rendered the breadwinner/homemaker ideal obsolete. Partly as a result of increased demand for labor, and partly as result of organized feminist efforts, women's opportunities for employment outside the home have improved, and most married women work for pay. Divorce rates have increased substantially, and a significant percentage of all children are born outside of wedlock. Public assistance for single parents has increased over time but remains relatively low, leaving many of these families below the poverty line. The costs of child rearing in general have increased, not only because of higher educational demands but also because the opportunity cost of women's time has risen.

During the last thirty years of the twentieth century, men's real wages remained relatively constant.[9] Women's contributions to family paychecks came to be seen as increasingly important to family welfare. Income inequality intensified differences between rich and poor. Child rearing came to be seen as an expensive undertaking. While the economic well-being of the elderly was protected by relatively generous benefits, the increased life expectancy of this group led to greater needs for expensive forms of direct care in homes, hospitals, and nursing homes. The combination of these trends led to increased stress on women, since traditional expectations concerning their roles as caregivers came into conflict with new desires and needs to participate in paid employment. Many women today face an uncomfortable choice between providing family care at high cost to themselves or settling for a lower level of family care than they consider right and good.[10]

This choice is complicated by a poor understanding of the changing relationship between the family and the economy. Because family work takes place outside the market economy, we tend to think of it as a noneconomic commitment, perhaps even a personal indulgence. But the work of raising children, maintaining healthy and happy adults, and caring for the sick and elderly has always been, and probably always will be, crucial to economic growth. Even though it is motivated largely by intrinsic reasons, it requires some level of economic support and reward.

OF CHILDREN AND PETS

Many people seem to think that parents, especially mothers, should pay most of the costs of raising children. These people think of children as pets. Parents have children for the same reasons that they acquire pets—because they provide companionship and love. Therefore, they should either take full responsibility for them or drop them off at the pound. Some wind up with beautiful golden retrievers with cheerful, trainable temperaments. Others are stuck with ugly, bad-tempered mutts. In any event, those who care for them are the ones who get the fun out of them; therefore, the caretakers—and not other taxpayers—should pay the costs.[11] All dog owners should use pooper scoopers, observe leash laws, and not ask the taxpayers for subsidies.

I love my pets. They include a beautiful white horse and a clever black dog, and I get a lot of pleasure from their company. But I would never argue that the time and money that I spend on them benefits anyone besides me. Nor would I ask society to help pay for their expense. My neighbors down the road are raising five children, as well as two dogs and four rabbits. Both parents work full time, splitting shifts so that one adult is always home. They probably get even more pleasure from their menagerie than I do from mine. There is another difference, though: the money, time, and love they devote to their children will benefit the rest of us.

According to one recent estimate, a middle-income family spends about $165,630 per child from birth to age eighteen.[12] Both childless individuals and deadbeat dads can take that money and put it into investments that offer them a much higher private rate of return. Private retirement benefits as well as social security payments are based on market earnings, which are much higher for individuals who have never taken time away from paid employment to raise a family. Who is going to pay the taxes to finance those future benefits? Whom are we going to hire to take care of us in our old age? Who else but those children down the road, when they grow up?

When parents devote time and money to the development of children's capabilities, they are engaged in socially productive work that yields benefits to others.[13] Some of these benefits are intangible, such as our collective sense of pride in a new generation of citizens. Other benefits are quite tangible, such as the taxes that today's children will pay when they grow up and enter the workforce, repaying our national debt and supporting our social security system. All citizens of this country implicitly enjoy a claim on the earnings of the younger generation, whether they have helped to rear them or not. Social security provides benefits based on paid work history or marital status by taxing the current working-age population. The time, energy, and effort devoted to producing these workers are not very generously rewarded; in fact, just the opposite is true. In an economy in which rewards are increasingly based on performance in paid employment, the costs and risks of parenthood are rising.[14] The direct costs of raising children— food, clothing, diapers, medical care, a bigger house, education—are the easiest to quantify. These generally increase, along with family income, because parents usually spend a percentage of their income, rather than a flat amount, on children. Parents today tend to spend more than they used to because they recognize the increased impact that educational credentials will have on their children's success. More and more young people are seeking university and postgraduate degrees. Partly as a result, they often remain at least somewhat dependent on their parents well past the age of eighteen.

Parenting imposes indirect as well as direct costs. Children affect virtually every decision parents make—where to live, how to spend time, what kinds of jobs to choose. Parents often give up potential income when they decide to cut back on their hours of paid work in order to spend time at home with their children. The effects can be substantial, because in today's labor market, taking time out from paid employment tends to hurt career chances and lower future earnings. The larger the potential salary, the greater the potential losses.

If mothers and fathers live together, they often share the burden of reduced market income. In fact, fathers may work longer hours on their jobs to make up for the deficits. But today, many women are raising children on their own: about a third of children are born out of wedlock, plus the risks of separation and divorce are high, with about one-half of marriages projected to end in divorce.[15] Child support agreements are difficult to negotiate and even more difficult to enforce. Women who choose to become mothers risk making themselves and their children vulnerable to poverty and other kinds of economic stress.[16]

Whether they actually become mothers or not, women who take time out of the paid labor market to devote themselves full time to meeting the needs of family members not only accumulate less labor market experience but also earn less money than men with comparable levels of education. As long as they are happily married, women who are housewives are generally compensated by receiving a share of their husband's income. But if their marriage crumbles or their husband dies, they are left vulnerable; even if they remain married, their fear of being left to fend for themselves may put them in a weak, even subservient position in the home.[17]

Statistical analyses have shown that motherhood tends to lower women's earnings even if they do not take much time out from paid work. Generally, the more children a woman has, the less she earns, even if she works the same amount of time and remains with one employer for the same length of time as a childless woman.[18] A number of factors could explain this pattern. Employers could have a bias against hiring or promoting mothers; alternatively, mothers might consciously or unconsciously behave in ways that signal less commitment to their careers. What is interesting is that the numbers show exactly the opposite effect for fathers: having children tends to increase men's earnings.[19]

Biological differences in themselves are less important than the tendency of mothers to take more personal responsibility for children and other dependents, which puts them in a weak position. Even if a woman starts out in a perfectly equal relationship with her spouse or partner, that equality is likely to erode over time. Individuals who specialize in providing care do not control the products of their labor. They acquire valuable experience, but it is not the kind of experience that an employer will pay for.[20] As Sylvia Ann Hewlett and Cornel West have noted:

> Of course, large numbers of well-meaning moms and dads may still elect to invest large quantities of money and time in child-raising, but for the first time in history their loving energies are not reinforced by enlightened self-interest. Instead, they must rely entirely on large reserves of altruistic love—large enough to last for more than two decades per child. This is a tall order in a society that venerates the market.[21]

THE COSTS OF ELDER CARE

Most people can exercise some choice over whether or not to rear children, and certainly one could argue that we would be better off in some ways if people had fewer children—up to a point. But the same penalties I described earlier also apply to the care of individuals at the other end of the dependency spectrum. We live in a society in which most of the elderly enjoy an economic safety net known as social security. However, many elderly people (especially women) continue to live in poverty and to suffer from health problems that require face-to-face, hands-on assistance. Money alone, in any case, does not meet their personal and emotional needs. We expect responsible adults to tend to, if not directly care for, their parents and other elderly relatives.

This expectation, however, is not backed up by any economic or legal sanctions, except where the elderly people in question control financial assets and can use the promise of a bequest to reward their children's behavior. Sadly, economic research has shown that strategic calculations seem to have a small but significant effect on adult children's behavior.[22] A more significant factor, however, is the extent of love, obligation, and reciprocity among family members. Deciding how to allocate responsibilities for care of an elderly person who needs personal assistance is not easy. Siblings often disagree about who should do what for Mom or Dad. The "good child's dilemma" comes into play: the first person who volunteers to provide assistance may be stuck with the job.

In my own family, things worked out remarkably well. My father cared for my mother when she was stricken with cancer of the pancreas. After she died, he remarried, and when his wife later succumbed to a serious illness, he cared for her, too. The McFarlin Oil Company never offered my father a pension, but he worked well past the age of seventy while looking after the company owner's surviving son, John, as well as his oil money. My father was rewarded by a substantial bequest when John died. After my father's second wife died, he married again, at the age of eighty.

His new wife, an old family friend, was not much younger than he. Still, she dedicated herself to virtually full-time care of him through a long and difficult period of debility before he died at age eighty-seven. I provided only occasional support and backup. My brother, who lived in the same area as they, helped out more. My sister, who had taken early retirement from her job, took on even more responsibility. Fortunately, we never fought or disagreed over who should provide care. We were pretty lucky.

Virtue is not always its own reward. The National Family Caregivers Association surveyed its members in 1997, asking them to describe positive and negative outcomes of caregiving, along with difficulties. An overwhelming majority, 70 percent, said that they had found an inner strength they had not known they possessed. However, more than 67 percent registered frustration, and 76 percent were troubled by the lack of consistent help from other family members. More than 60 percent complained of depression.[23] They also paid an economic penalty. A study by Brandeis University's National Center for Women and Aging and the National Alliance for Caregivers reported that two-thirds of those acting as caregivers for elderly relatives (providing more than eight hours a week in unpaid care) had lost out at work by forgoing promotions and training opportunities. Not surprisingly, approximately three-fourths of all home caregivers for people age fifty or older are women—spouses, daughters, sisters, and friends.[24]

It is estimated that approximately 25 percent of all U.S. workers in 1996 provided at least some care for an ailing parent, and the demand for such assistance is projected to increase. The demographic pressures are intensifying, since low fertility rates are contributing to an increase in the elderly population's relative size. Also, the number of people older than eighty-five—the neediest group—is increasing, and on average, half of this group needs some help with personal care. Wives will probably continue to play an especially important role in caring for aging spouses because women's life expectancy is greater than men's.[25]

However, there is reason to believe that the supply of unpaid labor for home elder care will soon decline. Unlike the women of my mother's generation, many of my peers are heavily invested in jobs and careers from which they cannot easily excuse themselves. Many of them live a long distance from their parents. The price, to them, of providing care has gone up. And while they may agree that they have an obligation to care, they are unlikely to agree that their obligation is any greater than that of their husbands or sons or brothers. We are likely to see more and more negotiation over the distribution of elder care responsibilities.

It is time to rethink the larger social organization of care, considering the special needs not just of children and the elderly but also of the ill and disabled. In addition to encouraging more equal sharing of care and a better balance between paid work and unpaid care responsibilities, we need to improve the quality of paid care services, structuring them in ways that encourage the development of personal connection and attentiveness to emotional needs. A full consideration of these issues is beyond this chapter's scope, but having explored the larger relationship between the family and the economy, we can take a closer look at issues particularly relevant to public support for child rearing.

PUBLIC SUPPORT FOR CHILD REARING

Child rearing provides important public benefits. That we offer relatively little public support for it—and often deliver that support in indirect and inconsistent ways—helps explain the anger that motivated the welfare reforms implemented in 1996. Many people said they disliked programs that gave people incentives "not to work."[26] However, that problem could have been viewed in reverse: very few programs, apart from welfare, provided much support for family work, which was not rewarded in the labor market. Increasingly, it came to seem that mothers living in poverty were the only ones who could afford to take time out of paid employment to stay home with their children.

This perception was inaccurate, based on a widespread misunderstanding of levels of public assistance, as well as the high visibility of welfare programs relative to the tax benefits that more affluent families enjoyed. However, the stresses and strains on low- and middle-income families with children are significant. Indeed, most families currently living in poverty are there because the private costs of raising children are so high. If we provided more generous, universal supports for families—as do most of the countries of northwestern Europe—we could dramatically reduce the percentage of children living in poverty. We could also produce happier, healthier, and more productive adults.

To say that children are public goods is not to say that everyone should raise them or that we need a greater number of them. Rather, it is to say that once they are brought into this world, we all have something to gain from fully developing their capabilities. Parents should take responsibility for their own children. By the same token, the public should accept responsibility for recognizing, rewarding, and supplementing parental efforts. This principle is reflected in many of our existing social policies, but economists seldom examine the ways in which the costs of child rearing are distributed.

U.S. Expenditures on Children and Families

Among other things, we allow families a dependent tax deduction and tax credits, offer public assistance for poor parents with young children, maintain a system of institutional and foster care for children whose parents cannot care for them, and provide public education. The economists Robert Haveman and Barbara Wolfe have calculated that in 1992, government spending accounted for about one-third of total expenditures on children. Their calculation probably underestimated parental contributions, because it did not fully account for the cost of the time that parents devote to child care, which substantially lowers lifetime earnings.[27]

Government expenditures on education per student have increased over time, but public support for parents of young children has declined. Between 1948 and 1960, the value of the federal tax exemption for dependents was so high that few families with children even paid income taxes. The real value of the exemption, however, was undermined by inflation between 1960 and 1985. The economist Eugene Steuerle has estimated that the tax rate of families with two children increased 43 percent over this period, while the average tax rate for families without children remained essentially unchanged.[28] The economist Ed Wolff has argued that the relative well-being of parents has declined over the past three or four decades.[29]

In 1998, Congress added a $500-per-child tax credit (for children sixteen or younger) to the income tax code. In 2001, this child tax credit was increased to $600 per child. While this was a move in the right direction, it has not counteracted the previous decline and has been of limited value to low-income families, who are eligible for only a portion of the amount.[30] If the value of the dependent tax exemption had remained at the same percentage of median family income at which it was originally set in the 1940s, it would amount to more than $7,000. In 1998, parents could subtract from their taxable income $2,700 for each dependent child under age eighteen, unless the parents had an extremely high income (more than $189,950 in aggregate gross income for a married couple filing jointly). The amount saved in taxes depended on which tax bracket the family was in. For families with incomes below the poverty line, who paid zero income taxes, the benefits were nil. For families in the 31 percent tax bracket (with what the Internal Revenue Service calls an adjusted taxable income of greater than $114,050 for a married couple filing jointly), the potential savings amounted to as much as $837 a year. If the child tax credit was added, a family in that bracket could receive $1,352 per child.

These tax savings amount to something similar to what northwestern European countries call a *family allowance*. But there are three big differences. First, countries such as France, Germany, and Sweden provide much higher benefits, including paid family leave from work. Second, they provide a lump-sum benefit that is the same for children in all families, rather than a benefit whose value goes up along with the income tax bracket a family is in. Finally, these countries also provide substantial in-kind services such as nationally funded health care, child care, and paid family leave from work.

In contrast, U.S. workers do not enjoy a right to paid family leaves. At best, they receive a guaranteed unpaid leave of twelve weeks to care for newborns or other needy family members, and this is available only to those who are employed by firms with more than fifty employees—approximately one-half of all workers. Children in low-income families are eligible for subsidized health services through Medicaid, but both take-up rates and overall quality of care are low. While many states provide subsidies for child care, these also fall short. In 1999, only 12 percent of children eligible for federal child care assistance received it.[31]

WHO GETS WHAT: THE REALITY OF INEQUALITIES

Uneven public provision contributes to unequal access. The higher a family's income, the more likely it is that the family can afford child care with an explicitly educational component. Only about 39 percent of three-year-olds from households with incomes between $10,000 and $20,000 attended center-based programs in 1999. By contrast, more than 58 percent of three-year-olds from households with incomes of more than $50,000 learned their ABCs in center-based programs.[32]

Income inequality among families translates into inequality among children. Analyses of household budgets have shown that most families spend about the same percentage of their income on their children—about 25 to 30 percent if they have one child and 35 to 50 percent if they have two children.[33] The distribution of private expenditures on children largely reflects the underlying distribution of income. The average income of the families in the richest 20 percent of families is more than ten times that of the bottom quintile. Thus, about ten times as much gets spent on the top fifth of children as on the bottom fifth.[34] Not surprisingly, most of the children in the bottom fifth live in families with incomes below the poverty line.

Limited Attention to Poor Families' Needs

We do provide a social safety net in the form of programs targeted specifically at poor families with children. These programs include the one commonly termed welfare, or Temporary Assistance to Needy Families (TANF), previously called Aid to Dependent Families with Dependent Children (AFDC). Much attention has focused on the reforms introduced in 1996, which imposed both a work requirement and a time limit for assistance. That the real value of the cash benefits provided has declined substantially over the past fifteen years is seldom mentioned.[35]

Poor families in which a parent is working for pay (and not receiving TANF) are eligible for the earned income tax credit (EITC). Unlike the other tax-linked family benefits previously described, the EITC is refundable, so families receive the benefit even if it is greater than the income taxes they owe. Childless families can receive a small refund, but much larger benefits are provided for families with one or two children. No benefits are provided for children beyond the first two. Expenditures on EITC now exceed those on TANF. While the amounts provided do not guarantee that working families with children will enjoy incomes over the poverty line, they provide a significant boost for low-wage earners.

Taken together, income tax exemptions, the child tax credit, TANF, and the EITC represent the main components of our public transfers in support of child rearing. One might suppose that they have a substantial equalizing effect, in keeping with principles of equal opportunity for children. Such is not the case. The amount of support received by poor families and their children—those in most need—does not add up to much more than that offered to affluent ones. Families in between get the least support of all.[36] Before looking at these numbers in more detail, it is useful to review how and why our policies of support for poor families have changed.

Inequalities in Tax Savings and Other Family Supports

Poor people in this country lack the shield of glib self-confidence that well-educated, affluent citizens often use to deflect criticism of their own entitlements. Ask a group of young professionals how many of them receive federal housing assistance. Very few will raise their hands. Then ask how many deduct the interest they pay on their home mortgages from their income taxes. Many will get huffy at the very idea that this could be considered public assistance. Yet this tax deduction costs the federal government more than twice as much as is spent on low-income housing assistance and low-rent public housing.[37] There are no limits or restrictions on it—the deduction applies to summer homes in Aspen and beach compounds in Key West as well as to homes for the middle class. This deduction is worth about $5,000 a year, on average, to taxpayers making more than $200,000.

Tax Savings
A look at family support policies yields similar results. The implicit family allowance paid per child in 2000 for a married-couple family with an adjusted gross income of more than $161,450 (the 36 percent tax bracket) amounted to $1,008 in tax savings per child, plus a $500 tax credit, for a grand total of $1,508 per child. In 2000, the maximum monthly benefit per TANF recipient in the median state amounted to slightly more—$1,684 a year. Single mothers receiving TANF, moreover, were subject to strict income and wealth eligibility requirements, time limits, and work requirements. None of these restrictions applied to affluent families enjoying the dependent tax exemption and child credit. Indeed, the affluent family previously described could have claimed another $1,008 in tax savings if one parent avoided paid work and therefore qualified as a dependent.[38]

Poor families eligible for the EITC fared better. Among families receiving the maximum benefit, the additional benefits that accrued from the first child in 2000 amounted to $2,000, and for the second child $1,535. In other words, EITC recipients with two children in 1998 could receive a slightly higher level of cash support per child (an average of $1,768) than either poor families on TANF or affluent families with $161,450 or more in taxable income. But since third and subsequent children receive no subsidy, EITC recipients raising larger families actually receive less per child than many affluent families of the same size.

What about in-kind benefits to poor families such as Medicaid and food stamps? If you count these in, however, you must also count tax expenditures that primarily benefit the affluent, such as the mortgage interest tax deduction previously described, Medicare (which provides health benefits to citizens sixty-five and older, regardless of income), and the tax exemption of employer contributions to health insurance and pensions from taxation.[39]

Government Supports for Child Care: Taxes and Other Issues

Federal support for child care can be compared more specifically. Like our implicit family allowance system, it takes two very different forms. Tax benefits are of primary relevance to nonpoor families. In 2000, the child care tax credit amounted to 20 to 30 percent of child care expenses (depending on family income level) up to $2,400 for one child younger than thirteen and $4,800 for two or more children if these expenses were incurred as a result of parental work for pay. Thus, it could offer as much as $720 per child. Since this credit is not refundable, it offered no tax benefit for most families unless they had at least $15,000 in income. No upper income limit was imposed on this credit, and as high-income families were more likely to spend money on child care, they were the most likely to benefit, as remains true.

A less well-known but more generous subsidy takes the form of dependent care pretax accounts, which allow working parents with child care expenses to set aside up to $5,000 per year in an employer-sponsored account that is exempt from income and payroll taxes. Employers have an incentive to set up such accounts because their payroll taxes are reduced. Here again, the value depends on the tax rate, but a family in the top federal income tax bracket in 2000 could garner a subsidy amounting to $1,980, not counting the effect of payroll taxes. In sum, the range of tax subsidies generated reimbursements ranging from $480 a year to a high of almost $2,000 (the benefit to a family in the highest tax bracket of a fully utilized dependent care tax account).

In the early 1990s, the cost of these tax expenditures far exceeded federal expenditures on programs aimed to serve low-income families. In 1993, the cost of the child and dependent care tax credit alone was $2.5 billion, compared to $1.7 billion spent on child care for AFDC recipients, transitional child care, at-risk child care, and the child care and development block grant.[40] Since that year, child care funding targeted to low-income families has been significantly increased, and program delivery has been reorganized as part of the changes to the larger welfare system legislated in 1996. Still, the amount of total entitlement expenditures authorized for 1999, $2.2 billion, remained slightly below the overall cost of the child and dependent care tax credit.[41]

Furthermore, most recent administrative effort has gone into providing child care for recipients of TANF as a way of encouraging transitions to paid employment. As a result, many of the working poor have found it difficult to find subsidized slots; families with an income above the poverty line but less than $40,000 a year remain the group least likely to receive assistance with child care costs.[42] As one expert has put it, "Concerns about the potential costs of that increased level of demand, along with concerns about the implications of future economic downturns, have made some states hesitant to expand their child care programs much beyond the welfare population."[43] Even states that allocated additional funds, such as Massachusetts and New York, have long waiting lists for low-income families.

Survivor's Insurance
Another, more telling example of benefits to relatively affluent families lies in a comparison between the treatment of single parents receiving welfare and those covered under a universal program. A provision of the social security system known as survivor's insurance provides benefits for families in which an adult member dies. If you pay social security taxes and happen to be run over by a truck tomorrow, your spouse and children under eighteen will receive a monthly check from the federal government.

The amounts of survivor's assistance are generous. In 2000, the average annual benefit per child was $6,728. The average annual benefit per widowed father or mother was $7,116. For a widowed father or mother with two children the total came to $20,573.[44] Compare this number with the maximum TANF benefit in the typical state for a family of three: $5,052.[45] The family receiving survivor's insurance does not have to qualify as poor to receive this help, and there is no requirement that the surviving spouse find a job. These benefits are financed by taxes on the working-age population, not by the contributions of those who directly benefit. If you were one of those economists who think that people's actions are entirely determined by some calculation of benefits and costs, you might worry about the fact that a mother is much better off murdering her husband than leaving him, as long as she can get away with it (either way, she needs a really good lawyer).

The economist Gary Becker, who writes a regular column for *Business Week,* was referring to welfare when he said, "It's bad for children to grow up in a family where all they know is that a check comes from the government every month. That's destructive of the child's self-respect and self-esteem."[46] Is it bad, then, for children if their families get a check from survivor's insurance or from a life insurance policy? Or, for that matter, from a trust fund set up by their grandparents? Do popular magazines or TV shows ever interview young middle-class widows or rich coupon clippers who are ashamed of receiving a monthly check?[47]

DIRECTIONS FOR CHANGE

We already have a family allowance system in the United States. It just happens to be a complicated, inconsistent, and inadequate one. We could simplify, improve, and expand this system. Greater public support for child rearing could increase economic efficiency by improving the development of children's capabilities and enhancing equality of opportunity. In principle, universal programs, supplemented by some targeted provisions for the poor, make sense. We could finance these expenditures in two ways: first, by taxing nonparents more heavily, in consideration of the economic benefits they will enjoy in their old age from taxes imposed on the working-age population, and second, by making implicit loans to children that would be repaid later, as the young people matured, entered the labor force, and began paying taxes.

Rather than providing a detailed blueprint of prescribed policies, I propose four priorities for change:

- *Offer consistent support for child rearing across income groups.* Rather than relying on the dependent tax exemption and tax credits as a way of providing family allowances, we should provide a simple lump-sum amount per child that is not determined by family income. If we want to impose requirements that parents engage in a certain amount of paid employment, these should be consistent across all income categories. This support should be keyed to the age of the child, with particular attention to the needs of families with infants, and should include paid family leaves from work of at least one year that encourage both mothers and fathers to devote time to active care.

- *Develop an effective safety net for children at risk of poverty.* In recent years, far more attention has been devoted to declining welfare rolls than to the persistently high rate of poverty among families with children. Significant improvements have taken place, including increased support for low-income parents through EITC and better health insurance coverage for children. However, more rapid progress in reducing, if not eliminating, persistent poverty among young children is needed. Assistance targeted to poor families, over and above what other families receive in the form of support for child rearing, could be conditioned on a number of factors, including participation in paid employment. However, neither sanctions nor time limits should be allowed to threaten children's welfare.

- *Provide greater public support for child care and early childhood education.* The structure and organization of our current public school system are relics of an earlier age. Despite considerable evidence that early interventions in childhood can improve developmental outcomes, we continue to subsidize college and university costs at a higher level than those for preschool.[48] We should provide greater public support for childcare, including universal pre-kindergarten programs for three- and four-year-olds similar to those in place in France and Sweden.[49] We might also consider synchronizing school schedules more closely with work schedules, eliminating the three-month summer vacation and instead offering students a series of two-week vacations staggered throughout the school year.

Universal prekindergarten programs would be more expensive than the income-tested assistance that has been widely proposed.[50] However, universal subsidies reflect the economic reasoning laid out earlier: public support comes as recognition of valuable work, not as charity. Furthermore, any benefit that is phased out as family incomes increase acts as an implicit tax on married women's labor force participation, thus indirectly reinforcing traditional gender roles.[51]

- *Reduce the cost to employees of cutting back on paid working time.* The primary policy instrument here would be paid family leave from work. Explicit incentives, such as allowing fathers paid leave for work that cannot be traded for maternity leave, could encourage paternal participation. In Sweden, for instance, parental leave can be shared or used by one parent, but one nontransferable month is reserved for the father and one for the mother, to encourage sharing.[52] During their child's first year, more than half of fathers use some leave. Fathers use nearly one-third of all paid temporary leave to stay home and care for sick children.[53] In the U.S. context, Sylvia Hewlett and Cornel West have called for a paid *and* compulsory leave for new fathers.[54]

Another policy instrument would be reduction of the penalties currently imposed on part-time employment. In France, where all work-related benefits are prorated by hours worked, part-time jobs are relatively better remunerated than in this country. At the same time, the French have made it illegal for most paid employees to put in more than thirty-five hours of work per week, thus discouraging the career "arms race" that occurs in the United States, where many professional and managerial workers are currently pressured to reduce the amount of time they devote to families and communities in order to meet their employers' expectations.[55]

In sum, parenting is essential, socially productive labor. It creates the productive capabilities that we call human capital, develops our culture, and creates our future. Parenting helps adults learn patience, humility, and love for others. Furthermore, without some kind of parenting, none of us would be here today. The United Nations Convention on the Rights of the Child, ratified by all nations of the world except for Somalia and the United States, stipulates that "parents have joint primary responsibility for raising the child, and the nation shall support them in this. The nation shall provide appropriate assistance to parents in child-raising."[56] More frank and open discussion of what kinds of assistance are appropriate could move U.S. policy in a more supportive direction. It could also do a great deal to remedy what seems to be a double standard of assistance for rich and poor.

14

Supporting a Dual-Earner/ Dual-Carer Society

Janet C. Gornick and Marcia K. Meyers

T he organization of market work and parenting in the United States has changed dramatically in recent decades, and the growth of maternal employment has been one of the most consequential of these changes. Both married and single mothers are much more likely to be employed now than they were forty years ago, with the most dramatic increase observed among mothers of young children. The traditional model of family life, with a male breadwinner and a female homemaker, has become the exception, not the rule. But rather than eliminating gender inequality, new work and family life arrangements have exacerbated inequality and created new and difficult problems for families. Some of the most formidable of these problems concern the care of children. With most parents in the workforce, society is facing a new and painful dilemma: if everyone is at work in the market, who will care for children?

While several other industrialized countries have enacted public provisions that help employed parents combine earning and caregiving, American families have been left largely on their own to craft private solutions and coping strategies. Some families accommodate by reducing the employment ties of one parent—most often of the mother. Other families cope by "split-shift" parenting—when one caregiver returns home from work, the other heads for the workplace. (This pattern of split-shift parenting is discussed later in the chapter.) Still other families place their children in out-of-home child care, and a growing number are doing so before their child's first birthday. For some, there is no available nonparental care, and children are simply left to care for themselves.

Although adults are valiantly trying to balance work and family, relying on these private solutions to adapt an outmoded model of gendered work to new realities has created new and vexing problems. Squeezed by the movement of mothers into the labor market, families are finding themselves increasingly time-poor. Employed mothers, in particular, often find themselves working very long hours in the labor market and the home. Women who reduce their labor force attachments to care for children incur substantial costs in terms of their earnings and career opportunities—costs that their male counterparts rarely pay. Because women's increase in market hours has not been matched by an increase in men's domestic and caregiving work, gender inequality remains entrenched in the home as well. Split-shift parenting creates other problems for families, increasing the risk of divorce and of compromises in parent-child relations. The current child care system, largely left to the private market, strains parents' finances, subjects children to care of dubious quality, and impoverishes many child care workers, nearly all of whom are women. Child care costs, combined with the limited availability of paid family leave and other public income supports for families, help explain why U.S. levels of economic insecurity and poverty are exceptionally high by international standards.

The problems just described are not unique to the United States, however. Families in all other industrialized countries are struggling to balance market demands with children's needs, women's concerns as mothers and as workers, and women's interests with men's interests. But many of these problems are more acute in the United States than in European countries with similar levels of economic development. American families are struggling more than their European counterparts, in part, because the United States has done much less than other rich countries to provide a package of government policies that helps resolve work-family conflicts.

We begin this chapter by documenting some of the prices that U.S. women, men, and children are paying as families struggle to craft private solutions to work-family conflicts without compromising either gender equality or economic security. Next, we argue that current debates about work-family issues have failed to provide satisfying solutions to these problems because they have created a false dichotomy between two opposing perspectives. One perspective gives primacy to women's care work and suggests that we may need to sacrifice gender equality for the sake of parenthood and children's well-being. An opposing view stresses women's attachment to the labor market and suggests that we may need to sacrifice children's and parents' interests for the sake of gender equality. Drawing on recent scholarship in Europe, we suggest a resolution to this false dichotomy by considering as an end vision a dual-earner/dual-carer society—that is, an earning, caring, egalitarian society. We then lay out the contours of a public policy package consistent with such a society, including gender egalitarian family leave rights, early childhood education and care, compatible public school schedules, working-time regulations, and income supports. We also examine policy provisions in twelve industrialized countries to provide policy lessons for the United States. In the final section, we comment on the prospects for change in the U.S. context.

PROBLEMS IN A "HALF-CHANGED WORLD"

U.S. parents are navigating uncertain new terrain between traditional expectations that mothers will bear full responsibility for caring for their children in the home and new expectations that all adults will pursue work in the market. Parents raising children in what has been termed a "half-changed world" are grappling with work-family conflicts that were rare even a single generation ago.[1] As families attempt to craft private solutions to these conflicts, they are often perpetuating or even exacerbating gender inequalities in the market and in the home.

Gender Inequalities in the Labor Market

One of the most significant problems associated with private solutions to work-family dilemmas is that they reinforce already deep gender inequalities in employment. Many women leave employment for months or years following childbirth. Others work in part-time jobs that are associated with lower hourly wages, reduced access to occupational and public social welfare benefits, restricted opportunities for advancement, and limited job security.[2] Still others select occupations that permit flexibility, trading "parenting time" for flat wage schedules, fewer benefits, and the absence of career ladders.

What is important is that these reductions in employment are linked to motherhood but, for the most part, not to fatherhood. In fact, the presence of children is associated with weaker labor market ties for women and *increases* in men's labor market attachment. Compared to nonfathers, fathers are more likely to be employed and to be employed full time, and they earn more per hour.[3] The differing effects of children on women's and men's employment outcomes is the primary factor underlying gender inequality in the labor market. Because labor market attachments are depressed by the presence of children for women but not for men, women pay steep economic penalties related to the care and nurturing of children.

Ann Crittenden has labeled the reduction in earnings due to women's disproportionate caregiving responsibilities the "mommy tax." Crittenden has estimated that the total lost earnings over the working life of a college-educated woman can easily top $1 million. In a middle-income family—for example, where a father earns $30,000 per year in full-time work and a mother $15,000 in part-time work— the mommy tax will still exceed $600,000.[4] While the mommy tax is the most punitive for highly educated women who could command high market wages, it still exacerbates gender inequality in the labor market at all levels of income. For families at the bottom of the skills and earnings distributions, particularly those headed by single mothers, it greatly heightens the risk of economic instability and poverty.

Gender Inequalities at Home

The evidence is mixed about whether women and men work the same number of *total* hours per week, considering time devoted to both paid market work and unpaid work in the home. What differs markedly between men and women is the proportion of their total workweek devoted to paid versus unpaid work. The gender gap in hours devoted to unpaid work has diminished in recent decades, as men's household labor has increased modestly and women's has declined substantially. Nevertheless, women continue to do the large majority of unpaid work in the home. As of the mid-1990s, the time women devoted to unpaid work was about twice that of men.[5]

The gender gap remains particularly wide with respect to unpaid time spent caring for children. Bianchi documented that the time U.S. married fathers spend with their children has risen in recent years. However, she estimated that they still spend just 56 percent of the time married mothers spend in primary child care activities, 45 percent of the time mothers spend in either primary or secondary activities, and about two-thirds the time in activities with children present.[6] Thus, married fathers' time with children still lags behind mothers' by a wide margin.

Where do women get the time for all this unpaid caregiving? Mothers who are employed appear to manage the time demands of the market and their children by reducing hours devoted to everything else. Employed mothers spend more than seven fewer hours per week on housework than their nonemployed counterparts. Per week, employed mothers also spend less time sleeping (fifty-five hours versus sixty-one), less time on personal care (sixty-nine hours versus seventy-four), and much less time in leisure activities (twenty-nine hours versus forty-one).[7] Many employed mothers, especially those with preschool-age children, face a severe time squeeze.

Split-Shift Parenting

One-quarter to one-third of parents now work nonstandard schedules, and a substantial share do so in order to arrange what Presser has called "split-shift" parenting. Split-shift (or "tag-team") parenting, like other aspects of the work-family balancing act, has a gendered cast. Mothers are four times as likely as fathers (44 percent versus 11 percent) to cite caregiving responsibilities as the primary reason for working nonstandard hours. And while men's likelihood of working evenings, nights, and weekends is unaffected by the presence or ages of children in the home, women are much more likely to work nonstandard hours when they have a preschool-age child. As Presser has observed: "Women generally are the adapters who arrange their work hours around those of their husbands rather than visa versa. . . . Men are acceptors: they are willing to care for children when mothers are employed."[8]

Is split-shift parenting a viable solution to the problem of balancing work and family obligations? Or is it one more symptom of the greater dilemma? Although split-shift parenting may help reduce gender inequalities in the provision of care for children and in housework, it does so at a high cost to workers and their families. A large body of research from Europe and the United States has shown that working nonstandard hours—especially night and rotation shifts—is associated with a variety of health problems. Furthermore, round-the-clock employment also has been shown to raise the likelihood of workplace accidents. What Presser has called the "social consequences" of nonstandard work schedules are also troublesome. Non-daytime employment has been associated with lower marital quality (especially when there are children), much higher divorce rates, and more limited parent-child interactions. There is also disturbing evidence that children whose parents work night and weekend shifts fare much more poorly in school than other children, in terms of both academic achievement and behavior problems.[9]

Child Care Costs for Parents, Children, and Providers

The movement of women from the home to the market when their children are young has greatly increased both the demand for and supply of nonparental child care. Like other solutions to work-family problems, these alternative care arrangements are overwhelmingly private—in both provision and financing. As with other private solutions, they create difficult problems and trade-offs for many families.

The use of overwhelmingly private nonparental care imposes steep financial costs on families. Among working families with children younger than thirteen, about half pay for child care during their working hours. Across all families, these costs average $286, or 9 percent of family earnings, per month. The costs of child care are substantial on average, and—because the distribution of these costs is highly unequal—they are extremely high for some families. Among families with children younger than five who have incomes at or below 200 percent of the federal poverty threshold, the half who pay for child care spend about 17 percent of family earnings. Among families at or below the poverty line, the one-third who pay for child care spend 23 percent of family earnings.[10]

Although American families are paying a lot for child care, the quality of care they are purchasing may not be very good. There is relatively little regulation of caregiver qualifications in private U.S. child care settings. The lack of public oversight, combined with persistent low wages for child care professionals, has produced a minimally educated and highly unstable caregiving workforce, with many workers cycling in and out of low-paid child care positions. Some child care centers report rates of staff turnover well in excess of 100 percent annually. The predictable result of these workforce issues is the provision of often very poor care to children. Observational studies of child care centers have concluded that only 15 percent of U.S. centers provide "good" care; in unregulated family child care and relative care, 50 percent to 69 percent has been assessed as "inadequate" or "fair" to "poor." Unfortunately, it is the children who are most developmentally vulnerable—those from poor communities and disadvantaged families—who are likely to receive the poorest care.[11]

The private child care solution to the work-family dilemma creates another, often overlooked gender penalty: it impoverishes a large, low-wage child care workforce dominated by women. U.S. child care workers are poorly paid and usually work without employment benefits or realistic opportunities for career advancement. The average full-time child care center worker earns between $13,125 and $18,988 annually, making child care professionals one of the most poorly paid groups of workers in the country. By way of comparison, the average earnings of child care workers are about the same—and those of family child care providers are barely half—of the wages earned by parking-lot attendants.[12]

Economic Insecurity and Poverty

The movement of many more women into the labor market during recent decades has created new time demands and other social pressures. We would have expected, however, that this increase in household labor supply was good for families' economic well-being. Indeed, throughout most of the 1990s, the United States experienced one of the most sustained periods of economic growth in recent history. Although many families fared very well during the 1990s, many others experienced a different economic reality even in the midst of the financial good times. Starting in the late 1990s, child poverty rates dipped slightly, but this drop was followed by the return of U.S. poverty rates similar to those of the 1970s. As of 2000, more than 18 percent of children ages six to seventeen and 22 percent of those younger than six were living in officially poor families.[13]

If everyone is now at work, why do so many U.S. families continue to live at the margins of self-sufficiency? Demographic and economic factors—including both the high percentage of children in single-parent families and the growth of low-wage employment since the 1970s—are part of the answer. The paucity of government assistance for families compounds these problems. Even before the welfare reforms of the 1990s, families relying on public assistance were among the poorest of the poor. Between 1994 and 1999, average welfare benefits declined by 30 percent, and receipt of welfare among poor families declined a remarkable 33 percent.[14]

Limited government assistance contributes to working families' poverty. The largest single source of help for working poor families is the earned income tax credit (EITC). Although the EITC has provided important assistance for low-earning families, it has not supplied enough to offset declining real incomes, and it has done little to help families manage the considerable expenses associated with employment. By one recent estimate, only about 15 percent of income-eligible families receive child care subsidies—with levels varying from 6 to 25 percent across states.[15] In the absence of assistance, child care costs can push near-poor families deeper into poverty.

Of particular importance for families with children, government programs provide very little in the way of income replacement for workers who withdraw from employment temporarily due to childbirth or other caregiving-related needs. Since 1993, the national Family and Medical Leave Act (FMLA) has granted workers in larger establishments the right to unpaid leave; however, publicly mandated maternity pay is available in only five states, covering less than a quarter of the labor market. Paid leave provided voluntarily by employers is offered to fewer than 4 percent of women employees. Thus, many parents cannot take advantage of their FMLA rights to care for their infants; nearly 80 percent of employees who have not taken FMLA leave when needed have cited an inability to afford unpaid leave as the reason for doing so.[16]

Swimming Upstream

Despite the evidence of deeply entrenched gender divisions in market and caregiving duties, many families express a desire to share earning and caring more equally. When asked if they would prefer to work more hours with more pay as opposed to the same or fewer hours with less pay, nearly one-quarter of U.S. mothers have indicated that they would like to have more hours of employment.[17] Men, on the other hand, have often expressed a desire to have more hours of time with their families. In a number of mostly qualitative studies, men have reported dissatisfaction with their responsibility for a disproportionately high share of economic provisions for their families and a disproportionately small role in caring for their children.[18]

Although many parents express the wish to share earning and caring more equally, and the desire to spend substantial time with their young children, those who try to do so are likely to find themselves swimming upstream in contemporary America. For parents whose resources allow them to reduce working time for caregiving, the penalties are likely to be social and professional. Women who choose to spend substantial time away from the workplace to care for young children often find themselves "mommy-tracked" away from the most lucrative career opportunities. In the context of gendered sex role expectations, men who make similar choices are likely to find themselves even more severely "daddy-tracked." Data from employer surveys, for example, have indicated that a majority of managers still believe that part-time working schedules and even brief parental leaves are inappropriate for men.[19] Parents with fewer resources are likely to have even more limited options. With little or no access to paid parental leave, low-earning parents often face a cruel choice between spending time at home with very young children and earning enough to meet their families' basic needs. The constrained choices of low-income women are evident in, for example, the fact that rates of leave-taking and the length of leaves increased most substantially among higher-income women after the FMLA's passage.[20]

RECONCILING EARNING, CARING, AND GENDER EQUALITY: THE DUAL-EARNER/DUAL-CARER SOCIETY

As noted earlier, two distinct perspectives have dominated academic and public discourse about work and family issues during the past four decades. Firstly, social scientists, policy analysts, and advocates have written extensively about changes in Americans' working behavior and about new problems for families who are attempting to balance work and family demands. Secondly, during this same period, American feminists have written volumes about the causes and consequences of gender inequality, both at home and in the labor market. Many have concluded that the two are inextricably linked, with labor market inequality resulting from gendered divisions of labor at home.

There has been surprisingly little interaction and agreement between these perspectives. Much of the work-family literature has stressed *women's* connection to their children and has located work-family conflict in women's lives. This perspective suggests that work-family conflict can be solved by crafting strategies—such as paid maternity leave, part-time work, job sharing, telecommuting, and flextime—that allow women both to work for pay and to spend time caring for their children. In contrast, much of the feminist literature has focused on enabling women to leave the home and strengthen their ties to the labor market—that is, to achieve parity with men. This perspective has emphasized policies that support women's employment, including out-of-home child care and the dismantling of employment barriers. While there is much overlap between these perspectives in terms of their concerns, productive engagement between them has been rather limited.

In recent years, European welfare state scholars have engaged in a parallel debate about the characteristics of the "woman-friendly welfare state." One group, writing from a "care perspective," has stressed support for women engaged in various forms of private caregiving. According to them, the state's ideal role is to grant women "the right to time for care" and to remunerate women for care work performed in the home—in other words, to lower the costs associated with women's unique role as care providers. Advocates of another view, the "women's employment" or "universal breadwinner" perspective, have alternatively argued that the primary aim of state policy should be to bolster gender equality in the labor market. These proponents have vigorously critiqued the care perspective, arguing that while it may value and reward women's unpaid work in the short run, it is ultimately counterproductive to reducing gender inequalities since it cements gendered divisions of labor into place. Care perspective proponents contend that failing to support women as caregivers disregards many women's desires to engage deeply in care work, denies women the options of remuneration for time spent at home, and deprives those in need of care of their caregivers' time.

Necessary Social Transformations

To reconcile these seemingly incompatible goals, we need to imagine fundamental transformations in both gender *and* market arrangements. One solution is the "dual-earner/dual-carer" society, as labeled by the British sociologist Rosemary Crompton.[21] The dual-earner/dual-carer society would differ from contemporary society in two important respects. First, men and women would engage *symmetrically,* as groups, in both paid work in the labor market and in unpaid work in the home.[22] In an earner/carer society, men and women would "halve it all," as the American psychologist Francine Deutsch has evocatively phrased it; the benefits and costs of parenting would be shared equally.[23] Second, the time allocated to caring would be not only degendered but *substantial.* In an earner/carer society, the majority of caring for very young children would be located in the home. Until children were old enough to enter educationally oriented care (at age two and a half or three), parents would be able to spend substantial time caring for their own children.[24]

The earner/carer society describes a *societal* arrangement; it is neither a prescription nor a mandate for individual families. It serves as a useful heuristic device for considering the provisions of modern welfare states. If we want to create an egalitarian society that values paid work in the market and caregiving work in the home, what role will the state need to play in providing support and reducing barriers for women and for men? While the earner/carer society would "halve it all" between women and men, such a society would be composed of men and women who choose various combinations of market and home time—depending on, for example, their preferences, their children's needs and life stages, and their extended families' resources. Likewise, while an earner/carer society would situate the bulk of care of very young children in the home, individual families would be free to make a variety of choices about their allocation of time to the market and to in-home caregiving.

What would it take to realize an earner/carer society? This shift would require transformations in the division of work between men and women, a more family-friendly labor market, and a new role for government. The most fundamental transformation would result from a reallocation of mothers' and fathers' time between market and caring work. For mothers *and* fathers to share the caring, men (on average) would need to shift an appreciable number of hours from labor market to home. For men *and* women to share the earning, women (on average) would need to shift a more modest number of hours from the home to the market.

For this compromise and adaptation to happen, both men and women would need the option to work reduced hours when their children were young, without undue penalties affecting wages, benefits, or professional opportunities. They would need flexibility in their work arrangements to attend to the routine and emergency aspects of family life. Also, they would need trusted and affordable resources outside the nuclear family to provide care for children during their own working hours.

Employers' Roles in Supporting Societal Shifts

Individual employers may help bring about some of these changes. Some employers in the public and private sectors have developed a number of exemplary policies to make the workplace more family friendly. However, these are exceptions. Moreover, employers have few, if any, incentives to absorb the costs that would result from a significant reallocation of parents' time from the workplace to the home for care of very young children or the costs associated with older children's out-of-home care. As it is, employers continue to enjoy a free ride on the unpaid work of parents, mostly mothers, who care for dependent family members without compensation and bear the substantial cost themselves. In the absence of mechanisms to forcefully shift these costs back onto employers, there is very little incentive for workplaces to direct substantial resources toward resolving work-family dilemmas.

We cannot expect families to solve these challenges on their own; nor can we rely on employers to bring about a fundamental transformation of work and family life. And allocating core services for working parents to consumer markets—as we now do with child care—produces substantial inequalities across families in financial burdens and in the quality of care received. An earner/carer society can be achieved only if government plays a more active role in supporting new alternatives and making these choices less costly for individuals and for employers.

PUBLIC POLICY IN SUPPORT OF A DUAL-EARNER/DUAL-CARER SOCIETY

Although U.S. families are left largely to their own devices to manage work and family demands, their counterparts in many continental and northern European countries are supported by a package of policies that allows parents to reduce their employment hours during their children's earliest years, creates incentives for men to assume a larger share of caregiving in the home, provides affordable substitute care for children while their parents are in the workplace, and ensures minimum levels of economic security. These policies provide a blueprint for a welfare state that would be consonant with an earner/carer society; we will address specific examples of them in the following section.

Family Leave

Family leave provisions are fundamental in helping parents secure sufficient time for caregiving when their children are young. To achieve this goal, leave policies must include both rights and benefits: granting parents the right to take time off to care for children without losing their jobs, and providing cash benefits (or wage replacement) to offset lost wages during leave periods.

Public family leave provisions consonant with the earner/carer model would have at least four components, all of which have been developed in many European countries. First, mothers would have maternity leave rights and benefits that guaranteed their option to take time off from work, with pay, around the time of a birth or adoption. Second, fathers would have paternity leave rights and wage replacement for some period around the time of a birth or adoption. Third, following their maternity and paternity leaves, both parents would be granted longer-term parental leave, with the right both to be away from the workplace and to receive cash benefits. Parental leave policies would support a combination of caregiving and market work during children's early years, up to, for instance, the third birthday (when many children would enter full-day preschool). Finally, throughout their children's lives, parents would be entitled to temporary paid leaves—often referred to in Europe as *leave for family reasons*—that would allow them to take brief interruptions from employment to care for a sick child or to respond to other family caregiving demands.[25]

Addressing Leave-Related Gender Inequality

The most vexing problems in the design of public family leave policies concern gender equality. If women use extensive leave benefits to take long absences from the workplace for caregiving reasons, leaves may exacerbate already substantial gender differentials in paid and unpaid work. An obvious first step toward gender equality is the extension of family leave benefits to mothers *and* fathers. It is equally important to design policies that create incentives to maximize the likelihood that men will use the benefits to which they are entitled, as women already do nearly everywhere.

Recent European experiences have suggested that two features of parental leave design may increase the incentives for men to take up their benefits. First, a high benefit rate—ideally, one that approaches the worker's full wage—is fundamental. Because men tend to have higher wages than women, it often makes economic sense, in the absence of full wage replacement, for mothers, rather than fathers, to withdraw from the labor market. Leaves that provide flat-rate or low to medium earnings-related benefits reinforce this gender differential. Full or high parental leave wage replacement rates maximize fathers' propensity to take advantage of leave rights and benefits.[26]

Second, men's incentives to take up leave increase when fathers' rights are granted on an individual basis or are otherwise nontransferable to their female partners. Policies that grant each parent his or her own period of leave create nontransferable rights, as do policies that reserve some portion of the family-based entitlement specifically for fathers. Either approach creates use-it-or-lose-it provisions for fathers; leave time that is not taken by the father is lost to the family.

Early Childhood Education and Care and Public School Scheduling

Early childhood education and care (ECEC) is a second essential support for parents combining earning and caring. If the family leave rights and benefits described thus far were extended to all parents, mothers and fathers could provide the bulk of very young children's care and arrange working schedules to provide a portion of older children's non-school-hours care. For older preschool-age children, however, and for school-age children during summers and school holidays, high-quality public ECEC is a crucial family support in two dimensions: it provides a safe and affordable alternative to parental care, and it provides an enriching experience for children.

ECEC policy consonant with an earner/carer society would reflect several principles that have been fully or partially developed here and abroad. First, ECEC would be universally available and affordable. Providing care as a universal child entitlement—that is, not categorically linked to parental employment—would improve both availability and affordability of care and provide a critical employment support to mothers and fathers. Second, ECEC would be available during both standard and nonstandard working hours. In the '24/7' U.S. economy, opening high-quality child care centers during the standard workweek would not be enough. With more affordable and acceptable child care options, parents who are currently working nonstandard hours in order to accommodate child care needs might be able to switch to more conventional hours. For those who could not or did not, a combination of off-hours child care and standard-hours early education experiences would be needed.

Third, the quality of publicly provided ECEC would be high. While the provision of high-quality care has obvious benefits for children, it is also important for the promotion of gender equality. Parents' decisions to substitute marketplace time for home time are influenced by both the cost of care relative to their wages and their perception of the quality differential between parental and substitute care. Care arrangements of uncertain caliber can compromise parents'—particularly mothers'—willingness and ability to commit to employment. The quality of care has other implications for the wages and benefits of the overwhelmingly female caregiving workforce. Child care providers' wages are the single largest economic input in child care production, and providers' education, training, and tenure are the most robust predictors of child care quality. A commitment to improving the quality of ECEC in the United States would necessarily include a commitment to raising the human capital and wages of some of the workforce's lowest-paid workers.

Although public schooling serves as de facto child care, children's care needs do not end when they enter school. Depending on their parents' employment schedules, children may need care before and after school, during school holidays, and during summer vacations. With more flexible working arrangements and extended family leave, parents could be available to provide part of this care. However, in countries with short school days or years, including the United States, this solution would still leave many hours of care uncovered. Policies to extend school hours and lengthen the school year to match parents' working schedules would provide another essential support for earner/carer families.

Regulated Working Time

For parents combining earning and caring, sufficient time for work in the market and caregiving in the home is often the scarcest of resources. The model of an earner/carer society assumes that both mothers and fathers will adjust their employment hours in order to provide care in the home—an option that is currently unavailable or prohibitively expensive (in terms of reductions in income and career opportunities) for many parents in the United States. Several of the European welfare states provide models for a more active state role in regulating working time to support earner/carer families. First, policies governing the length of the legal workweek can shorten overall hours, such as changing from the current U.S. legal standard of 40 hours to perhaps 37.5 or 35 hours, or adding "right to time off" policies that guarantee parents the right to work part time while their children are young. Second, labor market regulations can protect employees electing to work less than full time from excessive wage and benefit penalties by requiring employers to provide equal pay and prorated benefits for part-time employees. Third, policies governing compensation can lessen the burden, and possibly the extent, of nonstandard-hours work among parents. Required wage bonuses for nonstandard work hours, for example, provide incentives for employers to shift workers from nonstandard to standard hours, and for the workers who do work these shifts, bonuses increase their financial rewards.

Economic Security for Families: Universal and Targeted Income Support

Public policies that secure family income are the fourth crucial element in a package of government support for an earner/carer society. A society that encourages men and women to engage symmetrically in market and caregiving work is a society that expects parents to be responsible for their families' economic support. It is also a society that allows parents to limit their hours of market work in order to devote time to their children's care and nurturing. This suggests that all parents, including single parents and low-earning parents, would not be expected to be more than "fully employed." That is, no parents would be forced to work very long hours, double shifts, or more than one job in order to meet their financial obligations to make up for low hourly earnings.

Adequate Income Support Policies

One principle for an income support policy in an earner/carer society has already been considered in our discussion of wage replacement rates for parental leaves. However, a combination of market work and paid parental leaves still would not guarantee economic security for families headed by very low earners. Income support policies fully compatible with an earner/carer society would incorporate at least four other principles that are evident in many other industrialized countries' social welfare systems.

First, these policies would socialize a portion of the exceptional expenses entailed in childrearing. Raising a child to adulthood costs middle-income American families about $165,000—or $8,500 to $10,000 per year, depending on the child's age.[27] The high costs of raising children are usually imposed during the earliest and least lucrative years of adults' working lives. Universal child allowances are a common mechanism through which European welfare states use the tax-and-transfer system to distribute this burden more equally across families of different types and throughout their life.

Second, they would provide a floor of income security for low-skilled workers without creating employment disincentives. The proportion of workers earning very low wages is exceptionally large in the United States, relative to other industrialized countries. Unless we were willing to deny parenthood to low-wage workers or to consign them and their children to poverty, low-earning parents in an earner/carer society would need supplemental forms of income assistance. In the United States, efforts to adopt guaranteed-income policies have often run aground on concerns about individual work disincentives (such as the substitution of public benefits for earnings) or the disincentives for job expansion (such as the incentive to mechanize low-skilled labor). Income security policies consistent with an earner/carer society would provide income benefits that encouraged and rewarded labor market attachment.

Third, income-support policies would adapt unemployment compensation to the realities of family and caregiving demands. All industrialized countries have provisions for income support during periods of temporary unemployment. The rules and institutional structure of these programs can severely disadvantage parents, and this is particularly true in the United States. Parents who reduce their working hours or interrupt their labor market attachments in order to provide caregiving in the home may find themselves with too few hours or weeks of covered employment to qualify for benefits. Parents who leave a job "voluntarily" for family-related reasons—such as a child's illness or the loss of a childcare arrangement—may find themselves categorically ineligible for unemployment benefits, regardless of their earnings history.

Fourth, these policies would ensure the income security of single parents. The model of an earner/carer society begins with the assumption that two adults share in children's support and care. Policies that aid parents and provide targeted benefits for those combining earning and caring may actually provide an incentive for more parents to remain actively involved in their children's care and support—whether the parents reside with the children or not. The reality in the United

States and in other industrialized countries, however, is that a large proportion of children spend part or all of their childhood with a single parent. Ensuring these families' economic security raises particularly difficult challenges. Two of the most important and effective principles for this support are, first, assurance that child support obligations are imposed and paid by noncustodial parents and, second, that custodial parents receive adequate payments, regardless of the absent parent's earning capacity or cooperation. European programs of "advanced maintenance" payments, which guarantee replacement of the absent parent's income for all families, provide useful models for child support policies compatible with an earner/carer society.

HOW ARE THE INDUSTRIALIZED COUNTRIES PERFORMING AGAINST THIS BLUEPRINT?

These policies provide a blueprint for a policy package that would support earner/carer families. A substantial body of research has suggested that these policies could advance the twin goals of supporting men's and women's reallocation of time between market and home and of promoting greater equality in employment opportunities. Unfortunately, the United States lags behind many other industrialized countries in their adoption. In this section, we compare family policies across twelve industrialized countries, as of the mid- to late 1990s.[28] We pay particular attention to describing policies that are consonant with an earner/carer society and to comparing U.S. provisions to those of other rich, industrialized countries.

For this analysis we have selected countries that represent three distinct welfare state approaches or regimes. Since the 1990 publication of Esping-Andersen's *Three Worlds of Welfare Capitalism,* it has been commonplace for comparative social policy scholars to focus on welfare state regimes, that is, groups of countries with similar policy characteristics. Esping-Andersen's three-part typology clusters countries into the social democratic welfare states (primarily the Nordic countries), the conservative welfare states (primarily, the continental European countries), and the liberal (or residual) welfare states (typified by the English-speaking countries of the United Kingdom and its former colonies).[29] In this study, the social democratic countries were represented by Denmark, Finland, Norway, and Sweden, the conservative countries by Belgium, France, Germany, Luxembourg, and the Netherlands, and the liberal countries by Canada, the United Kingdom, and the United States.

Family Leave Provisions

Nearly all industrialized countries in this comparison sample provide generous parental leave during the first year of childhood, and many provide more extensive leave for family reasons after that period. The United States stands virtually alone in the lack of *any* national program for paid leave.

Table 14-1 provides a detailed comparison of three forms of family leave—maternity, paternity, and parental leave—across the twelve countries.[30] National policies granted maternity leave rights and publicly funded benefits in most of them; the United States failed to provide wage replacement in its national laws. The most substantial benefits for mothers are provided in two social democratic countries that have consolidated maternity and parental leave schemes. Drawing on their combined maternity and parental leave rights and benefits, Norwegian mothers are entitled to one year of leave at 80 percent wage replacement (or forty-two weeks at full wage replacement), while Swedish mothers could take a year of leave, with most wages replaced, plus three additional months at a lower rate. The five conservative countries provide somewhat shorter maternity leaves—generally, about four months—but they pay relatively high replacement rates (80 percent to 100 percent). Among the liberal countries, only Canada and the United Kingdom have countrywide policies of paid maternity leave, and in both countries benefits are low by cross-national standards.

Paternity and Parental Leaves

Short-term paid paternity leave is far more limited. Fathers in the social democratic countries can claim two to four weeks of paid paternity leave at the same rates paid to mothers; in the conservative countries, fathers in Belgium, Luxembourg, and the Netherlands are granted two to four days paid leave at 100 percent wage replacement. While fathers' rights to short-term paternity benefits are extremely limited, all countries now extend longer-term benefits to fathers through parental

TABLE 14-1. Family Leave—Maternity, Paternity, and Parental Leave Provisions (Approximately 2000)[31]
(Currency amounts in 2000 U.S. dollars, PPP-adjusted)

	Maternity Leave Benefits (paid)	Paternity Leave Benefits (paid)	Parental Leave Benefits (unpaid and paid)	Incentives for Fathers' Take-up
Social Democratic Countries				
Denmark	18 weeks. 100% of wages up to flat rate ceiling of DKK 2,758 [US $321] per week, equal in practice to about 60% prior wages. Due to collective agreements, many employers "top up," so 80% of parents receive 100% wage replacement.	2 weeks (ten days). Benefit is same as maternity pay.	Paid leave: Parents may share 10 weeks of parental leave. Benefit level same as maternity leave. Extended to 12 weeks if father takes 2 weeks. As with maternity leave, 80% receive full wage. Following parental leave, each parent entitled to 26 weeks of additional childcare leave (13 weeks if after 1st birthday). Benefit level is 60% of parental leave benefit level; sometimes supplemented by local authorities. Available until child's 9th birthday.	"Use it or lose it": 2 weeks of leave added to the 10 weeks of parental leave and designated for the father (for a total of 12 weeks); if he does not take them, they are lost to the family. Individual, nontransferable entitlement: The child care leave is granted to each parent and may not be transferred.
Finland	18 weeks [105 days]. Benefit based on graduated replacement rate: approximately 70% at low income, 40% at medium income, 25% at high income (equal, on average, to approximately 66%).	3 weeks [18 days]. Benefit is same as maternity pay.	Paid leave: Parents may share 26 weeks [158 days] of parental leave. Benefit level is 66% of earnings, flat rate if not employed. Following parental leave, family entitled to 108 weeks home care leave, on the condition that the child is not in public childcare. Benefit paid at a low flat rate of approximately FIM 2,900 [US $475] per month. Available until child's 3rd birthday.	
Norway	Paid leave: Parents may share 52 weeks of leave at 80% of wages, or, alternatively, 42 weeks at 100% of wages. (9 weeks exclusively for the mother, 4 exclusively for the father). Benefits subject to maximum income of NOK 290,261 [US $26,876] per year. Benefit can be paid while parent is employed 50%–90% time, and leave time is extended accordingly. Available until child's 3rd birthday.			"Use it or lose it": 4 weeks of leave are designated for the father; if he does not take them, they are lost to the family.
Sweden	Paid leave: Parents may share 65 weeks [15 months] of leave. Benefit level is 80% of earnings for 52 weeks [12 months]; flat rate for remaining 13 weeks [3 months], at approximately SEK 1,800 [US $187] per month. Earnings-related benefit subject to maximum income of approximately SEK 270,000 [US $28,000] per year. Benefit can be paid while parent is employed part-time and leave is extended accordingly. Available until child's 8th birthday.			"Use it or lose it": 4 weeks of leave are designated for the father; if he does not take them, they are lost to the family.

(continued on page 392)

	Maternity Leave Benefits (paid)	Paternity Leave Benefits (paid)	Parental Leave Benefits (unpaid and paid)	Incentives for Fathers' Take-up
			Conservative Countries	
Belgium	15 weeks, 82% of wages for first 4 weeks [1 month], plus 75% of wages thereafter. Benefits during first month not subject to ceiling; thereafter, benefits subject to maximum income of approximately $95/day.	3–4 days. 100% of wages.	Paid leave: Each parent entitled to 13 weeks [3 months] full-time leave, or up to 26 weeks [6 months] of half-time leave. Parents taking leave receive flat rate benefit payment of BF 20,400 [US $551] per month. Available until child's 4th birthday.	Individual, nontransferable entitlement: Father has his own leave entitlement that may not be transferred. However, the low replacement rate is a disincentive to take-up.
France	16 weeks for first 2 children, 26 weeks for third and subsequent children. 100% of wages, up to maximum of FF 387 [US $59] per day.	No paid paternity leave.	Paid leave: Parents may share 156 weeks [3 years] of leave. No benefit paid for first child; benefit level is flat rate FF 3,024 [US $462] per month for second and subsequent children. Benefit can be paid at reduced rate while parent is employed part time. Available until child's 3rd birthday.	
Germany	14 weeks. 100% of wages.	No paid paternity leave.	Paid leave: Parents may share 156 weeks [3 years] of leave. Benefit is flat rate of DM 600 [US $309] per month for 2 years or up to DM 900 [US $464] per month for 1 year. Benefits are income-tested, but majority of families qualify (during the first six months, then the income limits are lower and about half qualify). Benefits can be paid during part-time employment of up to 30 hours per week. Paid leave can be used until child's 2nd birthday; 3rd year of leave may be used until child is 8 years old.	
Luxembourg	16 weeks. 100% of wages.	2 days. 100% of wages.	Paid leave: Each parent entitled to 26 weeks [6 months] full-time leave; one parent can receive flat rate of LF 60,000 [US $1,471] per month. Benefit can be paid at half rate if parent works part time. One parent must take parental leave directly following maternity leave; other can take leave until child is 5 years old.	Individual, nontransferable entitlement: Father has his own leave entitlement that may not be transferred. However, the low replacement rate is a disincentive to take-up.
Netherlands	16 weeks. 100% of wages, up to daily maximum of 310 guilders [US $154] per day.	2 days. 100% of wages.	Unpaid leave: Each parent entitled to leave of the equivalent of 13 weeks [3 months] at their usual hours of work per week. Standard take-up is 26 weeks [6 months] at 50% working time. Available until child's 8th birthday.	Individual, nontransferable entitlement: Father has his own leave entitlement that may not be transferred. However, the absence of wage replacement is a disincentive to take-up.

	Maternity Leave Benefits (paid)	Paternity Leave Benefits (paid)	Parental Leave Benefits (unpaid and paid)	Incentives for Fathers' Take-up
Liberal Countries				
Canada	15 weeks. 55% of previous average insured earnings, up to a maximum benefit of C $413 [US $350] a week. Plus family supplement for low-income earners (less than C $25,921 [US $21,967]) raises replacement rate to 80%.	No paid paternity leave.	Paid leave: Parents may share 35 weeks of parental leave; combined maternity [15 weeks] and parental benefit cannot exceed 50 weeks. Benefit rate is same as for maternity (55% up to a maximum of C $413 [US $350] a week.) Parents can continue to work, earning the greater of C $50 [US $42] per week or 25% of their weekly benefit rate without affecting their parental benefits. Available until child's 1st birthday.	
United Kingdom	Statutory Maternity Pay (stricter eligibility): 6 weeks at 90% of wages, plus 12 weeks at flat rate (£60.20 [US $92]) a week. Maternity Allowance (broader eligibility): 18 weeks. Paid at lesser of 90% of wages or flat rate (£60.20 [US $92] a week).	No paid paternity leave.	Unpaid leave: Each parent entitled to 13 weeks full-time leave per child. No more than 4 weeks can be taken in any given year. Available until child is 5 years old.	Individual, nontransferable entitlement. Father has his own leave entitlement that may not be transferred. However, the absence of wage replacement is a disincentive to take-up.
United States	No national policy of paid maternity leave. Some benefits paid under temporary disability insurance (TDI) laws in 5 states: California, Hawaii, New Jersey, New York, Rhode Island. Approximately 23% of the U.S. population resides in these states. Maximum duration: 26–52 weeks; average duration: 5–13 weeks. Maximum weekly benefits: $170–$487; average weekly benefits: $142–$273.	No paid paternity leave.	Unpaid leave: Each parent entitled to 12 weeks family and medical leave (if employer has 50+ employees and work history requirements fulfilled). Available until child's 1st birthday. Several states extend federal leave; generally, state laws broaden coverage (including smaller employers) and/or increase duration. California enacted paid parental leave in 2002. Pays approximately 55% wage replacement for 6 weeks, subject to earnings cap.	Individual, nontransferable entitlement: Father has his own leave entitlement that may not be transferred. However, the absence of wage replacement is a disincentive to take-up.

Source: Table based on material presented in J.C. Gornick and M.K. Meyers, *Families That Work: Policies for Reconciling Parenthood and Employment* (New York: Russell Sage Foundation, 2003).

leave policies, although in some cases (the Netherlands, United Kingdom, and United States), parental leave is unpaid. In Denmark, for example, following mothers' maternity leave, parents are entitled to share approximately three additional months of parental leave (in practice, about 80 percent receive full pay); Finnish parents may share six months at about two-thirds pay. Parents in both of these countries also have further rights to leave, also paid, but at lower rates. In general, these benefits can be "fractioned," or distributed, over longer periods of time—for example, until the child's third birthday in Norway, and until the eighth or ninth birthday in Sweden and Denmark, respectively. This offers parents the opportunity to take up these benefits later in their children's lives if they choose to do so.

Paternity and parental leave rights and benefits are very limited in the liberal regime countries. None offer specific provisions for paternity leave, and only Canada offers cash payments for parental leave-takers during the first year following birth; following a recent doubling of the duration of parental leave benefits, parents can now share thirty-five weeks of paid leave. Until 1993, United States lacked any national policy for parental leave. With the passage of the Family and Medical Leave Act, parents in firms with at least fifty employees were granted rights to twelve weeks of unpaid, job-protected leave at the time of childbirth or adoption.[32]

The social democratic countries stand out as leaders in creating incentives for fathers to take up leave rights. In addition to the comparatively high replacement rates, three of these countries include a use-it-or-lose-it component in the family's shareable benefits. In most of the conservative and all of the liberal countries, policies that create incentives for fathers' leave are weak. While rights to parental leave or benefits are fully individualized (fathers have their own rights) in Belgium, Luxembourg, the Netherlands, the United Kingdom, and the United States, fathers' incentives to take the leave to which they are entitled are clearly weakened by the low or nonexistent wage replacement.[33]

Program Funding
A key characteristic of the European leave programs is that they are all funded through either social insurance schemes or general tax rev-

TABLE 14-2. Public Maternity and Parental Leave Expenditures and Financing
(Approximately 2000)[34]

	Maternity and Parental Leave Expenditures, 1998	Financing of Maternity Leave	
	Per Employed Woman (in 2000 US dollars, PPP-adjusted)	Contribution Framework	Contributors
Social Democratic Countries			
Denmark	$594	Funded by employers and government.	Employers pay whole cost for first 2 weeks; local government whole cost from third week on.
Finland	$673	Funded through sickness insurance fund.	Employers; employees; government; government pays substantialsubsidy.
Norway	$808	Funded through global social insurance fund.	Employers; employees; government; government pays substantialsubsidy.
Sweden	$608	Funded through sickness insurance fund.	Employers and government.
Conservative Countries			
Belgium	$234	Funded through global social insurance fund.	Employers; employees; government (paid from sickness and invalidity fund).
France	$431	Funded through health care insurance fund.	Employers; employees; government.
Germany	$465	Funded through health care insurance fund.	Employers; employees; government; employers pay a substantial share as they are required to top-up public benefit.
Luxembourg	$414	Funded through sickness insurance fund.	Employers; employees; government.
Netherlands	$67	Funded through general unemployment fund.	Employers; employees; government.
Liberal Countries			
Canada	$152	Funded through unemployment insurance fund.	Employers; employees.
United Kingdom	$75	Funded through global social insurance fund.	Employers; employees; government; government pays substantial subsidy.
United States	$0	In states with programs, funded through temporary disability insurance (TDI) funds.	In states with programs, various combinations of employer and employee contributions.

Source: Table based on material presented in J.C. Gornick and M.K. Meyers, *Families That Work: Policies for Reconciling Parenthood and Employment* (New York: Russell Sage Foundation, 2003).

enues (Table 14-2). Nearly everywhere, maternity benefits are paid out of consolidated sickness and maternity funds or social insurance funds that finance a broader array of programs; in most cases government subsidies fill in some of the costs. A crucial feature of these funding arrangements is that none mandate employers to provide wage replacement for their own employees—as is sometimes advocated in the United States. Furthermore, when the insurance funds do draw heavily on employer contributions, employers do not face "experience rating," meaning that their premiums are not determined by the usage

TABLE 14-3. Institutional Arrangements and Entitlements for
Publicly Supported Early Childhood Education and Care
(Approximately 2000)[35]

	Primary Public ECEC Institutions	Entitlement for Children Age 0–2	Entitlement for Children Age 3–School-Age
Social Democratic Countries			
DK	*Vuggestuer:* for children age 6–36 months; *Bornehaver:* for children age 3–6 years; *Aldersintegrerede institutioner:* for children 6 months–6 years; *Bornehaveklasser:* half-day, preprimary through school system for children age 6.	Yes, from age 1 or younger.	
FI	*Paivahoito* for children age 0–6; 6-*vuotiaiden esiopetus* (preschool) for 6-year-olds.	Yes.	
NW	*Barnehage:* children age 0–5.	No.	
SW	*Forskola:* for children age 0–6; *Forskoleklass:* preschool through school system for children age 6.	Yes, from age 1.	
Conservative Countries			
BE	*Kinderdagverblijf* (Flemish) and *crèche* (French): for children age 0–36 months; *Kleuterschool* (Flemish) and *Ecole Maternelle* (French): for children age 2.5–5.	No.	Yes, from 30 months.
FR	*Crèche:* for children age 0–36 months; *Ecole Maternelle:* for children age 2–5 years.	No.	Yes, from 30 to 36 months.
GE	*Krippe:* for children 0–36 months; *Kindergarten:* for children age 3–5 years.	No.	Yes, from age 3 (part-day).
LX	*Foyer de Jour:* includes crèche (0–36 months), *jardin d'enfants* (2–3 years), and *groupes scolaires* (4–12 years); *Enseignement Prescolaire:* compulsory preprimary for children age 4; *Education précoce:* optional preprimary for children age 3.	No.	Yes, from age 4.
NL	*Kinderopvang, Gastouderopvang* and *Peuterspeelzaal:* for children age 2 months–3 years old, and sometimes older children as well. *Bassischool* for children age 4–5.	No.	Yes, from age 4.
Liberal Countries			
CN	Market-based care main option for children below age 5. Public preprimary (usually part-day) available for 4-year-olds in some provinces.	No.	
UK	Market-based care main option for children below age 4. Part-day public nursery education: 4- and some 3-year-olds.	No.	Yes, from age 4 (part-day).
US	Market-based care main option for children below age 5. Public pre-K and Head Start for some children age 4.	No.	

Source: Table based on material presented in J.C. Gornick and M.K. Meyers, *Families That Work: Policies for Reconciling Parenthood and Employment* (New York: Russell Sage Foundation, 2003).

rates of their own employees (a tax scheme that the United States, alone, applies to unemployment insurance). Not surprisingly, the so-cial democratic countries invest the most in maternity and parental leave ($594 to $808 per employed woman); spending levels are lower in the conservative countries ($67 to $465) and in the two liberal countries ($75 to $152).[36] While public expenditures are substantial for these programs, when considered per capita the cost of paid leave is surprisingly modest, even in the generous social democratic countries.

Early Childhood Education and Care

Provisions for early childhood education and care vary dramatically across these industrialized countries, in both institutional arrangements and in service levels. The United States and other liberal countries stand apart from the countries of Europe in their heavy reliance on private market and family arrangements to provide ECEC until the start of public school.

The social democratic countries provide care until the start of school through a single public system, usually under the authority of the social welfare system (Table 14-3). Care is provided primarily through child care centers and, to a lesser extent, organized family day care schemes and public preschool programs for older children.[37] ECEC is generally provided as a right in the social democratic countries, although the extent and nature of the ECEC entitlement varies.

The conservative countries are more diverse in their organization of public care. In Belgium and France, public ECEC is provided through a dual system of child care centers for younger children and preprimary schools for children from the age of two and a half or three until the start of primary school.[38] Care for the younger children is not universal, but preprimary services are universally available, and take-up is nearly 100 percent for the older preschool-age children. ECEC provisions are more restricted in other conservative countries. Germany, Luxembourg, and the Netherlands provide a limited amount of public child care for children before the start of preprimary or primary school, with priority given to children in socially deprived families; ECEC for older children is provided through part- or full-day educational programs.

In the liberal countries, including the United States, child care for the under-threes is provided through mostly private child care centers and family day care homes. A limited number of subsidies provided to help low-income parents cover all or a portion of this private care. The

TABLE 14-4. Enrollment in Publicly Supported Early Childhood Education and Care (Approximately 2000)[39]

	Share of Children Served in Publicly Financed Care, Under Age 1	Share of Children Served in Publicly Financed Care, Ages 1, 2 Years	Share of Children Served in Publicly Financed Care, Ages 3, 4, 5 Years	Usual Hours of Operation, Preprimary Programs	Share of Children Served in Publicly Financed Care, Age 6 Years— in Countries Where Primary School Starts at Age 7	Age of Start of Compulsory Schooling
Social Democratic Countries						
Denmark	15%	74%	90%	7:00 A.M. to 6:00 P.M. all year.	98%	7
Finland	Few	22%	66%	7:00 A.M. to 5:00 P.M. all year.	92%	7
Norway	2%	37%	78%	Full day (41 or more hours per week).	Not applicable.	6
Sweden	Few	48%	82%	6:30 A.M. to 6:00 P.M. all year.	93%	7
Conservative Countries						
Belgium	15%	42%	99%	8:30 A.M. to 3:30 P.M. with after-school care available. Wednesday afternoon closed.	Not applicable.	6
France	Few	20%	99%	8:40 A.M. to 4:30 P.M. during term time. Wednesday afternoon closed.	Not applicable.	6
Germany	Few	5%	77%	Generally morning or afternoon sessions during school year, without lunchtime.	Not applicable.	6
Luxembourg	Few	3%	67%	8 A.M. to 4 P.M. but usually closed for two-hour lunch each day and Tuesday and Thursday afternoons.	Not applicable.	4
Netherlands	17%		71%	Child care full day; preschool (for 4+-year-olds during term time) 8:30 A.M. to 2:00 P.M.	Not applicable.	5
Liberal Countries						
Canada	Few	5%	53%	Part day, part year.	Not applicable.	5–6
United Kingdom	Few	2%	77%	Varies by type of program, from 2.5 to 6.5 hours per day.	Not applicable.	5
United States	Few	6%	53%	Usually part day, part year.	Not applicable.	5–6

Source: Table based on material presented in J.C. Gornick and M.K. Meyers, *Families That Work: Policies for Reconciling Parenthood and Employment* (New York: Russell Sage Foundation, 2003).

majority of care remains private, however, in both the source of financing (families) and provision (market or private entities). None of these countries extend guarantees for public childcare, and all heavily target and/or means-test public subsidies. Public provision in the liberal countries is more extensive for children from age four to the start of primary school, through various forms of (usually part-day) preprimary programs under the auspices of national, regional or local educational authorities. Preprimary programs are limited in availability, however, and often targeted to low-income or otherwise disadvantaged families.

Variations in child care and school institutions have critical implications for the levels of ECEC provision (Table 14-4). The social democratic countries are relatively high in inclusion for the under-threes, and the share of older children in public care varies from nearly two-thirds in Finland to 90 percent in Denmark. Among the conservative countries, variety in institutional arrangements translates into considerable variation in enrollments. Belgium provides full-day child care services for a large number of children under age three and for nearly all children ages three to five. In France, Germany, Luxembourg and the Netherlands, in contrast, services for the under-threes are more limited but available for two-thirds or more of those in the older age group.

Extent of Program Inclusiveness

In terms of inclusiveness, parents in the United States and other liberal countries consistently receive the least from government—particularly when their children are young. For children under age three, fewer than 5 percent receive public child care (this includes those in public care and those in care with public subsidies other than tax credits).[40] Between ages three and five, about half to three-quarters are in some form of publicly supported care, including child care, preschool, or public school; by age five, most children in these countries are in public school. Both preprimary services and the first year of public school are often only part-day, however, leaving employed parents to find private care during the remainder of their working hours.

Extensive systems of public ECEC in many of the European countries translate into substantial investments in children (Table 14-5).[41] Sweden spends nearly $5,000 and Denmark over $4,000 per year for

TABLE 14-5. Spending on Early Childhood Education and Care, per Child
(Middle 1990s) (in 2002 U.S. dollars, PPP-adjusted)[42]

Social Democratic Countries	
Denmark	$4,050
Finland	$3,189
Sweden	$4,950
Conservative Countries	
France	$3,161
Netherlands	$1,369
Liberal Countries	
United Kingdom	$780
United States 1997	$548
United States 2000	$679

Source: Table based on material presented in J.C. Gornick and M.K. Meyers, *Families That Work: Policies for Reconciling Parenthood and Employment* (New York: Russell Sage Foundation, 2003).

each child under school age. Spending in the conservative countries is lower, largely due to lower enrollment of children under age three in public care. The liberal countries spend much less per child. The United States spends the least of the seven countries for which we have data, investing only $548 per child under school age via direct provisions, subsidies, and tax credits combined. Between 1997 and 2000, spending in the United States rose substantially—to $679 per child under school age—but it remains well below the level of expenditure in any of these comparison countries.

As noted above, parents' need for substitute care does not stop when their children enter primary school. The extent of this need varies with the standard school day and school year, and on this dimension, U.S. schools provide less assistance than those in many other countries. The American school day, which averages between six and seven hours, is slightly shorter than the school day in some other countries. Even more dramatically, American children generally attend school about 180 days per year, while children in most European countries spend 190–200 days per year in school; that adds up to as many as four additional weeks when parents must find care for their children.[43]

Regulated Working Time

During the 1990s, in several European countries, legislation combined with collective bargaining shortened the standard workweek—generally to the range of thirty-five to thirty-nine hours. The motivations have been varied, including creating jobs, supporting families, and strengthening gender equality in divisions of labor. While Europeans have debated the benefits of a shorter workweek, a number of factors have combined to lengthen annual working time in the United States.[44]

The social democratic countries are especially family-friendly. In Denmark, for example, which reported the lowest annual hours in Europe as of 1998, working time reduction remains an active issue; the explicit focus is to meet the needs of families. In Sweden, working time reduction remains at the top of the public policy and collective bargaining agendas, as "a way to improve the well-being of workers and increase equality between men and women." As of 2000, normal weekly hours in these four countries ranged from thirty-seven (in Denmark) to just over thirty-nine (in Finland).[45]

Activity is under way in the conservative countries as well. In 1997, prominent labor and academic leaders called for Belgium to shift to a thirty-five-hour workweek, and in 2000, the thirty-five-hour workweek became law in France.[46] By 2000, all five of these countries had reduced the normal workweek to below forty hours.

Along with efforts to shorten working hours for all workers, some European countries have adopted policies specifically aimed at freeing parents' time for caregiving. In Sweden, for example, all parents have the right to work just six hours per week, with job protection (and prorated remuneration), until their children reach the age of eight.[47] In 2001, Germany passed a law granting the right to work part time to all workers in establishments with more than fifteen employees; the Netherlands has established a similar right for employees in enterprises of ten or more workers. Belgium grants employees the right to work 80 percent of the time for five years. And France has enacted a right to part-time work exclusively for parents. In most cases, these regulations give employers a safety valve in that they can refuse a change on certain business grounds, but those grounds are often subject to judicial review.

No similar efforts to reduce working time were evident in the United States during this period. The workweek in the United States fell steadily during the nineteenth and early twentieth centuries, until the five-day, forty-hour week became the legal standard in the 1930s. In recent years, the United States has seen no substantial reduction in working hours, and Americans currently report the longest work hours, both weekly and annually, among these twelve countries. Scholars attribute some of these excess work hours to weak labor market regulations or collective agreements, including the lack of rules establishing maximum work hours or minimum vacation days, both of which are common elsewhere.[48]

Protections for Part-Time Workers

The United States also lags behind its European counterparts in employment protections for part-time workers. In Europe, there has been a gradual extension of employment protections to part-time workers through rulings established using European sex discrimination legislation combined with collective bargaining. Supranational organizations have taken the lead in this policy movement.[49] The 1994 Part-Time Work Convention and Recommendation of the ILO, for example, called for measures to ensure that part-time workers receive the same protection as full-time workers with respect to the right to organize, occupational safety and health, wages, maternity protection, sick leave, and holidays. The Council of the European Union's Directive on Part-Time Work, adopted in 1997, has even broader language, requiring that "in respect of employment conditions, part-time workers shall not be treated in a less favourable manner than comparable full-time workers solely because they work part-time."[50] That is interpreted to mean nondiscrimination in pay and benefits, as well as advancement opportunities.

The United States has not followed its European counterparts in the extension of protections to part-time workers. Partly for this reason, the United States has a comparatively large pay gap between part-time and otherwise similar full-time workers and larger differentials in access to health insurance and other employment-based benefits.[51]

Economic Security for Families

One of the most fundamental functions of the welfare state is the assurance of economic security for both those who are attached to the labor market and those who are not. In the provision of support for families with children, the United States is an exceptional laggard by international standards on at least four dimensions.[52]

First, nearly all of the countries surveyed here, other than the United States, provide universal cash transfers to families with children in the form of family or child allowances. These benefits are designed to partially offset or socialize the costs of rearing children and are typically provided regardless of parents' work history or current income.

Second, child support policies in other countries are more effective in ensuring income replacement for custodial single parents. In many countries, private child support payments are replaced or guaranteed by the state when absent parents cannot or do not pay. The United States has become more aggressive in its efforts to collect child support from noncustodial parents, but none of the states ensure that custodial parents receive child support assistance in the form of advance or guaranteed payments if the noncustodial parent does not pay. In actuality, just the opposite is true for many of the poorest U.S. families. Parents on public assistance are obligated to cooperate with the collection of child support, but the collections are retained by the state; at state discretion, the custodial parent may receive all of the collection, a small pass-through (typically $50), or nothing.[53]

Third, means-tested social assistance programs are less restrictive, and more generous, in most other industrialized countries. The main form of cash assistance for families with children in the United States, Temporary Assistance for Needy Families (TANF), is both extremely limited in coverage and very meager in benefit levels. In contrast, means-tested assistance programs in other countries usually serve broader and more diverse populations—blending single- and dual-parent families, and families with and without paid workers—and benefit levels are generally higher, as well as indexed to changes in prices or wages. When combined with other forms of cash assistance, such as child allowances and advance payments of child support, these means-tested benefits ensure that families with children have a minimum level of income and a cushion against poverty due to unemployment or very-low-wage work.

Fourth, the United States lags behind its European counterparts in protections for temporarily unemployed workers, especially with respect to the economic security of families with children.[54] Typically, disqualifications for "voluntary job separations" are less stringent than they are in the United States—where, in all but five states, the disqualification lasts for the entire unemployment spell. Unemployment compensation is more widely available to part-time workers elsewhere, including those currently seeking part-time work, than in the United States. And many of these countries—including Finland, France, Germany, the Netherlands, Sweden, and the United Kingdom—have unemployment assistance programs, which specifically provide means-tested cash assistance for unemployed workers who are not eligible for insurance-based benefits, either because they fail to meet the eligibility requirements or because they have exhausted their benefits.

Variation in the generosity of provisions for family income is evident in public spending on cash benefits for families (Table 14-6).[55] When family allowances for children, family support benefits, single-parent cash benefits, paid family leave, and refundable tax credits for families (e.g., the United States' EITC) are considered together, the social democratic countries spend substantial, and relatively similar, amounts on cash benefits for families. Across the four countries, spending averages about 2 percent of GDP, or just about $1,850 per child per year. Expenditures in the conservative countries are much more varied, ranging from a low of 0.8 percent of GDP in the Netherlands to a high of 2.4 percent in Luxembourg. Across these five countries, per child spending averages just over $2,200 per year.

Among the liberal countries, the United Kingdom spends about the same amount, per child, as do the less generous of the conservative European countries. The United States lags quite dramatically, spending only 0.5 percent of GDP or about $650 per child per year.

PROSPECTS FOR CHANGE IN THE UNITED STATES

Since the United States falls far behind many other rich, industrialized countries in the provision of support to families—in particular to

TABLE 14-6. Expenditures on Cash Benefits for Families, 1998 (in 2000 U.S. dollars, PPP-adjusted)[56]

	As a Percentage of GDP	Per Child Under Age 18
Social Democratic Countries		
Denmark	1.5%	$1,822
Finland	1.9%	$1,883
Norway	2.2%	$2,249
Sweden	1.6%	$1,417
Conservative Countries		
Belgium	2.1%	$2,265
France	1.5%	$1,390
Germany	2.0%	$2,247
Luxembourg	2.4%	$4,270
Netherlands	0.8%	$884
Liberal Countries		
Canada	0.8%	$793
United Kingdom	1.7%	$1,557
United States	0.5%	$650

Source: Table based on material presented in J.C. Gornick and M.K. Meyers, *Families That Work: Policies for Reconciling Parenthood and Employment* (New York: Russell Sage Foundation, 2003).

earner/carer families—we may have much to learn from our European counterparts. However, translating European-style policy configurations to the United States would require a substantial mobilization of political support and the exercise of political will. Given current political trends, is the development of policies that support an earner/carer society politically feasible in the United States? Furthermore, are U.S. policy makers even willing to look abroad for lessons about family policy?

Support for any form of social policy expansion may seem unlikely in the wake of the 1996 welfare reform, which not only reversed the sixty-one-year-old entitlement to public assistance for families with children but also drastically reduced cash benefits. While welfare reform may be read as a sign of social policy retrenchment, it may also, paradoxically, signal support for new forms of government assistance to low-income families. Alongside the public assistance cuts, Congress authorized a large expansion in child care subsidy assistance for the working poor, expanded the EITC, and expanded health insurance for children in low-income families. These federal policy reforms provide encouraging evidence that support for expanding some forms of family policy can coexist with widespread opposition to traditional public assistance.

Federal and state policy makers are also considering policies that benefit families more widely. Many of the initiatives that have received the most attention over the past twenty years—including allowances or refundable tax credits for families, paid family leave, and universal preschool—are similar in design to the universal policies in European countries. This suggests that now, more than ever, U.S. policy makers have much to gain from studying European family policy designs.

The European experience also provides encouraging evidence that family policies are economically feasible, even in fiscal hard times. In recent years, the U.S. press has frequently characterized European welfare states as undergoing severe, across-the-board social policy retrenchment. Many of these countries are, in fact, *increasing* commitments in several areas of social provision. Expansions were particularly great during the 1980s and 1990s in the policy areas we have outlined, including child care and parental leave.[57] These programs remain politically popular, partly because they are effective in shoring up women's employment and reducing child poverty, and partly because their financing avoids unduly burdening employers.

As more U.S. families struggle to combine employment and parenthood, the possibility that government could do more to help families is resonating with a broad spectrum of society. Americans are often characterized as deeply suspicious of government intrusions into private life, but recent surveys have suggested that U.S. parents believe government is not doing enough to provide work-family support. Large majorities support paid family leave, and they want it to be publicly financed; substantial majorities of Americans also say they support amendments to worktime regulation that would extend workers' options for choosing between pay and working time. Americans express support for government assistance with child care, after-school programs, and longer school days and school years.[58]

For a new approach to family policy to become a reality, Americans will need to translate their support for these policies into political demands. In *The Missing Middle,* Theda Skocpol envisioned mobilization of these demands through broad political alliances that transcend age, race, and class divisions in their support for reforms similar to the package we have described in this chapter. By aligning interests on both social insurance and family benefits, along with shifting the focus of social policy from means-tested programs for the disadvantaged to universal supports, she suggested that "there are bright prospects for a new progressive politics focused on social supports for all working parents."[59]

Expanding our vision of family policy to support an earner/carer world also has the potential to close other political cleavages. Formulating leave, child care, and labor market policies that explicitly extend benefits to fathers as well as mothers has the potential to engage men in support of family policy. Designing policies as supports for both employment and caring, shared equally by women and men, holds promise for closing the schism between feminists oriented to reducing gender differentials and advocates focused on rewarding caregiving in the home and supporting children's well-being. The earner/carer framework may also engage conservatives who have traditionally opposed expanding government support for families. The model of an earner/carer society supports the employment of women, including low-income women; it encourages parents to spend time with their children; and it strengthens fathering—three elements of the contemporary conservative agenda. By building political bridges across these long-standing divides, the model of an earner/carer society may help reenergize support for U.S. family policy development.

NOTES

Introduction: Societal Crossroads
Jody Heymann

1. James Madison, letter to W.T. Barry, August 4, 1822, in G.P. Hunt, ed., *The Writings of James Madison*, vol. 9 (New York: G.P. Putnam's Sons, 1910).
2. Alexis de Tocqueville, *Democracy in America*, vol. 2 (New York: Vintage Books, 1945), 99.
3. S.J. Heymann, *The Widening Gap: Why Working Families Are in Jeopardy and What Can Be Done About It* (New York: Basic Books, 2000).
4. At the beginning of the twentieth century, families bore the economic cost of children, but they also bore most of the economic benefits. Children began to labor early on farms and in homes, and their wages and services helped their family members, young and old. In contrast, when today's children begin working, they will be supporting other families financially through their taxes (including retirement taxes), as well as practically, through their labor.

Changes in the Demographics of Families over the
Course of American History
Donald J. Hernandez

1. D.J. Hernandez, *America's Children: Resources from Family, Government, and the Economy* (New York: Russell Sage Foundation, 1993).
2. J. Qvortrup, "From Useful to Useful: The Historical Continuity of Children's Constructive Participation," *Sociological Studies of Children* 7 (1995): 49–76; V. A. Zelizer, *Pricing the Priceless Child: The Changing Social Value of Children* (New York: Basic Books, 1985).
3. V.K. Oppenheimer, *The Female Labor Force in the United States*, Population Monograph Series no. 5, Institute of International Studies (Berkeley: University of California Press, 1970).
4. K. Anderson, "A History of Women's Work in the United States," in A.H. Stromberg and S. Harkness, eds., *Women Working: Theories and Facts in Perspective* (Mountain View, CA: Mayfield, 1988); C. Goldin, *Understanding the Gender Gap: An Economic History of Working Women* (Oxford: Oxford University Press, 1990); A. Kessler-Harris, *Out to Work: A History of Wage-Earning Women in the United States* (Oxford: Oxford University Press, 1982); B. Reskin and H.I. Hartmann, eds., *Women's Work, Men's Work: Sex Segregation on the Job* (Washington, DC: National Academy Press, 1986).
5. S. Ruggles, "The Rise of Divorce and Separation in the United States, 1880–1990," *Demography* 4 (1997): 455–66.

6. Ibid.; S.S. South, "Economic Conditions and the Divorce Rate: A Time-Series Analysis of the Postwar United States," *Journal of Marriage and the Family* 47 (1985): 31–41.

7. R.D. Conger, G.H. Elder Jr., F.O. Lorenz, K.J. Conger, R.L. Simons, L.B. Witbeck, J. Huck, and J.N. Melby, "Linking Economic Hardship to Marital Quality and Instability," *Journal of Marriage and the Family* 52 (1990): 643–56; R. Conger and G.H. Elder Jr., *Families in Troubled Times: Adapting to Change in Rural America* (Hawthorne, NY: Aldine de Gruyter, 1994); G.H. Elder Jr., R.D. Conger, E.M. Foster, and M. Ardelt, "Families Under Economic Pressure," *Journal of Family Issues* 13 (1992): 5–37; J.K. Liker and G.H. Elder Jr., "Economic Hardship and Marital Relations in the 1930s," *American Sociological Review* 48 (1983): 343–59.

8. Hernandez, *America's Children*.

9. Ibid.

10. W.J. Wilson, *The Truly Disadvantaged: The Inner City, the Underclass, and Public Policy* (Chicago: University of Chicago Press, 1987).

11. U.S. Department of Labor, Bureau of Labor Statistics, *Handbook of Labor Statistics, Bulletin 2340* (August 1989), Table 16; and calculated from *Employment and Training Report of the President, 1982* (Washington, DC: U.S. Government Printing Office, 1982), Tables A-4, A-13, and A-16; and calculated by the author from Current Population Survey data from the U.S. Census Bureau.

12. "Ozzie and Harriet family" refers to television portrayals in the 1950s of families in which the father was the breadwinner and the mother stayed at home.

13. Hernandez, *America's Children*.

14. P.H. Jacobson, *American Marriage and Divorce* (New York: Rinehart, 1959); K. Davis, "The American Family in Relation to Demographic Change," in C.F. Westoff and R. Parke Jr., eds., *Demographic and Social Aspects of Population Growth*, vol. 1 of Commission Research Reports, U.S. Commission on Population Growth and the American Future (Washington, DC: Government Printing Office, 1972).

15. C. Bose, *Women in 1900: Gateway to the Political Economy of the 20th Century* (Philadelphia: Temple University Press, 2001).

16. F.D. Blau and M.A. Ferber, *The Economics of Women, Men, and Work* (Englewood Cliffs, NJ: Prentice-Hall, 1986); R.A. Rosenfeld, *Farm Women: Work, Farm, and Family in the United States* (Chapel Hill: University of North Carolina Press, 1987); M.M. Wright, " 'I Never Did Any Fieldwork, but I Milked an Awful Lot of Cows': Using Rural Women's Experience to Reconceptualize Models of Work," *Gender and Society* 9 (1995): 216–35.

17. Bose, *Women in 1900*.

18. U.S. Congress, *Alternative Measures of Poverty*, staff study prepared for the Joint Economic Committee (Washington, DC: Government Printing Office, 1989), 10.

19. J.K. Galbraith, *The Affluent Society* (Boston: Houghton Mifflin, 1985), 323–24.

20. Citro and Michael, *Measuring Poverty*; L. Rainwater, *What Money Buys: Inequality and the Social Meanings of Income* (New York: Basic Books, 1974).

21. Rainwater, *What Money Buys*.

22. Hernandez, *America's Children*. The insights in this section, additional literature, and a comprehensive review of existing U.S. studies and original research by Rainwater suggest that the measure of relative poverty using poverty thresholds be set at one-half of median family income in specific years and adjusted for family size. See Expert Committee on Family Budget Revisions, *New American Family Budget Standards* (Madison, WI: Institute for Poverty Research, 1980); V. Fuchs, "Towards a Theory of Poverty," in *The Concept of Poverty* (Washington, DC: Chamber of Commerce of the United States, 1965); Rainwater, *What Money Buys*; Hernandez, *America's Children*. More recently, three advantages and two drawbacks of the relative approach were identified and discussed by the Panel on Poverty and Family Assistance established at the request of the U.S. Congress by the National Research Council of the National Academy of Sciences.

See C.F. Citro and R.T. Michael, *Measuring Poverty: A New Approach* (Washington, DC: National Academy Press, 1995).

The first advantage is that relative measures are easy to understand and calculate, making them especially compelling for comparisons across countries where it is difficult to develop analogous expert family budgets or other types of poverty thresholds. The second advantage is that they do not represent any type of family budget per se but, instead, refer to a point, usually one-half the median, of an income or expenditure distribution. The third advantage is that they are self-updating, thereby averting the need for periodic revisions that are often controversial because expert or political views differ regarding the content of a minimally adequate family budget.

The first drawback of relative measures is that they present too much of a moving target for policies to reduce poverty. But the panel pointed out that this argument can be overstated and that a measure based on the percentage of the median is appropriate and public policies can, indeed, lead to reductions in poverty so measured. In fact, a relative measure calculated as 50 percent of adjusted median disposable income for eight Western nations in the latter half of the 1980s indicated that child poverty varied from a high of 27 percent in the United States to a low of 3 percent in Sweden, and that government tax and transfer programs reduced child poverty across eight countries by an average of 7.9 percentage points, and in France and the United Kingdom by 18 to 20 percentage points. See T. Smeeding and B.B. Torrey, "Revisiting Poor Children in Rich Countries" (working paper, Center for Policy Research and Luxembourg Income Study, Syracuse University, March 1995).

The second drawback is that if real median family income declined from one year to the next, then the value of the relative poverty threshold would decline and the measured poverty rate would fall, even if the level of real income remained unchanged among families toward the bottom of the income distribution. See Citro and Michael, *Measuring Poverty*. One solution might be a decision rule never to adjust a relative poverty threshold downward, an approach consistent with general expectations and planning goals of economic policy makers that incomes will rise over the longer run. Since 1947, real median income has fallen seven times, for periods ranging from one to four years, but the corresponding periods of recovery required to reach or surpass the previously recorded historic highs have generally been about as long as the periods of decline. For example, following the five declines between the late 1940s and the early 1970s, each of which lasted one or two years, record highs were documented during the first year of income increase (four times) or during the third year of increase (once). Similarly, following the two declines during the early 1980s and the early 1990s, which lasted three or four years, record highs were documented either three or four years following the low.

The current analysis assessing long-term trends at approximately ten-year intervals shows that periodic declines in median family income were not an issue after 1949 because declines were not occurring during the years for which relative poverty was measured; instead, median family income was at historical highs during these years. Furthermore, the first advantage cited by the Panel on Poverty and Family Assistance regarding international comparisons also applies to the changes over the sixty years studied here. The relative poverty measure is easy both to understand and to calculate, and it would be difficult to develop historically comparable family budgets or other poverty thresholds for 1939 to 1999 that would be widely accepted.

23. U.S. Census Bureau, *Poverty Status of People, by Age, Race, and Hispanic Origin: 1959 to 2000,* www.census.gov/hhes/poverty/histpov/hstpov3.html, Table 3 (last revised February 15, 2002; accessed February 26, 2002).

24. J.M. McNeil, *Workers with Low Earnings: 1964 to 1992,* series P-60, no. 178, *Current Population Reports, Consumer Income* (Washington, DC: U.S. Bureau of the Census, 1992) and unpublished Census Bureau tabulations kindly provided by J.M. McNeil.

25. D.J. Hernandez, "Poverty Trends," in G.J. Duncan and J. Brooks-Gunn, eds., *Consequences of Growing Up Poor,* (New York: Russell Sage Foundation, 1997).

26. U.S. Census Bureau, Population Division, Population Projections Branch, maintained by Laura K. Yax (Population Division), www.census.gov/population/www/projections/natsum-T3.html (last revised August 2, 2002).

27. D.J. Hernandez and E. Charney, eds., *From Generation to Generation: The Health and Well-Being of Children in Immigrant Families* (Washington, DC: National Academy Press, 1998); D.J. Hernandez and K. Darke, "Socioeconomic and Demographic Risk Factors and Resources Among Children in Immigrant and Native-Born Families: 1910, 1960, 1990," in Hernandez and Charney, *From Generation to Generation.*

28. D.J. Hernandez, ed., *Children of Immigrants: Health, Adjustment, and Public Assistance* (Washington, DC: National Academy Press, 1999).

29. Hernandez and Charney, *From Generation to Generation.*

30. Hernandez and Charney, *From Generation to Generation;* A. Portes and R.G. Rumbaut, *Legacies: The Story of the Immigrant Second Generation* (New York: Russell Sage Foundation, 2001); R.G. Rumbaut, "The Crucible Within: Ethnic Identity, Self-Esteem, and Segmented Assimilation Among Children of Immigrants," *International Migration Review* 28 (1994): 748–94; R. Rumbaut, "Ties That Bind: Immigration and Immigrant Families in the United States," in A. Booth, A.C. Crouter, and N. Landale, eds., *Immigration and the Family: Research on U.S. Immigrants* (Mahwah, NJ: Lawrence Erlbaum, 1997); R. Rumbaut and W.A. Cornelius, eds., *California's Immigrant Children: Theory, Research, and Implications for Educational Policy* (San Diego: Center for U.S.-Mexican Studies, University of California, San Diego, 1995).

31. Hernandez and Charney, *From Generation to Generation;* Hernandez, *Children of Immigrants.*

32. J.P. Shonkoff and D.A. Phillips, eds., *From Neurons to Neighborhoods: The Science of Early Childhood Development* (Washington, DC: National Academy Press, 2000).

33. Committee on Economic Development, *Preschool for All: Investing in a Productive and Just Society: A Statement on National Policy* (New York: Committee for Economic Development, Research and Policy Committee, 2002); Shonkoff and Phillips, *From Neurons to Neighborhoods.*

34. H.B. Presser and A.G. Cox, "The Work Schedules of Low-Educated American Women and Welfare Reform," *Monthly Labor Review,* April 1997, 25–30.

35. U.S. Census Bureau, Health Insurance Coverage: 2000, www.census.gov/hhes/www/hlthin00.html, Tables 4, 6, 8, and 9 (last revised January 18, 2002; accessed March 6, 2002).

Changing Work and Family Lives: A Historical Perspective
Eileen Boris

1. M. Anderson, "Second Annual Report of the Director of the Women's Bureau for the Fiscal Year Ended June 30, 1920," in U.S. Department of Labor, *Reports of the Department of Labor, 1920* (Washington, DC: GPO, 1921). The standard history of the Women's Bureau remains J. Sealander's *As Minority Becomes Majority: Federal Reaction to the Phenomenon of Women in the Work Force, 1920–1963* (Westport, CT: Greenwood Press, 1983); see also K.A. Laughlin, *Women's Work and Public Policy: A History of the Women's Bureau, U.S. Department of Labor, 1945–1970* (Boston: Northeastern University Press, 2000).

2. "Plans for the Thursday Morning Session—American Women as Citizens," memo to Miss Miller from Adelia Kloak, January 5, 1948, box 6, folder 133, Frieda Miller Papers (A-37), Schlesinger Library, Radcliffe Institute for Advanced Study, Harvard University.

3. For the most compelling analysis of how "gender—racialized gender—constitutes a central piece of the social imagery around which . . . social policies are built," see A. Kessler-Harris, *In Pursuit of Equity: Women, Men, and the Quest for Economic Citizenship in Twentieth-Century America* (New York: Oxford University Press, 2001), 5.

4. For this insight I am indebted to S. Michel. See our essay, "Social Citizenship and Women's Right to Work in Postwar America," in P. Grimshaw, K. Holmes, and M. Lake, eds., *Women's Rights and Human Rights: International Historical Perspectives,* (New York: Palgrave, 2001), 199–219. For an extended discussion of the workings of public-private welfare state regimes, see G. Esping-Andersen, *Three Worlds of Welfare Capitalism* (Princeton, NJ: Princeton University Press, 1990). For a feminist version, see J.S. O'Connor, A.S. Orloff, and S. Shaver, *States, Markets, Families: Gender, Liberalism and Social Policy in Australia, Canada, Great Britain and the United States* (New York: Cambridge University Press, 1999).

5. E. Brooks-Higginbotham, "African-American Women's History and the Metalanguage of Race," *Signs: Journal of Women in Culture and Society* 17 (1992): 251–74.

6. For recent trends, see J. Heymann, *The Widening Gap: Why America's Working Families Are in Jeopardy and What Can Be Done About It* (New York: Basic Books, 2000); M.K. Nelson and J. Smith, *Working Hard and Making Do: Surviving in Small Town America* (Berkeley: University of California Press, 1999).

7. W. Schneider, "Government by Gender Gap," *National Journal,* May 19, 2001, 1534; S.E. Howell and C.L. Day, "Complexities of the Gender Gap," *Journal of Politics* 62 (2000): 858–74; M. Schlesinger and C. Heldman, "Gender Gap or Gender Gaps? New Perspectives on Support for Government Action and Policies," *Journal of Politics* 63 (2001): 59–94.

8. See M. Willrich, "Home Slackers: Men, the State, and Welfare in Modern America," *Journal of American History* 87 (2000): 460–89.

9. See K. Anthony, *Mothers Who Must Earn* (New York: Survey Associates, 1914).

10. M.S. Gustafson, *Women and the Republican Party, 1854–1924* (Urbana: University of Illinois Press, 2001); M.S. Gustafson, K. Miller, and E.I. Perry, eds., *We Have Come to Stay: American Women and Political Parties, 1880–1960* (Albuquerque: University of New Mexico Press, 1999).

11. J.T. Patterson, *America's Struggle Against Poverty, 1900–1994* (Cambridge, MA: Harvard University Press, 1994), 3–34.

12. T. Skocpol, *Protecting Mothers and Soldiers: The Political Origins of Social Policy in the United States* (Cambridge, MA: Harvard University Press, 1992); M. Grossberg, *Governing the Hearth: Law and Family in Nineteenth-Century America* (Chapel Hill: University of North Carolina Press, 1985); N.F. Cott, *Public Vows: A History of Marriage and the Nation* (Cambridge, MA: Harvard University Press, 2000).

13. J. ten Broek, "California's Dual System of Family Law: Its Origin, Development, and Present Status," parts 1–3, *Stanford Law Review* 16 (1964): 257–317, 900–81; for the classic statement, see 17 (1965): 614–82. For a synthesis, see E. Boris and P. Bardaglio, "Gender, Race, and Class: The Impact of the State on the Family and the Economy, 1790–1945," in N. Gerstel and H.E. Gross, eds., *Families and Work* (Philadelphia: Temple University Press, 1987), 132–51.

14. M.B. Katz, *In the Shadow of the Poorhouse: A Social History of Welfare in America* (New York: Basic Books, 1986). For more on the role of religion, see S.W. Carlson-Thies, "Charitable Choice: Bringing Religion Back into American Welfare," *Journal of Policy History* 13 (2001): 109–32; S. Traverso, *Welfare Politics in Boston, 1910–1940* (Amherst: University of Massachusetts Press, 2003).

15. E.C. Green, *This Business of Relief: Confronting Poverty in a Southern City, 1740–1940* (Athens: University of Georgia Press, 2003).

16. C.E. Bose, *Women in 1900: Gateway to the Political Economy of the Twentieth Century* (Philadelphia: Temple University Press, 2001), percentages from 40–41.

17. For this insight, see R.D.G. Kelley, *Race Rebels: Culture, Politics, and the Black Working Class* (New York: Free Press, 1994), 31–32.

18. A. Kessler-Harris, *A Woman's Wage: Historical Meanings and Social Consequences* (Lexington: University Press of Kentucky, 1990); A. Baron, "Gender and Labor History: Learning from the Past, Looking to the Future," in A. Baron, ed., *Work Engendered: Toward a New History of American Labor* (Ithaca, NY: Cornell University Press, 1991), 1–46.

19. J. Jones, *Labor of Love, Labor of Sorrow: Black Women, Work, and the Family in America* (New York: Basic Books, 1985); K. Anderson, *Changing Woman: A History of Racial Ethnic Women in America* (New York: Oxford University Press, 1996), 153–219.

20. On the construction of children's worth in this period, see V. Zelizer, *Pricing the Priceless Child* (New York: Basic Books, 1985).

21. G. Riley, *Divorce: An American Tradition* (New York: Oxford University Press, 1991), 124.

22. L. Gordon, *Pitied but Not Entitled: Single Mothers and the History of Welfare* (New York: Free Press, 1994), 21.

23. S.P. Breckinridge, "Neglected Widowhood in the Juvenile Court," *American Journal of Sociology* 16 (1910): 54.

24. L.B. Glickman, *A Living Wage: American Workers and the Making of Consumer Society* (Ithaca, NY: Cornell University Press, 1997).

25. "Report of the Massachusetts Commission on the Support of Dependent Minor Children of Widowed Mothers, House Number 2075, January, 1913," in G. Mink and R. Solinger, *Welfare: A Documentary History of U.S. Policy in the Twentieth Century* (New York: New York University Press, 2002), 27–28.

26. Skocpol, *Protecting Mothers and Soldiers,* 424–79; G. Mink, *The Wages of Motherhood: Inequality in the Welfare State, 1917–1942* (Ithaca, NY: Cornell University Press, 1995), 27–52. See also J.L. Goodwin, *Gender and the Politics of Welfare Reform: Mothers' Pensions in Chicago, 1911–1929* (Chicago: University of Chicago Press, 1997); M. Ladd-Taylor, *Mother-Work: Women, Child Welfare, and the State, 1890–1930* (Urbana: University of Illinois Press, 1994), 135–66.

27. Quoted in U.S. Congress, Senate, *Conference on Care of Dependent Children: Proceedings,* 60th Congress, 2nd session, 1909, S. Doc. 721, 36.

28. Skocpol, *Protecting Mothers and Soldiers,* 424.

29. S. Michel, "The Limits of Maternalism: Policies Toward American Wage-Earning Mothers During the Progressive Era," in S. Michel and S. Koven, eds., *Mothers of a New World: Maternalist Politics and the Origins of Welfare States* (New York: Routledge, 1993), 277–320.

30. F. Kelley, "Married Women in Industry," *Proceedings of the Academy of Political Science* 1 (1910): 90–96.

31. Kelley testimony reported in "Forbid Home Work and End Child Labor," *New York Globe,* Dec. 7, 1912, clipping in scrapbook, "New York Factory Investigating Commission, 1912–1913," box 57, papers of the National Child Labor Committee, Library of Congress, Washington, D.C.

32. For a discussion of African American women's engagement in Progressive reform as part of interracial coalitions, in which they engaged in public health campaigns and gained resources for their schools and churches, see G.E. Gilmore, *Gender and Jim Crow: Women and the Politics of White Supremacy in North Carolina, 1896–1920* (Chapel Hill: University of North Carolina Press, 1996); for more on their self-help efforts, see also T. Hunter, *To "Joy My Freedom": Southern Black Women's Lives and Labors After the Civil War* (Cambridge, MA: Harvard University Press, 1997). In addition, see E. Boris, "The Power of Motherhood: Black and White Activist Women Redefine the 'Political,' " in Koven and Michel, eds., *Mothers of a New World,* 213–45; Gordon, *Pitied but Not Entitled.*

33. P.A. Schechter, *Ida B. Wells-Barnett and American Reform, 1880–1930* (Chapel Hill: Uni-

versity of North Carolina Press, 2001). On white women's political activities, see R. Edwards, *Angels in the Machinery: Gender in American Party Politics from the Civil War to the Progressive Era* (New York: Oxford University Press, 1997).

34. For a comprehensive history of day care, see S. Michel, *Children's Interests/Mothers' Rights: The Shaping of America's Child Care Policy* (New Haven, CT: Yale University Press, 1999), 50–90; Katz, *Shadow of the Poorhouse*, 130–31.

35. W.I. Trattner, *Crusade for the Children: A History of the National Child Labor Committee and Child Labor Reform in America* (Chicago: Quadrangle Books, 1970).

36. Michel, *Children's Interests*, 85.

37. Lathrop quoted in L.H. Feder, "The Relation of Private Case Working Agencies to Programs of Public Welfare," *Social Forces* 9 (1931): 517–18.

38. On criteria for morality and cleanliness, see Breckinridge, "Neglected Widowhood," 55. Michel summarized studies that reveal how implementation led mothers into employment; see *Children's Interests*, 84. See also Ladd-Taylor, *Mother-Work*, 148–52; J. Goodwin, "An American Experiment in Paid Motherhood: The Implementation of Mothers' Pensions in Early Twentieth-Century Chicago," *Gender and History* 4 (1992): 323–42; Traverso, *Welfare Politics in Boston*, 27–51.

39. Willrich, "Home Slackers," 472.

40. A.R. Ingra, "Likely to Become a Public Charge: Deserted Women and the Family Law of the Poor in New York City, 1910–1936," *Journal of Women's History* 11 (2000): 59–81, quotation on 62.

41. Willrich, "Home Slackers," 460–89. For more on this court, see M. Willrich, *City of Courts: Socializing Justice in Progressive Era Chicago* (New York: Cambridge University Press, 2003).

42. J. Novkov, *Constituting Workers, Protecting Women: Gender, Law, and Labor in the Progressive Era and New Deal Years* (Ann Arbor: University of Michigan Press, 2001), 24, quotation on 28. See also K.K. Sklar, "The Historical Foundations of Women's Power in the Creation of the American Welfare State, 1830–1930," in Koven and Michel, eds., *Mothers of a New World*, 43–93.

43. *Muller v. Oregon*, 208 U.S. 412 (1908). I have discussed this case in E. Boris, "Reconstructing the 'Family': Women, Progressive Reform, and the Problem of Social Control," in N. Frankel and N.S. Dye, eds., *Gender, Class, Race, and Reform in the Progressive Era* (Lexington: University Press of Kentucky, 1991), 71–86. The best discussion of the minimum wage is V. Hart's *Bound by Our Constitution: Women, Workers, and the Minimum Wage* (Princeton, NJ: Princeton University Press, 1994).

44. Kessler-Harris, *In Pursuit of Equality*, 28–34; E. Boris, *Home to Work: Motherhood and the Politics of Industrial Homework in the United States* (New York: Cambridge University Press, 1994), 118–20, 163–77. See also S. Lehrer, *Origins of Protective Labor Legislation for Women, 1905–1925* (Albany: State University of New York Press, 1987).

45. 261 U.S. 525 (1923). See V. Hart, "No Englishman Can Understand: Fairness and Minimum Wage Laws in Britain and America, 1923–1938," in B. Holden-Reid and J. White, eds., *American Studies: Essays in Honour of Marcus Cunliffe*. (London: Macmillan, 1990), 249–66.

46. U.S. Department of Labor, *Seventh Annual Report of the Director of the Women's Bureau, for the Fiscal Year Ended June 30, 1925* (Washington, DC: GPO, 1926), 2.

47. For an expression of this position by a Women's Bureau ally, see S. Breckinridge, "The Home Responsibilities of Women Workers and the 'Equal' Wage," *Journal of Political Economy* 31 (1923): 521–43. See also Kessler-Harris, *Woman's Wage*, 6–56.

48. E. Zaretsky, "The Place of the Family in the Origins of the Welfare State," in B. Thorne and M. Yalom, eds., *Rethinking the Family: Some Feminist Questions* (New York: Longman, 1982), 188–224.

49. E.K. Abel, *Hearts of Wisdom: American Women Caring for Kin, 1850–1940* (Cambridge, MA: Harvard University Press, 2000).

50. Ibid., 160, 162–65.
51. B. Hoffman, *The Wages of Sickness: The Politics of Health Insurance in Progressive America* (Chapel Hill: University of North Carolina Press, 2001), 6–23; D. Bender, "Inspecting Workers: Medical Examination, Labor Organizing, and the Evidence of Sexual Difference," *Radical History Review* 80 (2001): 51–75; A. Tone, *The Business of Benevolence: Industrial Paternalism in Progressive America* (Ithaca, NY: Cornell University Press, 1997).
52. K. Lindenmeyer, *"A Right to Childhood": The U.S. Children's Bureau and Child Welfare, 1912–46* (Urbana: University of Illinois Press, 1997).
53. A. Kessler-Harris, "The Paradox of Motherhood: Night Work Restrictions in the United States," in U. Wikander, A. Kessler-Harris, and J. Lewis, eds., *Protecting Women: Labor Legislation in Europe, the United States, and Australia, 1880–1920* (Urbana: University of Illinois Press, 1995), 337–57.
54. Skocpol, *Protecting Soldiers and Mothers,* 512–22, quotation on 513; C. Gordon, *Dead on Arrival: The Politics of Health Care in Twentieth-Century America* (Princeton, NJ: Princeton University Press, 2003), 13–14, 154, 180–81, 213–14.
55. M. Ladd-Taylor, " 'My Work Came Out of Agony and Grief': Mothers and the Making of the Sheppard-Towner Act," in Koven and Michel, eds., *Mothers of a New World,* 321–42, quotation on 330.
56. American Social History Project, *Who Built America? Working People and the Nation's Economy, Politics, Culture, and Society* (New York: Worth, 2000), 2:368–77; D.M. Figart, E. Mutari, and M. Power, *Living Wages, Equal Wages: Gender and Labor Market Policies in the United States* (New York: Routledge, 2002), 92–94; V.W. Wolcott, *Remaking Respectability: African American Women in Interwar Detroit* (Chapel Hill: University of North Carolina Press, 2001), 170; A. Kessler-Harris, *Out to Work: A History of Wage-Earning Women in the United States* (New York: Oxford University Press, 1982), 250; L. Scharf, *To Work and Wed: Female Employment, Feminism, and the Great Depression* (Westport, CT: Greenwood Press, 1980), 43–65; A. Kessler-Harris, "Providers: An Exploration of Gender Ideology in the 1930s," *Gender and History* 1 (1989): 31–49.
57. For a recent synthesis of the Great Depression's impact, see N. Lichtenstein, *State of the Union: A Century of American Labor* (Princeton, NJ: Princeton University Press, 2002), 25–30, quotation on 30. See also Kessler-Harris, *In Pursuit of Equity,* chapters 2–3.
58. R. Edsforth, *The New Deal: America's Response to the Great Depression* (Oxford: Blackwell, 2000); A. Badger, *The New Deal: The Depression Years, 1933–1940* (London: Macmillan, 1989).
59. For the divided nature of the American welfare state, see Suzanne Mettler, *Dividing Citizens: Gender and Federalism in New Deal Public Policy* (Ithaca, NY: Cornell University Press, 1998) and R.C. Lieberman, *Shifting the Color Line: Race and the American Welfare State* (Cambridge, MA: Harvard University Press, 1998). Both studies offer cogent analyses of federalism.
60. Lichtenstein, *State of the Union.*
61. J.L. Klein, *For All These Rights: Business, Labor, and the Shaping of America's Public-Private Welfare State* (Princeton, NJ: Princeton University Press, 2003).
62. Quoted in Kessler-Harris, *In Pursuit of Equity,* 123.
63. D. King, *Actively Seeking Work? The Politics of Unemployment and Welfare Policy in the United States and Great Britain* (Chicago: University of Chicago Press, 1995).
64. S. Mettler has recalculated the percentage and sex of those covered; see *Dividing Citizens,* 198–201.
65. In addition to the studies cited in note 63, see Kessler-Harris, *In Pursuit of Equity;* E. Boris, "The Racialized Gendered State: Constructions of Citizenship in the United States," *Social Politics* 2 (1995): 170–72.
66. Kessler-Harris, *In Pursuit of Equity,* 142, gives the figures of 3 million domestic workers and 3.5 million agricultural ones.
67. Quoted in Klein, *For All These Rights,* 116.

68. Ibid., 116–17.
69. Ibid. See also A. Derickson, "Health Security for All? Social Unionism and Universal Health Insurance, 1935–1958," *Journal of American History* 80 (1994): 1333–56; C. Gordon, "Why No National Health Insurance in the U.S.? The Limits of Social Provision in War and Peace, 1941–1948," *Journal of Policy History* 9 (1997): 277–87.
70. Lindenmeyer, *"A Right to Childhood,"* 182–95; on New Deal relief programs that addressed health care, see Klein, *For All These Rights*.
71. N. Lichtenstein, "From Corporatism to Collective Bargaining: Organized Labor and the Eclipse of Social Democracy in the Postwar Era," in G. Gerstle and S. Fraser, eds., *The Rise and Fall of the New Deal Order, 1930–1980* (Princeton, NJ: Princeton University Press, 1989), 122–52; S. Jacoby, *Modern Manors: Welfare Capitalism Since the New Deal* (Princeton, NJ: Princeton University Press, 1997); B. Stevens, "Labor Unions, Employee Benefits, and the Privatization of the American Welfare State," *Journal of Policy History* 2 (1990): 233–60.
72. Figart, Mutari, and Power, *Living Wages,* 105, 107.
73. Remarks at FLSA hearings, 1937, quoted in Hart, *Bound by Our Constitution,* 166.
74. Figart, Mutari, and Power, *Living Wages,* 112–13; see also Mettler, *Dividing Citizens,* 191–92; Kessler-Harris, *In Pursuit of Equity,* 101–12.
75. Regarding women, see Kessler-Harris, *In Pursuit of Equity*.
76. Asked whether the FLSA would "force" southern housewives to "pay [their] negro girl eleven dollars a week," President Roosevelt replied that no wage and hour bill would "apply to domestic help," as quoted in Hart, *Bound by Our Constitution,* 166. Women industrial workers understood that the FLSA was not about affording a maid but, as one textile operative told her congressman in 1938, "how she could get $15.00 a week to support a family on," as quoted in Mettler, *Dividing Citizens,* 194.
77. Mettler, *Dividing Citizens,* 201–5.
78. Ibid., 144–50.
79. Lieberman, *Shifting the Color Line,* 180–81.
80. P.H. Douglas quoted by Mettler, *Dividing Citizens,* 127.
81. Mettler, *Dividing Citizens,* 126–28, 143–58; D.M. Pearce, "Toil and Trouble: Women Workers and Unemployment Compensation," *Signs* 10 (1985): 439–59.
82. Social Security Board quoted in Kessler-Harris, *In Pursuit of Equity,* 139.
83. Kessler-Harris, *In Pursuit of Equity,* 161.
84. J. Quadagno, *The Transformation of Old Age Security: Class and Politics in the American Welfare State* (Chicago: University of Chicago Press, 1988), 72.
85. A. Kessler-Harris, "Designing Women and Old Fools: The Construction of the Social Security Amendments of 1939," in L.K. Kerber, A. Kessler-Harris, and K.K. Sklar, eds., *U.S. History as Women's History: New Feminist Essays* (Chapel Hill: University of North Carolina Press, 1995), 87–106.
86. Kessler-Harris, *In Pursuit of Equity,* 142.
87. Ibid., 149.
88. See Social Security Administration, "History of the Provisions of Old-Age, Survivors, and Disability Insurance," http://www.ssa.gov/OACT/HOP/hopi.htm#302 (accessed February 3, 2002). Nonetheless, many domestics continued to be paid under the table, as "Nannygate" controversies during the Clinton years testify. See Grace Chang, *Disposable Domestics* (Boston: South End Press, 2000), 55–59.
89. Quoted in Gordon, *Pitied but Not Entitled,* 254.
90. E. Boris, "When Work Is Slavery," in G. Mink, ed., *Whose Welfare?* (Ithaca, NY: Cornell University Press, 1999), 37–38; see also N. Rose, *Workfare or Fair Work: Women, Welfare, and Government Work Programs* (New Brunswick, NJ: Rutgers University Press, 1995), 73–75.
91. Mettler, *Dividing Citizens,* 169–70.
92. J. Goodwin, " 'Employable Mothers' and 'Suitable Work': A Re-evaluation of Welfare

and Wage Earning for Women in the Twentieth-Century United States," *Journal of Social History* 29 (1995): 253–74.

93. Mettler, *Dividing Citizens,* 138–40, 158–65.

94. Quoted in Michel, *Children's Interests,* 120; see also Mettler, *Dividing Citizens,* 119.

95. Quoted in Michel, *Children's Interest,* 140, but see 138–41.

96. W.M. Tuttle Jr., *"Daddy's Gone to War": The Second World War in the Lives of America's Children* (New York: Oxford University Press, 1993), 71.

97. L. Weiner, *From Working Girl to Working Mother: The Female Labor Force in the United States, 1820–1980* (Chapel Hill, NC: University of North Carolina Press, 1985), 95; S. Hesse-Biber and G. Lee Carter, *Working Women in America: Split Dreams* (New York: Oxford University Press, 2000), 34–35; K. Anderson, "Last Hired, First Fired: Black Women Workers During World War II," *Journal of American History* 69 (1982): 82–97.

98. S.M. Evans, *Born for Liberty: A History of Women in America* (New York: Free Press, 1989), 224; M.F. Berry, *The Politics of Parenthood: Child Care, Women's Rights, and the Myth of the Good Mother* (New York: Viking, 1993), 106–7; Michel, *Children's Interests,* 134–35.

99. Berry, *Politics of Parenthood,* 107.

100. Michel, *Children's Interests,* 193–95; E. Stoltzfus, *Citizen, Mother, Worker: Debating Public Responsibility for Child Care After the Second World War* (Chapel Hill: University of North Carolina Press, 2003).

101. As Michel notes on 142–45 in *Children's Interests,* these workplace facilities were child-centered, down to the size of furniture and fixtures. They offered preschool education to children of "working people of modest means," as one center administrator explained (quotation on 143), along with nutrition and additional broad-based care. They anticipated the philosophy behind the Great Society's Head Start program as described in E. Zigler and S. Muenchow, *Head Start: The Inside Story of America's Most Successful Educational Experiment* (New York: Basic Books, 1992). Open twenty-four hours, they accommodated parents' shift schedules. When picking up their children, parents also could obtain reasonably priced precooked meals to take home. See A. Kesselman, *Fleeting Opportunities: Women Shipyard Workers in Portland and Vancouver During World War II and Reconversion* (Albany: State University of New York Press, 1990), 74–89.

102. K. Anderson, *Wartime Women: Sex Roles, Family Relations, and the Status of Women During World War II* (Westport, CT: Greenwood Press, 1981), 50; S. Strasser, *Never Done: A History of American Housework* (New York: Pantheon, 1982), 282–99.

103. S.J. Kleinberg, *Women in the United States, 1830–1945* (New Brunswick, NJ: Rutgers University Press, 1999), 309–14.

104. Women's Bureau, U.S. Department of Labor, "Maternity Protection of Employed Women," *Bulletin,* no. 240 (Washington, DC: GPO, 1952), 8–9; J.M. Elkin, "The 1946 Amendments to the Railroad Retirement and Railroad Unemployment Insurance Acts," *Social Security Bulletin,* December 1946, 23–33, 49–50; see also S.B. Kamerman, A.J. Kahn, and P. Kingston, *Maternity Policies and Working Women* (New York: Columbia University Press, 1983), 34–35, 78; Dorothy Sue Cobble, *The Other Women's Movement: Workplace Justice and Social Rights in Modern America* (Princeton, NJ: Princeton University Press, 2004), 127–31.

105. "Maternity Relief for Government Employees," remarks of Mr. Langer, *Congressional Record—Senate,* vol. 94, pt. 1, 80th Congress, 2nd session, 1948, 140810, reprinting testimony of F. Miller and M. Eliot from the Women's and Children's Bureaus; "Langer to Reintroduce His Bill for 60-Day Maternity Leaves," *Evening Star* (Washington, DC), December 7, 1948; "Providing Maternity Leave for Government Employees," *Report (to Accompany S. 784),* Senate, calendar no. 1579, 89th Congress, 2nd session, report no. 1525.

106. "Maternity Protection of Employed Women," 3, 11–15.

107. Ibid., 25–26, 29.

108. These positions can be found in *Maternity Leave for Government Employees,* Hearings Before a Subcommittee of the Committee on Post Office and Civil Service, United States Senate, 80th Congress, 2nd session on S. 784, February 17 and 18, 1948 (Washington, DC: GPO, 1948), quotation on 36–37.

109. For two examples of this reevaluation, see S. Coontz, *The Way We Never Were: American Families and the Nostalgia Trap* (New York: Basic Books, 1992); J. Weiss, *To Have and to Hold: Marriage, the Baby Boom, and Social Change* (Chicago: University of Chicago Press, 2000).

110. Memo to Miss Plunkett from L.H. Dale, "Inequity in Federal Internal Revenue Code," May 8, 1951, folder 2-0-1-2, box 20, Office of Director, General Correspondence, 1948–63, papers of the U.S. Women's Bureau, RG86, National Archives; statement of Hon. L.K. Sullivan, U.S. Congress, House Committee on Ways and Means, *General Revenue Revision: Hearing Before the Committee on Ways and Means,* 83rd Cong., 1st session, June and July 1953, 32.

111. The best account of the tax deduction for childcare is in Stoltzfus, *Citizen, Mother, Worker,* 199–212. Women qualified for the deduction by passing a means test that reinforced the necessity rationale for women's wage earning that the bureau has continued to the present.

112. For a discussion of the need for women's labor, see National Manpower Council, *Womanpower* (New York: Columbia University Press, 1997).

113. For example, see G. Lemke-Santangelo, *Abiding Courage: African American Migrant Women and the East Bay Community* (Chapel Hill: University of North Carolina Press, 1996); V.L. Ruiz, *From Out of the Shadows: Mexican Women in Twentieth-Century America* (New York: Oxford University Press, 1998).

114. D.C. Hamilton and C.V. Hamilton, *The Dual Agenda: The African American Struggle for Civil and Economic Equality* (New York: Columbia University Press, 1997).

115. Kessler-Harris, *In Pursuit of Equity,* chapters 5–6.

116. J. Quadagno, *The Color of Welfare: How Racism Undermined the War on Poverty* (New York: Oxford University Press, 1994); M. Brown, *Race, Money, and the American Welfare State* (Ithaca, NY: Cornell University Press, 1999), 203–93.

117. Weiner, *From Working Girl to Working Mother;* C.B. Costello and A.J. Stone, eds., *The American Woman, 2001–2002: Getting to the Top* (New York: Norton, 2001), Figure 4-1: "Women in the Labor Force, 1948–1998," 227; on the crisis in social reproduction, see, for example, A.R. Hochschild, *The Time Bind: When Work Becomes Home and Home Becomes Work* (New York: Metropolitan Books, 1997); see also A.R. Hochschild and A. Machung, *The Second Shift* (New York: Viking, 1989).

118. "The Report of the President's Commission on the Status of Women," in M. Schneir, ed., *Feminism in Our Time: The Essential Writings* (New York: Vintage, 1994), 43.

119. Quoted in Kessler-Harris, *In Pursuit of Equality,* 215.

120. Figart, Mutari, and Power, *Living Wages,* 143–75, 184–93; S.M. Evans and B.J. Nelson, *Wage Justice: Comparable Worth and the Paradox of Technocratic Reform* (Chicago: University of Chicago Press, 1989); L.M. Blum, *Between Feminism and Labor: The Significance of the Compatible Worth Movement* (Berkeley: University of California Press, 1991).

121. For more about the deliberate addition of "sex," see C. Harrison, *On Account of Sex: The Politics of Women's Issues, 1945–1968* (Berkeley: University of California Press, 1988), 176–82; C. Deitch, "Gender, Race, and Class Politics and the Inclusion of Women in Title VII of the 1964 Civil Rights Act," *Gender and Society* 7 (1993): 183–203; J. Freeman, "How Sex Got into Title VII: Persistent Opportunism as a Maker of Public Policy," *Law and Inequality: A Journal of Theory and Practice* 9 (1991): 163–85; L.J. Rupp and V. Taylor, *Survival in the Doldrums: The American Women's Rights Movement, 1945 to the 1960s* (New York: Oxford University Press), 176–79.

122. NOW, "Bill of Rights," reprinted in A. Jaggar and P. Rothenberg, eds., *Feminist Frameworks,* 3rd ed. (New York: McGraw-Hill, 1992), 159. On earlier labor feminists, see

D.A. Deslippe, *"Rights, Not Roses": Unions and the Rise of Working-Class Feminism, 1945–1980* (Urbana: University of Illinois Press, 2000); Cobble, *The Other Women's Movement.*

123. M.G. Fried, ed., *From Abortion to Reproductive Freedom: Transforming a Movement* (Boston: South End Press, 1990); D. Roberts, *Killing the Black Body: Race, Reproduction, and the Meaning of Liberty* (New York: Vintage, 1997).

124. S. Michel, "The Benefits of Race and Gender: Retirement in Postwar America," unpublished paper in author's possession, 1999, 15.

125. In *Children's Interests,* Michel presents the most compelling discussion; see 236–80.

126. L. Vogel, *Mothers on the Job: Maternity Policy in the U.S. Workplace* (New Brunswick, NJ: Rutgers University Press, 1993); I draw on Boris and Michel, "Social Citizenship," 211–13.

127. G. Mink, *Welfare's End* (Ithaca, NY: Cornell University Press, 1998). During the late 1960s, however, Congress strengthened work requirements for preschool-age children's mothers, the same group whose labor force participation was rising in the population at large. Some feminist defenders of welfare rights charged that such social policy efforts discounted poor women's competency as mothers. Source: F.F. Piven and R. Cloward, *Poor People's Movements;* Boris, "When Work Was Slavery."

128. R. Solinger, *Beggars and Choosers: How the Politics of Choice Shapes Adoption, Abortion, and Welfare in the United States* (New York: Hill & Wang, 2001), 139–82.

129. J. Karaagac, *Between Promise and Policy: Ronald Reagan and Conservative Reformism* (Lanham, MD: Lexington Books, 2000); A. E. Busch, *Ronald Reagan and the Politics of Freedom* (Lanham, MD: Rowman & Littlefield, 2001).

130. Mink, *Welfare's End;* R. Kent Weaver, "Ending Welfare as We Know It: Policymaking for Low-Income Families in the Clinton/Gingrich Era," in M. Weir, ed., *The Social Divide: Political Parties and the Future of Activist Government* (Washington, DC: Brookings Institution Press, 1998), 361–416.

131. Mink, *Welfare's End.*

132. M. Olasky's *Tragedy of American Compassion* (Washington, DC: Regnery, 1992) served as a bible for this position. For more on the Progressives, see Katz, *In the Shadow of the Poorhouse;* for more on the conservative revolution, see M.B. Katz, *The Undeserving Poor: From the War on Poverty to the War on Welfare* (New York: Pantheon, 1989); M.B. Katz, *The Price of Citizenship: Redefining the American Welfare State* (New York: Metropolitan Books, 2001); for recent Medicare reform, see http://www.medicare.gov/ (accessed January 2, 2004).

Civil Society: Changing from Tight to Loose Connections
Robert Wuthnow

1. For a historical overview, see T. Bender, *Community and Social Change in America* (Baltimore, MD: Johns Hopkins University Press, 1982).

2. R. Wuthnow, Arts and Religion Survey, machine-readable data file, Princeton University, 1999. This survey of 1,530 adults was conducted for the author by the Gallup Organization.

3. The most ambitious attempt to assemble data on the decline of community involvement is R.D. Putnam, *Bowling Alone: The Collapse and Revival of American Community* (New York: Simon and Schuster, 2000).

4. R. Wuthnow, Civic Involvement Survey, machine-readable data file, Princeton University, 1999. This survey of 1,528 adults was conducted for the author by the Gallup Organization.

5. Ibid.

6. C.S. Fischer, "Ambivalent Communities: How Americans Understand Their Locali-

ties," in Alan Wolfe, ed., *America at Century's End* (Berkeley: University of California Press, 1991).

7. Social consequences of this form of recruitment are discussed in M. Hechter, *Internal Colonialism: The Celtic Fringe in British National Development* (New Brunswick, NJ: Transaction, 1998).

8. W.R. Scott and J.W. Meyer, *Institutional Environments and Organizations: Structural Complexity and Individualism* (Beverly Hills, CA: Sage, 1994).

9. Wuthnow, Civic Involvement Survey, my analysis.

10. Ibid.

11. On changes in families and communities of residence, see especially B.N. Adams, *Kinship in an Urban Setting* (Chicago: Markham, 1968); C.S. Fischer, "The Dispersion of Kinship Ties in Modern Society: Contemporary Data and Historical Speculation," *Journal of Family History* 7 (1982): 353–75; E. Shanas, "Social Myth as Hypothesis: The Case of the Family Relations of Old People," *Gerontologist* 19 (1979): 3–9.

12. Wuthnow, Civic Involvement Survey, my analysis.

13. This point is condensed from my book *Loose Connections: Joining Together in America's Fragmented Communities* (Cambridge, MA: Harvard University Press, 1998), chapter 3.

14. Wuthnow, Civic Involvement Survey, my analysis.

15. Discussed in R. Wuthnow, "The Changing Character of Social Capital in the United States" (unpublished paper, Department of Sociology, Princeton University, 1997).

16. These observations are from my book *Acts of Compassion: Helping Others and Caring for Ourselves* (Princeton, NJ: Princeton University Press, 1991).

17. V.A. Hodgkinson and M.S. Weitzman, *Giving and Volunteering in the United States: Findings from a National Survey* (Washington, DC: Independent Sector, 1996), Table 1.10.

18. Putnam, *Bowling Alone,* 130.

19. Hodgkinson and Weitzman, *Giving and Volunteering,* Table 1.10; A. Greeley, "The Tocqueville Files: The Other Civic America," *The American Prospect,* (May-June 1997).

20. Wuthnow, Civic Involvement Survey, my analysis.

21. Wuthnow, *Loose Connections,* Table 2.

22. Wuthnow, Civic Involvement Survey, my analysis.

23. Ibid.; R. Wuthnow, *God and Mammon in America* (New York: Free Press, 1994).

24. J.J. Corbin, "A Study of Factors Influencing the Growth of Nonprofits in Social Services," *Nonprofit and Voluntary Sector Quarterly* 28 (1999): 296–314.

25. Wuthnow, *Loose Connections,* Table 7.

26. Hodgkinson and Weitzman, *Giving and Volunteering,* 42.

27. M.C. Dufour and K.G. Ingle, "Twenty-five Years of Alcohol Epidemiology," *Alcohol Health and Research World* 19 (1995): 77–78; B. Marvel, "Religion of Sobriety," *Dallas Morning News,* June 10, 1995, 1C.

28. K. Butler, "Adult Children of Alcoholics," *San Francisco Chronicle,* February 20, 1990, D7; S. Wuthnow, "Working the ACOA Program," in R. Wuthnow, ed., *"I Come Away Stronger": How Small Groups Are Shaping American Religion* (Grand Rapids, MI: Eerdmans, 1994), 179–204.

29. "News Summary," *New York Times,* July 16, 1988, 1.

30. R. Wuthnow, *Sharing the Journey* (New York: Free Press, 1994), chapter 3.

31. Ibid.

32. N.L. Rosenblum, *Membership and Morals: The Personal Uses of Pluralism in America* (Princeton, NJ: Princeton University Press, 1998); R. Wuthnow, "How Religious Groups Promote Forgiving: A National Study," *Journal for the Scientific Study of Religion* 36 (2000): 124–37.

33. Wuthnow, Civic Involvement Survey, my analysis.

34. G. Gallup Jr. and D.M. Lindsay, *Surveying the Religious Landscape: Trends in U.S. Beliefs* (Harrisburg, PA: Morehouse Publishing, 1999), 15.

35. W.C. Roof, *Spiritual Marketplace: Baby Boomers and the Remaking of American Religion* (Princeton, NJ: Princeton University Press, 1999).
36. Ibid. Such observations are drawn mainly from qualitative interviews and through comparisons among younger and older people, including some comparisons of survey data; see also my book *After Heaven: Spirituality in America Since the 1950s* (Berkeley: University of California Press, 1998).
37. M. Chaves, M.E. Konieczny, K. Beyerlien, and E. Barman, "The National Congregations Study: Background, Methods, and Selected Results," *Journal for the Scientific Study of Religion* 38 (1999): 458–76.
38. R. Wuthnow, "Reassembling the Civic Church: The Changing Role of Congregations in American Civil Society," unpublished paper, Department of Sociology, Princeton University, 2000.
39. For examples of nonprofit organizations linked in interorganizational networks, see Wuthow, *Loose Connections.*
40. Reviewed in Putnam, *Bowling Alone,* chapter 9.
41. These results are from my analysis of the Civic Involvement Survey using logit regression analysis in which age, gender, race, education, family income, being employed, living in a central city area, and living in a suburb were included as control variables.
42. R. Wuthnow, Religion and Politics Survey, machine-readable data file, Princeton University, 2000. The survey included 5,603 respondents. Of those who had not attended a class or lecture in the previous year about social or political issues, 33 percent of those who had read about social or political issues on the Internet during the previous year had contacted an elected official during this time, compared with 17 percent of those who had not read about issues on the Internet.
43. W.J. Wilson, "Rising Inequality and the Case for Coalition Politics," *Annals of the American Academy of Political and Social Science* 568 (2000): 78–99.
44. D.S. Massey, A.B. Gross, and K. Shibuya, "Migration, Segregation, and the Concentration of Poverty," *American Sociological Review* 59 (1994): 425–45.
45. My analysis of a national survey of nearly thirty thousand cases conducted by R.D. Putnam, Social Capital Benchmark Survey, 2000, Roper Center, Storrs, CT.
46. Wuthnow, *Sharing the Journey.*
47. Wuthnow, "Changing Character of Social Capital."
48. P.F. Nardulli, J.K. Dalager, and D.E. Greco, "Voter Turnout in U.S. Presidential Elections: An Historical View and Some Speculation," *P.S.: Political Science and Politics* 29 (1996): 122–133.
49. Wuthnow, Civic Involvement Survey.

Inequalities at Work and at Home: Social Class and Gender Divides
Jody Heymann

1. D. Hernandez and D. Myers, *America's Children: Resources from Family, Government, and the Economy* (New York: Russell Sage Foundation, 1993).
2. D. Hernandez, "Children's Changing Access to Resources: A Historical Perspective," in K. Hansen and A. Garey, eds., *Families in the U.S.: Kinship and Domestic Politics* (Philadelphia: Temple University Press, 1998).
3. Hernandez and Myers, *America's Children.*
4. Hernandez, "Children's Changing Access."
5. A. Kessler-Harris, *Out to Work: A History of Wage-Earning Women in the United States* (New York: Oxford University Press, 1982).
6. C. Goldin, *Understanding the Gender Gap: An Economic History of American Women* (New York: Oxford University Press, 1990).
7. Before the war, for example, three out of five school districts refused to hire married

women; after the war, only one out of five refused. Before the war, 50 percent of school districts fired women who married while employed; after the war, only 10 percent did. When the marriage bars eroded, the rise in wage labor by married women commenced in earnest.

8. Hernandez and Myers, *America's Children;* Bureau of the Census, *Statistical Abstract of the United States: 1998,* 118th edition (Washington, DC: U.S. Government Printing Office, 1998).

9. Workmen's compensation, the first of these to be enacted on a wide scale, had been adopted by ten states as of 1911 and by forty-two states as of 1920; all fifty states now have such laws. At a state level, California was the first to establish mandatory old-age assistance, in 1929, and Wisconsin instituted the first compulsory unemployment insurance, in 1932. See P. Day, *A New History of Social Welfare* (Boston: Allyn & Bacon, 1997). The Social Security Act of 1935 turned income support for the elderly and unemployment insurance into federal policies and programs.

10. S.J. Heymann, *The Widening Gap: Why Working Families Are in Jeopardy and What Can Be Done About It* (New York: Basic Books, 2000).

11. J. Currie and D. Thomas, "Does Head Start Make a Difference?" *American Economic Review* 85, no. 3 (1995): 341–64.

12. R. McKay, L. Condell, and H. Ganson, *The Impact of Head Start on Children, Families and Communities: Final Report of the Head Start Evaluation, Synthesis, and Utilization Project* (Washington, DC: CSR, 1985); S. Andrews, J. Blumenthal, D. Johnson, A. Kahn, C. Ferguson, T. Lasater, P. Malone, and D. Wallace, "The Skills of Mothering: A Study of Parent Child Development Centers," *Monographs of the Society for Research in Child Development* 47, no. 6 (1982): 1–83; W. Barnett, "Long-term Effects of Early Childhood Programs on Cognitive and School Outcomes," *The Future of Children* 5, no. 3 (1995): 25–50; F. Campbell and C. Ramey, "Effects of Early Intervention on Intellectual and Academic Achievement: A Follow-up Study of Children from Low-Income Families," *Child Development* 65, no. 2 (1994): 684–98; H. Garber, *The Milwaukee Project: Preventing Mental Retardation in Children at Risk* (Washington, DC: American Association on Mental Retardation, 1988); D. Johnson and T. Walker, "A Follow-up Evaluation of the Houston Parent-Child Development Center: School Performance," *Journal of Early Intervention* 15, 3 (1991): 226–36.

13. K. Shulman, "The High Cost of Child Care Puts Quality Care Out of Reach for Many Families," issue brief, Children's Defense Fund, Washington, D.C., 2000.

14. Data on Head Start enrollment reported by Craig Turner, Head Start Bureau, in a telephone interview by Maria Palacios on March 7, 2000, based on *Head Start Program Information Report* (September 1998–June 1999) and data from Head Start Bureau databases.

15. J. Posner and D. Vandell, "Low-Income Children's After-School Care: Are There Beneficial Effects of After-School Programs?" *Child Development* 65, no. 2 (1994): 440–56; U.S. Department of Education, *Safe and Smart: Making After-School Hours Work for Kids* (Washington, DC: U.S. Department of Education, 1998). Available at: http://www.ed.gov/pubs/SafeandSmart (accessed July 6, 2000).

16. C. Snow, *Preventing Reading Difficulties in Young Children* (Washington, DC: National Research Council and National Academy of Sciences, 1998).

17. D. Morris, B. Shaw, and J. Perney, "Helping Low Readers in Grades 2 and 3: An After-School Volunteer Tutoring Program," *Elementary School Journal* 91, no. 2 (1990): 133–50.

18. J.L. Richardson, K. Dwyer, K. McGuigan, W.B. Hansen, C. Dent, C.A. Johnson, S.Y. Sussman, B. Brannon, and B. Flay, "Substance Abuse Among Eighth-Grade Students Who Take Care of Themselves After School," *Pediatrics* 84, no. 3 (1989): 556–66; D. Blyth and N. Leffert, "Communities as Contexts for Adolescent Development: An Empirical Analysis," *Journal of Adolescent Research* 10, 1 (1995): 64–87.

19. J. Fox and S. Newman, *After-School Crime or After-School Programs: Tuning in the Prime Time for Violent Juvenile Crime and Implications for National Policy* (Washington, DC:

Fight Crime Invest in Kids, 1997); P. Schinke, M. Orlandi, and K. Cole, "Boys and Girls Clubs in Public Housing Developments: Prevention Services for Youth at Risk," *Journal of Community Psychology,* OSAP special issue (1992); U.S. Department of Education, *Safe and Smart.*

20. M. Sickmund, H. Snyder, and E. Poe-Yamagata, *Juvenile Offenders and Victims: 1997 Update on Violence* (Washington, DC: U.S. Department of Justice, Office of Juvenile Justice and Delinquency Prevention, 1997).

21. U.S. Department of Education, *Safe and Smart.*

22. General Accounting Office, *Welfare Reform: Implications of Increased Work Participation for Childcare* (Washington, DC: General Accounting Office, 1997).

23. R. Bradley, S. Rock, B. Caldwell, P. Harris, and H. Hamrick, "Home Environment and School Performance Among Black Elementary School Children," *Journal of Negro Education* 56, no. 4 (1987): 499–509; B. Iverson, G. Brownlee, and H. Walberg, "Parent-Teacher Contacts and Student Learning," *Journal of Educational Research* 74, 6 (1981): 394–96; D. Stevenson and D. Baker, "The Family-School Relation and the Child's School Performance," *Child Development* 58, 5 (1987): 1348–57.

24. T. Keith, P. Keith, G. Troutman, P. Bickley, P. Trivette, and K. Singh, "Does Parental Involvement Affect Eighth-Grade Student Achievement? Structural Analysis of National Data," *School Psychology Review* 22, no. 3 (1993): 474–76; P. Fehrmann, T. Keith, and T. Reimers, "Home Influences on School Learning: Direct and Indirect Effects of Parental Involvement on High School Grades," *Journal of Educational Research* 80, no. 6 (1987): 330–37.

25. A. Reynolds, "Comparing Measures of Parental Involvement and Their Effects on Academic Achievement," *Early Childhood Research Quarterly* 7, no. 3 (1992): 441–62; J. Griffith, "Relation of Parental Involvement, Empowerment, and School Traits to Student Academic Performance," *Journal of Educational Research* 90, no. 1 (1996): 33–41; S. Christenson, T. Rounds, and D. Gorney, "Family Factors and Student Achievement: An Avenue to Increase Students' Success," *School Psychology Quarterly* 7, no. 3 (1992): 178–206; D. Miller and M. Kelley, "Interventions for Improving Homework Performance: A Critical Review," *School Psychology Quarterly* 6, no. 3 (1991): 174–85; J. Comer, "Home-School Relationships as They Affect the Academic Success of Children," *Education and Urban Society* 16, no. 3 (1984): 323–37; J. Fantuzzo, G. Davis, and M. Ginsburg, "Effects of Parental Involvement in Isolation or in Combination with Peer Tutoring on Student Self-concept and Mathematics Achievement," *Journal of Educational Psychology* 87, no. 2 (1995): 272–81.

26. To reflect the efforts of the remarkable group of research assistants, students, and other team members I have had the privilege to lead, I often use the terms *we* and *our* to refer to my research team's efforts. This work would not have been possible without them. Ultimate responsibility for findings and opinions in this chapter rest with me.

27. I. Kristensson-Hallstrom, G. Elander, and G. Malmfors, "Increased Parental Participation on a Pediatric Surgical Day Care Unit," *Journal of Clinical Nursing* 6 (1997): 297–302; P.R. Mahaffy, "The Effects of Hospitalization on Children Admitted for Tonsillectomy and Adenoidectomy," *Nursing Research* 14, no. 1 (1965): 12–19; J. Bowlby, *Child Care and the Growth of Love* (Baltimore: Penguin Books, 1965); J. Robertson, *Young Children in Hospitals* (New York: Basic Books, 1958); S.J. Palmer, "Care of Sick Children by Parents: A Meaningful Role," *Journal of Advanced Nursing* 18, no. 2 (1993): 185–91; G. van der Schyff, "The Role of Parents During Their Child's Hospitalization," *Australian Nurses Journal* 8, no. 11 (1979): 57–58, 61.

28. M. Taylor and P. O'Connor, "Resident Parents and Shorter Hospital Stay," *Archives of Disease in Childhood* 64, no. 2 (1989): 274–76.

29. S.J. Heymann, S. Toomey, and F. Furstenberg, "Working Parents: What Factors Are Involved in Their Ability to Take Time Off from Work When Their Children Are Sick?" *Archives of Pediatrics and Adolescent Medicine* 153, no. 8 (1999): 870–74.

30. S.J. Heymann, A. Earle, and B. Egleston, "Parental Availability for the Care of Sick Children," *Pediatrics* 98, no. 2, pt. 1 (1996): 226–30; Heymann, Toomey, and Furstenberg, "Working Parents: What Factors Are Involved"; Heymann, *The Widening Gap;* S.J. Heymann and A. Earle, "The Impact of Welfare Reform on Parents' Ability to Care for Their Children's Health," *American Journal of Public Health* 89, 4 (1999): 502–5.

31. Still, the middle class is significantly more affected than the wealthy, who have far greater opportunities to insulate their families.

32. J. Gornick and M. Meyers, *Early Childhood Education and Care (ECEC): Cross-National Variation in Service Organization and Financing* (New York: Columbia Institute for Child and Family Policy, 2000).

33. National Center for Education Statistics, "Expenditures per Student for Early Childhood Education, 1993," Table 55-4. Available at: http://nces.ed.gov/pubs/ce/c97p55.pdf (accessed July 11, 2000).

34. Urban Institute, *Children's Budget Report: A Detailed Analysis of Spending on Low-Income Children's Programs in Thirteen States* (Washington, DC: Urban Institute, 1998).

35. David and Lucile Packard Foundation, *The Future of Children: Caring for Infants and Toddlers* (Los Altos, CA: David and Lucile Packard Foundation, 2001).

36. Gornick and Meyers, *Early Childhood Education and Care.*

37. National Center for Education Statistics, "Historical Summary of Public Elementary and Secondary School Statistics: 1869–70 to 1996–97," Table 39. Available at: http://nces.ed.gov/pubs2000/digest99/d99to39.html (accessed July 11, 2000).

38. World Data on Education: A Guide to the Structure of National Education Systems (Paris: UNESCO, 2000).

39. Twentieth-first Century Community Learning Centers. Available at: http://www.ed.gov/21stcclc/index.html (accessed June 14, 2001).

40. U.S. Bureau of the Census, "Resident Population Estimates of the United States by Age and Sex: April 1, 1990, to July 1, 1999, with Short-Term Projection to November 1, 2000," (Washington, DC: U.S. Bureau of the Census). Available at: http://www.census.gov/population/estimates/nation/intfile2-1.txt (accessed January 2, 2001).

41. National Center for Education Statistics, *Digest of Education Statistics 1997,* report no. 98-015 (Washington, DC: U.S. Department of Education, 1997).

42. J. Treasand and R. Torrecilha, "The Older Population," in R. Farley, ed., *State of the Union: America in the 1990s,* vol. 2: *Social Trends* (New York: Russell Sage Foundation, 1995).

43. Bureau of the Census data. Available at: http://www.census.gov/population/projections/nation/detail (accessed January 21, 2000); U.N. Department of Economic and Social Development Statistical Division, *1991 Demographic Yearbook* (New York: United Nations, 1992).

44. Bureau of the Census, *1990 Census of Population and Housing: Social, Economic, and Housing Characteristics* (Washington, DC: Bureau of the Census, 1992).

45. L.F. Berkman, "The Relationship of Social Networks and Social Support to Morbidity and Mortality," in S. Cohen and S.L. Syme, eds., *Social Support and Health* (Orlando: Academic Press, 1985); L.F. Berkman, T.E. Oxman, and T.E. Seeman, "Social Networks and Social Support Among the Elderly: Assesment Issues," in R.B. Wallace and R.F. Woolson, eds., *The Epidemiologic Study of the Elderly* (New York: Oxford University Press, 1992); L.F. Berkman and S.L. Syme, "Social Networks, Host Resistance and Mortality: A Nine-Year Follow-up Study of Alameda County Residents," in A. Steptoe and J. Wardle, eds., *Psychosocial Processes in Health: A Reader* (Cambridge: Cambridge University Press, 1994).

46. Women, Infants, and Children (WIC) is a program providing education, nutritional supplementation, and access to health services for low-income pregnant and breast-feeding women and for preschool-age children.

47. V.R. Fuchs, ed., *Women's Quest for Economic Equality* (Cambridge, MA: Harvard University Press, 1988).

48. Institute for Women's Policy Research, *Status of Women in the States* (Washington, DC: Institute for Women's Policy Research, 1996).

49. J. Waldfogel, "The Family Gap for Young Women in the United States and Britain: Can Maternity Leave Make a Difference?" *Journal of Labor Economics* 16, no. 3 (1998): 505–45; J. Waldfogel, "Women Working for Less: Family Status and Women's Pay in the U.S. and the U.K.," working paper no. D-94-1, Malcom Wiener Center for Social Policy, Harvard University, 1994.

50. Fuchs, *Women's Quest*.

51. Heymann and Earle, "Impact of Welfare Reform"; Heymann, Toomey, and Furstenberg, "Working Parents"; S.J. Heymann and A. Earle, "Parental Availability for the Care of Sick Children," *Pediatrics* 98, no. 2 (1996): 226–30.

52. International Labour Organization, *Maternity Protection at Work: Revision of the Maternity Protection Convention (Revised), 1952 (No. 103), and Recommendation, 1952 (No. 95), Report 5, No. 1* (Geneva: International Labour Office, 1997).

53. J. Heymann, A. Earle, S. Simmons, S. Breslow, and A. Kuehnhoff, *The Work, Family, and Equity Index: Where Does the United States Stand Globally?* (Boston: The Project on Global Working Families, 2004); Clearinghouse on International Developments in Child, Youth and Family Policies, "New Twelve-Country Study Reveals Substantial Gaps in U.S. Early Childhood Education and Care Policies," issue brief, Institute for Child and Family Policy, New York, 2001; J.C. Gornick, M.K. Meyers, and K.E. Ross, "Supporting the Employment of Mothers: Policy Variation Across Fourteen Welfare States," *Journal of European Social Policy* 7, no. 1 (1997): 45–69; UNESCO 2000, *World Data on Education: A Guide to the Structure of National Education Systems* (Paris: UNESCO, 2000), 157–65; labor codes from Natlex database, published by the International Labor Organization, available at: http://natlex.ilo.org.

54. J.B. Elshtain, "Freedom and Opportunity," in J. Rogers and J. Cohen, eds., *Can Working Families Ever Win? A New Democracy Forum on Helping Parents Succeed at Work and Caregiving* (Boston: Beacon Press, 2002).

When There Is No Time or Money: Work, Family,
and Community Lives of Low-Income Families
Lisa Dodson and Ellen Bravo

1. International Labour Organization, "Americans Work Longest Hours Among Industrialized Countries," press release, September 6, 1999, available at: http://www.ilo.org/public/english/bureau/inf/pr/1999/29.htm (accessed November 5, 2001); J. Schor, *The Overworked American: The Unexpected Decline of Leisure* (New York: Basic Books, 1991).

2. A.R. Hochschild, *The Time Bind: When Work Becomes Home and Home Becomes Work* (New York: Henry Holt, 1997); P. Moen and Y. Yu, "Having It All: Overall Work/Life Success in Two-Earner Families," in T. Parcel, ed., *Research in the Sociology of Work*, vol. 7 (Greenwich, CT: JAI Press, 1999); F. Schwartz, "Management Women and the New Facts of Life," *Harvard Business Review*, January-February 1989, 65–76; N. Rankin, "Fixing Social Insecurity," in S. A. Hewlett, N. Rankin, and C. West, eds., *Taking Parenting Public: The Case for a New Social Movement* (Lanham, MD: Rowman and Littlefield, 2002).

3. P. Osterman, "Work/Family Programs and the Employment Relationship," *Administrative Science Quarterly*, December 1995; E. Galinsky and J.T. Bond, "Helping Families with Young Children Navigate Work and Family Life," in E. Appelbaum, ed., *Balancing Acts: Easing the Burdens and Improving the Options for Working Families* (Washington, DC: Economic Policy Institute, 2000).

4. Wider Opportunities for Women, "Six Strategies for Family Economic Self-

Sufficiency: The Self-Sufficiency Standard, 2001," available at: http://www.sixstrategies .org/sixstrategies/selfsufficiencystandard.cfm (accessed November 5, 2001).

5. See, for example, J. Heymann, *The Widening Gap: Why America's Working Families Are in Jeopardy and What Can Be Done About It* (New York: Basic Books, 2000); K. Edin and L. Lein, *Making Ends Meet: How Single Mothers Survive Welfare and Low-Wage Work* (New York: Russell Sage Foundation, 1997); and L. Dodson, *Don't Call Us Out of Name: The Untold Lives of Women and Girls in Poor America* (Boston: Beacon Press, 1999).

6. The research methodology consisted of the following five steps: (1) analysis of secondary contextual data; (2) local theme-gathering focus groups (29 parents, 16 employers, and 18 community informants interviewed); (3) interviews (97 parents, 60 employers, and 45 community informants interviewed); (4) initial data analysis; (5) interpretive focus groups (41 parents, 14 employers, and 21 community informants from the participants in focus groups and individual interviews).

7. D. Belle, *The After-School Lives of Children: Alone and with Others While Parents Work* (Mahwah, NJ: Lawrence Erlbaum, 1999); B.M. Miller, S. O'Connor, S.W. Sirignano, and P. Joshi, *"I Wish the Kids Didn't Watch So Much TV": Out-of-School Time in Three Low-Income Communities* (Wellesley, MA: Center for Research on Women, Wellesley College, 1997); T.J. Long and L. Long, "Latchkey Children," in L.G. Katz, ed., *Current Topics in Early Childhood Education,* vol. 5 (Norwood, NJ: Ablex, 1984).

8. L. Bailyn, R. Drago, and T. Kochan, *Integrating Work and Family Life: A Holistic Approach* (Cambridge, MA: Sloan Work–Family Policy Network, 2001).

9. K. Schulman, "The High Cost of Childcare Puts Quality Care Out of Reach for Many Families," available at: http://www.childrensdefense.org/head-resources.htm (accessed November 26, 2001).

10. L. Giannarelli and J. Barsimantov, "Childcare Expenses of America's Families," available at: http://www.newfederalism.urban.org/html/op40/occa40.html (accessed November 1, 2001).

11. D. Blau and E. Tekin, "The Determinants and Consequences of Childcare Subsidies," *Poverty Research News* 5, no. 3 (2001): 3; Childcare Bureau, "Access to Childcare for Low-Income Families," available at: http://www.acf.dhhs.gov/programs/ccb/research/ ccreport.htm (accessed October 31, 2001); "Only 10 Percent of Eligible Families Get Child Care Help, New Report Shows," Department of Health and Human Services News press release, October 19, 1999.

12. H. Presser, "Some Economic Complexities of Child Care Provided by Grandmothers," *Journal of Marriage and the Family* 51 (1989): 581–91; A.R. Roschelle, *No More Kin: Exploring Race, Class, and Gender in Family Networks* (Thousand Oaks, CA: Sage, 1997).

13. A. Collins and B. Carlson, "Child Care by Kith and Kin: Supporting Family, Friends, and Neighbors Caring for Children," Children and Welfare Reform issue brief 5, available at: http://www.edrs.com, ED423080; M. Brown-Lyons, A. Robertson, and J. Layzer, *Kith and Kin—Informal Child Care: Highlights from Recent Research* (New York: National Center for Children in Poverty at Columbia University, 2001).

14. A. Wilkins, "Childcare Experiences of Former TANF Recipients," National Conference of State Legislatures, August 2001, available at: http://www.ncsl.org/statefed/ WELFARE/CC2001.htm (accessed December 7, 2001); Belle, *After-School Lives of Children;* K. Westra and J. Routley, "Arizona Cash Assistance Exit Study," Arizona Department of Economic Security, Office of Evaluation, January 2000, available at: http:// www.de.state.az.us/links/reports/exitstudy.html (accessed November 7, 2001); A. Brayfield, S.G. Deich, and S.L. Hofferth, *Caring for Children in Low-Income Families: A Substudy of the National Child Care Survey, 1990* (Washington, DC: Urban Institute Press, 1993); E. Galinsky and J.T. Bond, "Helping Families with Young Children Navigate Work and Family Life," in J.P. Shonkoff and D.A. Phillips, eds., *From Neurons to Neighborhoods: The Science of Early Childhood Development* (Washington, DC: National Academy Press, 2000). For other child care evaluation studies, see B. Hershfield and

K. Selman, eds., *Child Day Care* (New Brunswick, NJ: Transaction Publishers, 1997); S. Hofferth, A. Brayfield, S. Deich, and P. Holcomb, *National Child Care Survey, 1990, Report 91–5* (Washington, DC: Urban Institute, 1991).

15. S.L. Hofferth, "Child Care, Maternal Employment, and Public Policy," *Annals of the American Academy of Political and Social Science* 563 (1999): 20–38.

16. L. Dodson, unpublished interviews and research findings, 1999.

17. M. Sing, H. Hill, and L. Mendenko, *Work, Welfare, and Family Well-Being* (Washington, DC: Mathematica Policy Research, 2001).

18. J.S. Litt, C.N. Fletcher, and M. Winter, "Health-Related Carework in Low-Income Households: The Special Case of Children with Disabilities," paper presented at the Conference on Carework, Inequality, and Advocacy, Irvine, California, August 17, 2001; Heymann, *Widening Gap;* P. Newacheck, B. Strickland, J.P. Shonkoff, J.M. Perrin, M. McPherson, M. McManus, C. Lauver, H. Fox, and P. Arango, "An Epidemiologic Profile of Children with Special Health Care Needs," *Pediatrics* 102, no. 1 (1998): 117–23; L. Montgomery, J. Kiely, and G. Pappas, "The Effects of Poverty, Race, and Family Structure on U.S. Children's Health: Data from the NHIS, 1978 Through 1980 and 1989 Through 1991," *American Journal of Public Health* 86, no. 10 (1996): 1401–5.

19. Studies have documented an increased prevalence of asthma among children from urban, minority, and low-income backgrounds. Prevalence rates among such children have been reported from 10 percent to 20 percent, whereas the prevalence for U.S. children overall is 6 percent. See M.E. Mansour, B.P. Lanphear, and T.G. DeWitt, "Barriers to Asthma Care in Urban Children: Parents Perspectives," *Pediatrics* 106, no. 3 (2000): 512–19. Nationally, 14 percent of working mothers who had received welfare for more than two years in the past and 11 percent of working mothers who had received welfare for two years or less had a child with asthma, compared with 7 percent of mothers who had never been on welfare. See S.J. Heymann and A. Earle, "The Impact of Welfare Reform on Parents' Ability to Care for Their Children's Health," *American Journal of Public Health* 89, no. 4 (1999): 502–5.

20. M. Meyers, H. Brady, and E. Seto, *Expensive Children in Poor Families: The Intersection of Childhood Disabilities and Welfare* (San Francisco: Public Policy Institute of California, 2000).

21. K.W. Hamlett, D.S. Pellegrini, and K.S. Katz, "Childhood Chronic Illness as a Family Stressor," *Journal of Pediatric Psychology* 17 (1992): 33–47; G.H. Landsman, " 'Real Motherhood,' Class and Children with Disabilities," in H. Ragone and F.W. Twine, eds., *Ideologies and Technologies of Motherhood: Race, Class, Sexuality, Nationalism* (New York: Routledge, 2000); Heymann, *The Widening Gap.*

22. J.S. Litt, C.N. Fletcher, and M. Winter, "Health-Related Carework in Low-Income Households: The Special Case of Children with Disabilities," paper presented at the Conference on Carework, Inequality, and Advocacy, Irvine, California, August 17, 2001.

23. L. Dodson, unpublished interviews and research findings, 1998.

24. E.M. Hallowell and J.J. Ratey, *Driven to Distraction: Recognizing and Coping with Attention Deficit Disorder from Childhood Through Adulthood* (New York: Simon & Schuster, 1995).

25. Heymann, *The Widening Gap.*

26. Dodson, unpublished interviews and research findings, 1998.

27. Litt, Fletcher, and Winter, "Health-Related Carework."

28. P. Loprest, "How Families That Left Welfare Are Doing: A National Picture," New Federalism: National Survey of America's Families, no. B-1 (Washington, DC: Urban Institute, 1999); Sing, Hill, and Mendenko, *Work, Welfare, and Family Well-Being;* H.J. Holzer and M.A. Stoll, *Employers and Welfare Recipients: The Effects of Welfare Reform in the Workplace* (San Francisco: Public Policy Institute of California, 2001).

29. J.R. Henly, "Barriers to Finding and Maintaining Jobs: The Perspectives of Workers

and Employers in the Low-Wage Labor Market," in J. Handler and L. White, eds., *Hard Labor: Women and Work in the Post-Welfare Era* (Armonk, NY: M.E. Sharpe, 1998).

30. Nationally, 30 percent of the working poor are clustered in service occupations, 15 percent in sales, and 15 percent as laborers or machine operators. See M. Kim, "Problems Facing the Working Poor," in E. Appelbaum, ed., *Balancing Acts: Easing the Burdens and Improving the Options for Working Families* (Washington, DC: Economic Policy Institute, 2000).

31. N.B. Coe, G. Acs, R.I. Lerman, and K. Watson, *Does Work Pay? An Analysis of the Work Incentives Under TANF* (Washington, DC: Urban Institute, 1998).

32. P. Anderson and B. Meyer, "The Extent and Consequences of Job Turnover," *Brookings Papers on Economic Activity—Microeconomics* 6 (1994): 177–248; H. Holzer and R. Lalonde, "Job Change and Job Stability Among Less-Skilled Young Workers," in D. Card and R. Blank, eds., *Finding Jobs: Work and Welfare Reform* (New York: Russell Sage Foundation, 2000).

33. T. Gladden and C. Taber, "Wage Progression Among Less Skilled Workers," in Card and Blank, eds., *Finding Jobs;* Holzer and Lalonde, "Job Change and Job Stability."

34. K.S. Newman, *No Shame in My Game: The Working Poor in the Inner City* (New York: Knopf, 2000).

35. Gladden and Taber, "Wage Progression Among Less Skilled Workers"; Karen Czapanskiy, "Parents, Children, and Work-First Welfare Reform, or Where Is the *C* in TANF?" *Maryland Law Review* 61 (2002).

36. Coe et al., *Does Work Pay?*

37. R. Batt and P.M. Valcour, "Workplace Flexibility, Work-Family Integration, and Employee Turnover," paper presented at the conference Work and Family: Expanding the Horizons, San Francisco, March 3–4, 2000.

38. J. Waldfogel, "The Family Gap for Young Women in the U.S. and U.K.: Can Maternity Leave Make a Difference?" *Journal of Labor Economics* 16, no. 3 (1998): 505–45; D.R. Dalton and D.J. Mesch, "The Impact of Flexible Scheduling on Employee Attendance," *Administrative Science Quarterly* 35 (1990): 370–87; Bailyn, Drago, and Kochan, *Integrating Work and Family Life.*

39. B. Grosswald, " 'I Raised My Kids on the Bus': Transit Shift Workers' Coping Strategies for Parenting," working paper no. 10, Center for Working Families, University of California, Berkeley, 1999.

40. L. White, "Quality Child Care for Low-Income Families: Despair, Impasse, Improvisation," in Handler and White, eds., *Hard Labor;* D.L. Vandell and B. Wolfe, "Child Care Quality: Does It Matter and Does It Need to Be Improved?" available at: http://www.aspe.hhs.gov/hsp/ccquality00/index.htm (accessed November 26, 2001).

41. For more detailed information on policy changes, see the following Web sites: http://www.communitychange.org regarding TANF, http://www.nelp.org regarding unemployment, http://www.nationalpartnership.org regarding family leave, http://www.childcarereaction.org and http://www.childrensdefense.org regarding child care, and http://www.aflcio.org and http://www.9to5.org regarding working families.

Addressing the Time Crunch of High Earners
Sylvia Ann Hewlett

1. Focus group, Cambridge, Massachusetts, February 12, 2001. Names and affiliations have been changed. The dialogue is based on tapes and interview notes, and it has been edited for clarity and space.

2. The High-Achieving Women 2001 survey was conducted in January 2001 by Harris Interactive under the auspices of the National Parenting Association. This nationwide survey was designed to explore the professional and private lives of highly educated,

high-earning women. The survey is featured in *Creating a Life: Professional Women and the Quest for Children* (New York: Miramax Books, 2002). The survey was conducted on-line and targeted the top 10 percent of women—measured in terms of earning power—and a small sample of men, for comparative purposes. Responding were nationally representative samples of 1,168 high-earning career women ages twenty-eight to fifty-five, highly educated high-earning noncareer women ages twenty-eight to fifty-five, and 472 high-earning men ages twenty-eight to fifty-five. Our analysis delineated two age groups: the older generation, ages forty-one to fifty-five, and their younger counterparts, ages twenty-eight to forty. We also distinguished between high earners (those earning more than $55,000 in the younger group or $65,000 in the older one), ultra-high earners (those earning more than $100,000), and "high-potential" women—highly qualified women who have left their careers mainly for family reasons.

3. This series of questions was asked of women only. While some women felt they shouldered most of the household and child care responsibilities, some felt these were shared. In households with both men and women employed full time or self-employed, 40 percent said they both cleaned the house, 39 percent shared preparing meals, 41 percent said they both did grocery shopping, 37 percent said they both helped with homework, 30 percent said they both took time off work for child sickness, and 25 percent said they both did organizing activities.

4. Vignettes contained in this chapter are based on follow-up interviews with respondents to the High-Achieving Women 2001 survey. As with the Cambridge focus group, names and other identifying information have been changed, and the dialogue is re-constructed, based on interview notes and e-mails. It has been edited for clarity and space.

5. The "good enough" mother and "good enough" parent are concepts developed by British psychologist D.W. Winnicott. Essentially, Winnicott asserted that babies do not need a perfect parent in order to develop a healthy personality, but they do need a "good enough" parent. See D.W. Winnicott, *The Family and Individual Development* (London and New York: Routledge, 1989). See also Bruno Bettelheim, *Good-Enough Parent* (New York: Knopf, 1987).

6. J.B. Schor, *The Overworked American: The Unexpected Decline of Leisure* (New York: Basic Books, 1992).

7. J.B. Schor, "Time Crunch Among American Parents," in S.A. Hewlett, N. Rankin, and C. West, eds., *Taking Parenting Public: The Case for a New Social Movement* (Lanham, MD: Rowman & Littlefield, 2002).

8. The picture is, of course, complicated by the fact that individuals often need to hold more than one of these jobs to get by. For a description of these trends and their consequences, see J. Heymann, *The Widening Gap: Why America's Working Families Are in Jeopardy and What Can Be Done About It* (New York: Basic Books, 2000).

9. J.A. Jacobs and K. Gerson, "Towards a Family-Friendly, Gender Equitable Work Week," *University of Pennsylvania Journal of Labor and Employment Law,* fall 1998, 458–59. See also J.A. Jacobs and K. Gerson, "Who Are the Overworked Americans?" *Review of Social Economy* 56, no. 4 (1998): 442–59.

10. See discussion in Jacobs and Gerson, "Towards a Family-Friendly," 467.

11. University of Texas, Houston, "Work/Family Task Force Report," May 1996, available at: http://worklife.uth.tmc.edu/wftfcost.html (accessed April 1, 2004).

12. B.L. Ware and B. Fern, "The Challenge of Retaining Top Talent: The Workforce Attrition Crisis," Integral Training Systems, Menlo Park, California, 1997, available at: http://www.itsinc.net/retention-research.htm (accessed April 1, 2004). See also J. Sullivan, "The Cost Factors and Business Impacts of Turnover," March 1998, available at: http://www.drjohnsullivan.com/articles/1998/net10.htm (accessed April 1, 2004). According to Anne Ruddy, the executive director of WorldatWork, a global network of human resource professionals, the bill for filling the slot of a high-level executive is about

three times the job's annual salary ("Friends of the Family," *Working Mother,* October 2000, 62).

13. American Management Association, "2000 AMA Staffing and Structure Survey," October 2000, 1.

14. Interview, December 20, 2000.

15. "100 Best Companies for Working Mothers," *Working Mother,* October 2000, 76–84.

16. T. Carbasho, "Despite Benefits' Costs Crunch, Family-Friendly Benefits Still Growing Trend," *Pittsburgh Business Times,* January 2, 2004, 15.

17. Interview, October 17, 2000.

18. Source: http://www.workingwoman.com (accessed February 10, 2001).

19. Source: http://www.workingwoman.com (accessed February 20, 2001).

20. K.H. Hammonds, "Family Values," *Fast Company,* December 2000, 169.

21. Jacobs and Gerson, "Towards a Family-Friendly," 462.

22. Source: http://www.lawyerslifecoach.com/newsletters/issues08 (accessed January 7, 2001).

23. In a recent article, DeGroot stressed the importance of attitudinal change. As she pointed out, even a generous benefits package with a rich array of options cannot help employees strike a meaningful, sustainable balance between professional and personal life unless there is a fundamental change in managers' mind-sets. See S.D. Friedman, P. Christensen, and J. DeGroot, "Work and Life: The End of the Zero-Sum Game," *Harvard Business Review,* November-December 1998, 119–29.

24. Interview with Sheila Kamerman. See the Clearinghouse on International Developments in Child, Youth and Family Policy at Columbia University, at: http://www.child policyintl.org.

25. See F.N. Schwartz, "Management Women and the New Facts of Life," *Harvard Business Review,* January-February 1989, 65–76.

26. See discussion in A. Crittenden, *The Price of Motherhood* (New York: Holt, 2001), 32.

27. "In 1979 parents who were employed full time in all sectors of the economy were granted the right to an unpaid partial leave of absence to at most three-quarters of full time until the child was 8 years old. (Civil servants have had this right since 1970.) That is, parents could reduce their hours of work to thirty hours per week with a right to return to full-time work after two months' notice to the employer." S.B. Kamerman and A.J. Kahn, *Child Care, Parental Leave, and the Under Threes: Policy Innovation in Europe* (New York: Auburn House, 1991), 188–89.

28. R. Mahony, *Kidding Ourselves* (New York: Basic Books, 1995), 18.

29. N. Rankin in "Leave-Taking Employees Need 'On-Ramps' to Ease Re-entry to Workplace, Experts Say," *Human Resources Report* 19, no. 43 (2000): 1181.

30. Its significance goes beyond preferences. Research has shown that parental presence is important for a child's health. For a summary of the literature showing the consequences of parents' caring for their children's health, see J. Heymann, A. Earle, and B. Egleston, "Parental Availability for the Care of Sick Children," *Pediatrics* 98, no. 2 (1996): 226–30.

31. S.I. Greenspan, "The Reasons Why We Need to Rely Less on Day Care," *Washington Post,* Outlook section, November 7, 1997, 3. See also S.I. Greenspan and J. Salmon, *The Four-Thirds Solution: Solving the Child-care Crisis in America Today* (New York: Perseus Books, 2001).

32. Consideration of other barriers to decreasing total professional hours, such as changes in workplace structure and evaluation and promotion processes, and how they could be overcome, are beyond the scope of this chapter.

33. A discussion of this evidence is beyond the scope of this chapter. Refer to works by Gornick and Waldfogel, among others. See, for example, E. Bardasi and J.C. Gornick, "Women and Part-Time Employment: Workers' Choices and Wage Penalties in Five Industrialized Countries," Luxembourg Income Study working paper no. 223, March 2000; J. Waldfogel, "The Effects of Children on Women's Wages," *American Sociology*

Review 62, no. 2 (1997): 209–17; Heather Joshi, "The Opportunity Costs of Childbearing: More than Mothers' Business," *Journal of Population Economics* 11 (1998): 161–83.

The National Story: How Americans Spend Their Time on Work, Family, and Community
David M. Almeida and Daniel A. McDonald

This project was supported by the MacArthur Foundation Research Network on Successful Midlife Development, the W.K. Kellogg Foundation, and the National Institute for Mental Health (MH19734) and the National Institute on Aging (AG16731, AG19239). The authors wish to thank Shevaun Neupert, Joyce Serido, and Amy Howerter for their assistance in preparing this chapter.

1. A. Rossi, ed., *Social Responsibility During Middle Adulthood* (Chicago: University of Chicago Press, 2001).
2. J.P. Robinson and G. Godbey, *Time for Life: The Surprising Ways Americans Use Their Time* (University Park, PA: Pennsylvania State University Press, 1997).
3. R.C. Barnett, "Toward a Review and Reconceptualization of the Work/Family Literature," *Genetic, Social, and General Psychology Monographs* 124 (1998): 125–82.
4. Rossi, *Social Responsibility*.
5. D.M. Almeida, D.A. McDonald, J. Havens, and P. Schervish, "Temporal Patterns in Social Responsibility," in A. Rossi, ed., *Social Responsibility During Middle Adulthood* (Chicago: University of Chicago Press, 2001).
6. Robinson and Godbey, *Time for Life*.
7. R.D. Putnam, *Bowling Alone: The Collapse and Revival of American Community* (New York: Simon & Schuster, 2000).
8. Ibid.
9. R.S. Weiss, "Men and the Family," *Family Process* 24 (1985): 49–58.
10. Rossi, *Social Responsibility*.
11. Barnett, "Toward a Review."
12. Rossi, *Social Responsibility*.
13. Putnam, *Bowling Alone*.
14. Rossi, *Social Responsibility*.
15. F.T. Juster and F.P. Stafford, *Time, Goods, and Well-Being* (Ann Arbor: Institute for Social Research, University of Michigan, 1985); Robinson and Godbey, *Time for Life*.
16. Almeida et al., "Temporal Patterns"; National Research Council, *Time Use Measurement and Research* (Washington, DC: National Academy Press, 2000).
17. G.L. Staines and J.H. Pleck, *The Impact of Work Schedules on the Family* (Ann Arbor: University of Michigan Press, 1983).
18. Rossi, *Social Responsibility*.
19. Putnam, *Bowling Alone*.
20. Robinson and Godbey, *Time for Life*.
21. Rossi, *Social Responsibility*.
22. Ibid.
23. D. Cantor, J. Waldfogel, J. Kerwin, M.M. Wright, K. Levin, J. Rauch, T. Hagerty, and M.S. Kudela, "Balancing the Needs of Families and Employers: Family and Medical Leave Surveys, 2000 Update," report submitted by Westat to the Department of Labor, 2001.
24. J.A. Levine and T.L. Pittinsky, *Working Fathers: New Strategies for Balancing Work and Family* (New York: Harcourt Brace, 1997).
25. J.H. Pleck, "Paternal Involvement: Levels, Sources, and Consequences," in M.E. Lamb, ed., *The Role of the Father in Child Development* (New York: Wiley, 1997).
26. Cantor, et al., "Balancing the Needs."

Challenges to Change
Christopher Beem

1. The labor movement, for instance, fostered and depended on a narrative of solidarity among working people. See, for example, P. Le Blanc, *A Short History of the U.S. Working Class: From Colonial Times to the Twenty-first Century* (Amherst, MA: Humanity Books, 1999). But again, I understand these three to be most relevant to our contemporary circumstance.

2. M. Sandel, *Democracy's Discontent: America in Search of a Public Philosophy* (Cambridge, MA: Belknap Press, 1996), 5.

3. Compare, for example, France. The French concept of *laïcité* is both deeply moral and culturally unifying, but it is also ardently secular and has developed as a reaction to the Roman Catholicism that so long dominated the culture.

4. It bears mentioning that one of the seminal works regarding the concept of American public, or civil, religion was Bellah's essay "Civil Religion in America," *Daedalus* 96 (1967): 1–21. The short accounting presented here does not, so far as I can see, differ in any significant way from Bellah's essay.

5. See C. Lasch, *Haven in a Heartless World: The Family Besieged* (New York: Basic Books, 1977).

6. See A. de Tocqueville, *Democracy in America,* trans. G. Lawrence, ed. J.P. Mayer (Garden City, NY: Anchor Books, 1969), 448. See also R. Wuthnow and T.L. Scott, "Protestants and Economic Behavior," in H. Stout and D.G. Hart, eds., *New Directions in American Religious History* (New York: Oxford University Press, 1997).

7. H.S. Commager, *The American Mind: An Interpretation of American Thought and Character Since the 1880s* (New Haven: Yale University Press, 1950), 3.

8. T. Skocpol, "Advocates Without Members: The Recent Transformation of American Civic Life," in T. Skocpol and M. Fiorina, eds., *Civic Engagement in American Democracy,* (Washington, DC: Brookings Institution Press; New York: Russell Sage Foundation, 1999), 495.

9. M. Winick, D. Graves, and R. Sicso, "Attorney Advertising in Texas: Regulations Mean Serious Business," *Texas Wesleyan Law Review* 3, no. 1 (1996): 234.

10. Lawyers who took advantage of the newfound right to advertise, such as Joel Hyatt, were quick to point out that during his days in Springfield, Illinois, Abraham Lincoln advertised his services. See American Bar Association Commission on Advertising, "Lawyer Advertising at the Crossroads: Professional Policy Recommendations" (Chicago: American Bar Association, 1995), 29–32.

11. This notion is reflected in and affirmed by Tocqueville in *Democracy in America.* Tocqueville believed that lawyers' natural conservatism and elitism countered the worst impulses of a democracy and made them the functional equivalent of the aristocracy. "Where lawyers are absolutely needed," he wrote, "as in England and the United States, and their professional knowledge is held in high esteem, they become increasingly separated from the people, forming a class apart." *Democracy in America,* 267.

12. 425 U.S. 748 (1976).

13. *Bates v. State Bar of Arizona,* 433 U.S. 350 (1977).

14. American Bar Association Commission on Advertising, "Lawyer Advertising at the Crossroads," 154.

15. Note also that all of these stadiums have been either renamed or demolished. Three Rivers Stadium is no more; in 2001, the Pittsburgh Pirates began playing at PNC Park. Mile High Stadium was demolished this year; in 2002, the Denver Broncos began playing in "Invesco Field @ Mile High." Riverfront Stadium, built in 1970, was renamed Cinergy Field in 1997, then demolished in 2002 to make way for the Great American Ball Park, so named by the Great American Insurance Company. Candlestick Park,

built in 1960, was renamed 3Com Park in 1995. For more on this fascinating history, see http://www.ballparks.com (accessed February 9, 2004).

16. Ibid.

17. Rising prices for these rights have proven that ARCO got quite a bargain. Staples paid $100 million for 20 years (or $5 million per year) for the naming rights to the new arena for the Los Angeles Lakers basketball team.

18. There are a few exceptions. The redesigned Lambeau Field (home of the Green Bay Packers) did not sell naming rights, and the new stadium for the Cleveland Browns football team opened in 1999 as the Cleveland Browns Stadium. Interestingly, both of these stadiums are publicly owned.

19. Cities accept these terms because they believe that sports franchises are engines for jobs and economic growth. After crunching the numbers, the economists Roger G. Noll and Andrew Zimbalist concluded that "a new sports facility has an extremely small and (perhaps even negative) effect on overall economic activity and employment. See R.G. Noll and A. Zimbalist, "Sports, Jobs and Taxes," *Brookings Review* 15, no. 3 (1997): 36.

20. Thus, for example, the city of Denver approved the end of the name "Mile High Stadium."

21. Quoted in R. Baker, "Stealth T.V.," *American Prospect,* February 12, 2001, 29.

22. N. Klein, *No Logo: Taking Aim at the Brand Bullies* (New York: Picador Press, 1999), 89.

23. Baker, "Stealth T.V.," 30.

24. Klein, *No Logo,* 102.

25. General Accounting Office (GAO), *Report HEHS-00-156: Commercial Activities in Schools* (Washington, DC: Government Printing Office), 22.

26. For example, a toothpaste company sponsored a unit on dental hygiene. Less benignly, one activist group reported on schools' use of nutrition-related curricula produced by McDonald's and potato chip companies. See http://www.corpwatch.org/issues/PID.jsp? articleid=3289 (accessed April 27, 2004).

27. GAO, *Commercial Activities in Schools,* 22.

28. National Gambling Impact Study Commission, *National Gambling Impact Study Commission Report* (Washington, DC: U.S. Government Printing Office, June 18, 1999), 2-1.

29. Contemporary arguments center much more on the fact that lotteries are, in effect, a regressive tax that affects poor people disproportionately and that advertising by the state is targeted in ways that reflect and abet this problem.

30. C.T. Clotfelter and P.J. Cook, *Selling Hope: State Lotteries in America* (Cambridge, MA: Harvard University Press, 1989), 36.

31. D. Nibert, *Hitting the Lottery Jackpot* (New York: Monthly Review Press, 2000), 36.

32. The story of legalized (as opposed to state-sponsored) gambling is obviously much more complex. However, circumstances here, too, have changed dramatically over the past thirty years. New Jersey passed a law allowing gambling in Atlantic City in 1977, and American Indian gaming exploded as a result of the 1988 Indian Gaming Regulatory Act.

33. Nibert, *Hitting the Lottery Jackpot,* 42.

34. Of course, a large part of this change is due to the fact that Americans lost their belief that gambling is a sin. This change, in turn, reflects the collapse of the quasi-Protestant public moral consensus. Catholicism and Judaism never had the same concerns about gambling, and as the new Protestant-Catholic-Jewish consensus developed in the second half of the twentieth century, social strictures around gambling began to wane.

35. For a thoroughly convincing account of the collapse of the civic republican tradition in American society, see Sandel, *Democracy's Discontent.* For more on the contemporary relationship between religion and economics in America, see R. Wuthnow, *Poor Richard's Principle: Recovering the American Dream Through the Moral Dimension of Work, Business, and Money* (Princeton: Princeton University Press, 1996).

36. National Sleep Foundation, "Less Sleep, More Work: An American Portrait" (Washington DC: National Sleep Foundation, 2001), 1.

37. R. Putnam, *Bowling Alone: The Collapse and Revival of American Community* (New York: Simon & Schuster, 2000), 189–215.

38. J. Schor, *The Overworked American: The Unexpected Decline of Leisure* (New York: Basic Books, 1992), 41.

39. Ibid., 29.

40. T. Skocpol, *The Missing Middle: Working Families and the Future of American Social Policy* (New York: Norton, 2000), 132.

41. See J.F. Sandberg and S.L. Hofferth, "Changes in Children's Times with Parents: U.S. 1981–1997," PSC Research Report no. 01-475, May 2001.

42. A. Fever, "America 24/7: No Matter the Time, Someone's Always Working," *New York Times,* April 4, 2001.

43. S.J. Heymann and A. Earle, "The Impact of Parental Working Conditions on School-Age Children: The Case of Evening Work," *Community, Work and Family* 4, no. 3 (2001): 317.

44. J. Heymann, *The Widening Gap: Why America's Working Families Are in Jeopardy—and What Can Be Done About It* (New York: Basic Books, 2000).

45. It is also quite possible that when corporations provide these kinds of services, parents feel constrained to use them, even if they would prefer to stay home themselves.

46. See their Web site, http://www.nascd.com (accessed February 9, 2004).

47. S. Hewlett and C. West, *The War Against Parents* (New York: Houghton Mifflin, 1998), 35.

48. Klein, *No Logo,* 312.

49. Ibid., 318.

The Paradox of Corporate Solutions:
Accomplishments, Limitations, and New Opportunities
Marcie Pitt-Catsouphes and Bradley K. Googins

1. U.S. Bureau of the Census, *Statistical Abstracts of the United States* (Washington, DC: Government Printing Office, 2001), 367, available at: http://www.census.gov/prod/2002pubs/01statab/labor.pdf.

2. See S. Lewis, "European Perspectives of Work and Family Issues," work-family policy paper, Center for Work and Family, Boston College, 1997; S. Lobel, "Quality of Life in Brazil and Mexico: Expanding Our Understanding of Work and Family Experiences in Latin America," work-family policy paper, Center for Work and Family, Boston College, 2000; G. Russell, "Work and Family Issues in Japan and the Republic of Korea," work-family policy paper, Center for Work and Family, Boston College, 2000.

3. See M. Pitt-Catsouphes, "Family-Friendly Workplaces," in *Work-Family Encyclopedia* (Chestnut Hill, MA: Center for Work and Family, Boston College, 2002), available at: http://www.bc.edu/wfnetwork.

4. Many thoughtful arguments have been advanced concerning the semantic implications of terms such as *work and family, work-family, work-life,* and *family-friendly.* In the interest of advancing our arguments about the importance of evaluating the contributions of the family-friendly workplace, we are, for now, glossing over the important conceptual distinctions between these terms. We hope that this is not distracting for the reader.

5. L. Bailyn, R. Drago, and T. Kochan, *Integrating Work and Family Life: A Holistic Approach,* report of the Sloan Work-Family Network (Cambridge, MA: Massachusetts Institute of Technology, 2001), available at: http://lsir.la.psu.edu/workfam/integrate.htm.

6. L. Litchfield and M. Pitt-Catsouphes, "Culture and Work/Life Balance: Findings from the *Business Week* Study" Research Highlight Series, Center for Work and Family, Boston College, 1999.

7. M. Fried, *Taking Time: Parental Leave Policy and Corporate Culture* (Philadelphia: Temple University Press, 1998).

8. See T. Allen, "Family-Supportive Work Environments: The Role of Organizational Perceptions," *Journal of Vocational Behavior* 58, no. 3 (2000): 414–35; E.E. Kossek and V. Nichol, "Understanding the Immediate Climate for Work/Family Integration: Assessing Congruence in the Supervisory and Subordinate Relationship Affecting Work/Family Outcomes," paper presented at the annual meeting of the National Academy of Management, Vancouver, British Columbia, 1995.

9. T. Bond, E. Galinsky, and J. Swanberg, *The 1997 National Study of the Changing Workforce* (New York: Families and Work Institute, 1997), 104.

10. R. Rapoport and L. Bailyn with D. Kolb, J. Fletcher, D.E. Friedman, S. Eaton, M. Harvey, and B. Miller, *Relinking Life and Work: Toward a Better Future* (New York: Ford Foundation, 1996), available at: http://www.cpn.org/sections/topics/work/index.html; L. Bailyn, D. Bengtse, F. Caree, and M. Tierney, "The Radcliffe-Fleet Work and Life Integration Project," in L. Casner-Lott, ed., *Holding a Job, Having a Life: Strategies for Change* (Scarsdale, NY: Work in America Institute, 2000), 35–49.

11. T. Kuhn, *The Structure of Scientific Revolutions* (Chicago: University of Chicago Press, 1962).

12. J. Williams, *Unbending Gender: Why Work and Family Conflict and What to Do About It* (New York: Oxford University Press, 1999).

13. A. Hochschild and A. Machung, *The Second Shift* (New York: Avon Books, 1990).

14. See also, for example, J. Pleck, "Paternal Involvement: Levels, Sources, and Consequences," in M. Lamb, ed., *The Role of the Father in Child Development* (New York: Wiley, 1997), 66–103.

15. E. Galinsky and A. Johnson, *Reframing the Business Case for Work-Life Initiatives* (New York: Families and Work Institute, 1998).

16. According to the Census Bureau, dual-earner couples are the most common structure of married-couple families. In 2000, 56 percent of all married couples were dual-earner couples; 21 percent, couples with only the husband in the labor force; 6 percent, couples with only the wife in the labor force; and 16 percent, couples with neither the husband nor the wife in the labor force. See U.S. Bureau of the Census, *Current Population Survey*, "America's Families and Living Arrangements: March 2000" (Washington, DC: Government Printing Office, 2000), 20–537. Available at: http://www.census.gov/prod/2001pubs/p20-87.pdf.

17. For a review related to these points, see E.E. Kossek and C. Ozeki, "Bridging the Work-Family Policy and Productivity Gap: A Literature Review," *Community, Work and Family* 2, no. 1 (1999): 7–32.

18. As described on its Web site, the "Families and Work Institute (FWI) is a nonprofit center for research that provides data to inform decision-making on the changing workforce, changing family and changing community." Information about the Families and Work Institute is available at: http://www.familiesandwork.org/about/index.html.

19. E. Galinsky, D.E. Friedman, and C.A. Hernandez, *The Corporate Reference Guide to Work-Family Programs*, report no. W91-01 (New York: Families and Work Institute, 1991).

20. *Juggling Work and Family*, Hedrick Smith Productions, Inc., produced in association with South Carolina Educational Television, 2001.

21. See R. Drago and R. Kashian, "Mapping the Terrain of Work/Family Journals," *Journal of Family Issues* 24, no. 4 (2003); A. Lilly, M. Pitt-Catsouphes, and B. Googins, *The Sloan Work and Family Research Network: Literature Database* (Chestnut Hill, MA: Center for Work and Family, Boston College, 2002), available at: http://www.bc.edu/wfnetwork.

22. Hewitt and Associates, *Work and Family Benefits Provided by Major U.S. Employers in 1997* (Lincolnshire, IL: Hewitt and Associates, 1998).

23. U.S. Department of Labor, *Employee Benefits in Medium and Large Private Establishments, 1997*, bulletin 2517 (Washington, DC: Bureau of Labor Statistics, 1999), available

at: http://www.bls.gov/ncs/ebs/sp/ebb10017.pdf; U.S. Department of Labor, *Employee Benefits in Medium and Large Private Establishments, 1997* (Washington, DC: Bureau of Labor Statistics, 2000), available at: http://data.bls.gov/servlet/SurveyOutputServlet.

24. E. Galinsky and J.T. Bond, *The 1998 Business Work-Life Study: A Sourcebook* (New York: Families and Work Institute, 1998).

25. Galinsky and Bond, *1998 Business Work-Life Study;* S. MacDermid, J.L. Hertzog, and K.B. Kensinger, with J.F. Zipp, "The Role of Organizational Size and Industry in Job Quality and Work-Family Relationships," *Journal of Family and Economic Issues* 22, no. 2 (2001): 191–216; M. Pitt-Catsouphes, P. Mirvis, and L. Litchfield, "Behind the Scenes: Corporate Environments and Work-Family Initiatives," Center for Work and Family, Boston College, 1995.

26. Galinsky and Bond, *1998 Business Work-Life Study.*

27. M. Pitt-Catsouphes, P. Mirvis, and S. Lewis, "Participation in Change: Work/Family Groups in Corporations," Center for Work and Family, Boston College, 1997.

28. E. Kelly and F. Dobbin, "Civil Rights Laws at Work: Sex Discrimination and the Rise of Maternity Leave Policies," *American Journal of Sociology* 105, no. 2 (1999): 455–92.

29. J. Goodstein, "Institutional Pressures and Strategic Responsiveness: Employer Involvement in Work-Family Issues," *Academy of Management Issues* 37, no. 2 (1994): 350–82.

30. Pitt-Catsouphes, Mirvis, and Litchfield, "Behind the Scenes"

31. S. Lobel and L. Fraught, "Four Methods for Providing the Value of Work/Life Initiatives," *Compensation and Benefits Review* 28, no. 6 (1996): 50–57.

32. B.B. Baltes, T.E. Briggs, J.W. Huff, J.A. Wright, and A. Neuman, "Flexible and Compressed Workweek Schedules: A Meta-Analysis of Their Effects on Work-Related Criteria," *Journal of Applied Psychology* 84, no. 4 (1999): 496–513.

33. S.J. Lambert, "Added Benefits: The Link Between Work-Life Benefits and Organizational Citizenship Behavior," *Academy of Management Journal* 43, no. 5 (2000): 801–15. In this study, Lambert and colleagues distributed surveys to a sample of 884 employees working at Fel-Pro, a manufacturing firm which had 2,000 employees at the time of data collection. The researchers report an overall response rate of 67.9 percent. Lambert found links between the availability of work-life benefits, perceptions of organizational support, and employees' organizational citizenship behaviors.

34. A. Konrad and R. Mangel, "The Impact of Work-Life Programs on Firm Productivity," *Strategic Management Journal* 21 (2000): 1225–37.

35. R. Pruchno, L. Litchfield, and M. Fried, "Measuring the Impact of Workplace Flexibility: Findings from the National Work/Life Measurement Project," Center for Work and Family, Boston College, 2000.

36. Catalyst, *A New Approach to Flexibility: Managing the Work/Time Equation* (New York: Catalyst, 1998), 59.

37. For a discussion of the employee-customer profit chain, see A. Rucci, S. Kirn, and R. Quinn, "The Employee-Customer Profit Chain at Sears," *Harvard Business Review* 76, no. 1 (1998): 82–98.

38. See, for example, S. Friedman, ed., "Case Studies," Wharton Work/Life Integration Project, University of Pennsylvania, 2001); and J. Casner-Lotto, ed., *Holding a Job, Having a Life: Strategies for Change* (Scarsdale, NY: Work in America Institute, 2000).

39. H. Bohen and A. Viveros-Long, *Balancing Jobs and Family Life: Do Flexible Schedules Help?* (Philadelphia: Temple University Press, 1981).

40. M. Tausig and R. Fenwick, "Unbinding Time: Alternate Work Schedules and Work-Life Balance," *Journal of Family and Economic Issues* 22, no. 2 (2001): 101–19.

41. Catalyst, *New Approach to Flexibility;* C. Higgins, L. Duxbury, and K. Johnson, "Part-Time Work for Women: Does It Really Help Balance Work and Family?" *Human Resource Management* 39, no. 1 (2000): 17–32.

42. L. Litchfield, "Final Report: Assessment of On-Site Child Care," unpublished report, Center for Work and Family, Boston College, 2001.

43. E.E. Kossek and C. Ozeki, "Bridging the Work-Family Policy and Productivity Gap: A Literature Review," *Community, Work and Family* 2, no. 1 (1999): 7–32.
44. As noted by Bond and associates, data gathered from employees about the availability of benefits may underestimate the actual availability, because employees may not be aware whether or not a certain type of benefit is offered by their employers unless or until the employees actually have a need for it. See Bond, Galinsky, and Swanberg, *1997 National Study of the Changing Workforce.*
45. S. MacDermid, J.L. Hertzog, and K.B. Kensinger, with J.F. Zipp. "The role of organizational size and industry in job quality and work-family relationships." *Journal of Family and Economic Issues* 22, no. 2 (2001): 191–216. Available at: http://www.census.gov/population/socdemo/gender/ppl-121/tab09.txt.
46. U.S. Bureau of the Census, *Statistical Abstracts,* 483.
47. M. Pitt-Catsouphes and L. Litchfield, "How Are Small Businesses Responding to Work and Family Issues?" in R. Hertz and N. Marshall, eds., *Working Families: The Transformation of the American Home* (Berkeley: University of California Press, 2001), 131–51.
48. Bond, Galinsky, and Swanberg, *1997 National Study,* 95, 101.
49. Ibid., 88, 90.
50. K. Christensen, "Contingent Work Arrangements in Family-Sensitive Corporations," Center for Work and Family, Boston College, 1995.
51. Bond, Galinsky, and Swanberg, *1997 National Study,* 99.
52. J. Glass and T. Fujimoto, "Employer Characteristics and the Provision of Family Responsive Policies," *Work and Occupations* 22, no. 4 (1995): 380–411.
53. Bond, Galinsky, and Swanberg, *1997 National Study,* 99.
54. E. Bankert and B. Googins, "Family-Friendly—Says Who?" *Across the Board* 33, no. 7 (1996): 45–49.
55. On factors limiting the effectiveness of work-family initiatives, see A. Campbell and M. Koblenz, "The Work and Life Pyramid of Needs: A New Paradigm for Understanding the Nature of Work and Life Conflicts," MK Consultants, Evanston, Illinois, 1997.
56. R. Drago, "Work and Family and the Social Contract," *Perspectives on Work* 4, no. 1 (2000): 16–18; T. Kochan, "Building a New Social Contract at Work: A Call to Action," *Perspectives on Work* 4, no. 1 (2000): 2–12.
57. F. Heuberger and L. Nash, eds., *A Fatal Embrace: Assessing Holistic Trends in Human Resources Programs* (New Brunswick, NJ: Transaction, 1994).
58. M.K. Judiesch and K.S. Lyness, "Left Behind? The Impact of Leaves of Absence on Managers' Career Success," *Academy of Management Journal* 42, no. 6 (1999): 641–51.
59. Pruchno, Litchfield, and Fried, "Measuring the Impact of Workplace Flexibility."
60. Galinsky and Johnson, *Reframing the Business Case.*
61. Corporate Work-Family Roundtable, "Corporations: Principles of Excellence," Center for Work and Family, Boston College, 1996.
62. B. Grosswald, D. Ragland, and J. Fisher, "Critique of U.S. Work-Family Programs and Policies," *Journal of Progressive Human Services* 12, no. 1 (2001): 53–75.
63. E. Kelly and F. Dobbin, "Civil Rights Laws at Work: Sex Discrimination and the Rise of Maternity Leave Policies," *American Journal of Sociology* 105, no. 2 (1999): 455–92.
64. See D. Meadows, "Leverage Points: Places to Intervene in a System," Sustainability Institute, Hartland, Vermont, 1999, for a discussion about the importance of using new paradigms when systemic change is needed. The summary is available at: http://en.wikipedia.org/wiki/Donella_Meadows%27_twelve_leverage_points_to_intervene_in_a_system.
65. See M. Pitt-Catsouphes, B. Googins, and I. Fassler, "Enhancing Strategic Value: Becoming a Company of Choice," work-family policy paper, Center for Work and Family, Boston College, 1998.
66. Additional information about Corporate Voices for Working Families can be found on the organization's Web site at: http://www.cvworkingfamilies.org/index.html.

67. See S. Lewis, "European Perspectives of Work and Family Issues," work-family policy paper, Center for Work and Family, Boston College, 1997.
68. A nonprobability, purposive sample was created to gather the opinions of a wide variety of individuals about the concept of a family-friendly society. The individuals who participated in this qualitative study included elected officials at the community level (for example, a mayor from a large city, a mayor from a small city, and members of a local school board), elected officials at the state level (for example, a governor and state representatives), and elected officials at the federal level (for example, a member of the House of Representatives); administrators in executive branches of the national governments of the United States and the United Kingdom (for example, a policy advisor at the national level and a director of a national agency); union leaders (for example, a leader of a national organization offering research and policy support to unions in the United States); researchers (for example, the director of an employment policy institute); human service providers (for example, the director of a nonprofit agency providing day services to elders needing care); business leaders (for example, members of a corporate membership group organized to support the development of work-family initiatives at the workplace); and employees from a metropolitan area in the northeastern region of the United States.
69. J. Brannen, "Researching Work-Family Issues: Starting from Home, Starting from Work, Starting from Somewhere Else," paper presented at the Work-Family Researchers Conference, San Francisco, March 3–4, 2000.

Public Opinion on Work and Family Policy: The Role of Changing Demographics and Unionization
Henry E. Brady and Laurel Elms

1. Survey question wordings and responses for ABC News/*Washington Post,* CBS News/*New York Times,* and Gallup items were obtained from the Roper Center for Public Opinion Research at the University of Connecticut. For more on the Roper Social and Political Trends data set, see H.E. Brady, R.D. Putnam, A.L. Campbell, L. Elms, S. Yonish, and D. Apollonio, *Roper Social and Political Trends Data, 1973–1994* (Storrs, CT: Roper Center for Public Opinion Research, University of Connecticut, 2001), individual surveys conducted by the Roper Organization, 1973–1994. The Roper Social and Political Trends data set combines more than two hundred surveys, conducted ten times every year, from 1973 to 1994. Among other things, the Roper surveys include an extensive battery of twelve items about political participation that provide the best information available about changes in participation over time.

 The American National Election Studies (NES), completed every biennium, provide a continuous time series from 1952 to 2000, and we draw on them to learn about public support for family policies. See V. Sapiro, S.J. Rosenstone, and the National Election Studies, *1948–2000 Cumulative Data File* (Ann Arbor: University of Michigan, Center for Political Studies, 2001).

 The General Social Surveys (GSS), completed every year or every other year from 1972 to 2000, offer detailed information on occupational groups, union membership, party identification, and family policies. See J.A. Davis, T.W. Smith, and P.V. Marsden, *General Social Surveys, 1972–2000,* 3rd version (Chicago, National Opinion Research Center, 2001/Ann Arbor, Inter-university Consortium for Political and Social Research, 2001).

2. For detailed discussions of the history and eventual passage of a national family leave law, see A. Bernstein, *The Moderation Dilemma: Legislative Coalitions and the Politics of Family and Medical Leave* (Pittsburgh, PA: University of Pittsburgh Press, 2001); S.K. Wisensale, *Family Leave Policy: The Political Economy of Work and Family in Amer-*

ica (Armonk, NY: M.E. Sharpe, 2001); and R.D. Elving, *Conflict and Compromise: How Congress Makes the Law* (New York: Simon & Schuster, 1995).

3. Bernstein, *Moderation Dilemma.*
4. Ibid.; Elving, *Conflict and Compromise.*
5. Bernstein, *Moderation Dilemma.*
6. Elving, *Conflict and Compromise.*
7. Bernstein, *Moderation Dilemma.*
8. Ibid.
9. L. Grundy and N. Firestein, *Work, Family, and the Labor Movement* (Cambridge, MA: Radcliffe Public Policy Institute, 1997).
10. S. Klueck Elison, "Policy Innovation in a Cold Climate," *Journal of Family Issues* 18 (1997): 30–54.
11. Bernstein, *Moderation Dilemma.*
12. Gallup questions asked in November 1989 and October 1990 about continuing health and other benefits during an unpaid family leave suggest at least majority support for this in the general population. Similar questions about treating men and women equally also suggest at least majority support.
13. The December 1986 question asked about "a bill that would require companies employing more than 15 people to grant up to 18 weeks of unpaid leave to employees," whereas the December 1992 question asked about "a bill that would require companies employing more than 50 people to grant up to 12 weeks of unpaid leave to employees."
14. We are somewhat restricted in how we can group occupations by the limited job classifications available in one of our main sources of survey data, the Roper Trends data set. The Roper occupation variable includes only ten options, lumping together some job types that we might otherwise choose to split into different categories. For example, service workers and protective workers are in a single category. In contrast, the NES and GSS surveys query respondents about their occupations in far greater detail.
15. We considered civilian nonfarm employment. Where possible, we dropped the small number of farm workers and farm and small business owners from the data sets. The Roper occupation categories follow the main groupings used by the U.S. Census for the most part, but Roper also includes a separate "owner—small retail store or business" category. Depending on the type of shop or business and the type of work performed by the owner, such small-business owners could be assigned to any of the four main occupation groups we examine. The Roper occupation codes do not contain additional details about what individuals in this owner group sell or do, so we excluded this small category (less than 3 percent of the entire sample) from our analysis. Not surprisingly, owners are less supportive of family leave than all of the other Roper occupation types (except the very small number of farmers), and virtually none of them report being members of a union. The Roper occupation variable did not distinguish between farm and nonfarm laborers, so we were not able to exclude farm workers for the Roper data. We also dropped members of the armed forces (again, except for the Roper data). In the 1990s, the white- and blue-collar groups each constituted slightly more than 30 percent of the workforce, while the managerial and professional category represented slightly more than 20 percent. The remaining 10 percent were service and protective workers.
16. Occupation is sometimes included in socioeconomic status measures. However, we consider occupation separately in our analysis, so it was excluded from the socioeconomic status measure.
17. The Roper education question was "What was the last grade of regular school that you completed—not counting specialized schools like secretarial, art or trade schools?" The household income question was "Now here is a list of income categories. (HAND RESPONDENT CARD.) Would you call off the letter of the category that best describes the combined annual income of all members of this household, including wages or salary, pensions, interest or dividends, and all other sources?"

18. Creating these quintiles is rather complicated for longitudinal data. One other possibility would be simply to use a fixed set of nominal categories, for example, to compare over time those who never finished high school with college graduates. Since socioeconomic status is ordinarily considered to be multidimensional—composed of education and income—we could even make combinations of nominal categories, such as those with graduate degrees and family incomes over $75,000 or high school dropouts with incomes below $15,000. The problem with this approach is that categories that look the same over time are not really the same. For one thing, the proportion of respondents in such categories will change substantially during the period under investigation. For example, in 1960, 41.1 percent of American adults had completed high school; by 1990 that figure had risen to 77.6 percent. See U.S. Bureau of the Census, *Statistical Abstract of the United States, 1996,* 116th ed. (Washington, DC: Government Printing Office, 1996), 159. Moreover, the meaning of such nominal categories changes over time. Obviously, as inflation erodes the value of the dollar, the purchasing power of any particular income is attenuated. At the same time, there has been steady escalation in the standard of living considered to be minimally adequate—or comfortably middle-class. See L. Rainwater, *What Money Buys: Inequality and the Social Meanings of Money* (New York: Basic Books, 1974), chapter 3.

    With respect to education, the rising level of education in the population has been accompanied by a transformation in the social meaning of any particular level of educational achievement. In fact, Nie, Junn, and Stehlik-Barry demonstrate that what matters for activity in politics is not the absolute level of educational attainment but the level of education relative to one's peers and, therefore, that a college degree was associated with much greater political activity a generation ago, when completing college was rarer than it is today. See N.H. Nie, J. Junn, and K. Stehlik-Barry, *Education and Democratic Citizenship in America* (Chicago: University of Chicago Press, 1996).

19. The content and number of response options for both the income and education questionnaire items also varied over time. The dollar amounts of the income response options changed frequently over time—there were six different sets of response options, with eight to eleven income ranges. When a respondent refused to answer this question, we used a measure of the interviewer's estimate of household income level. However, this estimate was available only for studies 74-03 through 86-10. For the education item, the response options changed once. For studies 73-09 through 78-02, the four categories recorded were no school, grade school (1–8), high school (9–12), and college (13–16+). For studies 78-03 through 94-06, the categories expanded to seven: no school, 0–8 years, 9–11, 12, 13–15, 16, and 17 or more years.

20. It is usually possible to get at least as many categories as one less than the sum of the number of categories from each measure. This follows if the first measure is scored 1 to m and the second 1 to n. Then the possible sums of the combined measure are all integers between 2 and $(m + n)$. This amounts to $(m + n - 1)$ categories. If the two measures are perfectly correlated, then there can be no more than $\min(m,n)$ categories (where m is the number of categories in the first measure and n is the number in the second measure), but in the usual case with imperfect correlation, the number of categories is at least $(m + n - 1)$ and usually more.

21. The initial decision to combine the measures immediately raised three additional issues. First, over what time period should we construct SES ranks? Second, how should each separate measure be scored to make maximum use of the information it contains? Third, how should the two scorings be combined? Because we want rankings for each separate national sample, the answer to the first question is that the index should be constructed separately for each study, and quintiles should be constructed for each study from this index. There is no doubt about this, but there is some question about how to obtain the information needed for scoring each measure separately and combining the two measures.

Our approach to scoring the separate measures and combining the two measures was to do a principal components analysis of the two measures for a group of studies covering a period of time (usually more than one study) during which we had, for each measure, items with the same categories. The principal components analysis "solves" the problem of scoring by forming z-scores from the raw data. It "solves" the problem of combining the two measures by taking the first principal component of these two measures. Invariably, the two measures contribute about equally to this first principal component, and the component explains about 70 to 73 percent of the variance in each measure for the Roper studies. We chose to analyze groups of studies because we worried that analyzing each study separately would lead, because of sample variability, to quite different principal components. This method led to very stable component loadings across studies.

The scores on the principal component from the two measures provided enough separate categories so that approximations to quintiles of between 16 and 24 percent per quintile were possible for the Roper data. Groups of exactly 20 percent for either data set could not be created directly because the discrete categories had many tied cases. To break these ties, we added a very small random number (on the order of .000001) to the principal component to break the ties. With this modification, true quintiles became possible because the people in the tied category were randomly divided into the two nearest quintiles, although each quintile includes some people who might really belong in the quintile above or below them. Because we do not have enough information to make the proper assignment, it is clearly better to assign ambiguous cases randomly to finish up a quintile than to have quintiles of uneven sizes.

22. All of the Roper interviews were conducted face-to-face with a representative sample of the population of the continental United States, age eighteen and older. Respondents' sex and race were coded by interviewers, rather than being ascertained through interview questions. From 1973 through 1976, respondents' ages were estimated by interviewers, but from 1977 through 1994, respondents were asked to specify their age ranges.

23. Married respondents selected the first option in the question "Are you married, single, widowed, separated or divorced?" The category of employed included both part- and full-time workers: "Are you at present employed, either full-time or part-time?"

24. Roper respondents were asked, "What is your religious affiliation, if any—Protestant, Catholic, Jewish or what?" Responses were coded into five categories: Protestant, Catholic, Jewish, other, and none.

25. The Roper party identification question was stated: "Regardless of how you may have voted in the past, what do you usually consider yourself—a Democrat, a Republican, some other party, or what?" In addition to Democratic and Republican identification, volunteered responses of "independent," no party affiliation, and "don't know" were recorded.

26. The Roper survey samples did not include individuals younger than eighteen. The bottom socioeconomic status quintile of a representative sample of all U.S. residents would contain both more children and more elderly than the overall population.

27. All Roper respondents, regardless of employment status at the time of the interviews, were asked, "Do you, or does anyone in your family living here at home belong to a labor union?"

28. Obviously, these simple data obscure complex social relationships that would involve a separate research enterprise to disentangle. For example, it is well known that the elderly have lower levels of education and that African Americans are disproportionately Protestant.

29. The lines displayed in Figure 10-3 as well as in Figures 10-4, 10-5, 10-6, 10-9, 10-10, 10-11, and 10-12 are loess curves with the smoothing parameter set to 0.30. Loess is a nonparametric smoothing technique that reduces the effect of outliers. For an applied

discussion, see W.G. Jacoby, "Loess: A Nonparametric, Graphical Tool for Depicting Relationships Between Variables," *Electoral Studies* 19 (1999): 577–613.

30. See United States Bureau of Labor Statistics, "Union Members in 2000," USDL 01-21, ftp://ftp.bls.gov/pub/news.release/History/union2.01182001.news, for an overview of unionization rates by occupation and other characteristics.

31. See M.B. MacKuen, R.S. Erikson, and J.A. Stimson, "Macropartisanship," *American Political Science Review* 86 (1989): 1,125–42.

32. The left-out groups were nonunion workers (for union members); all nonworkers, including unemployed (for the four occupational groups); men (for women); top quintile (for the four socioeconomic status quintiles); people ages eighteen to twenty-nine (for the three age groups); and those without children younger than eighteen (for those with children younger than eighteen).

33. "If you had a say in making up the federal budget this year, for which of the following programs would you like to see spending increased and for which would you like to see spending decreased . . . Child care?" The response categories were *increased, same,* or *decreased.* The other question was: "Do you think government should provide child care assistance to low and middle income working parents, or isn't it the government's business?"

34. The exact GSS wording in 1996 was: "Should employers offer this option: Offer paid time off to new parents?"

35. For the other issues, the difference between union member and nonunion worker support was as follows: NES health care item, 5.5 percent; GSS health care item, 4.3 percent; NES item on funding for child care, 2.9 percent; NES item on funding for child care for low- and middle- income workers, -2.8 percent. The range was -2.8 percent to 5.5 percent, and the average was about 2.5 percent.

36. The NES question was as follows: "There is much concern about the rapid rise in medical and hospital costs. Some people feel there should be a government insurance plan which would cover all medical and hospital expenses for everyone. Suppose these people are at one end of a scale, at point 1. Others feel that all medical expenses should be paid by individuals, and through private insurance plans like Blue Cross. Suppose these people are at the other end, at point 7. And of course, some people have opinions somewhere in between at points 2, 3, 4, 5, 6. Where would you place yourself on this scale, or haven't you thought much about this?" The data in the text summarize results for 1984, 1988, 1992, 1994 and 1996.

The GSS question was very similar, except that it was on a five-point scale: "In general, some people think that it is the responsibility of the government in Washington to see to it that people have help in paying for doctors and hospital bills. Others think that these matters are not the responsibility of the federal government and that people should take care of these things themselves." Respondents are handed a card with five categories, with the first labeled "I strongly agree it is the responsibility of government to help"; the third, "I agree with both answers"; and the fifth, "I strongly agree people should take care of themselves." They are then asked, "Where would you place yourself on this scale, or haven't you made up your mind on this?" The results in the text summarize results for 1975, 1983, 1984, 1986, 1987, 1988, 1989, 1990, 1991, 1993, 1994, 1996 and 1998.

37. Supporters were respondents who chose points 1, 2, or 3 on the NES scale and points 1 or 2 on the GSS scale.

38. The survey asked: "Now here is a list of things some people do about government or politics. (HAND RESPONDENT CARD.) Have you happened to have done any of those things in the past year? (IF 'YES') Which ones?" The list of activities was as follows: "Written your congressman or senator; Attended a political rally or speech; Attended a public meeting on town or school affairs; Held or run for political office; Served on a committee for some local organization; Served as an officer of some club or organization; Written a letter to the paper; Signed a petition; Worked for a political party; Made a

speech; Written an article for a magazine or newspaper; Been a member of some group like the League of Women Voters, or some other group interested in better government."

39. R.D. Putnam, *Bowling Alone: The Collapse and Revival of American Community* (New York: Simon & Schuster, 2000).

Work, Family, and Children's Consumer Culture
Juliet Schor

For research assistance on trends in commercialization, I thank Eli Lambert, Leah Plunkett, and Anna White; for bibliographic assistance, Shauna Shames and Suzy Conway of Countway Library, Harvard Medical School; for financial assistance on commercialization trends, the Center for a New American Dream; and for general project support, the Philanthropic Collaborative.

1. J. Schor, *The Overworked American: The Unexpected Decline of Leisure* (New York: Basic Books, 1992).
2. J.T. Bond, E. Galinsky, and J.E. Swanberg, *The 1997 National Study of the Changing Workforce,* report no. 2 (New York: Families and Work Institute, 1998).
3. A. Hochschild, *The Time Bind: When Work Becomes Home and Home Becomes Work* (New York: Metropolitan, 1997).
4. On requirements for occupational success, see J. Waldfogel, "The Effect of Children on Women's Wages," *American Sociological Review* 62 (1997): 209–17; J. Waldfogel, "Understanding the 'Family Gap' in Pay for Women with Children," *Journal of Economic Perspectives* 12, no. 1 (1998): 137–56; J. Williams, *Unbending Gender: Why Family and Work Conflict and What to Do About It* (New York: Oxford University Press, 2000).
5. For more on the complementarity perspective, see R.C. Barnett and C. Rivers, *She Works/He Works* (San Francisco: HarperCollins, 1996); S. Chira, *A Mother's Place: Choosing Work and Family Without Guilt or Blame* (New York: HarperPerennial, 1998); F.J. Crosby, *Juggling: The Unexpected Advantages of Balancing Career and Home* (New York: Free Press, 1991).

   Despite their apparent differences, the conflict and complementarity strands of literature are not contradictory. There are overall positive impacts from combining roles, engaging in satisfying market work, and convergence in gender roles that have been identified in the literature. However, at the margin, the temporal and intensity demands from work are excessive, and in conflict with household and family needs. (To put the situation in economic language, total utility is positive, but marginal utility is negative.) Indeed, if there is not a functional "market" to determine working hours and intensity of work (as I argued in *The Overworked American*), then there can be a persistent disequilibrium in which workplace demands exceed employees' preferences and exert persistent negative impacts on the family or household economy. In such a situation, employees do not have the opportunity to optimize their choice of working hours or intensity of work along a continuum (as standard economic theory assumes they do). Instead, employees are forced into all-or-nothing choices in that either they retain the job and work more than is preferred or they quit. In this view, persistent work-family conflict is caused by employers' failure to offer a "complete market" in hours and intensity of work.

   A second possible (although, I believe, less plausible) cause of work-family conflict is a disjuncture between the preferences of employees and the needs of those who depend on them for unpaid services. Parents could be working more hours than are compatible with children's well-being because, at the margin, they enjoy working more than caretaking or because they prefer earning income to caring for children. This is the argument of conservatives who believe mothers should not hold paying jobs.
6. On children and consumerism, see E. Chin, *Purchasing Power: Black Kids and American*

Consumer Culture (Minneapolis: University of Minnesota Press, 2001); S. Kline, *Out of the Garden: Toys and Children's Culture in the Age of TV Marketing* (London: Verso, 1993); E. Seiter, *Sold Separately: Parents and Children in Consumer Culture* (New Brunswick: Rutgers University Press, 1993); S.R. Steinberg and J.L. Kincheloe, eds., *Kinderculture: The Corporate Construction of Childhood* (Boulder, CO: Westview Press, 1998).

7. J. McNeal, "Tapping the Three Kids' Markets," *American Demographics* 20 (1998): 36.

8. B. Horovitz, "Targeting the Kindermarket," *USA Today,* March 3, 2000, 1.

9. See http://www.teenresearch.com.

10. J. McNeal, *Kids as Customers* (New York: Lexington Books, 1992), Table 3-4.

11. S. Reese, "Kidmoney: Children as Big Business," *Education and Arts Policy Review* 99, no. 3 (1998): 37–40.

12. See Kaiser Family Foundation report, "Kids and Media at the New Millennium," November 1999, Tables 7 and 8-A, 19–20. Available at: http://www.kkf.org/entmedia/1535-index.cfm.

13. M. Gladwell, "The Coolhunt," in J.B. Schor and D.B. Holt, eds., *The Consumer Society Reader* (New York: New Press, 2000), 360–74.

14. M.B.W. Tabor, "Schools Profit from Offering Pupils," *New York Times,* April 5, 1999, 1.

15. On Channel One, see R. Fox, *Harvesting Minds: How TV Commercials Control Kids* (Westport: Praeger, 1996). A parallel Internet effort—ZapMe!—has recently withdrawn from the market. ZapMe! "gave" schools computers in exchange for guaranteeing four hours per day of pupil use. Students were exposed to advertising on the site, their movements were tracked, and demographic information was collected, which was then sold for residential direct mail marketing. For more on ZapMe!, see A. Molnar, "ZapMe! Linking Schoolhouse and Marketplace in a Seamless Web," *Phi Delta Kappan,* April 2000, 601–3.

16. Corporations are also providing "curricula," which they send unsolicited to teachers and schools. Oil companies write environmental curricula, and junk-food companies produce nutrition curricula. See Consumers' Union, *Captive Kids: A Report on Commercial Pressures on Kids at School* (Yonkers, NY: Consumers' Union, 1995).

17. See, for example, the kids and commercialism material on http://www.newdream.org and the commercial alert section of http://www.essential.org.

18. On the American Psychological Association stance, see A.D. Kanner and T. Kasser, "Stuffing Our Kids: Should Psychologists Help Advertisers Manipulate Children?" (2000), available at: http://www.commercialalert.org/psychology/stuffingourkids.html. An earlier version of this paper appeared in the February 2000 issue of *The California Psychologist.*

19. The Academy's Web site, http://www.aap.org, contains numerous articles and press releases warning parents about the adverse health impacts of television. See also American Academy of Pediatrics Committee on Communications, "The Commercialization of Children's Television," *Pediatrics* 89, no. 2 (1992): 343–44; W.H. Dietz and V.C. Strasburger, "Children, Adolescents, and Television," *Current Problems in Pediatrics* 21, no. 1 (1991): 8–32; D.G. Singer and W. Benton, "Caution: Television May Be Hazardous to a Child's Mental Health," *Developmental and Behavioral Pediatrics* 10, no. 5 (1989): 259–61.

20. "Watch Out for Children: A Mothers' Statement to Advertisers," at http://www.rebelmothers.org.

21. Question wording was not always ideal (for instance, question 1 may be described as leading). Table 11-1 as presented in this chapter is also available at http://www.newdream.org.

22. Again, question wording was not ideal, in particular because of the double use of the word *pressures*. This will be corrected if there is a resurvey.

23. See also A.D. Walsh, R.N. Laczniak, and L. Carlson, "Mothers' Preferences for Regulating Children's Television," *Journal of Advertising* 27, no. 3 (1998): 23–36.

24. For an uncritical view, see McNeal, *Kids as Customers.*

25. For some interesting and sophisticated critiques of these ideas, see H. Jenkins, ed., *The Children's Culture Reader* (New York: New York University Press, 1998).

26. P. Ariès, *Centuries of Childhood: A Social History of Family Life* (New York: Knopf, 1962). Ariès argued that before the sixteenth century, children were regarded as "miniature adults" (in contrast to today's dominant paradigms that define childhood as a separate stage of human development). Aspects of the Ariès thesis remain controversial, such as the nature of affective relations between parents and children, and the extent of maltreatment of children and how it affected infant mortality. On these, see L.A. Pollock, *Forgotten Children: Parent-Child Relations from 1500 to 1900* (Cambridge: Cambridge University Press, 1983). However, these debates are not central to this discussion.

27. N. Postman, *The Disappearance of Childhood* (New York: Random House, 1984).

28. V. Zelizer, *Pricing the Priceless Child: The Changing Social Value of Children* (New York: Basic Books, 1985).

29. For other literature in this genre, see especially N. Field, "The Child as Laborer and Consumer: The Disappearance of Childhood in Contemporary Japan," in S. Stephens, ed., *Children and the Politics of Culture* (Princeton, NJ: Princeton University Press, 1995), as well as S. Stephens, ed., "Introduction," *Children and the Politics of Culture* (Princeton, NJ: Princeton University Press, 1995).

    Following Ariès, Postman contended that childhood emerged with the spread of literacy. In the oral culture of the Middle Ages, childhood ended at about age seven, when full speech was achieved. By contrast, a culture based on literacy requires a longer developmental period in which children gradually learn to discipline their bodies and repress their physical energies—prerequisites for long hours of reading and studying. The spread of literacy led to age-based schooling in the form of primary schools, and to the spatial and social isolation of children. Children were thought of no longer as miniature adults, but as unformed ones. Eventually, literacy was supplemented by moral education, the teaching of manners, and inculcation of discipline. Childhood also functioned as a stage in which youth were protected from and kept ignorant of a host of shameful and negative features of adult society, such as violence, cruelty, sickness, death, and, most importantly, sex. This was in contrast to the earlier era in which children were fully exposed to adult society. It has also been argued that by the twentieth century, adults had adopted a more humane and empathic attitude toward children.

30. As evidence for his thesis, Postman cited trends such as the eroticization of children, the rise in juvenile crime rates, the rise of sexual activity, drug, and alcohol use among youth, a decline in children's games, and the disappearance of specialized clothing styles for children.

31. On childhood as a carefree period, see Postman, *Disappearance of Childhood,* 67. On the sacralization of childhood, see Zelizer, *Pricing the Priceless Child.* As both Postman and Zelizer understood, social class has always figured prominently in constructions of childhood. Childhood was mainly a project of the middle class, which could afford that extra-*commercium* space for its children. Among the working class and the poor, isolation from the market economy came later and was never as complete.

32. For an argument that this is nostalgic and false in the case of adults, see D. Miller, "Introduction," in D. Miller, ed., *Acknowledging Consumption* (London: Routledge, 1995).

33. On toys in the United States, see G. Cross, *Kids' Stuff: Toys and the Changing World of American Childhood* (Cambridge, MA: Harvard University Press, 1997).

34. D. Cook, "The Rise of the Toddler as Subject and as Merchandising Category in the 1930s," in Mark Gottdiener, ed., *Consumers, Commodification and Media Culture* (Lanham, MD: Rowman & Littlefield, 2000); D. Cook, "The Visual Commoditization of Childhood: A Case Study of a Children's Clothing Trade Journal, 1920s–1940s," *Journal of Social Science* 3, nos. 1–2 (1999): 21–40; D. Cook, "The Other 'Child Study,' " *Sociological Quarterly* 41, no. 3 (2000): 487–507.

35. On children and consumption patterns, see also Postman, *Disappearance of Childhood.*

36. Retailers allowed the shoplifting because it complemented actual consumer expenditures; they gave easy credit, even when the husbands' approval was in doubt or had been explicitly denied, because it expanded sales. See E.S. Abelson, *When Ladies Go A-Thieving* (New York: Oxford University Press, 1989); R. Ohmann, *Selling Culture* (London: Verso, 1996); E.D. Rappaport, *Shopping for Pleasure: Women in the Making of London's West End* (Princeton, NJ: Princeton University Press, 2000).

37. On advertising targeting mothers, see R. Marchand, *Advertising the American Dream: Making Way for Modernity, 1920–1940* (Berkeley: University of California Press, 1985): 228–32; E. Seiter, *Sold Separately: Parents and Children in Consumer Culture* (New Brunswick, NJ: Rutgers University Press, 1993), chapters 2–3.

38. For accounts of marketing trends, see D.S. Acuff, *What Kids Buy and Why* (New York: Free Press, 1997); G. del Vecchio, *Creating Ever-Cool: A Marketer's Guide to a Kid's Heart* (Gretna, LA: Pelican, 1998).

39. On advertising's undermining of adult authority, see L. Coco and R. Nader, *Children First: A Parent's Guide to Fighting Corporate Predators* (Washington, DC: Corporate Accountability Research Group, 1996).

40. This research is described in detail in J. Schor, *Born to Buy: Marketing and the Transformation of Childhood and Culture* (New York: Scribner's, 2004).

41. For more on Nickelodeon's programming strategy and antiadult bias, see ibid.

42. An example is a Nickelodeon ad with a smiling child in an SUV. The text reads: "A nation of kids and they Drive purchases; Kids influence 62% of family SUV and minivan purchases! Nickelodeon owns 50% of the K2-11 GRP's in Kids' Commercial TV." See *Adbusters Magazine* 30 (2000): 22.

43. For more on the influence market, see Horovitz, "Targeting the Kindermarket."

44. I am indebted to Eli Lambert for this point.

45. On children's recognition of Joe Camel, see P.M. Fischer, M.P. Schwartz, J.W. Richards Jr., A.O. Goldstein, and T.H. Rojas, "Brand Logo Recognition by Children Aged 3 to 6 Years: Mickey Mouse and Old Joe the Camel," *Journal of the American Medical Association* 266, no. 22 (1991): 3145–53; C.L. Hays, "The Media Business: Advertising," *New York Times,* March 26, 1998, 5.

46. Marketers use the language of "owning" children: "If you own this child at an early age, you can own this child for years to come"; "Hey, I want to own the kid younger and younger." Quoted in G. Ruskin, "Why They Whine: How Corporations Prey on Our Children," *Mothering* 97 (1999): 41–50.

47. On mothers' labor force participation rates, see L. Leete and J. Schor, "The Great American Time Squeeze," briefing paper, Economic Policy Institute, Washington, DC, 1992; J. Schor, *The Overspent American: Upscaling, Downshifting and the New Consumer* (New York: Basic Books, 1998).

48. For the Current Population Survey results, see Council of Economic Advisers, "Families and the Labor Market, 1969–1999: Analyzing the 'Time Crunch,' " Council of Economic Advisers, Washington, DC, May 1999, 3–4.

49. Leete and Schor, "The Great American Time Squeeze."

50. Ibid.

51. For a discussion of trends in parental time with children, see J. Schor, "The Time Crunch Among American Parents," in S. Hewlett, N. Rankin, and C. West, eds., *Taking Parenting Public* (Lanham, MD: Rowman & Littlefield, 2002).

52. Kaiser Family Foundation, "Kids and Media," Table 8-F, 24.

53. Ibid.

54. E.H. Woodward, "Media in the Home 2000," survey series no. 7, Annenburg Public Policy Center, University of Pennsylvania, 2000, 16.

55. Kaiser Family Foundation, "Kids and Media." See also Singer and Benton, "Caution: Television." However, compare the rates reported in Woodward, "Media in the Home."

56. For citations and review articles, see J. Schor, "Should Children Be Protected from Mar-

keters? The Commercialization of American Childhood," Boston College, August 2002; Schor, *Born to Buy.*

57. For information on the AAP's campaign on media, see http://www.aap.org/family/mediaimpact.htm.

58. On imperfections in the market, see, for example, Schor, *Overworked American.*

59. K. Greve, "The Impact of Parental Working Hours on Discretionary Expenditures on Children in Upper Income Families," A.B. thesis, Department of Economics, Harvard University, 1995.

60. B. Sutton-Smith, *Toys as Culture* (New York: Gardner Press, 1986), chapter 3.

61. T. Kasser, *The High Price of Materialism* (Cambridge, MA: MIT Press, 2002).

62. T. Robinson, M.N. Saphir, H.C. Kraemer, A. Varady, and K.F. Haydel, "Effects of Reducing Television Viewing on Children's Requests for Toys: A Randomized Controlled Trial," *Journal of Developmental Behavioral Pediatrics* 22 (2001): 179–94.

63. For earlier studies, see, for example, R.P. Adler, G.S. Lesser, L. Merengoff, T.S. Robertson, J.R. Rossiter, and S. Ward, *The Effects of Television Advertising on Children* (Lexington, MA: Heath, 1980).

64. The cross-country analysis is reported in J. van Erva, *Television and Child Development,* 2nd ed. (Mahwah, NJ: Erlbaum, 1998), 100. For a full discussion of the literature on research regarding marketing's impact on children's consumerism, see M.E. Goldberg, "A Quasi-Experiment Assessing the Effectiveness of TV Advertising Directed to Children," *Journal of Marketing Research* 27 (1990): 445–54; Schor, *Born to Buy.*

65. M. Dolliver, "What Do I Want to Be When I Grow Up? Filthy Rich!" *Adweek,* October 5, 1998.

66. Woodward, "Media in the Home," Figure 3.7.

67. On the negative effects of materialism on well-being, see Kasser, *High Price of Materialism;* T. Kasser and R.M. Ryan, "A Dark Side of the American Dream: Correlates of Financial Success as a Central Life Aspiration," *Journal of Personality and Social Psychology* 65, 2 (1993): 410–22.

68. E. Galinsky, *Ask the Children: What America's Children Really Think About Working Parents* (New York: Morrow, 1999), 339–40.

69. For this argument, see Schor, "Should Children Be Protected from Marketers?"

Europe Advanced While the United States Lagged
Sheila B. Kamerman

1. In this paper, I use the term "working parents" or "working families" to refer to labor force status, not to imply that parenting, by itself, is not work.

2. Usually included here are maternity, paternity, and parental leaves and benefits, child or family allowances, child-conditioned tax benefits, child-conditioned social insurance benefits, child-conditioned housing benefits, early childhood care and education benefits and services, advanced maintenance or guaranteed minimum child support, child welfare services, parent education, child and family support and preservation services, special benefits and services for children with disabilities, school meals, home help and home health services, maternal and child health care, and family law.

3. Among the OECD countries, those that do not provide a child or family allowance are South Korea, Mexico, Turkey, and the United States.

4. MISSOC (Mutual Information System on Social Protection in the Member States of the European Union), European Commission, Brussels, 2002; Social Security Administration (SSA), *Social Security Programs Throughout the World, 1999* (Washington, DC: Government Printing Office, 1999).

5. A. Gauthier, *The State and the Family* (Oxford: Oxford University Press, 1996); M. Gordon, *Social Security Programs in Industrial Countries* (New York: Cambridge University

Press, 1988); S.B. Kamerman and A.J. Kahn, eds., *Family Policy: Government and Families in Fourteen Countries* (New York: Columbia University Press, 1978); S.B. Kamerman and A.J. Kahn, "Investing in Children: Government Expenditures for Children and Their Families in Western Industrialized Countries," in G.A. Cornia and S. Danziger, eds., *Child Poverty and Deprivation in the Industrialized Countries, 1945–1995* (Oxford: Oxford University Press, 1997).

6. Belgium, Greece, Italy, Portugal, and Spain are the EU countries where the benefit is linked to employment.

7. Gauthier, *State and the Family;* Gordon, *Social Security Programs.*

8. SSA, *Social Security Programs;* R. Titmuss, *Problems of Social Policy* (London: HMSO and Longmans Green, 1950).

9. Kamerman and Kahn, "Investing in Children."

10. A.J. Kahn and S.B. Kamerman, eds., *Child Support: From Debt Collections to Social Policy* (Newbury Park, CA: Sage, 1988).

11. A policy of providing advanced maintenance payments had been introduced in the late 1930s in Denmark and Sweden, in 1976 in Austria, and in the 1980s in France, Germany, and Norway. See S.B. Kamerman and A.J. Kahn, *Income Transfers for Families with Children: An Eight-Country Study* (Philadelphia: Temple University Press, 1983).

12. J. Bradshaw, J. Ditch, H. Holmes, and P. Whiteford, *Support for Children: A Comparison of Arrangements in Fifteen Countries* (London: HMSO, 1993); Kahn and Kamerman, *Income Transfers.*

13. S. Pedersen, *Family, Dependence, and the Origins of the Welfare State* (New York: Cambridge University Press, 1993), 413.

14. H. Land, "The Child Benefit Fiasco," in K. Jones, ed., *Yearbook of Social Policy* (London: Routledge and Kegan Paul, 1977).

15. A family wage is a wage designed to support a male breadwinner, his wife, and two children. Several countries have enacted a family wage as a minimum wage in the past, including Australia, New Zealand, and the Netherlands, but no country currently supports such a wage.

16. Gauthier, *State and the Family.*

17. H. Immervoll, H. Sutherland, and K. DeVos, "Reducing Child Poverty in the European Union: The Role of Child Benefits," in K. Vleminckx and T. Smeeding, eds., *Child Well-Being, Child Poverty, and Child Policy in Modern Nations* (Bristol: Policy Press, 2001); Kahn and Kamerman, *Income Transfers;* S.B. Kamerman, M. Newman, J. Waldfogel, and J. Brooks-Gunn, "Social Policies, Family Types, and Child Outcomes in Selected OECD Countries," OECD working paper, 2003.

18. For more information about global developments and developments in the OECD countries, see S.B. Kamerman, "From Maternity to Parental Leave Policies: Women's Health, Employment, and Child and Family Well-Being," *Journal of the Medical Women's Association* 55, no. 2 (2000): 98–99. See also S.B. Kamerman, "Parental Leaves: An Essential Ingredient in Early Childhood Care and Education," in L. Sherrod, ed., *Social Policy Report* (Ann Arbor, MI: Society for Research in Child Development, 2000); SSA, *Social Security Programs.* For more information about the EU countries, see P. Moss and F. Deven, eds., *Parental Leaves: Progress or Pitfall?* (Brussels: CBGS, 1999).

19. They were enacted at a time when the United States was also enacting protective legislation for women, but in relation to shorter working hours, rather than maternity protection. See S.B. Kamerman, A.J. Kahn, and P. Kingston, *Maternity, Policies and Working Women* (New York: Columbia University Press, 1983).

20. Gauthier, *State and the Family.*

21. Of some interest, four of the five U.S. states with temporary disability insurance (TDI) policies in place enacted their legislation during or shortly after World War II (between 1941 and 1950). Only Hawaii enacted its law later (1969). The history of these policies— why they were enacted and where, and why none were enacted subsequently—has yet

to be told. As a result of federal legislation enacted in 1978, these TDI policies cover pregnancy and maternity, typically providing new mothers a cash benefit for six to twelve weeks at those times, while they are away from work.

In Canada, a job-protected maternity leave of at least seventeen weeks was enacted by the federal government and the provinces during the 1970s, and through the 1971 unemployment insurance reform legislation, the federal government provided a cash benefit during that leave. Adoption was included in 1984, and an additional ten-week paid parental leave was added in 1990. For details, see M. Baker, "Canada," in S.B. Kamerman and A.J. Kahn, eds., *Family Change and Family Policies in Great Britain, Canada, New Zealand, and the United States* (New York: Oxford University Press, 1997); M. Baker, *Canadian Family Policies* (Toronto: University of Toronto Press, 1995); and S.B. Kamerman, *Maternity and Parental Benefits and Leaves: An International Review* (New York: Columbia University Center for the Social Sciences, 1980). In January 2001, the parental leave was extended to fifty-two weeks. See D.S. Lero, "Research on Parental Leave Policies and Children's Development: Implications for Policy Makers and Service Providers," Center of Excellence and Early Childhood Development, Montreal, February 14, 2003. Available at: http://excellence-earlychildhood.ca (accessed April 13, 2004).

22. Leaves provided as a result of collective bargaining agreements or voluntarily by employers may supplement the statutory provision and raise the benefit level or extend its duration.

23. D. Levine, *Poverty and Society* (Rutgers, NJ: Rutgers University Press, 1988), 55.

24. S. Koven and M. Koven, *Mothers of a New World* (New York: Routledge, 1993).

25. Gauthier, *State and the Family.*

26. ILO, *Equal Opportunities and Equal Treatment for Men and Women Workers: Workers with Family Responsibilities* (Geneva: ILO, 1980; 1981; 1997); *Equal Opportunities and Equal Treatment for Men and Women in Employment* (Geneva: ILO, 1985); *Maternity Benefits in the Eighties* (Geneva: ILO, 1985); *Maternity Protection at Work* (Geneva: ILO, 1997).

27. Two years later, women working in agriculture were included as well.

28. ILO, *Equal Opportunities,* 1980; 1981; 1985.

29. See ILO Web site: http://www.ilo.org/public/english/bureau/inf/pr/2000/28/htm.

30. SSA, *Social Security Programs.*

31. Ibid.

32. ILO, *Maternity Benefits,* 1.

33. S.B. Kamerman and A.J. Kahn, *Child Care, Family Benefits, and Working Parents* (New York: Columbia University Press, 1981).

34. European Commission Network on Child Care and Other Measures to Reconcile Employment and Family Responsibilities, *Leave Arrangements for Workers with Children* (Brussels: European Commission, 1994); see also Moss and Deven, *Parental Leaves.*

35. See also http://www.childpolicyintl.org/table111.pdf and Kamerman, "Parental Leave Policies." In *Social Policy Report* (Ann Arbor, MI: Society for Research in Child Development, 2000).

36. Because of space constraints, I have not discussed paternity leaves, but these are a minor add-on to the primary maternity and parental leave policies.

37. Only in Sweden is there high use of parental leave by fathers; that is partly in response to the governments' strong efforts to encourage such behavior. Recently, there is a growing effort to increase fathers' use of parental leaves by including a "use it or lose it" provision—namely, if fathers do not use a portion of the parental leave (now months), it is a lost benefit.

38. These services include center day care, family day care, pre-kindergarten, kindergarten, nursery schools, play groups, drop-in centers, and so on.

39. S.B. Kamerman, *Early Childhood Education and Care: An International Overview* (Paris: OECD, 2000), available at: http://www.childpolicyintl.org; S.B. Kamerman, ed., *Early*

Childhood Education and Care (New York: Institute for Child and Family Policy, 2001); OECD, *Starting Strong: Early Childhood Education and Care* (Paris: OECD, 2001).

40. Kamerman, *Early Childhood Education.*

41. Compulsory education for primary school was enacted in Britain in 1870, in France in 1882, in Sweden in 1842, in Italy in 1860, and in Germany and the United States in the 1870s and 1880s.

42. M. Kellmer-Pringle and S. Naidoo, *Early Child Care in Britain* (New York: Gordon and Breach, 1975); J. Tizard, P. Moss, and J. Perry, *All Our Children: Pre-School Services in a Changing Society* (London: Temple Smith/New Society, 1976).

43. M. David and I. Lezine, *Early Child Care in France* (New York: Gordon and Breach, 1975); F. Pistillo, "Preprimary Education and Care in Italy," in P.P. Olmsted and D.P. Weikart, eds., *How Nations Serve Young Children* (Ypsilanti, MI: High/Scope Press, 1989).

44. L. Gunnarsson, B.M. Korpi, and U. Nordenstam, *Early Childhood Education and Care Policy in Sweden* (Stockholm: Ministry of Education and Science, 1999).

45. Ibid.

46. Furthermore, in the United States, as in several other countries, there was an additional factor—namely, the division of responsibilities between federal and state governments, with the allocation of responsibility for education assigned to state governments.

47. S.B. Kamerman and A.J. Kahn, "Social Policy and Children in the United States and Europe," in J. Palmer, T. Smeeding, and B. Torrey, eds., *The Vulnerable* (Washington, DC: Urban Institute, 1988); Kamerman and Kahn, *Family Change and Family;* Kahn and Kamerman, *Child Support.*

48. Just as Germany had established old age, sickness, and maternity benefits in the early 1880s, Britain had invented unemployment insurance in 1911, but this benefit became generally established only in the period between the world wars.

49. G. Esping-Andersen, *Social Foundation of Postindustrialized Economy* (New York: Oxford University Press, 1999); G. Esping-Andersen, *Why We Need a New Welfare State* (New York: Oxford University Press, 2002); S.B. Kamerman, "Welfare States, Family Policies, and Early Childhood Education, Care, and Family Support: Options for the Central and Eastern European (CEE) and Commonwealth of Independent States (CIS) Countries."

50. Kahn and Kamerman, *Income Transfers.*

51. Of course, if in the post–September 11, 2001 era there are significant constraints imposed on immigration, the situation may change.

52. U.S. House of Representatives Committee on Ways and Means, *The Green Book 2000: Background Material on Programs Under the Jurisdiction of the Committee on Ways and Means* (Washington, DC: Government Printing Office, 2000).

53. C.J. Ruhm, "The Economic Consequences of Parental Leave Mandates: Lessons from Europe," *Quarterly Journal of Economics* 113 (1998): 285–317.

54. The relevant federal legislation was the Economic Opportunity Amendments of 1971, which made provision for comprehensive child development services for all children. The act was passed by the Congress but vetoed by President Richard Nixon.

Eliminating Economic Penalties on Caregivers
Nancy Folbre

This chapter draws from my book *The Invisible Heart: Economics and Family Values* (New York: The New Press, 2001) and from an article co-authored with Paula England entitled "Reforming the Social Contract: Public Support for Child Rearing in the U.S.," in G. Duncan and L. Chase-Lansdale, eds., *For Better or Worse: The Effects of Welfare Reform on Children* (New York: Russell Sage, 2002).

1. J. Stiglitz, *Economics of the Public Sector* (New York: Norton, 1988), 218.
2. R. Putnam, *Bowling Alone: The Collapse and Revival of American Community* (New York: Simon and Schuster, 2000).
3. Economists' views on care-related intrinsic motivations are discussed in P. England and N. Folbre, "The Cost of Caring," *Annals of the American Academy of Political and Social Science* 561 (1999): 39–51. See also Folbre, *Invisible Heart: Economics and Family Values.*
4. On caregiving and humans' biological makeup, see S.B. Hrdy, *Mother Nature: Natural Selection and the Female of the Species* (London: Chatto & Windus, 1999); E. Sober and D.S. Wilson, *Unto Others: The Evolution and Psychology of Unselfish Behavior* (Cambridge, MA: Harvard University Press, 1998).
5. The classic formulation of this view can be found in G.S. Becker and G. Stigler, "De Gustibus Non Est Disputandum," *American Economic Review* 67, no. 1 (1977): 76–90. See also M. Friedman and R. Friedman, *Free to Choose: A Personal Statement* (New York: Harcourt Brace, 1980).
6. N. Folbre, *Who Pays for the Kids? Gender and the Structures of Constraint* (New York: Routledge, 1994).
7. Ibid.
8. C. Goldin, *Understanding the Gender Gap: An Economic History of American Women* (New York: Oxford University Press, 1990).
9. J. Heintz and N. Folbre, *The Ultimate Field Guide to the U.S. Economy* (New York: The New Press, 2000), 34.
10. P. England, M. Budig, and N. Folbre, "The Public Benefits and Private Costs of Caring Labor," *Social Problems* 49, no. 4 (2003): 455–73.
11. For a good example of this point of view, see E. Burkett, *The Baby Boon: How Family-Friendly America Cheats the Childless* (New York: Free Press, 2000).
12. M. Lino, "Expenditures on Children by Families, Annual Report, U.S. Department of Agriculture, Center for Nutrition Policy and Promotion, 2000.
13. N. Folbre, "Children as Public Goods," *American Economic Review* 84, no. 2 (1994), 86–90.
14. Folbre, *Who Pays for the Kids?*; P. England and N. Folbre, "The Cost of Caring," *Annals of the American Academy of Political and Social Science* 561 (1999): 39–51.
15. D.J. Hernandez, *America's Children: Resources from Family, Government, and the Economy* (New York: Russell Sage Foundation, 1993).
16. L. Weitzman, *The Divorce Revolution: The Unexpected Social and Economic Consequences for Women and Children in America* (New York: Free Press, 1985).
17. B.R. Bergmann, "The Economic Risks of Being a Housewife," *American Economic Review* 7, no. 2 (1981): 81–86. See also P. England and G. Farkas, *Households, Employment, and Gender* (New York: Aldine, 1986).
18. J. Waldfogel, "The Effects of Children on Women's Wages," *American Sociological Review* 62, no. 2 (1997): 209–17.
19. M. Budig and P. England, "The Wage Penalty for Motherhood," *American Sociological Review* 66, no. 2 (2001): 204–25.
20. For more details, see A. Crittenden, *The Price of Motherhood* (New York: Metropolitan Books, 2001).
21. S.A. Hewlett and C. West, *The War Against Parents: What We Can Do for America's Beleaguered Moms and Dads* (New York: Houghton Mifflin, 1998), 36.
22. D. Bernheim, A. Schleifer, and L.H. Summers, "The Strategic Bequest Motive," *Journal of Political Economy* 93 (1985): 1045–76.
23. National Family Caregivers Association, "A Profile of Caregivers," member survey, 1997, available at: http://www.nfcacares.org/survey.html.
24. S. Rimer, "Study Details Sacrifices in Caring for Elderly Kin," *New York Times,* November 27, 1999, 9.

25. P. Arno, C. Levine, and M. Memmnott, "The Economic Value of Informal Caregiving," *Health Affairs* (March/April 1999), 182–88.

26. Martin Gilens, *Why Americans Hate Welfare* (Chicago: University of Chicago Press, 1999).

27. R. Haveman and B. Wolfe, "The Determinants of Children's Attainments: A Review of Methods and Findings," *Journal of Economic Literature* 33 (1995): 1831. For an alternative estimate of the value of parental time, see N. Folbre, "Valuing Parental Time: New Estimates of Expenditures on Children in the United States," paper presented at the meeting of the Allied Social Science Association, Atlanta, January 3–5, 2002.

28. For Steuerle's estimates, see Children's Defense Fund—Minnesota, "Family Tax Policies," available at: http://www.cdf-mn.org/family.htm (accessed November 19, 1999); see also L. Whittington, "Taxes and the Family: The Impact of the Tax Exemption for Dependents on Marital Fertility," *Demography* 29, no. 2 (1992): 215–26.

29. E. Wolff, "The Economic Status of Parents in Postwar America," paper prepared for the meeting of the National Parenting Association, September 20, 1996, available from Department of Economics, New York University.

30. For more discussion of family support issues, see Hewlett and West, *War Against Parents.*

31. U.S. Department of Health and Human Services, *Access to Child Care for Low Income Working Families,* available at: http://www.acf.dhhs.gov/news/press/2000/ccstudy.htm.

32. National Center for Education Statistics, *The Condition of Education 2000* (Washington, DC: Government Printing Office, 2000), Table 2-1.

33. D. Betson, "Alternative Estimates of the Cost of Children from the 1980–86 Consumer Expenditure Survey," special report no. 51, Institute for Research on Poverty, University of Wisconsin, Madison, 1990.

34. I. Garfinkel, "Economic Security for Children: From Means Testing and Bifurcation to Universality," in I. Garfinkel, S.S. McLanahan, and J.L. Hochschild, eds., *Social Policies for Children* (Washington, DC: Brookings Institution, 1996).

35. G. Mink, *Welfare's End* (Ithaca, NY: Cornell University Press, 1998).

36. Garfinkel, "Economic Security for Children."

37. R. Albelda, N. Folbre, and the Center for Popular Economics, *The War on the Poor: A Defense Manual* (New York: The New Press, 1996), 14.

38. The figure for the maximum TANF benefit in the median state is from U.S. House Ways and Means Committee, *Green Book 2000,* 106th Congress, 2nd session (Washington, DC: Government Printing Office, 2000), 390. Available at: http://www.access.gpo .gov/congress/wm001.html.

39. Citizens for Tax Justice, *The Hidden Entitlements,* part 3-1, available at: http://www.ctj .org/hid_ent/part-3/part3-1.htm

40. National Academy of Science, *Child Care for Low Income Families* (Washington, DC: National Academy Press, 1996). Available at: http://www.nap.edu/readingroom/books/ childcare.

41. U.S. House Ways and Means Committee, *Green Book 1998,* 105th Congress, 2nd session (Washington, DC: Government Printing Office, 1998), 684. Available at: http://www .access.gpo.gov/congress/wm001.html.

42. S. Hofferth, "Caring for Children at the Poverty Line," *Children and Youth Services Review* 12, no. 1/2 (1995): 1–31.

43. S. Long, "Childcare Assistance Under Welfare Reform: Early Responses by the States," Urban Institute, 1999. Available at: http://www.urban.org/url.cfm?ID-900265.

44. Social Security Bulletin, *Annual Statistical Supplement 2001* (Washington, DC: Government Printing Office, 2001), Table 5-A. Available at: http://www.ssa.gov/statistics/ Supplement/2001/5a.pdf.

45. Committee on Ways and Means, *Green Book 2000,* Table 7–10, 390.

46. G. Becker, quoted in R. Pear, "Thousands to Rally in Capital on Children's Behalf," *New York Times,* June 1, 1996, 10.

47. Kaus and others have insisted that social security pays benefits only to workers, but that is not true if you define workers as Kaus does, namely, as those who actually earn a wage. Spouses and survivors who have never worked for a wage enjoy substantial benefits.

48. L. Karoly, P.W. Greenwood, S.S. Everingham, J. Hoube, M.R. Kilburn, C.P. Rydell, M. Sanders, and J. Chiesa, *Investing in Our Children: What We Know and Don't Know About the Costs and Benefits of Early Childhood Interventions* (Santa Monica, CA: Rand, 1998); Children's Defense Fund, *The State of America's Children Yearbook, 1999* (Boston: Beacon Press, 1999).

49. French American Foundation, *Ready to Learn: The French System of Early Education and Care Offers Lessons for the United States* (New York: French American Foundation, 1999).

50. B. Bergmann and S. Helburn, *America's Child Care Problem: The Way Out* (London: Palgrave, 2002).

51. E. McCaffery, *Taxing Women* (Chicago: University of Chicago Press, 1997).

52. L. Haas, *Equal Parenthood and Social Policy: A Study of Parental Leave in Sweden* (Albany: State University of New York Press, 1992).

53. S.B. Kamerman and A.J. Kahn, "Child and Family Policies in an Era of Social Policy Retrenchment and Restructuring," paper presented at the Luxembourg Income Study Conference on Child Well-Being in Rich and Transition Countries, September 30–October 2, 1999.

54. Hewlett and West, *War Against Parents,* 244.

55. M. Harrington, *Care and Equality: Inventing a New Family Politics* (New York: Knopf, 1999).

56. For more information, see the Web site of the United States Fund for UNICEF at: http://www.unicefusa.org/infoactiv/rights.html.

Supporting a Dual-Earner/Dual-Carer Society
Janet C. Gornick and Marcia K. Meyers

1. We thank Peggy Orenstein for the phrase "a half-changed world." See her book *Flux: Women on Sex, Work, Love, Kids and Life in a Half-Changed World* (New York: Doubleday, 2000), for an account of women's struggles to balance family with self-sufficiency in a society filled with conflicting pressures.

2. See L. Bassi, "Policy Implications of Part-Time Employment, Part of a Symposium on Part-Time Employment and Employees," *Journal of Labor Research* 16, no. 3 (1995): 315–18; Employee Benefits Research Institute (EBRI), "Part-Time Work: Characteristics of the Part-Time Work Force: Analysis of the March 1992 Current Population Survey," working paper P-55, 1993; J.C. Gornick and J.A. Jacobs, "A Cross-National Analysis of The Wages of Part-Time Workers: Evidence from the United States, the United Kingdom, Canada, and Australia," *Work, Employment and Society* 10, no. 1 (1996); R.A. Rosenfeld, "Women's Part-Time Employment: Individual and Country-Level Variation," paper presented at the meeting of RC28, International Sociological Association, Durham, North Carolina, August 11, 1993; C. Tilly, *Short Hours, Short Shrift: Causes and Consequences of Part-Time Work* (Washington, DC: Economic Policy Institute, 1990).

3. On fathers' employment patterns, see J.C. Gornick, "Gender Equality in the Labor Market," in D. Sainsbury, ed., *Gender Policy Regimes and Welfare States* (Oxford: Oxford University Press, 1999), 210–42. On fathers' earnings, see S. Lundberg and E. Rose, "The Effects of Sons and Daughters on Men's Labor Supply and Wages," *Review of Economics and Statistics* 84, no. 2 (2002): 251–68.

4. A. Crittenden, *The Price of Motherhood: Why the Most Important Job in the World Is Still the Least Valued* (New York: Metropolitan Books, 2001).

5. On the gender gap related to unpaid work, see J. Gershuny and J.P. Robinson, "Historical Changes in the Household Division of Labor," *Demography* 25, no. 4 (1988): 537–52; S.M. Bianchi, M.A. Milkie, L.C. Sayer, and J.P. Robinson, "Is Anyone Doing the Housework? Trends in the Gender Division of in Household Labor," *Social Forces* 79, no. 1 (2000): 191–228; S.M. Bianchi, "Maternal Employment and Time with Children: Dramatic Change or Surprising Continuity?" *Demography* 37, no. 4 (2000): 401–14; J.P. Robinson and G. Godbey, *Time for Life* (University Park, PA: Pennsylvania State University Press, 1997). For data on the mid-1990s, see Bianchi et al., "Is Anyone Doing the Housework?"

6. On the gender gap in care for children, see Bianchi, "Maternal Employment"; Robinson and Godbey, *Time for Life*. On married fathers' time use, see Bianchi, "Maternal Employment."

7. On employed mothers' time use, see Robinson and Godbey, *Time for Life*; Bianchi, "Maternal Employment." For the specific comparisons cited, see Bianchi, "Maternal Employment."

8. On split-shift parenting and women's nonstandard work hours, see H.B. Presser, *Working in a 24/7 Economy: Challenges for American Families* (New York: Russell Sage Foundation, 2003). On women with preschoolers, see H.B. Presser, "Job, Family, and Gender: Determinants of Nonstandard Work Schedules Among Employed Americans in 1991," *Demography* 32, no. 4 (1995): 577–98. Quote from H.B. Presser, "Can We Make Time for Children? The Economy, Work Schedules, and Childcare," *Demography* 26, no. 4 (1989): 531.

9. On nonstandard work hours and health problems, see International Labour Organization (ILO), *Conditions of Work Digest: Working Time Around the World,* vol. 14 (Geneva: ILO, 1995); H.B. Presser, "Toward a 24-Hour Economy," *Science* 284 (1999): 1778–79. On the relation to accidents, see T. Kauppinen, "The 24-Hour Society and Industrial Relations' Strategies. European Industrial Relations Association," European Foundation for the Improvement of Living and Working Conditions, Dublin, 2001. On "social consequences," see Presser, *Working in a 24/7 Economy*. On marital and family consequences, see Presser, "Toward a 24-Hour Economy." On children's school-related difficulties, see J. Heymann, *The Widening Gap: Why America's Working Families Are in Jeopardy—and What Can Be Done About It* (New York: Basic Books, 2000).

10. L. Giannarelli and J. Barsimantov, *Child Care Expenses of America's Families* (Washington, DC: Urban Institute, 2000).

11. Children's Foundation, *Child Care Licensing Study* (Washington, DC: Children's Foundation, 2000). On child care staff turnover rates, see M. Whitebook, C. Howes, and D. Phillips, *Who Cares? Child Care Teachers and the Quality of Care in America* (Oakland, CA: Child Care Employee Project, 1989). On the quality of care in child care centers, see S. Helburn, M.L. Culkin, C. Howes, D. Bryant, R.M. Clifford, R. Cryer, D. Peisner-Feinberg, and S. Kagan, "Cost, Quality, and Child Outcomes in Child Care Centers," Department of Economics, University of Colorado, 1995; E. Galinsky, C. Howes, S. Kontos, and M. Shinn, *The Study of Children in Family Child Care and Relative Care* (New York: Families and Work Institute, 1994).

12. M. Whitebook, "Child Care Workers: High Demand, Low Wages," *Annals of the American Academy of Political and Social Science* 563 (1999): 146–61.

13. M. Shirk, N. Bennet, and J.L. Aber, *Lives on the Line: American Families and the Struggle to Make Ends Meet* (Boulder, CO: Westview Press, 1999).

14. M. Meyers, J.C. Gornick, and L.R. Peck, "Packaging Support for Low-Income Families: Policy Variation Across the United States," *Journal of Policy Analysis and Management* 20, no. 3 (2001): 457–83.

15. U.S. Department of Health and Human Services, *Access to Child Care for Low-Income Families* (Washington, DC: Government Printing Office, 1999).

16. U.S. Department of Labor, *Balancing the Needs of Families and Employers: The Family and Medical Leave Surveys, 2000 Update,* available at: http://www.dol.gov/asp/fmla/main2000.htm (accessed January 15, 2000).

17. Authors' calculations, based on data from the International Social Survey Programme, available at: http://www.issp.org (accessed January 15, 2000). On mothers' preference for more employment hours, see J.C. Gornick and M.K. Meyers, *Families That Work: Policies for Reconciling Parenthood and Employment* (New York: Russell Sage Foundation, 2003).

18. On men's views toward their work-family balancing, see, for example, R.C. Barnett and C. Rivers, *He Works, She Works: How Two-Income Families Are Happier, Healthier and Better Off* (New York: Harper Collins, 1996); S. Coltrane, *Family Man: Fatherhood, Housework, and Gender Equity* (Oxford: Oxford University Press, 1996); F.D. Deutsch, *Halving It All: How Equally Shared Parenting Really Works* (Cambridge, MA: Harvard University Press, 1999); J. Levine and T.L. Pittinsky, *Working Fathers: New Strategies for Balancing Work and Family* (New York: Harcourt Brace, 1997).

19. On "mommy-tracking" and "daddy-tracking," see Crittenden, *Price of Motherhood.*

20. On higher-income women's leaves, see K. Ross, "Labor Pains: Maternity Leave Policy and the Labor Supply and Economic Vulnerability of Recent Mothers," Ph.D. dissertation, Syracuse University, 1999.

21. R. Crompton, "Discussions and Conclusions," in R. Crompton, ed., *Restructuring Gender Relations and Employment: The Decline of the Male Breadwinner* (Oxford: Oxford University Press, 1999), 201–14. While we prefer the full label—the "dual-earner/dual-carer" society—as it stresses a vision of time allocation *between* family members, we will shorthand this as the "earner/carer" society (or model) from here on out. In either case, our intention is to encompass single as well as coupled parents. Clearly, single parents also struggle to balance earning and caring, sometimes alone and sometimes working with other family members.

22. This chapter's analysis of the earner/carer model focuses on heterosexual couples because we are concerned with problems of gendered divisions of labor within families. It is important to note that an earner/carer society would include and support same-sex as well as heterosexual couples. In fact, same-sex couples raising children could serve as a model, in that paid and unpaid work hours are not allocated within couples according to gendered expectations.

23. Deutsch, *Halving It All.*

24. The assumption that earner/carer parents would provide substantial care for their own children should not be read as an indictment of substitute care for young children. A large and growing body of research has identified the earliest months of life as a critical developmental period. While research on the effects of substitute care, in general, has found that children benefit from high-quality early childhood education and care, studies of the effects on very young children have reached mixed conclusions. We suggest here that parents should have the right to choose how to spend their own time during the first months after childbirth and the right to decide the type of care that their children will receive.

25. It is important that family leave provisions support and remunerate time spent caring for all family members—including, for example, disabled and elderly adults. However, for our purposes, we are focusing on child-related provisions.

26. P. Moss and F. Deven, "Parental Leave in Context," in P. Moss and F. Deven, eds., *Parental Leave: Progress or Pitfall?* (Brussels: NIDI/CBGS Publications, 1999), 35:45–68.

27. U.S. Department of Agriculture (USDA), *Expenditures on Children by Families,* miscellaneous publication no. 1528-2000 (Washington, DC: Center for Nutrition Policy and Promotion, USDA, 2001).

28. The choice of countries and the time period is determined by the requirements of the larger study from which this chapter is drawn. This study analyzes policy provision and

labor market and other outcomes using data from the Luxembourg Income Study (LIS), available at: http://www.lisproject.org (accessed 2001). LIS includes microdata for each of the twelve countries as of the mid 1990s. For a literature review of policy impacts, see Gornick and Meyers, *Families That Work*.

29. G. Esping-Andersen, *Three Worlds of Welfare Capitalism* (Princeton, NJ: Princeton University Press, 1990). In the social democratic regime, entitlements draw on the principle of the universal rights of social citizenship, and policies stress full employment for both men and women. In the conservative regime, entitlements are based on work performance, and policies are both status-preserving and compatible with the idea of subsidiary (that is, the primacy of community and family provision). In the liberal countries, entitlements derive primarily from assessments of individual need, and important categories of benefits are means-tested.

30. This policy typology is standard in cross-national family leave research. See, for example, Organization for Economic Development and Development (OECD), "Long-Term Leave for Parents in OECD Countries," chapter 5 in *Employment Outlook* (Paris: OECD, 1995). Maternity leave is granted only to mothers for a limited period around the time of childbirth. Paternity leave is granted only to fathers, also for a limited period around the time of childbirth. Parental leave is long-term leave available to parents—mothers and fathers—to allow them to take care of an infant or young child over a longer period of time. This is usually granted in addition to, and typically following, the maternity and paternity leave.

31. All durations are expressed as weeks, to help with interpretation. Where authors converted from days, years, or months, original duration is given in square brackets. All currency amounts expressed as 2000 U.S. dollars, adjusted for purchasing power parities.

"Use-it-or-lose-it" days were implemented in Denmark in 1999, Norway in 1993, and in Sweden in 1995.

Danish parental leave was reformed in March 2002. The entitlement was increased to thirty-two weeks (to be shared between parents) at same pay as maternity leave; 80 percent of employers still top up. Other changes increased the flexibility of parents' take-up options.

Finnish parents can replace the home care leave payment with payment for a private child care provider. Finland introduced incentives for fathers' take-up in 2003.

Norwegian parents can use cash benefits to pay for private child care (for children ages one or two) if the child is not in a public slot. In addition to paid parental leave, each parent is entitled to (according to Law of Work Conditions) one year's leave without salary.

As of 2002, French fathers are entitled to eleven working days (two weeks), paid at the same rate as the maternity benefit. French parents on parental leave working 50 percent time receive 66 percent of the full benefit; parents working 50–80 percent time receive 50 percent of the full benefit.

As of January 2001, the Netherlands government offers subsidies to employers who provide paid leave, to defray some of the costs.

Canadian maximum pertains to benefit level, not maximum covered earnings. Maximum benefit of US $413 a week converts to approximately US $17,500 per year, or equivalent to 55 percent of about US $32,000 in earnings. Also, the national government pays benefits, but rights to take leave are established at the provincial level.

As of 2003, maternity leave benefits in the United Kingdom were extended from eighteen to twenty-six weeks; fathers are entitled to two weeks paid paternity leave, paid at same rate as statutory maternity pay.

32. As of 2002, one state—California—grants paid parental leave. California provides six weeks of leave to both mothers and fathers, paid at approximately 55 percent wage replacement, subject to an earnings cap.

33. Several countries also provide other forms of leave for family reasons, i.e., temporary paid leave throughout children's years at home. The most extensive provisions are in place in the social democratic countries, although generous provisions are also available in Germany. As with other forms of leave, leave for family reasons raises issues about incentives for fathers' participation. The strongest incentives for fathers to take up these rights and benefits are in Norway and Germany, where the rights are both individualized and highly paid. In the United States women or men covered under the Family and Medical Leave Act can take leave for family reasons to care for a parent, spouse, or child, but the leave remains unpaid.

34. Expenditure data are from OECD's Social Expenditures Database (SOCX). These data include expenditures on "maternity and parental leave" as a single line item. Totals include both public and mandated private spending; thus, expenditures in Germany include both the social insurance payments and the mandated employer top-up. Expenditure data pertain to 1998 except for Luxembourg (1990) and the Netherlands (1989), where later data are not available.

35. In Denmark, an estimated 87 percent of municipalities guarantee places for all children between ages one and five; national law mandates child care slots be provided within three months of parent request (or shorter, following parental leave); few children are on waiting lists.

    In Finland, every child under school age has an unconditional right to day care provided by the local authority once the mother or father's period of parental allowance comes to an end, irrespective of the parents' financial status or whether or not they are in paid work.

    In Norway, universal access is a political priority and access varies by location.

    Swedish municipalities are required to provide fee-paying spaces for all children ages one to twelve whose parents work or are in school. Spots must be made available "without unreasonable delay"—defined as 3 to 4 months. An estimated 95 percent of municipalities are able to meet this requirement. As of 2001, children of unemployed parents also have the right to services.

    In Luxembourg, preprimary school *(education précoce)* for three-year-olds will be available in all communes by 2005.

    In the United Kingdom, by 2004, part-time nursery school is planned for all three-year-olds. The Sure Start program provides comprehensive services for children ages zero to three in deprived areas; its goal is to extend services to one-third of poor families by 2004.

36. These expenditures correspond to 1998 and are reported in 2000 PPP-adjusted U.S. dollars.

37. The term *child care centers* refers to care in organized centers that may be public, publicly supported private organizations, or fully private in funding and service provision; *family day care* refers to care that is provided in home settings that is regulated and may be financed by the public sector. We use the term *child care* inclusively to refer to child care centers and day care homes, as distinct from preprimary programs.

38. *Preprimary* (or *preschool*) refers to care provided with public funds specifically as an educational service before the start of primary school education. Providers may be public or publicly supported private organizations.

39. In Sweden, this does not include additional enrollments in family child care, which may be publicly subsidized and supervised.

    In Finland, although few children under age one were in child care, as of 2000, 97 percent of children under age three received some form of family support, through leave, home care allowance, or child care.

    In France, an estimated 9 percent of children under age three are in crèche (mostly under age two) and 11 percent are in *école*.

In Germany, approximately 80 percent of three- to five-year-olds are in care part time.

For the Netherlands, the 71 percent figure reflects an average of 17 percent of three-year-olds in public care and 99 percent of four- and five-year-olds in preprimary or primary school.

In the United States, the 53 percent figure is based on estimates of approximately 6 percent of children in subsidized arrangements and 47 percent in prekindergarten or kindergarten.

40. For more information on financing mechanisms, see M.K. Meyers and J.C. Gornick, "Public or Private Responsibility? Early Childhood Education and Care, Inequality, and the Welfare State," *Journal of Comparative Family Studies* 34, no. 3 (2003): 379–411.

41. Cross-nationally comparable ECEC expenditure data were available only for seven countries. These expenditures are given in 2000 PPP-adjusted U.S. dollars.

42. Spending estimates are for approximately 1995 (unless otherwise noted), converted to 2000 U.S. dollars adjusted for purchasing power parity.

Total spending calculated per child of relevant ages given country-specific institutions and available data: day care, nursery and preprimary education for children zero to four in the United Kingdom; federal and state child care subsidies, Head Start, and state prekindergarten programs for children zero to four in the United States; crèche and *école maternelle* for children zero to five in France; public child care for children zero to four in the Netherlands; public care for children zero to six in Sweden, Finland, and Denmark.

For Finland, this does not include the private care allowance received by an estimated 2 percent of zero- to six-year-old children.

For the United Kingdom, this does not include recent expansions of Sure Start and public nursery schools.

43. For a detailed discussion of school schedules across these countries, see J.C. Gornick, M.K. Meyers, and K.E. Ross, "Supporting the Employment of Mothers: Policy Variation Across Fourteen Welfare States," *Journal of European Social Policy* 7, no. 1 (1997): 45–70; Gornick and Meyers, *Families That Work*.

44. For a detailed discussion of working time regulations across these twelve countries, see Gornick and Meyers, *Families That Work*.

45. On Sweden, see 32 HOURS (Action for Full Employment and the Shorter Work Time Network of Canada) newsletter, 1998, and on Belgium and France, see 32 HOURS newsletter, 2000. Both available at: http://www.web.net/32hours/ (accessed January 15, 2000).

46. Ibid.

47. Gornick and Meyers, *Families That Work*.

48. On Americans' work hours, see Gornick and Meyers, *Families That Work*. On weak U.S. regulations, see J.A. Jacobs and J.C. Gornick, "Hours of Paid Work in Dual Earner Couples: The U.S. in Cross-National Perspective," *Sociological Focus* 35, no. 2 (2002): 169–87.

49. On European part-time workers, see M. Smith, C. Fagan, and J. Rubery, "Conceptualizing Part-Time Work: The Value of an Integrated Comparative Perspective," in J. O'Reilly and C. Fagan, eds., *Part-Time Prospects: An International Comparison of Part-Time Work in Europe, North America and the Pacific Rim* (New York: Routledge, 1998), 35–56. On supranational organizations, see P. Bolle, "Part-Time Work: Solution or Trap?" *International Labour Review* 136, no. 4 (1997): 557–79.

50. International Labour Organization (ILO), "C175 Part-Time Work Convention, 1994," available at: http://www.itcilo.it/english/actrav/telearn/global/ilo/law/iloc175.htm (accessed April 7, 2004); Council of the European Union, "Council Directive 97/81/EC of 15 December 1997. Framework Agreement on Part-time Work," 1997, available

at: http://europa.eu.int/comm/employment_social/soc-dial/social/parttime_en.htm (accessed 2001).

51. On U.S. part-time workers, see Gornick and Jacobs, "A Cross-National Analysis." On the pay gap, see E. Bardasi and J.C. Gornick, "Women's Part-Time Employment Across Countries: Workers' 'Choices' and Wage Penalties," in B. Garcia, R. Anker, and A. Pinelli, eds., *Women in the Labour Market in Changing Economies: Demographic Consequences,* Studies in Demography Series (Oxford: Oxford University Press, 2003).

52. For a more detailed treatment of cash benefits for families in these countries, see J.C. Gornick, "Income Maintenance and Employment Supports for Former Welfare Recipients: The United States in Cross-National Perspective," in E. Ganzglass and K. Glass, eds., *Rethinking Income Support for the Working Poor: Perspectives on Unemployment Insurance, Welfare, and Work* (Washington, DC: National Governors' Association Center for Best Practices, 1999), 49–90.

53. U.S. child support policies may even reduce the amount of assistance received by the poorest families on public assistance. Recent research suggests that aggressive state efforts to collect child support may lead to a net loss of income because noncustodial parents withdraw informal support to the parent of the child.

54. Gornick, "Gender Equality in the Labor Market."

55. Expenditures data are from the OECD Social Expenditure Database. For further analyses of cash benefit expenditures on families in these countries, see J. Gornick, "Social Expenditures on Children and the Elderly, 1980–1995: Shifting Allocations, Changing Needs," in A.H. Gauthier, C. Chu, and S. Tuljapurkar, eds., *The Allocation of Private and Public Resources Across Generations* (Dordrecht: Kluwer Publications, forthcoming).

56. Expenditures include cash benefits for families, i.e., programs targeted to families (family allowances for children, family support benefits, and single-parent cash benefits), as well as paid family leave and refundable tax credits for families. Approximately 60 percent of the expenditures in the United States are accounted for by the EITC.

57. J.C. Gornick and M.K. Meyers, "Lesson-Drawing in Family Policy: Media Reports and Empirical Evidence About European Developments," *Journal of Comparative Policy Analysis: Research and Practice* 3, no. 1 (2001): 31–57.

58. On support for publicly financed family leave, see "What Grown-Ups Understand About Child Development," survey results, Zero to Three: National Center for Infants, Toddlers and Families, Washington, DC, 2000, available at: http://www.zerotothree .org. On support for the choice of pay or working time, see S. Hewlett and C. West, *The War Against Parents: What We Can Do for America's Beleaguered Moms and Dads* (New York: Houghton Mifflin, 1998). On support for government assistance, see the Mott Foundation 1998, Lake Sosin Snell Perry 1998 and *Wall Street Journal/*NBC 1998 polling data available at: http://www.childrensdefense.org/cc_polls.htm (accessed 2001). On support for longer school days and years, see Hewlett and West, *War Against Parents.*

59. T. Skocpol, *The Missing Middle: Working Families and the Future of American Social Policy* (New York: Norton, 2000), 143.

CONTRIBUTORS

David Almeida is Associate Professor of Human Development at Pennsylvania State University. His research interests center on the general question of how daily experiences within the family and other social contexts, such as work and leisure, influence individual health and well-being.

Christopher Beem is a program officer for the Johnson Foundation in Racine, Wisconsin. He is also Executive Director of the Foundation's Work, Family and Democracy Project. His most recent book is *The Necessity of Politics: Reclaiming American Public Life* (University of Chicago Press, 1999). He earned his Ph.D. in ethics and society from the University of Chicago Divinity School in 1994.

Eileen Boris, Hull Professor of Women's Studies and Director of the Center for the Study of Women and Social Justice at the University of California, Santa Barbara, specializes in gender, race, labor, and the welfare state. A prize-winning author, she currently is writing a history of housekeepers, health aides, and personal attendants in the home workplace.

Henry E. Brady is Class of 1941 Monroe Deutsch Professor of Political Science and Public Policy at the University of California, Berkeley, and faculty director of Berkeley's Survey Research Center. He has written on political participation, elections, and social welfare policy in America and other countries. In 2004 he was elected to the American Academy of Arts and Sciences.

Ellen Bravo was national director of 9to5, National Association of Working Women, for eleven years and is now their lead speaker. She also teaches at the University of Wisconsin-Milwaukee. Among her publications is *The Job/Family Challenge: A 9to5 Guide (Not for Women Only)*. She served on the Congressional Commission on Leave.

Lisa Dodson teaches and conducts research about wage-poor America and work and family issues in the sociology department of Boston College and has written the award-winning book *Don't Call Us Out of Name: The Untold Lives of Women and Girls in Poor America* (1999) as well as other recent ethnographic articles.

Laurel Elms is a doctoral candidate at the University of California, Berkeley. Her dissertation focuses on measuring and explaining aggregate changes in partisan and ideological identifications.

Nancy Folbre is Professor of Economics at the University of Massachusetts at Amherst. Her recent books include *Family Time: The Social Organization of Care,* co-edited with Michael Bittman (Routledge, 2004) and *The Invisible Heart: Economics and Family Values* (The New Press, 2001). She is an associate editor of the journal *Feminist Economics*.

Bradley K. Googins, executive director of the Center for Corporate Citizenship at Boston College since 1997, is also an associate professor with the Carroll School of Management. In 1990 he founded the Center for Work and Family at Boston College, which he directed for six years. Dr. Googins, the author of several books and monographs, earned his Ph.D. in social policy from Brandeis University and his M.S.W. and B.A. from Boston College.

Janet Gornick is Associate Professor of Political Science at the City University of New York and Associate Director of the Luxembourg Income Study. With Marcia Meyers, she is co-author of *Families That Work: Policies for Reconciling Parenthood and Employment* (Russell Sage, 2003), a cross-country study of family leave, child care, and working time policies.

Donald J. Hernandez is Professor of Sociology at the University of Albany. Dr. Hernandez is the author of *America's Children: Resources from Family, Government, and the Economy,* the first national study of children to document the timing, magnitude, and reasons for revolutionary changes experienced by children since the Great Depression in family composition, parent's education, father's and mother's work, and family income and poverty.

Sylvia Ann Hewlett is the author, most recently, of *Creating a Life*. She is Director of the Gender and Public Policy Program at the School of International and Public Affairs at Columbia University and also the founding president of the Center for Work-Life Policy, a nonprofit organization which seeks to develop policies that enhance work-life balance.

Jody Heymann, M.D., Ph.D. is founding director of the Project on Global Working Families and an Associate Professor at the Harvard School of Public Health and Harvard Medical School. She is the author of more than ninety publications, including *The Widening Gap: Why America's Working Families Are in Jeopardy and What Can Be Done About It* and *Global Inequalities at Work: Work's Impact on the Health of Individuals, Families, and Societies.*

Sheila B. Kamerman is the Compton Foundation Centennial Professor for the Prevention of Child and Youth Problems at the Columbia University School of Social Work and the director of the Columbia Institute on Child and Family Policy. Her most recent book, co-edited with Alfred J. Kahn, is *Beyond Poverty: Social Exclusion and Children.*

Daniel A. McDonald received his Ph.D. in Family Studies and Human Development from the University of Arizona, where he currently is a research specialist in Cooperative Extension. He has published on temporal patterns of parent-child tensions, temporal patterns of social responsibility, and the daily interweave of fathers' work and home experiences.

Marcia K. Meyers is Associate Professor of Social Work and Public Affairs at the University of Washington. She has published extensively on the topics of U.S. social policy and, most recently, a cross-national study of work/family reconciliation policy, with Janet C. Gornick, called *Families That Work: Policies for Reconciling Parenthood and Employment*.

Marcie Pitt-Catsouphes is an assistant professor at Boston College. She is Director of the Sloan Work and Family Research Network and also a co-principal investigator for the study "Understanding the First Job: The Nurturing Families Study." Some of her recent publications include "Recasting the Work-Family Agenda as a Corporate Social Responsibility" (co-authored with B. Googins) and "Organizational Justice: Employee Access to Flexible Schedules" (co-authored with J. Swanberg, J. Hertzog, and K. Drescher-Burke).

Juliet Schor is Professor of Sociology at Boston College and author, most recently, of *Born to Buy: The Commercialized Child and the New Consumer Culture* (Scribner, 2004). She is also a founding member of the Center for a New American Dream (www.newdream.org).

Robert Wuthnow is Andlinger Professor of Sociology and Director of the Center for the Study of Religion at Princeton University. He is the author of more than twenty books about American religion and culture, including *Loose Connections: Joining Together in America's Fragmented Communities* and *Saving America? Faith-Based Services and the Future of Civil Society*.

ACKNOWLEDGMENTS

We want to thank all the contributors who took time from their busy schedules to meet, wrestle with one another's ideas, revise their own, and really invest in this subject. Their commitment to the critical importance of the relationships among work, family, and democracy has been impressive. Neither the engagement of all the contributors nor this edited volume would have been possible without the generous support and vision of the Johnson and the David and Lucile Packard Foundations. We are deeply indebted to them both. This effort was built on research initiated by Jody Heymann's research group with generous support from the William T. Grant Foundation, the National Institute for Child Health and Development, and the Canadian Institute for Advanced Research. Ongoing support for the Work, Family and Democracy initiative by the Ford Foundation contributed importantly to its continued development.

A project of this magnitude relies on the skills and commitment of many people. Among these, the research and staff assistance on this project of six stand out. This volume is far better because of the hard work of Alison Earle, Jennifer Eckerman, Aron Fischer, Bora Lee, Kate Penrose, Stephanie Simmons, and Noa Walsky. We are grateful for all of their contributions. The environs of the Johnson Foundation's Wingspread Conference Center offered an ideal setting in which to grapple with these ideas and problems. We are grateful to all the staff at Wingspread for their efforts and hospitality. In particular, we wish to thank Barbara Schmidt, Wendy Butler, and Linda Stengel for their unfailing support.

This volume is dedicated to Ann and Phil Heymann and Ray and Marilyn Beem. Without both her parents, Jody might have stumbled, given the era in which she grew up, into spending her life either solely on the kind of employment our society has defined as "work" or solely on the equally full-time job of child rearing. With their endless support, she has been blessed with the joyful chaos of trying to do both in a society whose institutions and supports have not yet caught up. Chris's parents have shown him time and again that a child's first and best advocates are his parents. Realizing the importance of families has been a driving force behind both their efforts.

INDEX